Oil Revolution

Through innovative and expansive research, *Oil Revolution* analyzes the tensions faced and networks created by anticolonial oil elites during the age of decolonization following World War II. This new community of elites stretched across Iran, Iraq, Saudi Arabia, Venezuela, Algeria, and Libya. First through their western educations and then in the United Nations, the Arab League, and the Organization of Petroleum Exporting Countries, these elites transformed the global oil industry. Their transnational work began in the early 1950s and culminated in the 1973 to 1974 energy crisis and in the 1974 declaration of a New International Economic Order in the United Nations. Christopher R. W. Dietrich examines how these elites brokered and balanced their ambitions via access to oil, the most important natural resource of the modern era.

CHRISTOPHER R. W. DIETRICH is Assistant Professor of History at Fordham University. He has been awarded fellowships from the Woodrow Wilson Foundation, the American Historical Association, the National History Center, Yale University, the University of Texas at Austin, and the Society for Historians of American Foreign Relations.

Global and International History

Series Editors

Erez Manela, *Harvard University*
John McNeill, *Georgetown University*
Aviel Roshwald, *Georgetown University*

The Global and International History series seeks to highlight and explore the convergences between the new International History and the new World History. Its editors are interested in approaches that mix traditional units of analysis such as civilizations, nations and states with other concepts such as transnationalism, diasporas, and international institutions.

Titles in the Series

Oil Revolution

*Anticolonial Elites, Sovereign Rights, and the
Economic Culture of Decolonization*

CHRISTOPHER R. W. DIETRICH

Fordham University

CAMBRIDGE
UNIVERSITY PRESS

CAMBRIDGE
UNIVERSITY PRESS

University Printing House, Cambridge CB2 8BS, United Kingdom

One Liberty Plaza, 20th Floor, New York, NY 10006, USA

477 Williamstown Road, Port Melbourne, VIC 3207, Australia

4843/24, 2nd Floor, Ansari Road, Daryaganj, Delhi – 110002, India

79 Anson Road, #06–04/06, Singapore 079906

Cambridge University Press is part of the University of Cambridge.

It furthers the University's mission by disseminating knowledge in the pursuit of education, learning, and research at the highest international levels of excellence.

www.cambridge.org
Information on this title: www.cambridge.org/9781107168619
DOI: 10.1017/9781316717493

First published 2017

Printed in the United States of America by Sheridan Books, Inc.

A catalogue record for this publication is available from the British Library.

ISBN 978-1-107–16861-9 Hardback
ISBN 978-1-316–61789-2 Paperback

For Verónica

What in short is the truth's cash-value in experiential terms?
William James

Contents

Figures

Acknowledgments

Morris Zapp, the antihero of David Lodge's novel *Small World*, provides some insight into one academic neurosis: "Scholars these days are like the errant knights of old, wandering the ways of the world in search of adventure and glory."[1] The quixotic sentence drips with irony, especially when uttered by such a notorious pedant. Delusions of grandeur aside, scholars are rarely thrill-seekers or glory-mongers. But Lodge's mockery of his character becomes poignant at the center of the sentence when, in the swift transition from simile to explanation, he lets Zapp utter truth. Scholarship requires one to wander and the wandering is often errant.

The generosity of the History Department and College of Liberal Arts at Fordham University, the History Department and the Institute for Historical Studies at the University of Texas at Austin, International Security Studies at Yale University, the Society for Historians of American Foreign Relations, the American Historical Association, and the National History Center allowed for long research trips, dedicated writing time, and errant wandering.

Others have made my research less errant. Archivists and librarians helped track down documents at a number of institutions: the OPEC library, the Bodleian Special Collections at Oxford, the Manuscripts Division of the Library of Congress, the OECD archives, the IMF archives, and the UN archives and libraries in New York and Geneva. In addition, I thank the staff at the National Archives of the United States, the National Archives of the United Kingdom, and the Johnson, Nixon,

---

[1] David Lodge, *Small World: An Academic Romance* (London: Secker and Warburg, 1984), 63.

and Ford presidential libraries. The Inter-Library Loan staff at Fordham also merits my deep gratitude.

Fordham University provided funds to workshop an early version of this book, for which I am thankful. This book has also benefited from discussions at the Columbia Seminar on Twentieth Century Politics and Society, Yale International Security Studies, the Institute for Historical Studies at the University of Texas at Austin, the Cold War Seminar and Remarque Institute at New York University, the European University Institute, the Ramapo College Global Studies Colloquium, the International and Comparative Law Center at Mississippi College, the Decolonization Seminar of the National History Center, and many annual meetings of the Society for Historians of American Foreign Relations.

Benevolence characterizes my mentors and peers. Mark Lawrence and Michael Stoff of the University of Texas at Austin provided sage advice, sharp critical eyes, and good humor as advisers. They and other scholars encouraged me to tackle important issues with clarity. Thanks for that to Mark Bradley, Giuliano Garavini, Bob Vitalis, Monica Kim, Craig Daigle, Marilyn Young, Ryan Irwin, Laurie Green, David Painter, Jeremi Suri, David Oshinsky, Bill Brands, Amy Offner, Petra Goedde, Brandon Wolfe-Hunnicutt, Bevan Sewall, Anand Toprani, Nate Citino, Victor McFarland, Jeremy Friedman, Paul Kramer, Frank Gerits, Douglas Little, James Goode, Roham Alvandi, John Darwin, Jason Parker, Philippa Levine, Paul Chamberlin, Nick Cullather, Brad Simpson, Joshua Davis, Marc-William Palen, Brett Bennett, Renata Keller, Jonathan Hunt, Sarah Steinbock-Pratt, Emily Brownell, Rachel Hermann and Wm. Roger Louis. My colleagues at Fordham – especially Asif Siddiqi, Kirsten Swinth, David Hamlin, Nicholas Paul, Maryanne Kowaleski, Mark Naison, Silvana Patriarca, Steven Stoll, Durba Mitra, Thierry Rigogne, Wolfgang Mueller, Saul Cornell, Susan Wabuda, Daniel Soyer, Sal Acosta, Doron Ben-Atar, Glenn Hendler, David Myers, Rosemary Wakeman, Carina Ray, and Michael Latham – have been supportive and, more importantly, kind.

Working at Cambridge University Press with Debbie Gershenowitz and her assistant, Kris Deutsch, has been an honor. The series editors – Erez Manela, John McNeill, and Aviel Roshwald – have been wonderful. The thorough comments of two anonymous reviewers pressed me to clarify my central arguments and my writing.

These people surely represent what is good about academic life, and many are also friends. Others whose company I enjoy are too many to list. Eli Wood and Asher Burk hosted me on research trips. Bernard Mommer provided an introduction at OPEC, photos from his personal collection, and a warm welcome in Vienna. My brother, Nathanael, has been a model of support. My parents, Rick and Robin, instilled from an early age what is mostly a healthy balance of optimism and pragmatism. Perhaps more importantly, they encouraged me to read and write ... and wander.

That I am a lucky person is confirmed to me every day by Verónica Jiménez Vega, for whom my love grows ever greater. She is the most spirited person I have ever met, with the possible exception of our son, Emiliano Dietrich-Jiménez. Without them my wandering may or may not have been less errant. But it wouldn't have been nearly as much fun.

Abbreviations

AAPSO	Afro-Asian People's Solidarity Organization
AJIL	*American Journal of International Law*
AOG	*Arab Oil & Gas*
CIEC	Conference on International Economic Cooperation
CWIHP	Cold War International History Project
DDRS	Declassified Documents Reference Service
DNSA	Digital National Security Archive
DOS	Department of State
ECAFE	United Nations Economic Commission for Asia and the Far East
ECLA	United Nations Economic Commission for Latin America
ECOSOC	United Nations Economic and Social Council
FRUS	*Foreign Relations of the United States*
GFL	Gerald Ford Presidential Library, Ann Arbor, MI
ICJ	International Court of Justice
IMF	International Monetary Fund
IMFA	Archives of the International Monetary Fund, Washington, DC
ION	*Inter-OPEC Newsletter*
ISIL	Indian Society of International Law, *The Asian-African States: Texts of International Declarations*
LBJL	Lyndon Baines Johnson Presidential Library, Austin, TX
LOC	Library of Congress, Washington, DC
MEED	*Middle East Economic Digest*
MEES	*Middle East Economic Survey*
NAM	Non-Aligned Movement

NARA	National Archives and Records Administration, College Park, MD
NIEO	New International Economic Order
NIEO: SD	UNITAR, *A New International Economic Order: Selected Documents, 1945–1975*
NSC	National Security Council
OAPEC	Organization of Arab Petroleum Exporting Countries
OAU	Organization of African Unity
OECD	Organization for Economic Cooperation and Development
OIC	OPEC Information Center, Vienna, Austria
OPEC	Organization of Petroleum Exporting Countries
PFAPC	*Papers of the First Arab Petroleum Conference*
PIW	*Petroleum Intelligence Weekly*
PPPUS	*Public Papers of the Presidents of the United States*
PSAPC	*Papers of the Second Arab Petroleum Conference*
RG 59	Record Group 59: Records of the Department of State
RNL	Richard Nixon Presidential Library, Yorba Linda, CA
ROAPE	*Review of Arab Petroleum Economics*
SDIPI	OPEC, *Selected Documents of the International Petroleum Industry*
SFAPC	*Study of the Fifth Arab Petroleum Conference*
UKNA	The National Archives of the United Kingdom, Kew, Richmond
UN	United Nations
UNA-G	Archives of the United Nations, Geneva, Switzerland
UNA-NY	Archives of the United Nations, New York, NY
UNCLS	UN Conference on the Law of the Sea
UNCTAD	UN Conference on Trade and Development
UNGA	UN General Assembly
UNITAR	UN Institute for Training and Research
UNOPI	UN Office of Public Information
UNSC	UN Security Council

Introduction

The Cash-Value of Decolonization

It was a cloudless afternoon in Benghazi on May 1, 1970. When Mahmood Maghribi stepped out of the front doors of the makeshift offices of the newly incorporated Libyan National Oil Corporation, the sun beat down on his face. He let his eyes adjust to the glare and then addressed the small group of reporters. He reminded them that when appointed by Muammar Qaddafi to manage the oil affairs of the Revolutionary Command Council two weeks earlier, he had demanded an immediate increase in the price of Libyan oil. There was "no room for emotions" about the right of the Libyan government to lower production to put pressure on the nation's foreign concessionaires, he now said. Recent resolutions by the Organization of Petroleum Exporting Countries and the United Nations General Assembly confirmed Libya's right to enforce its sovereignty. He paused and let his words hang in the shimmering air. Then he gestured to the south, to the barren desert sparsely spotted with oases and oil rigs, and to the north, where tankers waited at Benghazi Port to carry their charge across the Mediterranean to the thirsty markets of Western Europe. "Our rights are clear and are supported by scientific facts," he concluded.[1]

Maghribi's strategy was to link the international right to sovereign resource control with Libya's geopolitical and structural advantages in the oil industry. It found quick success. By October 1970, each of Libya's foreign oil concessionaires had given in to the demands written by Maghribi and signed by Qaddafi for higher prices, a higher tax rate, and greater Libyan revenues. The victory was like a starting pistol for the

---

[1] "Maghribi Warns Oil Companies against Resisting Libya's Price Demands," *PIW* 13: 28 (May 1, 1970), 2–3.

other members of OPEC. The oil nations negotiated new rules in Tehran and Tripoli in early 1971, which enshrined what Maghribi and others considered the sovereign right to control production and prices. By the middle of 1972, Libya, Algeria, and Iraq had nationalized oil production. By early 1973, Saudi Arabia and Iran had also squeezed agreements out of their foreign concessionaires for partial nationalization.

The pace of change, already swift, reached breakneck speed during the Yom Kippur War of October 1973. When the Nixon administration rearmed the Israeli army with Project Nickel Grass in the middle of that month, the Arab oil nations announced an embargo on the United States, general supply cuts, and a 70 percent increase in the posted price of Persian Gulf oil. The other OPEC members saw the financial opportunity and followed suit. By late December 1973, they had quadrupled the posted price of Persian Gulf oil. It was the first time that the OPEC nations set the price of oil, a power once reserved exclusively for multinational oil companies such as Exxon, Mobil, or British Petroleum, and subject to joint determination after the 1971 Tehran and Tripoli agreements. Thus began what was known in the United States, the industrialized countries, and

FIGURE 0.1 Mahmood Maghribi presents his credentials to UN Secretary General U Thant, February 4, 1971.
Source: UN Photo/ARA. Courtesy of United Nations Photo Library, Photo No. 240683.

most of the world as "the energy crisis." Libya and the OPEC nations, however, gave this a different name: "the oil revolution."

Oil Revolution is a history of oil and decolonization in the mid-twentieth century that ends with the 1973–74 energy crisis and its immediate aftermath. Throughout the crisis, officials from the OPEC nations argued that their collective control of prices distilled a long-brewing anticolonial discontent into an internationally sanctioned takeover of their nations' raw materials. They couched their victories as part of a massively influential but often forgotten vision of what this book calls "sovereign rights" – a diplomacy and, more broadly, a transnational political program that sought to use state power over natural resources to create what actors at the time described as "an economic equivalent of decolonization" or, more simply, "fair prices." Algerian Foreign Minister Abdelaziz Bouteflika summarized the standard position for 1,500 representatives from ninety-five Asian, African, and Latin American countries gathered in Peru for the 1971 meeting of the UN Conference on Trade and Development: "The Third World countries, on the whole, lived through the battle that the oil producing countries had to fight. World opinion acknowledged therein a decisive progress in the establishment of new economic relations based on justice."[2]

Such claims were built in the previous quarter century, in which decolonization forever transformed international society. They were newly important because the OPEC nations presented their oil price increases as a broader diplomatic achievement for the Third World. When Algerian president Houari Boumedienne called for a special session of the UN General Assembly in 1974 to discuss rising oil prices, he also framed his proposal in those terms. The poor nations needed "to follow the example of OPEC by uniting and presenting a common front" to end the "systematic plundering" that had characterized their economic life since the age of empire, he said. African, Asian, and Latin American leaders from over fifty nations responded by lauding OPEC, their oratory pouring forth for nearly three weeks in April 1974. The foreign minister of Tunisia captured their shared assumption in a simple declarative sentence: "Oil is at last being sold at a fair price on the international market." The delegates finished the session by passing a Program of Action for a New International Economic Order. At its broadest, the New Order called upon nations to make communal use of their

---

[2] "OPEC Presented as Example to Follow at the 'Group of 77' Conference of Lima," *AOG* 1: 4 (November 16, 1971), 18.

sovereignty "to correct the inequalities and redress the existing injustices" of international capitalism, described as "the remaining vestige of alien and colonial domination."[3]

But what exactly did economic justice or emancipation mean? Who determined what a fair price was? More broadly, how did decolonization influence the post–World War II international economy? One iteration of sovereign rights diplomacy in a line of many, Libyan oil policy in 1970 posed those enduring questions. It also shifted the locus of power and the distribution of profits in the international oil industry. Furthermore, it set off the most concentrated nonviolent transfer of global wealth in human history. In doing so, it also spurred a transformation of the political landscape of international capitalism in a crucial era of flux.

On that late afternoon in May 1970, though, the fuller consequences of Maghribi's actions lay over the horizon, like the markets that craved Libyan oil. For the moment he had a clear remit from Qaddafi and the Libyan Revolutionary Command Council for an important but difficult task: to use Libya's sovereign right, an intellectual and political tradition born of the age of decolonization, to squeeze price increases out of the concessionaires. His success in doing so was not foretold. In fact, past failures dimmed his hopes. He had come of age in an era marked by arguments about sovereign rights, but they had often been powerless. It would be "unwise" for any one country "to embark upon such a step alone," he had written in his 1966 George Washington University doctoral thesis on oil and "the new concept of 'transnational law.'" In particular, the disastrous experience of Iran under Prime Minister Mohammed Mossadegh from 1951 to 1953 had set a trend that was "still too clear to be ignored." Maghribi had also faced failure firsthand – as a young in-house lawyer for the American multinational Esso Libya, he had been fired, jailed, and deported in 1967 when he defied orders and organized student and dockworker strikes during the Arab–Israeli war.[4]

As a matter of fact, many observers discounted Maghribi and the government he worked for as radicals on the margins of respectable international politics. But the significance of his rights-based vision was not lost on Sir Eric Drake in the summer of 1970. During the Mossadegh crisis, Drake had managed the great Abadan Refinery, and he had

---

[3] "Focus on Oil at the UN Special Session on Raw Materials." *AOG* 3: 62 (1974), 5–6; UNOPI, Official Record, *Weekly News Summary*, April 12, 1974, WS/655; United Nations, *Yearbook of the United Nations, 1974* (New York, 1975), 306.

[4] Mahmood S. Maghribi, *Petroleum Legislation in Libya* (SJD Thesis, George Washington University, June 1966), 72–3, 180–7.

absconded to the company's headquarters in neighboring Iraq with the refinery's accounting books just before Iranian officials took control. Nearly twenty years later, now the director of British Petroleum, he warned U.S. officials and oil executives gathered in New York for an emergency meeting that grave consequences would result if the Libyans were successful. Like Maghribi had, Drake turned to the historical example of the Iranian prime minister. This was "the most important week in the history of the oil industry since Mossadegh."[5]

The seeds of that moment in 1970 and all that followed were sown a generation earlier, as the references to the 1951 Iranian nationalization imply. That is where *Oil Revolution* starts, in the first years of an age that was defined by the end of imperial rule across the globe. But decolonization was not just a massive structural change. It was also a movement. Maghribi, for example, described the "cruel and dark era" of European conquest as the most prominent feature of his father's and grandfather's lives. Decoloniza- tion, the freedom from that darkness, was the feature that molded his own. For him, as for others, decolonization entailed much more than the achieve- ment of political independence from a colonial master. Instead, the rise of national assertion was an ongoing project. After all, the structures that upheld colonial power had not washed away with formal independence, and nowhere did postcolonial power exert itself with greater vigor than in the material world of economics. Leaders from Latin America, Africa, Asia, and the Middle East confronted that problem in the quarter century before the energy crisis and the New International Economic Order.[6]

Such a history of decolonization and oil presents daunting challenges of explanation. The 1973–74 price increases were a product of immense forces: the evolution of energy-dependent consumer and industrial soci- eties across the world, technological trends favoring oil over other sources of energy, the concentration of accessible oil in fewer and fewer hands, and the training of anticolonial elites like Maghribi, not to mention the geopolitics of decolonization, nationalism, and the Cold War and the regional politics of the Middle East. Added to these large-scale factors were contingencies and disruptions that accumulated over time, such as the international response to the Iran oil crisis from 1951 to 1953, the participation of the Arab League in the 1955 Bandung Summit, the 1959 Arab Petroleum Congress and the 1960 formation of OPEC,

---

[5] Wilmott to Ellingworth, "Libyan Oil," October 23, 1970, Foreign and Commonwealth Office: Commodities and Oil Department, folder 435, UKNA.
[6] Maghribi, *Petroleum Legislation in Libya*, 3–4.

the 1967 Arab oil embargo, the 1969 Libyan revolution, the 1971 Tehran and Tripoli agreements, the 1971 British withdrawal from the Persian Gulf, the 1972 Iraqi nationalization, the 1973 Arab–Israeli war, and the rise and fall of the New International Economic Order.

Oil Revolution tells the story of those intersecting pathways by weaving together multiple contexts, ranging from national politics to international organizations to broader global intellectual and political trends. The contemporary argument that the energy crisis was also an oil revolution reminds us that it was in fact a product of a peculiar combination of economic, political, and intellectual circumstances – built by the actions and inactions of decision makers in international organizations, the oil-producing nations, the large multinational oil corporations, and the oil-consuming nations over two generations. In other words, the energy crisis was an episode in which the singularities of the moment were chronically bound up with persistent ways of thinking about the world.

Of particular interest for this book is one purposeful way of thinking: the collective culture of "economic emancipation," as styled by the Non-Aligned Movement and then as part of the New International Economic Order. Embedded within that phrase and others like it was a progressive interpretation of recent international history, a unified theory of colonial oppression and liberation. A world of people like Maghribi subscribed to and acted upon that basic belief. It led them to pose questions about imperialism and statehood, about international inequality and reparative justice, and about the global distribution of wealth. The book thus begins with what was to them the most important transformation of their era: decolonization.

Any study of decolonization must depart from a set of basic assumptions. When empires faded away and nations rose to take their place after 1945, this was in itself a development of unprecedented scale and scope and profound significance. But it was made even more meaningful by the fact that colonizers and colonized alike hardly imagined it possible in the previous half century. The 1919 establishment of the League of Nations mandate system and the 1945 creation of the UN trusteeship system assumed colonial durability. But independence and nationhood became a sweeping new norm in the following generation, as UN membership grew from 45 nations in 1945 to 144 by 1975.[7]

---

[7] On the introduction of former colonies into the international system, see: Rupert Emerson, *From Empire to Nation: The Rise to Self-Assertion of Asian and African Peoples* (Cambridge, MA.: Harvard University Press, 1960); Wm. Roger Louis, "The Imperialism of

Yet if decolonization marked the birth of a different world, its etymology also inherently notes that the aftermaths of colonialism were many and the sources of trouble for new nations vast. This book argues that decolonization was an ongoing struggle to define the relationship of new states to international society, and that there is an intellectual, political, and cultural history of that struggle. Its narrative is one skein that winds through the entanglements of the decolonizing world: the rise and fall of the program of sovereign rights diplomacy that was born in the 1950s, came of age in the 1960s, and died in the 1970s.

Decolonization was a pendular process in international history – a moment in which one set of ideas and practices gained momentum as another lost it. The sense of forward motion was palpable to those who felt it, and a program of sovereign rights both embodied the problems of a world in transition and envisioned the future. Its expansion over time and space required a new sort of agent to traverse the decolonizing world: "the anticolonial elite." Maghribi was one of the tens of thousands of people across the globe that formed this new international class, some of whom became hubs around which ideas of sovereign rights and postcolonial independence arose and crystallized into policy.

From Latin American economists to Middle Eastern oil ministers, the anticolonial elites I write about here had different professions, nationalities, ethnicities, life experiences, and opinions. But several characteristics bound them together. As was Maghribi, they were elite in their personal formation, by which I mean they were wealthy or politically connected enough to enroll in postgraduate education in their own countries, Western Europe, and the United States in a time when the great majority of men and women from their countries had no such opportunity (see Appendix I). Access to education and then professional opportunity, in turn, combined with the rise of decolonization and air transportation to make their spatial sweep vast. Their lives stretched from the classrooms and libraries of universities in London, Paris, New York, and Washington, D.C. to hallways and meeting rooms of the United Nations and OPEC to regional and international summits – from the New York Hilton to the Kuwait Sheraton, from Addis Ababa and

Decolonization," *Journal of Imperial and Commonwealth History* 22: 3 (1994), 462–511; Odd Arne Westad, *The Global Cold War: Third World Interventions and the Making of Our Times* (New York: Cambridge University Press, 2005); Giuliano Garavini, *After Empires: European Integration, Decolonization, and the Challenge from the Global South, 1957–1986* (Oxford University Press, 2012).

Bandung to Geneva and Vienna (see Appendix II). They distinguished themselves as lawyers, diplomats, editors, authors, functionaries, and economists in their national governments and in institutions headquartered in the United States, Europe, Latin America, the Middle East, Asia, and Africa. They met in person and corresponded often. The records of their interactions suggest the mutual nature of their endeavors, the level of talent on hand, and their self-awareness.

Another characteristic of the anticolonial elite was their attempt to spread their views about the international order. Public diplomacy was part of sovereign rights. The elites most often communicated with each other in English or French at their meetings, and their associations rushed to translate other material into those languages. Their newsletters, pamphlets, conference minutes, interviews, articles, and resolutions circulated freely and were often retailed by international organizations or interest groups. In many cases their work was part of ambitious projects funded and directed by institutions like the Carnegie Foundation or university academic departments, and in others it was conducted under the auspices of commissions created by international organizations such as the United Nations, OPEC, the Non-Aligned Movement, and the Arab League, or by smaller groups including national bar associations, regional economic working groups, or private consulting firms.

Anticolonial elites were thus widely dispersed, but they also occupied a common political and intellectual terrain. As they tried to understand and shape the complex conditions at hand, they created and reproduced networks of affiliation that made it possible for them to pose their challenges to international capitalism. They developed expertise, created policies, and mobilized language that rang true to each other.

The output of this determined set of voices led to an influence that was new to the second half of the twentieth century. To be sure, anticolonial dissent had shaped political life in Latin America, Asia, Africa, and the Middle East since the nineteenth century. But if the ferment surrounding divisions of wealth and power had a long history, the anticolonial elites' forerunners eked out a precarious existence on the margins of imperial society. Relations between colonial subjects and masters overshadowed others, a circumstance that forged a closed circuit that had barely begun to crack open in the first half of the twentieth century. It was only when the end of empire was nigh that anticolonialism could crystallize into a definitive arc. It was then that Maghribi and others came of age and began to use international institutions and conferences to establish a common agenda. From the 1950s on, they would face each other and their former rulers more frequently, more overtly, and on different platforms than ever before.[8]

The anticolonial elites also shared a profound feeling of vulnerability, especially in the face of the continuation of economic relations that had been established in the colonial era. They inherited many problems from the past, some of which were of a global economic order, even as their rise to self-assertion created a situation with no historical template with which to address those problems. They thus entered debates about the international economy with verve and made a passion out of the counteraction of economic subjugation. They sought to turn the spotlight onto what they considered a less formal, but no less important, form of discrimination and inequality.

Despite their vast differences in experience and setting, this highly developed sense of a common heritage of subjugation brought them a measure of common identity. Richard Wright, for example, described the elites who attended the Afro-Asian summit in Bandung, Indonesia, in 1955 as representative of "[t]he despised, the insulted, the hurt, the dispossessed – in short the underdogs of the human race." Many of the new elites were colonial subjects or former colonial subjects, and all of them expressed their familiarity with imperial oppression. In other words, for this international group of people, the imperial past was never really the past.[9]

Rarely, then, were anticolonial elites attracted to sovereign rights purely through cold, rational analysis. Rather, they used their capacity to analyze for political ends. Relatedly, although individuals tended to develop their expertise on narrow subjects, they trusted their own enthusiasm enough to generalize about pressing problems based on the evaluations of their peers.

At the center of attention in this book, then, stand the ideas and deeds of this new international class of anticolonial elites – their impressions of what decolonization meant and how it related to international capitalism, the changes they sought, and the policies they found desirable. In their sum, the anticolonial elites were an internationalist intelligentsia who saw themselves simultaneously as actors and theorists of an incomplete project

---

[8] Cemil Aydin, *The Politics of Anti-Westernism in Asia: Foundations of World Order in Pan-Islamic and Pan-Asian Thought* (New York, Columbia University Press, 2007); Erez Manela, *The Wilsonian Moment: Self-Determination and the International Origins of Anti-Colonial Nationalism* (New York: Cambridge University Press, 2007).

[9] Richard Wright, *The Color Curtain: A Report on the Bandung Conference* (New York: World Publishing, 1956), 11.

of liberation. Their shared cast of mind flowed from decolonization and was formed under the assumption that decolonization itself was best understood in the context of the long colonial era that preceded it. Their ideas of the past became a standpoint from which they made sense of the possibilities of decolonization to overhaul all sorts of international relationships in the future, including economic ones.

Anticolonial elites concerned with oil, too, took full part in the sovereign rights program, for oil was always part of the debates through which anticolonial elites envisioned an economic sequel to decolonization. This book explains that sovereign rights was entwined with the oil industry from the beginning. It also points out that the mutual feedback between decolonization and the question of international economic justice was nowhere more consequential than in discussions about oil. Just as the production of oil has always been eminently political, at the very least, so too did decolonization always have an economic character. In fact, the influence of decolonization in economic thought and practice set the stage for some of the most important episodes of twentieth-century international history, including the oil revolution.

Oil became important to the history of decolonization in part because it is different from phosphates, bananas, copper, coffee, tin, or other major commodities traded on a global scale. Simply put, oil is more precious to humans because it penetrates more deeply than any other natural resource into the inner workings of the modern global economy. After World War II, especially, energy consumption soared and oil drove the continued economic growth of the industrialized nations and the programs of rapid development of the poor nations. The oil industry is also a key site to study the influence of decolonization because of its unique geographical concentration. Throughout this history, oil was accessible in very few areas of the world, many of which lay in or across nations that had experienced some sort of past subjugation. In addition, as *Oil Revolution* reveals, the concessions that governed ownership, production, and price until the 1970s were considered by and large unfair agreements by anticolonial oil elites.

Oil thus held a unique but telling place in the global political economy. In fact, it is precisely because of its unique value, function, and concentration that it became a prism through which sovereign rights was projected. Control over oil became, by the time Qaddafi appointed Maghribi, a marker of the extent to which anticolonial elites could use decolonization to change international economic practice. The link between decolonization, oil, and sovereign rights is thus another red thread that runs through this book. It connects the early days of decolonization to the onset of the oil revolution and the New International Economic Order a quarter century later.

This emphasis on oil does not deny the obvious fact, however, that the struggle to understand and shape decolonization was always multidimensional and multilayered: political, economic, and cultural on the one hand, and local, national, and international on the other. Actually, the story that follows affirms the messiness and dislocation that comes with any major global transformation like decolonization. Yet at the same time, certain patterns endured within that dynamic range of perspectives, and at the core of this study are three observations about the way decolonization engulfed debates about the oil industry and, more broadly, discussions about justice under postwar international capitalism. First, as they move in a variety of directions, ideas and information have power. Second, nations lie ensnared not just in each other's histories but in the history of a larger international community. Third, anticolonial elites, with different degrees of consequence, spoke a gospel of economic emancipation. Their vision of international order had at its heart, always, a redistributive notion of economic justice.

The story of the anticolonial oil elites and sovereign rights is one of politics and diplomacy, as discussed above. But there is also another level of analysis, as is alluded to above in the discussion of the graininess of decolonization. *Oil Revolution* is also a history of what is called here "the economic culture of decolonization": the conditions of economic possibility that came with the end of empire and the rise of self-assertion of the so-called Third World in the 1950s and after. Above all, there emerged among the anticolonial elites a way of looking at the possibilities of independence, including in the international economy. The vision included beliefs about international law, the rights of sovereign nations, and an emphasis on the power of decolonization to change other relationships. A particular reading of history, which emphasized the overthrow of empire, formed a part of the anticolonial elite's shared vision as well. This was another constant among these agents as they shaped attitudes and policies: they denounced past colonialism as a vicious system of repression and exploitation and were ever aware of its ghosts.[10]

---

[10] This framework of culture and power, which emphasizes the ability of a particular interest to set and control the agenda on a given topic, draws from Steven Lukes, *Power:*

The intensity of that denunciation meant that even somewhat abstract issues, including the legal and economic doctrines that became crucial to the foreign policies of the anticolonial elites, were imbued with a deeply personal – that is to say a cultural and moral – perspective. The anticolonial elites' prolific body of rights–based writing and policy, which was conditioned by even as it forged the economic culture of decolonization, enriches our understanding of twentieth-century international history because of its legal, economic, diplomatic, and historical content. It is also interesting for its window into major diplomatic events. But on the cultural level it is perhaps most interesting because of the moral tenor of the anticolonial elites' international politics and diplomacy. The emotion involved meant that the economic culture of decolonization was never monolithic. This entails, in turn, that the history of the oil revolution is subject to all the contingencies that characterize life in modern international society. There were no guarantees that their ideas would find influence, and the anticolonial elites often felt as if they were fighting a losing battle. Even as they jointly propagated an economic equivalent to decolonization, they knew that the possibilities of applying sovereignty changed according to circumstance. Still, in the hands of the anticolonial elite, sovereign rights fostered the emergence of a shared culture that united an international community around a common set of problems and a common sense of purpose.

No less important than decolonization itself, in other words, was the way in which people fathomed its possibilities. This book asserts that anticolonial elites were moving forces in that history of understanding, and that they created their own intellectual tradition and their own culture. They carried intention and circumstance, ideas and reality, across a wide geographical and temporal base. They believed in the interconnectedness of nations and people in international society. The praise of national independence and international unity were basic assumptions that were inseparable in their mind-set, and they found their collective experience indispensable. In short, people such as Maghribi and Mossadegh were certain that their histories were slices of a whole.

To track the circulation of the anticolonial elites' arguments and the information they shared with each other is to visualize one example of

A Radical View, 2nd edn (New York: Palgrave Macmillan, 2004 [1974]); and Pierre Bourdieu and Loïc Wacquant, *The State Nobility: Elite Schools in the Field of Power* (Palo Alto, CA: Stanford University Press, 1998).

exactly how decolonization penetrated many aspects of mid-twentieth-century international life. Most important in this book are the two fields that intersected at the center of the economic culture of decolonization to form the core of the sovereign rights program: international law and development economics. Law and economics came together because each field formed a fertile seedbed for the growth of the other. Under the circumstances of decolonization, in turn, the legal assertion of the doctrine of "permanent sovereignty over natural resources" was meant to correct the economic problem of "unequal exchange." In the 1950s, the problem of unbroken imperial economic inequality gained an increased profile for anticolonial elites at the same time as the juridical independence of former colonies became more normal. The elites thus embarked on their project of economic emancipation by creating what Maghribi called "the new transnational law."[11]

The new transnational law that arose within that ever-expanding world community became a connective element among elites, and was consistently invoked by international lawyers who worked for the oil-producing countries, the United Nations, and OPEC. Although they drew inspiration from a number of different legal and economic traditions, in particular from Latin America, anticolonial oil elites used decolonization to forge their own political path. Their actions to consolidate the right to sovereignty and thus improve upon their nations' economic statuses became the units by which they measured progress. As the threat of unequal exchange and the right to permanent sovereignty became enshrined as legitimate currents of thought, the sovereign rights program had a precise intention – to bring raw material supplies under national control and use that control to overturn the unfair economic relations that characterized the past.

Sovereign rights thus was more than a set of beliefs or a method of analysis. It also became a means to action. Leaders in the United Nations, the Non-Aligned Movement, the Arab League, OPEC, and elsewhere discussed in great detail how permanent sovereignty could further their national and collective interests. Their enduring interchange became the basis for their shared culture of dissent from the 1950s to the 1970s. Sovereign rights diplomacy became identified with a specific set of ideas,

---

[11] For introductions to these concepts, see: Robert A. Packenham, *The Dependency Movement: Scholarship and Politics in Development Studies* (Cambridge, MA.: Harvard University Press, 1998); Kamal Hossain and Subrata Roy Chowdhury (eds.), *Permanent Sovereignty over Natural Resources in International Law: Principle and Practice* (New York: Pinter, 1984); Nico Schrijver, *Sovereignty over Natural Resources: Balancing Rights and Duties* (New York: Cambridge University Press, 2008).

language, and practices that sought to come to terms with the wrenching experience of decolonization. Like the principles of self-determination, racial equality, equality before law, and human rights to which it bears relation, sovereign rights became an *idée fixe* that encompassed fundamental values the elite international class had in common. In this way, sovereign rights was at the same time cultural and diplomatic.

Another aspect of the economic culture of decolonization and sovereign rights diplomacy was that the elites' basic ideas about law and economics helped forge alliances that otherwise might not have been possible. The anticolonial elites, including those who developed an expertise about oil, translated their individual experiences into international society, and expressed their disaffections and desires as a group. Attending to the specifics of their ideas, arguments, and policies is a way to think about how a certain understanding of justice became influential in international society. This focus points to another vital cultural dimension of the following story: the power of legal and economic regimes to enforce traditional hierarchies, the countervailing potential of decolonization to forge different futures, and in the elites' recognition of each.

The economic culture of decolonization and the sovereign rights program existed along the edges of international society for most of the period under consideration here. But by exploring their movement on the periphery, and by shifting the traditional axes of nation-based historical inquiry from the vertical to the horizontal, this book comes to approximate a history of mid-century international life. The discovery and discussion of new possibilities amidst old obstacles played a central part in anticolonial elites' and others' attempts to take in hand the immensity, as well as to understand the effects of decolonization on traditional questions of wealth, power, and diplomacy. As the sovereign rights program became durable, it became a means, first, of calling up the historical suffering of the bulk of the world at the hands of empires; second, of setting the independent future in opposition to the imperial past; third, and most critically, of drawing a picture of what exactly liberation meant in international capitalist society.

But what did liberation mean, exactly? How much did sovereign rights shape political choices and the international economy? What were the precursors to what U.S. Secretary of State Henry Kissinger called in 1975

---

[12] Memorandum of Conversation, November 16, 1975, L. William Seidman Files, box 312, GFL.

"the unholy alliance of OPEC and the Third World," and why did they command attention when and where they did?[12]

There are no easy answers to these questions. This is in part because novel meanings of justice were being woven into the fabric of international society. It is also in part because the ad hoc nature of decolonization resulted in a jumble of contradictions. How could it be otherwise?

There are thus certain caveats to this description of anticolonial elites and their sense of sovereign rights overcoming economic injustice. For one, the anticolonial elites were . . . elites. Some were less rich than others – elites from low-population Arab oil states were fantastically wealthy – but none suffered from want or hunger. The general critique of elite movements shared by thinkers from Rousseau to Foucault thus applies. Men whose political and intellectual formation occurred in the West were a miniscule fragment of the people they claimed to represent, and they rarely consulted their constituencies before doing what they thought best.

At the extreme end of this problem lies the question of authoritarianism. The acts of the governments of many of the anticolonial elites caused unfathomable suffering among their and others' peoples. It also goes without saying that their claims to similarity could be problematic because, like most political programs, sovereign rights was a complex and, most of the time, unwieldy one. The elites came from a disparate range of backgrounds and had distinct national, social, and ethnic identities. Factional identities changed, the meaning of ideas and policies were fought over. That problem, exacerbated by the vitality with which nations worked their way into coexistence, is evident even in the multitude of labels for even their largest categories: the Third World, the Afro-Asian bloc, the Non-Aligned Movement, the G-77, the periphery, the LDCs, to name just a few. Often described as moderate or radical by themselves and others, different blocs also disagreed on the practical question of means. Disagreement and suspicion always existed near the surface of solidarity and often overwhelmed it. Both OPEC and the Organization of Arab Petroleum Exporting Countries, for example, were born as much of conflict as consensus. Hidden inside the labyrinth of economic anticolonialism were catacombs of controversy.[13]

---

[12] Memorandum of Conversation, November 16, 1975, L. William Seidman Files, box 312, GFL.

[13] For the contemporary and academic use of the "Third World" and other descriptors, see: Garavini, *After Empires*, 11–12; Paul T. Chamberlin, *The Global Offensive: The United States, the Palestine Liberation Organization, and the Making of the Post-Cold War Order* (New York, Oxford University Press, 2012), 4–5, 269; Mark T. Berger, "After the

These limits and tensions, of which the anticolonial elites were aware, are an indissoluble part of the story. The elites, including those concerned with oil, struggled to cooperate but they were locked together. The problems and, often, contradictions that swarm around their policies and ideas are vexing, but it will not do to disparage the oil elites as opportunistic or to stigmatize sovereign rights or the economic culture of decolonization as merely convenient. That would underestimate the forces at play. Rather, if we are to understand the era and its meaning, we should struggle with the tensions that lay within the anticolonial elites' shifting understanding of who they were and what they stood for.

Two other broad tensions that marked the lives of the anticolonial elites from the 1950s to the 1970s are worth noting. The first lay in the fact that they lived caught between seemingly irreconcilable opposites: the imperial past and the sovereign present. The elites worked in concert to build a consensus around sovereign rights because they believed that national independence was not an end but a means to a better and richer future. The end of empire pointed to a sharp break with the past. Change was the essence of decolonization. Yet the imperial past had not been put to rest with independence, as Maghribi and many others stated. This created a psychology of striving and frustration.

The second notable tension is that between national interest and international camaraderie. It draws from the first. There were many consequences when former colonial powers, the Cold War superpowers, and postcolonial leaders and groups consecrated the national state as the elemental political unit to supplant colonial rule. Many of the results of nationalism are well-known. Time and time again, leaders have violently marginalized ethnic and sectarian minorities within their states and fought bloody external battles with their neighbors. More important here is an aspect of nationalism that is less commonly studied. The clashing interests of nations and groups of nations often undermined the possibilities of communal success through the sovereign rights program. If the

Third World? History, Destiny and the Fate of Third Worldism," *Third World Quarterly* 25: 1 (2004), 9–39; Mark Atwood Lawrence, "The Rise and Fall of Nonalignment," in *The Cold War in the Third World*, ed. Robert J. McMahon (New York: Oxford University Press, 2013); Robert B. Rakove, *Kennedy, Johnson, and the Nonaligned World* (New York: Cambridge University Press, 2013). For OPEC and OAPEC: Nathan J. Citino, *From Arab Nationalism to OPEC: Eisenhower, King Saud, and the Making of U.S.-Saudi Relations*, 2nd edn (Bloomington: Indiana University Press, 2005), 145–65; Christopher R. W. Dietrich, "'Arab Oil Belongs to the Arabs': Raw Material Sovereignty, Cold War Boundaries, and the Nationalisation of the Iraq Petroleum Company, 1967–1973," *Diplomacy & Statecraft* 22 (2011), 471–3.

new international community served as a point of union – a channel for the movement of ideas and a magnet for policy – national interests also functioned as a barrier to collective action.[14]

Like any set of people, beliefs, and action that change over time, the anticolonial elites, the economic culture of decolonization, and sovereign rights diplomacy cannot be defined in a phrase. But it is less viable to have no labels than cursory ones, and concepts predicated on tension are more useful than those that steamroll it. The dialectic between state-centered political decolonization and the internationalist language of economic decolonization, a simultaneous attempt to look inward and outward, is one leitmotif of this book. The tension between the heroic expectations for the present and the angry discourse of past victimization, a simultaneous attempt to look forward and backward, is the other. The experience of the oil elites from the 1950s to the 1970s reveals that these strains of coexistence wound tighter as time passed.

One key to understanding the international twentieth century lies in these contradictory impulses. Buried at the heart of the sovereign rights program, they extended the range and deepened the pathos of the economic culture of decolonization. A more complex understanding of them makes it possible to grasp at the positive and negative premises of the anticolonial elites. A study of their history reminds us that the elites were ultimately debating about the kind of world in which they *wished* to live.

Their endeavors to understand and shape that world are explored here in eight chronological chapters. Chapter 1 is a creation story of the sovereign rights program. Unequal exchange, the economic theory of global inequality put forward by Argentine economist Raúl Prebisch at the 1949 meeting of the UN Economic Commission for Latin America, captured the imagination of development economists and other elites in the early 1950s. At the same time, the Iran oil crisis led nationalist lawyers in the UN General Assembly to propose permanent sovereignty as a means to right the problem of economic injustice. When the assumptions of development economics became closely bound to the emergence of the new transnational law, the result was an emerging moral theory of international wealth redistribution.

Chapter 2 charts the course of sovereign rights as it became an intellectual and political compass for oil elites. The actions of the Arab League

---

[14] Recently, see Frederick Cooper, *Citizenship between Empire and Nation: Remaking France and French Africa, 1945–1960* (Princeton University Press, 2014).

between 1955, when its president, Abdel Khalek Hassouna, attended the Afro-Asian summit in Bandung, the 1959 Arab Petroleum Congress organized by the Arab League's Mohammed Salman, and the creation of OPEC in 1960 saw oil elites move into wider circles of engagement, even as sovereign rights began to govern their political and intellectual lives. The emphasis on control over the supply and the price of oil became embedded in that emerging international society.

Sovereign rights became a medium of all sorts of relationships. Chapter 3 recounts the first five years of OPEC in the context of the anticolonial community. It also examines the character, mechanisms, and impacts of sovereign rights in the oil industry. The program resonated emphatically, and oil elites such as Francisco Parra, Fuad Rouhani, and Feisal al-Mazidi became active participants in meetings of the Arab Oil Congresses, the Non-Aligned Movement, and the UN Conference on Trade and Development. But attempts to enact permanent sovereignty also caused friction, as revealed by the enmity between gradualists and insurrectionists during OPEC's royalty negotiations from 1962 to 1965.

Chapter 4 chronicles another schism, the 1967 Arab oil embargo. While the embargo brought the emancipatory political thought of some oil elites to the forefront, the project encountered abject failure when disagreements among the Arab OPEC members and between the Arab and non-Arab members marred any sense of solidarity. The gradualist monarchies in Saudi Arabia, Kuwait, and Libya all broke the embargo. The non-Arab members, Iran and Venezuela, used the embargo to grab a share of Arab markets. OPEC's experts in Vienna continued to tout anticolonial law and economics, while they desperately pretended the Arab–Israeli problem did not exist.

Chapter 5 reveals how a number of factors, including imperial and Cold War geopolitics, enabled key OPEC members to increase national control over oil after 1967. It and the chapters that follow also consider more closely the role of U.S. diplomacy, as circumstances abetted the convergence of oil elites around the sovereign rights program and, in turn, the program became powerful enough to gain the attention of American diplomats.

In the face of a financial crisis caused in part by the investment policies of gradualist oil nations, Great Britain announced in 1968 that it would withdraw its forces from the Persian Gulf. American presidents Lyndon Johnson and Richard Nixon sought to fill the "British vacuum" by granting more power to the Shah of Iran. That decision gave political leverage to Iranian officials, who amended the concept of permanent sovereignty even as they appropriated it in their ongoing revenue negotiations with the Iran oil consortium. In a remarkable parallel action, Ba'athist Iraq exploited relations with governments in both Cold War camps to develop the ability to independently produce its oil.

Those breakthroughs in turn enabled a second generation of oil elites, who came of political age in the 1950s and 1960s, to act more decisively. Chapter 6 reconstructs the international politics of the OPEC nations between 1970, when Mahmood Maghribi and his colleagues in Iraq, Algeria, Saudi Arabia, and Iran scrapped the traditional bargaining process, culminating in the Tehran and Tripoli agreements of 1971. The Cold War considerations of the Nixon administration again emboldened the sovereign rights program. Yet, as the strategy of Saudi oil minister Ahmed Zaki Yamani suggests, the gravitational force of the economic culture of decolonization played out against deep differences in political attitude and international allegiance.

Chapter 7 narrates the heyday of oil power between 1971 and 1973, marked by the pressure for partial ownership by Saudi Arabia and Iran and successful nationalizations by Algeria, Libya, and Iraq. The oil producers used their newfound political cohesion and market power to take control of the price of oil in this period. As they did so, they developed permanent sovereignty as a self-conscious and collective discourse of progress, and exuberantly pinpointed their particular policies on a broader map of decolonization.

Chapter 8 discusses the cascading global effects of oil power after October 1973. The energy crisis became firmly enmeshed with sovereign rights when the UN General Assembly passed its 1974 resolution in favor of a New International Economic Order in April 1974. From that perspective, the oil elites proposed a major realignment toward economic justice in the world. But there was a wrinkle in how oil price control represented the ideas at play. Escalating oil bills and the rise of "sovereign debt" severely limited the sovereign rights program as a collective vision.

The OPEC nations had harnessed the economic culture of decolonization into a successful diplomacy, but they could not be unambiguous champions of sovereign rights. The program had always been at variance with itself, and the energy crisis polarized its tensions when rising oil prices hit the nations of the "non-oil Third World" the hardest. Their joint crisis of sovereign debt was out of tune with the rights-driven solidarity of the New International Economic Order. The success of sovereign rights, at least in part, thus led to its marginalization. The

conclusion explores the meaning of that Pyrrhic victory for our understanding of twentieth-century international history.

When the international class of elites reflected on these realities and the
stunning shifts that accompanied them, they clutched at something profound about the economic culture that came into existence with the
advent of decolonization. In its investigation into the perspectives that
emanated from what W. E. B. Du Bois called "the world at Algeciras,"
this book argues strongly for considering history as it manifests itself on
the global periphery.[15]

The narrative that follows makes a number of contributions. First, it
reminds us that decolonization transformed, among many other things,
the global oil industry. This insight builds on the work of historians who
have laid bare the corporatist assumptions of the American, British, and
French men that constructed the "postwar petroleum order" and, increasingly, tapped into the complex triangular relations between foreign oil
companies, Western governments, and nationalist movements in Europe,
Latin America, South Asia, and the Middle East. Their interpretations
throw a powerful light on local visions and, in doing so, they caution
against the conflation of particular experiences with broader international
agendas. That warning should be heeded – bluntly handcuffing together
experiences of diverse origins and orientation threatens to flatten the
peaks and troughs of national topographies. After all, the nationalism in
Iran under Mohammed Mossadegh in the early 1950s was not that of the
Shah of Iran, much less that of Mahmood Maghribi in Libya or his
counterparts in Ba'athist Iraq, in the early 1970s.[16]

---

[15] W. E. B. Du Bois, "The African Roots of War," *Atlantic Monthly* 115 (May 1915), 707–14.

[16] On the postwar petroleum order, see Daniel Yergin, *The Prize: The Epic Quest for Oil, Money and Power* (New York: The Free Press, 2008 [1991]), 391–544. On corporatism in U.S. foreign oil policy: Michael B. Stoff, *Oil, War, and American Security: The Search for a National Policy on Foreign Oil, 1941–1947* (New Haven, CT: Yale University Press, 1980); David S. Painter, *Oil and the American Century: The Political Economy of U.S. Foreign Oil Policy, 1941–1954* (Baltimore: Johns Hopkins University Press, 1986); Aaron David Miller, *Search for Security: Saudi Arabian Oil and American Foreign Policy, 1939–1949* (Chapel Hill: University of North Carolina Press, 1980); Irvine Anderson, *Aramco, the United States, and Saudi Arabia: A Study of the Dynamics of Foreign Oil Policy, 1933–1950* (Princeton University Press, 1981). Historians of U.S. foreign policy, pan-Arabism, the Arab-Israeli conflict, and individual producers include: Nathan J. Citino, *From Arab Nationalism to OPEC: Eisenhower, King Saud, and the Making of U.S.–Saudi Relations*, 2nd edn (Bloomington: Indiana University Press, 2005); Steve Galpern, *Money, Oil, and Empire in the Middle East: Sterling and Postwar Imperialism, 1944–1971* (Cambridge University Press, 2009); Victor McFarland, "The United States,

But caution regarding difference over time and space does not mean chucking the key of similarity. Separate national accounts, while intimate, should not be cleaved from the international community of which each was a part. The book thus reminds us that the age of decolonization was one of great international commingling. The separation of nations into distinctive elements is an important part of that history, yet this was also an era in which people and groups interacted with each other across borders more intensely than ever before. The story of sovereign rights is found less in the canonical enclosures of nations than in the world between, and the search for an economic equivalent to decolonization reveals much about decolonization an international story of transition that was an ongoing process. Decolonization had a revolutionary influence on all sorts of international norms – including those regulating the production of commodities, international law, and the international economy – and its effects have yet to be fully explored.

Second, and relatedly, the book argues that the history of modern international society is an important arena of investigation in its own right. This is important because both corporatist and nationalist historians of oil illuminate an important assumption about the politics of international capitalism that merits further investigation: American and other Western

Saudi Arabia, and Oil in the 1970s," PhD dissertation, Yale University (2013); Anand Toprani, "Oil and Grand Strategy: Great Britain and Germany, 1918–1941," PhD dissertation, Georgetown University (2012); Brandon Wolfe-Hunnicut, "The End of the Concessionary Regime: Oil and American Power in Iraq, 1958–1972," PhD dissertation, Stanford University (2011); Mark Seddon, "British and U.S. Intervention in the Venezuelan Oil Industry: A Case Study of Anglo-U.S. Relations, 1941–1948," PhD thesis, University of Sheffield (2014); Uri Bialer, *Oil and the Arab-Israeli Conflict* (New York: Palgrave Macmillan, 1998); Mary Ann Heiss, *Empire and Nationhood: The United States, Great Britain, and Iranian Oil, 1950–1954* (New York: Columbia University Press, 1997); Stephen G. Rabe, *The Road to OPEC: United States Relations with Venezuela, 1919–1976* (Austin: University of Texas Press, 1982). Political scientists have theorized the effect of oil production on the societies of producing nations and ethnographers have examined the link between oil production and local affairs: Hazem Bablawi, *The Rentier State in the Arab World* (Berkeley: University of California Press, 1990); Terry Lynn Karl, *The Paradox of Plenty: Oil Booms and Petro-States* (Berkeley: University of California Press, 1997); Benjamin Smith, *Hard Times in the Lands of Plenty: Oil Politics in Iran and Indonesia* (Ithaca, NY: Cornell University Press, 2007); Thad Dunning, *Crude Democracy: Natural Resource Wealth and Political Regimes* (New York: Cambridge University Press, 2008); Fernando Coronil, *The Magical State: Nature, Money, and Modernity in Venezuela* (University of Chicago Press, 1997). For scholarship that discusses the formation of OPEC, see: Benjamin Shwadron, *The Middle East, Oil, and the Great Powers*, 3rd edn (New York: Wiley, 1974); Ian Seymour, *OPEC: Instrument of Change* (London: Macmillan, 1980); Ian Skeet, *OPEC: Twenty-Five Years of Prices and Politics* (New York: Cambridge University Press, 1988).

policymakers hoped that corporate oil control would ensure a cheap and stable energy supply and acclimate postwar international capitalism to the rising tide of decolonization. American diplomacy in particular sought to publicly divorce international economics – the business concerns of supply, demand, and price – from the rise of decolonization. The oil elites remarried those issues through a long-term project of reform. That program, and the culture from which it sprung, changed international society and had a tremendous effect on the international economy.[17]

Close historical scrutiny of the ideas and culture of the anticolonial oil elites makes sense, especially given the considerable evidence that broader schools of thought shaped attitudes, debates, and policies about the international distribution of wealth and power in other times and places. To explore their debates about decolonization and international capitalism is to discover a world of common referents, a vision whose circulation and adaptation began on the periphery of international society. In turning my attention to the longer history of the economic culture of decolonization, I also build on new trends in the writing of the international history of the twentieth century. The non-European world is less relegated to the margins of history than ever before, and a number of scholars have shrewdly observed that the anticolonial rabble-rousers of the twentieth-century world had constructive plans and lasting impacts. American, Soviet, and European policymakers were not unique in their universal claims or outsized influence, nor were there collective attempts to define progress exceptional.[18]

[17] On international society: Akira Iriye, *Cultural Internationalism and World Order* (Baltimore: Johns Hopkins University Press, 2000); Andrew Hurrell, *One Global Order: Power, Values, and the Constitution of International Society* (New York: Oxford University Press, 2007); Daniel Gorman, *The Emergence of International Society in the 1920s* (New York: Cambridge University Press, 2012). On decolonization and Cold War client states, see: Mark Bradley, *Imagining Vietnam and America: The Making of Postcolonial Vietnam, 1919–1950* (Chapel Hill: University of North Carolina Press, 2000); Robert J. McMahon, *Colonialism and Cold War: The United States and the Struggle for Indonesian Independence, 1945–49* (Ithaca, NY: Cornell University Press, 1981).

[18] In addition to the previously cited work on oil, see: Alison Fleig Frank, *Oil Empire: Visions of Prosperity in Austrian Galicia* (Cambridge, MA: Harvard University Press, 2007); Robert Vitalis, *America's Kingdom: Mythmaking on the Saudi Oil Frontier* (Palo Alto, CA: Stanford University Press, 2006); Melani McAlister, *Epic Encounters: Culture, Media, and U.S. Interests in the Middle East since 1945* (Berkeley: University of California Press, 2005); Timothy Mitchell, *Carbon Democracy: Political Power in the Age of Oil* (New York: Verso, 2011). Historians of the Cold War have engaged in transnational projects that emphasized the effects of the Soviet–American rivalry on other regions and vice-versa. See: Jeremi Suri, *Power and Protest: Global Revolution and the Rise of Détente* (Cambridge, MA: Harvard University Press, 2003); Thomas Borstelmann, *The Cold War and the Color Line: American Race Relations in the Global Arena* (Cambridge, MA: Harvard University Press, 2003);

This insight about decolonization is especially true in the field of international law. As historians have recently shown, international lawyers were actors of diplomatic consequence in the twentieth century. In the world of oil, anticolonial elite lawyers did more than gain new expertise and create knowledge through their studies and jobs. Their common enterprise was not just the intellectual one of an "invisible college" connected by academic journals and conferences, as the lawyer Oscar Schachter wrote. Rather, they used legal arguments to write their nationalism as a legitimate force into the international community. They were engaged in an ongoing process of communication and collaboration, through which they used international law to publicly pursue the sovereign rights program. In turn, the program took a general understanding about the influence of decolonization on international law and applied it to the specific question of national raw material control. In this sense, the anticolonial elites' ideas moved from academic into official channels. Of the utmost importance, a larger group of anticolonial elites understood international law as a means to an end. Their work in enshrining concepts like permanent sovereignty and changing circumstances into the international canon always had the broader goal of pressing for an economic equivalent to decolonization.[19]

Tanya Harmer, *Chile and the Inter-American Cold War* (Chapel Hill: University of North Carolina Press, 2011). Likewise, historians of empire have become more attuned to stories that occurred on the periphery, as well as the connections that yoked decolonization to the Cold War. See, for example: Ryan Irwin, *The Gordian Knot: Apartheid and the Unmaking of the Liberal World Order, 1960–1970* (New York: Oxford University Press, 2012); Chamberlin, *The Global Offensive*; Lien-Hang T. Nguyen, *Hanoi's War: An International History of the War for Peace in Vietnam* (Chapel Hill: University of North Carolina Press, 2012). One influential field has discussed the rise of modernization theory. See: Nick Cullather, *The Hungry World: America's Cold War Battle against Poverty in Asia* (Cambridge, MA.: Harvard University Press, 2010); Nils Gilman, *Mandarins of the Future: Modernization Theory in Cold War America* (Baltimore: Johns Hopkins University Press, 2003); Michael E. Latham, *The Right Kind of Revolution: Modernization, Development, and US Foreign Policy from the Cold War to the Present* (Ithaca, NY: Cornell University Press, 2011); Bradley R. Simpson, *Economists with Guns: Authoritarian Development and U.S.-Indonesian Relations, 1960–1968* (Palo Alto, CA: Stanford University Press, 2008); Amy L. S. Staples, *The Birth of Development: How the World Bank, Food and Agriculture Organization, and World Health Organization Changed the World, 1945–1965* (Kent State University Press, 1998).

[19] Oscar Schachter, "The Invisible College of International Lawyers," *Northwest University Law Review* 72: 2 (1977), 217–26. On the new history of international law, see: Samuel Moyn, "Knowledge and Politics in International Law," *Harvard Law Review* **129**: 8 (June 2016), 2164–89; Benjamin Coates, *Legalist Empire: International Law and American Foreign Relations in the Early Twentieth Century* (New York: Oxford University Press, 2016); David Kennedy, *A World of Struggle: How Power, Law, and Expertise Shape Global Political Economy* (Princeton University Press, 2016); Sundhya Pahuja, *Decolonising*

Third, and relatedly, the book reveals the influence of a broader array of forces behind the energy crisis than some accounts have suggested. In doing so, it warns against interpretations of the energy crisis or any other economic crisis that reduces complex political and cultural relations to mechanistic considerations of market behavior or structure. This is not to say that economic and geological imperatives were trivial. They provide the crucial context to this story. Demand outstripped supply and world reserves became concentrated in a limited number of countries by the early 1970s. Those conditions allowed the OPEC nations to enforce quantum price leaps. But an overemphasis on the market – and the models, theories, and laws such a social science is meant to reveal as true across time – risks placing the energy crisis above its context.[20]

Anticolonial internationalists, including the oil elites, did not conceive of their work in such a limited frame of reference. The economics of supply and demand, moreover, does not preclude recognition that sovereign rights assumed historically specific stakes and contours. In fact, what is most striking about the energy crisis and the rise of the New International Economic Order is that each surfaced from a gradual but decisive accumulation of ideas, politics, and policy.

In these ways and others, the work of an array of impressive scholars serves as my point of departure. But I hope the story I tell is different. The circulation and influence of the ideas, politics, and culture of elites from other eras and locations have been studied closely. It is time for the anticolonial elites of the mid-twentieth century to follow them out of the shadows.[21]

International Law: Development, Economic Growth, and the Politics of Universality (New York: Cambridge University Press, 2011); Antony Anghie, *Imperialism, Sovereignty, and the Making of International Law* (New York: Cambridge University Press, 2004); Martti Koskenniemi, *The Gentle Civilizer of Nations: The Rise and Fall of International Law, 1870–1960* (New York: Cambridge University Press, 2001).

[20] This critique of "economism" as the prejudicial tendency to understand economic thought through the creation of binary oppositions builds on the insights of political economists Fred Block and Albert O. Hirschman. See: Fred Block, "Political Choice and the Multiple 'Logics' of Capital," *Theory and Society* 15: 1/2 (January 1986), 175–92; Albert O. Hirschman, "Rival Interpretations of Market Society: Civilizing, Destructive or Feeble," *Journal of Economic Literature* (December 1982), 94–5.

[21] Lynn Hunt, *Politics, Culture, and Class in the French Revolution* (Berkeley: University of California Press, 1984); J. G. A. Pocock, *The Machiavellian Moment: Florentine Political Thought and the Atlantic Republican Tradition* (Princeton University Press, 2009); Daniel Rodgers, *Atlantic Crossings: Social Politics in a Progressive Age* (Cambridge, MA: Belknap, 1998); Emily S. Rosenberg, *Spreading the American Dream: American Economic and Cultural Expansion, 1890–1945* (New York: Hill and Wang, 1982).

In this book's epigraph, the American philosopher William James urges scholars to test what he called the "cash-value" of ideas by demanding to know whether it matters if they are true. In searching for the cash-value of decolonization, the pages that follow stand by that enterprise. They also add to it: illusions and even delusions have real outcomes. Foregrounding that interpretation privileges the intended but unrealized effects of actions alongside the more common concern with unintended consequences. It also moves against our natural human tendency to record success stories. Without the anticolonial elites' production of ideas and proposals, without their work in framing the debates over international law and the international economy, the energy crisis could not have transpired in the way that it did. It is not possible to write a history of the energy crisis without careful examination of how the devotees to sovereign rights moved about in the international current, how they framed and defined the issues that were important to them, and how those issues intersected with the aspirations of the OPEC nations.

Oil Revolution also suggests another benefit of expanding the cash-value thesis into the realm of expectations. If we look at the space between intentions and consequences, the attempt to measure the verification of truth over time becomes even more interesting. With every change, there is a gain and there is a loss. As the entries on the balance sheet piled up from the 1950s to the 1970s, sovereign rights became a ferment of what had been, what was, and what might be. When trying to explain the energy crisis as a historical event, the addition of such a contingent sensibility to the cash-value thesis means a great deal because it helps sort out how the principles of the economic culture of decolonization interacted with the puzzles the oil elites faced.

That story, about principles and puzzles, reveals an ambiguity from which no one can escape entirely in such human questions of rights, fairness, and justice. Any absolutist pretenses in the drama that follows, then, should not exclude that fundamental ambivalence and all its promise. Because the sovereign rights program unveiled itself in several forms, through different actors, and with numerous revisions, I am cautious in my claims. All conclusions are provisional, just as it is for provisional reasons that we retrieve them.

I

One Periphery

The Creation of Sovereign Rights, 1949–1955

*In this scheme, it is Latin America's position to act as part of the periphery
of the world economic system, in the specific role of producing food and
raw materials for the large industrial centers.*[1]
Raúl Prebisch, 1949

Every state has an unlimited right to dispose of its resources as it sees fit.[2]
Djalal Abdoh, 1952

When George Kennan visited Venezuela in February 1950, neither
"dollar-rich" Caracas nor the Venezuelan model of sovereignty
impressed him. "Here was a tropical country in the subsoil of which
reposed great quantities of a liquid essential to the present stage of
industrialization," he wrote in his journal. Venezuelan control over that
liquid rubbed him the wrong way. The price Western oil companies paid
into "the coffers of the Venezuelan government" was no more than
"ransom to the theory of state sovereignty." It was ransom, he said,
because Venezuelans "had not lifted a finger to create this wealth, would
have been incapable of developing it, and did not require it for its own
needs." The cold warrior also made due note of the "Communist-
dominated labor unions who control the workers in the oil fields," but
upon his return to Washington his written report emphasized less the

---

[1] Raúl Prebisch, "El Desarrollo Económico de la América Latina y Algunos de sus Princi-
pales Problemas," *El Trimestre Económico* 16 (1949), 348.
[2] UNGA, Official Records, Seventh Session, Second Committee, December 10, 1952, A/C.2/
SR.231.

threat of communism than the need for the United States to protect inexpensive access to "our" raw materials.[3]

Kennan already had begun to disengage from the Cold War, but his critique of Venezuela's application of state sovereignty to oil production was wrapped up in a related consensus. In that calculus, Western European and American planners defined what Venezuelans and other Latin Americans considered their inalienable right as a potential threat to US economic productivity, which was the key material and ideological weapon in the containment of communism. The passage of the US Defense Production Act the same year made global oil supply an official consideration of national security. In the following decades officials persistently invoked the link between oil consumption and the greater well-being of the "Free World." That connection reflected and shaped an international economy in which raw material producers and industrial nations had specific roles.[4]

The belief in the need to control the supply of raw materials applied especially to oil, historian and State Department adviser Herbert Feis wrote in 1946: "Enough oil within our certain grasp seemed ardently necessary to greatness and independence in the twentieth century." That year planners projected that Western Europe would be importing 80 percent of its oil from the Middle East by 1951. The prediction was nearly correct; the NATO countries obtained about 75 percent of their oil from the Persian Gulf by 1953. The United States, its allies, and multinational

---

[3] George Kennan, Diary Notes of Trip to South America, February 28, 1950, George F. Kennan Papers, Seeley G. Mudd Manuscript Library; Stephen G. Rabe, *The Killing Zone: The United States Wages Cold War in Latin America* (New York: Oxford University Press, 2012), 23.

[4] Historians with widely different interpretations of the origins of the Cold War agree on this point of productivity, as put forward by Charles Maier, *In Search of Stability: Explorations in Historical Political Economy* (Cambridge University Press, 1987), 121–52. On oil, the "Free World," and the Cold War, see: David S. Painter, "Oil and World Power," *Diplomatic History* 17 (Winter 1993), 159–70. Although certain parts of the nascent "Third World" received development aid from the United States in the late 1940s and 1950s, it was either because of their proximity to the Soviet Union and China or the pervasive belief that poverty facilitated the spread of communism. When this was not the case, other strategic and economic concerns applied. See: Robert J. McMahon, *The Cold War on the Periphery: The United States, India, and Pakistan* (New York: Columbia University Press, 1994), 22–3, 47–8; Nicholas J. Cullather, *Illusions of Influence: The Political Economy of United States–Philippines Relations, 1942–1960* (Stanford University Press, 1994), 36–59; Nicholas J. White, "Reconstructing Europe through Rejuvenating Empire: The British, French, and Dutch Experiences Compared," *Past and Present* 210 (2011), 211–36; Robert E. Wood, "From Marshall Plan to the Third World," in Melvyn P. Leffler and David S. Painter, eds., *The Origins of the Cold War: An International History*, 2nd edn (London: Routledge, 2005), 239–50.

corporations had arrived, in the decades since World War I, at a structure to secure that flow. Through a fine-spun series of cartel arrangements, five American companies – Socony-Vacuum (later Mobil), Standard Oil of California (Chevron), Standard Oil of New Jersey (Exxon), the Texas Company (Texaco), and Gulf – along with the British-owned Anglo-Iranian Oil Company (later British Petroleum), and Royal Dutch/Shell controlled over 90 percent of oil reserves outside of the United States, Mexico, and the Communist countries. The same companies, known as the Seven Sisters, accounted for nearly 90 percent of world oil production, owned almost 75 percent of world oil-refining capacity, and provided about 90 percent of the oil traded in international markets.[5]

Economists, journalists, and policymakers in the West widely echoed Kennan's position in explaining the economic and national security benefits of this structure, as well as the threat of nationalism to it. For Kennan, the ominous doctrine of state sovereignty had other repugnant repercussions. He even blamed that set of political beliefs for what he perceived as a loss of traditional culture. Oil wealth had turned Venezuela into a modern-day Goldsmith's Deserted Village, a place where "the prolonged enjoyment of unearned income" and "delusions of popular nationalism" decayed culture and debauched the citizenry.[6]

The Iranian representative to the United Nations, Djalal Abdoh, found insulting the idea that sovereign control was delusional or corrosive. He believed that the control of oil by multinational corporations had been made anachronistic by decolonization: corporate control and exploitation moved against the political stream of "the modern world," he told members of the Economic and Financial Committee of the UN General Assembly in 1952. If Kennan and other Western policymakers assumed certain areas would provide low-cost raw materials to the benefit of the greater international economy, anticolonial elites like Abdoh darkened that vision with the *bête noire* of colonial continuity. Like Kennan, he believed the world was cleft in two. Unlike Kennan, he measured that

---

[5] Michael B. Stoff, *Oil, War, and American Security: The Search for a National Policy on Foreign Oil, 1941–1947* (New Haven, CT.: Yale University Press, 1980), 1. The literature on this period is voluminous. For an introduction, see: Anand Toprani, "The French Connection: A New Perspective on the End of the Red Line Agreement, 1945–1948," *Diplomatic History* 36: 2 (April 2012), 261–7. For detailed descriptions of each of the companies' holdings, see US Congress, Senate, Select Committee on Small Business, *The International Petroleum Cartel: Staff Report to the Federal Trade Commission* (Washington, DC: US Government Printing Office, 1952), 21–33.

[6] George Kennan, Diary Notes of Trip to South America, February 28, 1950, George F. Kennan Papers, Seely G. Mudd Manuscript Library.

FIGURE 1.1 Djalal Abdoh, then a deputy of the Majlis, at the San Francisco Conference, at which the United Nations was founded, April 25, 1945.
Source: UN Photo/Rosenberg. Courtesy of the United Nations Photo Library, Photo No. 84190.

divide on a material basis by which unfair mechanisms enriched one half of the globe and impoverished the other. The dominant forces that concerned him were not directly associated with the Cold War struggle for global primacy. Neither was the question of sovereignty viewed as a capitalist-socialist disagreement over the sanctity or vulgarity of private property. Instead, he insisted that the prolongation of imperial economic thralldom stood against the new era of decolonization.[7]

From Abdoh's perspective, the right of a nation to control its resources was not a misdirected theory, as Kennan believed, but the conquest of a venal past. He and his counterparts worked in the United Nations to enshrine in international law a specific principle: permanent sovereignty over natural resources. This chapter examines the way in which their attempt to fashion permanent sovereignty as an imprescriptible right of nation-states was an early stirring of what would become the international sovereign rights program. The urgent preoccupation with

[7] UNGA, Official Records, Seventh Session, Second Committee, December 10, 1952, A/C.2/SR.231.

sovereign rights in the United Nations, which drew on the legal thought of Abdoh's Latin American interlocutors, provided common ground on which elites of different backgrounds built a long-term project.

In that context, permanent sovereignty was quickly linked to the economic doctrine of unequal exchange. Here again a Latin American interpretation, this one of global economic inequality, gave voice to a rising belief of sameness. By the mid-1950s, permanent sovereignty and unequal exchange had combined to become shorthand for discussions about global structural inequality and the common Third World drive to overcome it. Articulated in many different spheres of international society – legal thought, development economics, social theory, and imperial history – the shared vision of sovereign rights created a propitious environment for the marriage of anticolonial law to development economics.

The union of development economics to the international law of decolonization centralized the anticolonial elite experience. A new sovereign rights program thus drew influence at its birth from the fact that the cultural basis of international politics, the hierarchical division of the world into the powerful and the powerless, had been radically altered by decolonization. One event captured that moment and drove the process forward: the Iran oil crisis of 1951 to 1953.

The Iran oil crisis galvanized sovereign rights by bringing into the open, on a scale almost larger than life, the problem of economic continuity amidst political change that marked the decolonizing world. The crisis began when Iranian Prime Minister Mohammed Mossadegh called on the Anglo-Iranian Oil Company to respect sovereign control in April 1951. When rebuffed, he nationalized the foreign conglomerate. Historians have discussed in detail the origins of oil exploration in Persia and then Iran, the unfavorable oil concessions signed in 1901 and 1933, the 1951 nationalization, the ensuing crisis, and the American role in the 1953 overthrow of Mossadegh. Less is known, in contrast, about the contours of international debate spurred on by the crisis. This is too bad, because Mossadegh employed what became an influential public diplomacy of "economic independence" that grabbed the attention of an array of anticolonial nationalists, including Djalal Abdoh's counterparts in the United Nations. They moved to legitimate the principle in international law, and their meetings in New York became the first touch points in what would become an expansive network of affiliation.[8]

---

[8] Mary Ann Heiss, *Empire and Nationhood: The United States, Great Britain, and Iranian Oil, 1950–1954* (New York: Columbia University Press, 1997); Ervand Abrahamian, *The*

One way to begin that story is with the political career of the Iranian prime minister himself. Mossadegh held a deep-seated enmity toward the Anglo-Iranian Oil Company and foreign control of Iranian oil more generally. He argued against new petroleum exploration by either Soviet or US companies when Josef Stalin refused to remove the Red Army from Azerbaijan in 1946. He was among legislators in the Iranian parliament, the Majlis, who pushed through a 1947 law that forbade new concessions to foreign companies and directed the government to renegotiate Anglo-Iranian's 1933 concession.

In the late 1940s, Mossadegh also followed closely the development of new deals between other producing nations and their foreign concession-aires. The standard concessionary agreements between the multinational oil companies and the producing countries, including Iran, had been for a fixed royalty rate per ton of oil produced. In 1943 and 1947, Venezuela passed new laws that changed the terms and resulted in the widely publicized "fifty-fifty" profit-sharing deal. When Mossadegh and other nationalists in the Majlis began to pressure the Anglo-Iranian Oil Company for a similar profit-sharing agreement, the company declined. Instead, in 1949 it offered Iran a contract known as the Supplemental Agreement, which guaranteed that annual royalty payments would not drop below £4 million, reduced the area in which it would drill, and pledged to train Iranians for administrative positions. All this was in return for an extension of the concession for another 60 years. The young Shah of Iran, Mohammed Reza Pahlavi, who had recently survived an assassination attempt, believed that he needed to accept the British offer to maintain revenues and political stability. His cabinet did so and then sent it on to the Majlis.[9]

The Shah's plan did not work, in large part because of a well-informed public opinion. "The 50–50 sharing of profits agreement … is well known in Tehran," one official in the US State Department wrote. "Public

---

Coup: 1953, the CIA, and the Roots of Modern US-Iranian Relations (New York: The New Press, 2013); James H. Bamberg, *The History of the British Petroleum Company: Volume II, The Anglo-Iranian Years, 1928–1954* (Cambridge University Press, 1994), 283–451. For interesting recent discussions from the perspective of Anglo-Iranian officials, see: Nathan J. Citino, "Internationalist Oilmen, the Middle East, and the Remaking of American Liberalism, 1945–1953," *Business History Review* 84: 2 (2010), 227–51; Neveen Abdelrehim, Josephine Maltby, and Steven Toms, "Corporate Social Responsibility and Corporate Control: The Anglo-Iranian Oil Company, 1933–1951," *Enterprise and Society* 12: 4 (2011), 824–62.

[9] Anthony Sampson, *The Seven Sisters*, (New York: Viking, 1975), 108–11; Louis Turner, *The Oil Companies in the International System* (London: George, Allen & Unwin, 1978), 47–52.

opinion in Iran would never accept anything less than a 50–50 arrangement," the Iranian ambassador in Washington said. The Majlis denounced the Supplemental Agreement and demanded that Anglo-Iranian begin splitting profits with Iran on a fifty-fifty basis, as American oil companies had also just agreed to do in Saudi Arabia. The legislative term ended before a vote could be taken. Accusations of royal bribery and fraud tainted the following elections. Mossadegh and others staged a sit-in that forced new elections, and he was elected prime minister. He immediately called for the establishment of an oil committee, which he chaired. The director of Iran's petroleum institute, Manucher Farmanfarmaian, later described their meetings: "Mossadegh did not care about dollars and cents or numbers of barrels per day. He saw the basic issue as one of national sovereignty. Iran's sovereignty was being undercut by a company that sacrificed Iranian lives for British interests."[10]

The feeling of lost sovereignty was broadly shared within Iran, as was the use of the language of decolonization to describe it. To take one instance, Anglo-Iranian's highest-ranking Iranian employee, Mostafa Fateh, wrote a 23-page letter to a member of the board of directors. The company needed to recognize that "the awakening of nationalism and political consciousness of the people of Asia" would eventually force them to compromise. This self-aware germination of a new consciousness, often described as an awakening or a rebirth, would become central to the economic culture of decolonization and the sovereign rights program. Phrases like Fateh's captured a sentiment that was flowering among anticolonial elites who believed that their politics drew not only on specific political or economic traditions but also on deeper human instincts of freedom and unity.[11]

Fateh was in some ways an archetypal anticolonial elite. He was trained in political science and economics at Columbia University, and graduated with an MA in political science in 1919. As others would later, he began his path to contemporary relations in the oil industry with a close study of national history. In 1928 he wrote an article for the *Bulletin of the School of Oriental Studies* on Persian taxation from the pre-Christian era of Darius to the tenth century. In it, the details of the

---

[10] Funkhouser to McGhee, "Discussions with British on AIOC," September 14, 1950, *FRUS 1950*, vol. V, doc. 38; Memorandum of Conversation, "Aid for Iran," April 26, 1950, *FRUS 1950*, vol. V, doc. 235; Farmanfarmaian, *Blood & Oil*, 241–2.

[11] Mostafa Elm, *Oil, Power, and Principle: The Iranian Nationalization and Its Aftermath* (Syracuse University Press, 1994), 75–6.

different tax programs were less important than their effect in creating a "highly organized and prosperous state" that survived interventions from the Greek, Arab, and Mongol empires. The article was nationalist in intention – the invading empires, unlike the governments led by native Persians, "had overwhelmed and massacred but never governed" the people of Iran.[12]

Nationalism remained on Fateh's mind throughout his career at Anglo-Iranian. In 1949 he summarized his views in a letter to a Majlis deputy. Iran had been "hoodwinked" in their 1933 concessionary contract, he wrote. The new company proposals in the Supplemental Agreement resembled those "of a covetous lender who exploits the dire needs of his neighbor by taking his collateral for giving him a loaf of bread." In 1956 he wrote a long Marxist-inspired study that analyzed the earlier nationalist movements that led to the 1932 annulment of the original 1901 oil concession as "unjust and contrary to the sovereign rights of Persia." (He was jailed in 1957 by the Shah's government for the effort.) British intelligence documents reveal that Fateh was playing a complex double game. But he also expressed a widespread sentiment, and the Majlis oil committee recommended nationalizing Anglo-Iranian, an option legislators unanimously approved in April 1951.[13]

The legislation contained provisions to audit the company and a process by which to weigh company claims for compensation, but the British government accused the Iranians of stealing their property. They demanded that the International Court of Justice arbitrate the dispute. Mossadegh rejected both the accusation and the demand. He believed that the court did not have jurisdiction over a fundamentally domestic issue. Here he posed an argument about domestic jurisdiction, which became one of several key concepts of the sovereign rights program.

He traveled to The Hague to address the ICJ. To the judges, he emphasized the history of British and Russian imperial competition over

[12] Columbia University, Annual Commencement, June 4, 1919, p. 29 (where he is listed as being from Cyprus); Mostafa Khan Fateh, "Taxation in Persia: A Synopsis from the Early Times to the Conquest of the Mongols," *Bulletin of the School of Oriental Studies* 4: 4 (1928), 742–3.

[13] Elm, *Oil, Power, and Principle*, 54–55; Sepehr Zabih, *The Communist Movement in Iran* (Berkeley: University of California Press, 1966), 61–2; Habib Ladjevardi, *Labor Unions and Autocracy in Iran* (Syracuse University Press, 1985), 42, 156; Ervand Abrahamian, *Iran Between Two Revolutions* (Princeton University Press, 1982), 188; James A. Bill, *The Eagle and the Lion: The Tragedy of American-Iranian Relations* (New Haven: Yale University Press, 1992), 467n20.

Iran, and took extra time to review the 1919 treaty granting Britain charge of national finances and the army. The British had used that position to "ensure their exclusive ownership of our oil," he argued. "So what should have been the source of our national wealth became ... the cause of serious and formidable problems." Mossadegh made clear that the debate turned on a simple question that emerged from that history of imperialism: if an agreement was made between a private company and a government, was nationalization a matter essentially within domestic or international jurisdiction? The Iranian government insisted on domestic jurisdiction as a principle of sovereignty, he continued: "The decision we have taken to nationalize expresses the political will of a free and sovereign people. Understand, then, we are calling on the terms of the [United Nations] Charter to ask you to refuse to intervene in the matter."[14]

The court ruled in Iran's favor in July 1952. But this was in practical terms a barren victory. Anglo-Iranian announced that it would sue any tankers carrying Iranian oil at their point of destination. The legal threat – supported by the British and American governments, as well as the other multinational oil companies – was remarkably effective and forced Iranian oil production down by 90 percent. As the other multinational oil companies increased production in Iraq, Kuwait, and Saudi Arabia to offset the production loss, the British government pressed its advantage. Their ambassador to the United Nations, Gladwyn Jebb, continued to assert that Iranian oil was "clearly the legal property of the Anglo-Iranian Oil Company."[15]

Mossadegh also traveled to New York to present his case to the UN Security Council. He infused his argument about domestic jurisdiction with an internationalist entreaty that placed Iran squarely in the global context of decolonization. "It is gratifying to see that the European powers have respected the legitimate aspiration of the people of India, Pakistan, Indonesia, and others who had struggled for the right to enter the family of nations on terms of freedom and complete equality," he began. The nationalization, by a country that had long held formal independence, sought the same objective, Mossadegh said: "Iran demands just that right ... It expects this exalted international tribunal and the

---

[14] ICJ, *Anglo-Iranian Oil Co.*, Oral Proceedings Concerning the Preliminary Objections, Déclaration du Dr. Mossadegh (Iran), June 9, 1952.

[15] ICJ, *Anglo-Iranian Oil Co.*, Press Release, July 7, 1952; Gasiorowski, "The 1953 Coup D'etat in Iran," 262–7.

great Powers to help it, too, to recover its economic independence, to achieve the social prosperity of its people, and thus to affirm its political independence."[16]

His argument drew a tight connection between decolonization – "political independence" – and the right to use sovereignty to impose economic control. Iran had remained nominally independent for much of its history, as Fateh had also noted. But for the prime minister, his nation also stood within the transformative vision of decolonization. For self-determination to be realized, "economic independence" needed to follow. Mossadegh, then, criticized not only the past actions of British imperialist pressure but also the engrained economic inequality it left behind. In the light of such a conception, the delegates from Yugoslavia and India supported Mossadegh in the Security Council. The oil concession naturally fell under Iran's jurisdiction, they agreed. The conflict between the company and the government "was an exclusively domestic matter."[17]

The argument was one of stark clarity, and it echoed down the rest of the century. It also reverberated across space. Mossadegh and other Iranian elites maintained with great consistency that the problem of Iranian oil was symptomatic of global imbalances resulting from imperialism. They also placed the Iranian crisis in other comparative frameworks. The disparity between Venezuelan and Saudi oil incomes, on the one hand, and Iranian income, on the other, he told one American official, was the starkest illustration of the "theft" committed by the Anglo-Iranian Oil Company. At a train stop in Philadelphia after the Security Council meeting, he lectured a 200-person crowd in Independence Square on the similarities between the Iranian nationalization and the universal idealism of the American Revolution. "An ancient nation with many centuries of recorded history and a great culture and civilization has every right to achieve its political and economic freedom," he declared. "It is also entitled to use its natural resources to eradicate the misery and poverty that are plaguing the lives of the Iranian people." He then symbolically touched the Liberty Bell.[18]

---

[16] Rouholla K. Ramazani, *Iran's Foreign Policy: A Study of Foreign Policy in Modernizing Nations* (Charlottesville: University of Virginia Press, 1975), 215.

[17] Alan W. Ford, *The Anglo-Iranian Oil Dispute of 1951–1952: A Study of the Role of Law in the Relations of States* (Berkeley: University of California Press, 1955), 126; Yuen-li Liang, "The Question of Domestic Jurisdiction in the Anglo-Iranian Oil Dispute Before the Security Council," *AJIL* 46: 2 (1952), 272–82.

[18] Memorandum of Conversation, October 11, 1951, *FRUS, 1952–1954*, vol. X, doc. 113; "Mossadegh Pleads Cause," *The Washington Post* (October 23, 1951), 11.

FIGURE 1.2 Iranian Prime Minister Mohammed Mossadegh examines the Liberty
Bell, c. 1951.
Source: Department of State, Harry S. Truman Library and Museum. Accession No. 66–8004.

The Anglo-Iranian nationalization was a crisis of immense proportions,
and its legality was becoming a fiery topic in international circles. It was in
that context that the UN General Assembly passed a resolution in December 1952 declaring that "the right of peoples free to use and exploit their
national wealth and resources is inherent in their sovereignty." The
resolution on permanent sovereignty meant, in part, to validate the Iranian nationalization. It was also about a broader set of principles, as the
discussion between Djalal Abdoh and several Latin American delegates
mapped out the early connection between decolonization and the sovereign rights program. In short, the UN conversations testify to a frame of
mind that bonded anticolonial elites together.[19]

---

[19] UNGA, Official Records, General Assembly Res. 626 (VII), December 21, 1952. The
resolution was commented upon in the contemporary legal literature: James N. Hyde,
"Permanent Sovereignty over Natural Wealth and Resources," *AJIL* 50 (1956), 854–67;
Edward D. Re, "Nationalization and the Investment of Capital Abroad," *Georgetown*

Delegates representing what one US commentator lumped together as the "whole Asian-Arab, Latin American, Soviet thesis" began their attempt to convert the concept of self-determination into a binding legal doctrine of national resource ownership in the UN General Assembly in 1950. UN Secretary General Trygve Lie noted at the beginning of the session that one quarter of the population of the world had gained political independence in the previous six years. The pressure toward "freedom and equality" would only continue to increase, he said, as indicated by the surge of support for a Draft Covenant on Civil and Political Rights. The concept of permanent sovereignty became a part of that debate when several representatives argued that enshrining self-determination in international law would hasten the liquidation of colonialism.[20]

The General Assembly passed the complicated task of establishing the right and defining the legal machinery of self-determination to Djalal Abdoh's Economic and Financial Committee, which began work in 1952. There, as part of the more sweeping objective of creating an international law that reflected the new reality of decolonization, the delegates from Uruguay and Bolivia proposed a resolution on permanent sovereignty. The revolutionary government of the latter had just nationalized its mining industries, an act US Secretary of State Dean Acheson feared would have "a bad effect in other countries." The Uruguayan, Angel Maria Cusano, brought the meeting to order by arguing that the "immense natural wealth" of poorer nations could help bring about "the ideal of economic independence." Luis Adolfo Siles, the Bolivian ambassador who would later describe the United Nations as a global forum for the oppressed, discussed "the bitter experience" of Iran when he seconded the proposal.[21]

The position of the Latin American ambassadors was the result of a century-long sensitivity to foreign intervention and gunboat diplomacy. In 1868 the Argentine diplomat Carlos Calvo had put forward what came to be known as the Calvo Doctrine, an argument that foreign contractors were subject to local law. The goal of the doctrine was to defuse the threat of foreign intervention caused by investor and settler disputes. Latin

Law Journal 42 (1953–4), 44–68; Arthur K. Kuhn, "Nationalization of Foreign-Owned Property in Its Impact on International Law," *AJIL* 45: 4 (1951), 709–12.

[20] UNGA, Official Records, "Introduction," *Annual Report of the Secretary General on the Work of the Organization, 1 July 1950–30 June 1951*, A/1844/Add.1.

[21] UNGA, Official Records, Seventh Session, Second Committee, December 11, 1952, A/C.2/SR.232; Luis Adolfo Siles, *Bolivia en la ONU* (La Paz: Imprenta del Estado, 1966).

American governments had inserted it as a provision in treaties, national constitutions, local legislation, and private contracts with foreign companies ever since. In discussing that right with Abdoh and other lawyers in the United Nations, they sought to use the momentum of decolonization to endow the doctrine with international status.[22]

Abdoh, who had served with Mossadegh in the Majlis in the 1940s, agreed with the South Americans' legal argument and saw the benefit of internationalizing it. His position was also a likely one, for intellectual reasons as well as political ones. Or, better, his intellectual preparation and the political world he came to inhabit were inseparable. Like Mostafa Fateh, he shared certain characteristics of the new international class of anticolonial elites. His 1937 doctoral thesis at the University of Paris law school had concentrated on the "concept of social need" in Iranian contract law. He was concerned in particular with the "moral element" of the 1928 Civil Code – the same code that Fateh had defended as the successor to centuries of Persian governance. One fine-tune contradiction worried him: the law outlawed violence to force consent but was silent about what he considered the subtler "defects of consent" that occurred in negotiations between unequal parties. That silence suggested to Abdoh the need to reconsider the notion of "unilateral will" as it related to contracts. In an argument that he would directly echo in his public rationale for the Iranian nationalization and for the adoption of the permanent sovereignty resolution at the United Nations, he held that any situation in which "a victim" was forced into an "unfair contract . . . by nature marred the validity of the contract." The rightful parting of an individual from his property could only happen based on free volition. The distinction between consent and will needed to disappear, he concluded.[23]

The implications of that discrepancy were not difficult to deduce in the case of Iranian oil. Abdoh defended Iran's "sovereign right" to nationalize its oil on Eleanor Roosevelt's NBC television show in May 1951. Roosevelt, who as a US delegate to the United Nations in the late 1940s had argued that the rights of nations had no place in discussions about the

---

[22] Kenneth A. Rodman, *Sanctity vs. Sovereignty: The United States and the Nationalization of Natural Resource Investments* (New York: Columbia University Press, 1988), 43; Kate Miles, *The Origins of International Investment Law: Empire, Environment and the Safeguarding of Capital* (New York: Cambridge University Press, 2013), 72, 97–9; Nico Schrijver, *Sovereignty over Natural Resources: Balancing Rights and Duties* (New York: Cambridge University Press, 2008), 180.

[23] Djalal Abdoh, L'élément psychologique dans les contrats suivant la conception iranienne (Thèse pour le doctorat, Université de Paris, Faculté de Droit, 1937), 7, 183–4, 219.

human rights of individuals, began the interview with a point-blank question: Why had Iran canceled the 1933 oil concession? Abdoh responded that the concession, a contract between a private corporation and a nation, was "subject to Iranian law." Furthermore, he told Roosevelt, a private contract could not restrict the "legislative right" of Iran to change it. The Iranian nation had been forced to consent to an unfair oil concession, and the nationalization righted that wrong. To write permanent sovereignty into international law through a UN amendment, then, was to safeguard the economic rights of vulnerable countries – in the language of his dissertation, to protect will from consent. "Thus, in nationalizing her oil, Iran is only exercising an indisputable sovereign right," he concluded. "It is because of their awareness and because the Iranian people have fully realized their rights that the oil industry was nationalized."[24]

Abdoh added to the UN committee that Mexico's 1938 oil nationalization had upheld the legitimacy of permanent sovereignty. The Mexican delegate to the committee, former Treasury Secretary Ramón Beteta, had been influential in his application of the Calvo Doctrine during that dispute. What US officials euphemistically called the "economic protection" of Latin America was for him no different than the recent Italian invasion of Ethiopia, he wrote in 1937. Employing a similar dialectic that Mossadegh would later use at the Security Council, he linked economic control to national independence. Speaking after Abdoh in 1952, he confirmed his belief in the "interrelationship between the economic development of the under-developed countries and the free exploitation of their own resources."[25]

Abdoh and the Latin Americans explicitly introduced a link between what they considered the international right to self-determination and resource ownership. Their interactions also resulted in an analogy that likened their experiences, a point that was not lost on them or the shrewdest international observers. Herbert Feis, the American economic historian who helped write US foreign oil policy in the 1940s, linked the Iran crisis to the contemporary Bolivian and decade-old Mexican

---

[24] "Crisis in Iran," Mrs. Roosevelt Meets the Public, May 27, 1951, NBC Television Collection, LOC.

[25] UNGA, Official Records, Seventh Session, Second Committee, December 10, 1952, A/C.2/SR.231; Ramón Beteta, "Los Principios de México en su Vida Internacional," *Memorias de la Secretaría de Relaciones Exteriores. Septiembre de 1937-Agosto de 1938*, vol. I (Mexico City: DAPP, 1938), 24–9; UNGA, Official Record, Seventh Session, Second Committee, December 13, 1952, A/C.2/238.

arguments about "the right to use their sovereign power to expropri-ate." That connection was cast in an intrepid light at the UN committee. No suitable method existed in the past for nations such as Bolivia or Iran to communicate their shared position of defiance, the Bolivian Adolfo Siles told Abdoh. That "unfortunate phase" had passed "largely due to the influence of the United Nations," an institution that was unique in history because it was a place where the poorer countries could "pro-mote respect for an international right." The significance of the United Nations resided in its existence as a medium for the language and experience of similarity. When his government nationalized its tin mines, the nation had "experienced the full feeling of economic inde-pendence" for the first time in its history. For that reason, Abdoh's concerns touched him as familiar: the "maneuvers" of Anglo-Iranian in the wake of nationalization mirrored that of the former owners of Bolivia's mines.[26]

Thirty-one states voted for the resolution on permanent sovereignty in December 1952. The presidents of the New York Stock Exchange and the Guarantee Trust Company joined the delegations from the United States and Western Europe in lamenting the outcome. Abdoh took umbrage with their opposition. The "habit of exploiting the economies of others" moved against the ideal of international cooperation based on state sovereignty, he said in a moving speech after the vote. "The Countries of the Middle East and Latin America have become conscious of their rights, and the existing state of affairs cannot be allowed to continue." Like Mossadegh in the Security Council, Abdoh was clear about the thrust of his message: permanent sovereignty was a right conferred by decolonization.[27]

There was idealism here, to be sure, but strategy too. In emphasizing permanent sovereignty as an international right, Abdoh surely hoped that international support for the oil nationalization would limit the likelihood of retaliation against Iran. It did not. A US-sponsored coup overthrew Mossadegh and reinstated the Shah in August 1953. Acrimony character-ized the subsequent negotiations about the future of Iranian oil. In the end, through a new concession with the newly instituted Iran Consor-tium, Iran received formal title to its oil and a fifty-fifty profit-sharing

---

[26] Herbert Feis, "Oil for Peace or War," *Foreign Affairs* 32: 3 (April 1954), 427; UNGA, Official Record, Seventh Session, Second Committee, December 11, 1952, A/C.2/SR.232.

[27] Re, "Nationalization of Investment," 49–52; UNGA, Official Records, Seventh Session, Second Committee, December 13, 1952, A/C.2/SR.238.

agreement. But contractual stipulations against sovereign rights revealed serious limits to that paper sovereignty. On the crucial question of jurisdiction, the 1953 contract moved arbitration to "a jurisprudence intermediate between public international law and private international law," a position opposite the one put forth by Mossadegh, Abdoh, and in the UN resolution.[28]

The coup also indicated the marginality of the sovereign rights position in its earliest days. The US National Security Council produced a paper on Middle Eastern oil the same year. Oil was "crucial to the strength" of European recovery and the Cold War battle against the Soviet Union. The Eisenhower administration would continue to support corporate arrangements to buffer those interests from the politics of anticolonialism. At the same time, the US government would verbally distance itself from private interests to avoid accusations that "the American system is one of privilege, monopoly, private oppression, and imperialism," as one US official put it.[29]

But the link between "the American system" and "imperialism" was one that would fester in the minds of anticolonial elites for the foreseeable future. This was in part because the nationalization had been a boomerang of a weapon for nationalist Iran. The experience of Mossadegh, in other words, provided a harsh lesson for other erstwhile nationalists. It would serve as a cautionary tale for years.

At the same time, though, the Iran oil crisis also helped bring to life the new international narrative of sovereign rights. In permanent sovereignty, the members of the Economic and Financial Committee forged a legal principle they believed would cultivate solidarity and encourage national and international projects to redress past and ongoing economic injustices – hopefully with more success than Mossadegh had. Other anticolonial lawyers could now turn to permanent sovereignty as a basic right of nations in the international community. That critical shift would continue to build on the idea of decolonization as a new but inevitable process.

The UN conversations about permanent sovereignty also reveal another important and lasting element of the economic culture of decolonization. The notion of an alliance of victims becoming an

---

[28] Abolbashar Farmanfarma, "The Oil Agreement between Iran and the International Oil Consortium: The Law Controlling," *Texas Law Review* 34: 2 (December 1955), 259–87.

[29] Quoted in Nathan J. Citino, *From Arab Nationalism to OPEC: Eisenhower, King Saud, and the Making of U.S.-Saudi Relations*, 2nd edn (Bloomington: Indiana University Press, 2005), 43.

alliance of agents colors the whole history of sovereign rights. The tendency toward convergence in the United Nations shrank the territorial, political, and cultural distance between elites enough to make that exchange possible. A concurrent overlap in economic thought, centered on the concept of unequal exchange, complemented and bolstered the rise of permanent sovereignty in international law. In this case, too, the Latin American experience would help shape the content of the new sovereign rights program.

For the small cluster of lawyers working on the permanent sovereignty resolution, the United Nations represented a spectacular opportunity to democratize global politics. It was at the UN too that the assertion of permanent sovereignty as a right fused with a popular economic theory about the material legacy of imperialism. This also happened in the early 1950s when a cluster of theories and information about international trade that had long floated around rather loosely found an articulate voice in a recent UN hire, the Argentine central banker Raúl Prebisch. After he seized on the doctrine of unequal exchange, also known as the terms of trade thesis, a core set of assumptions quickly became influential among development economists. Crucially, the doctrine also helped other anticolonial elites understand and explain the inclusive vision of decolonization discerned by Mossadegh, Abdoh, and the others.

Prebisch outlined the basic argument for unequal exchange in his 1949 keynote address to the first conference of the UN Economic Commission for Latin America. The raw material exporting nations of Latin America had been left with economies that relied on the sale of raw materials and the import of finished goods, Prebisch said. That historical imbalance led to the exportation of raw materials at subdued prices vis-à-vis finished products. Subsequently, the low prices of raw materials curtailed the potential for development in Argentina and, more broadly, Latin America.

Relative costs, price trends, and other dry economic technicalities encased the argument. But there was more to the argument than macroeconomic analysis. Prebisch also said that unequal exchange was connected to the same sort of question of decolonization and international justice that concerned Mossadegh and the UN delegates in 1952. In the neat columns of his trade tables, he found a trend that pointed to deep-rooted causes for international economic inequalities. The lack of national control over raw material production led to endemically low prices, he believed, and international trade thus enriched industrialized nations at the expense of Latin American raw material producers. This

FIGURE 1.3 "Executive Secretaries of ECLA, ECAFE, and ECE Give Press Conference at UN Headquarters," June 4, 1952. Raúl Prebisch is on the far left and Gunnar Myrdal is on the far right.
Source: UN Photo/MB. Courtesy of the United Nations Photo Library, Photo No. 333462.

relationship, which he termed unequal exchange, played the crucial role in Latin American poverty: "From there come the differences, so accentuated, in the quality of life of the masses of those countries and these."[30]

The doctrine of unequal exchange was thus more than just academic analysis. It was an ethical appeal to reconsider an international economy unfairly tilted by dint of history. Prebisch arrived at this posture along what was a familiar course for anticolonial elites. As it had for Mostafa Fateh and Djalal Abdoh, Prebisch's concern with inequality began early in a career that initially dealt with domestic questions. In his first published article as a professional economist in 1920, he discussed the rising costs of

---

[30] Raúl Prebisch, *The Economic Development of Latin America and Its Principal Problems* (New York: UN, 1949), 10–11. Hans Singer developed a similar thesis simultaneously: Hans Singer, "The Distribution of Gains between Investing and Borrowing Countries," *American Economic Review* 40: 2 (1950), 473–85. In the economic literature, this is known as the Prebisch-Singer thesis. For an introduction, see: H. W. Arndt, *Economic Development: The History of an Idea* (University of Chicago Press, 1987), 49–87.

living for the Argentine "working class" as something "felt in the flesh."
In a 1924 article he condemned the private "hoarding of land" in Argentina as an "obstacle to national development and social justice." By the
time he had become an established national figure in the mid-1930s, he
had transferred that ethics to Argentina's foreign economic relations
through his systematic critique of the Ottowa trade accords.[31]

But if Prebisch had limited his analysis to Argentina or even to Latin
America in 1949, unequal exchange may not have been so influential. By
then he was ready to go further: the commercial trends he described
formed part of a larger order. He devised stark yet universal descriptors –
"center" and "periphery" – to identify a worldwide hierarchy. He did so
in a way that invited a connection to the nascent law of permanent
sovereignty. That correlation would catch on in part because Prebisch's
terms were both specific and vague. When used to interpret the historical
price trends for raw materials, a forceful and clear dichotomy emerged
between the center and the periphery. Yet a plurality of the world's nations
and aspiring nations – lands that otherwise had disparate political, cultural,
and geographical histories – formed Prebisch's periphery. The spatial
ambiguity of the periphery also lent it an expansive territorial application,
which aligned with the argument put forth by the UN diplomats, namely
that economic liberation was a next step in the process of decolonization.

Prebish explicitly made the argument a global one. If the collective
benefits of trade gradually reached throughout the industrial world, he
said, they did not "extend into the periphery of the world economy."
Here was the significance of the theory for Prebisch and for the elites that
would use it: "the periphery of the world economy."[32]

The more advanced theoretical content of the argument, and this was
another crucial insight, further suggested the validity of such a sweeping
application. Here Prebisch indicated the broader nature of the Argentine
and Latin American experience through his explicit contradiction of the
classical theory of comparative advantage. Taking a position against
what he called the "false universality" shared by Smith, Ricardo, Mill,
Marshall, Keynes, and others, he argued that international trade was not

---

[31] Reel 1, Envelope 1, doc. B-1920, Raúl Prebisch, Archivo de Trabajo, microfilm; Reel 1,
Envelope 2, doc. B-1924, Raúl Prebisch, Archivo de Trabajo, microfilm; Reel 1, Envelope
4, doc. C-1933, Raúl Prebisch, Archivo de Trabajo, microfilm.
[32] Prebisch, "El Desarrollo Económico," 349. The idea of an inevitable "favorable interest
of providence in international trade" has been traced by one economic historian to the
fourth century A.D.: Jacob Viner, *The Role of Providence in the Social Order* (Princeton
University Press, 1972), 36.

advantageous for all. Rather, it favored the technological advancement and industrial productivity of the nations of the center, which in turn forged a potent legacy in which the value of raw materials declined as productivity rose. The allegedly "natural" operation of trade was anything but, Prebisch said. Comparative advantage was not a scientific law with absolute or universal scope. Instead it was an outcome of policy derived from past power relations. It followed that the wealth of the center had less to do with the benefits derived from the expansion of commerce than with the inequitable structure of that commerce.[33]

Prebisch was among the first to grasp the massive economic implications of decolonization and its potential to challenge international conventions. But his insight was not invented of new cloth. The early surge of the doctrine of unequal exchange among development economists, and the link anticolonial elites would find between it and permanent sovereignty, occurred within a dynamic intellectual environment.

The underlying question of global economic injustice had, after all, been raised before. Imperialism, capitalism, and poverty were standbys of international thought, and unequal exchange built on a whole body of contemporary political-economic ideas. But while Prebisch and other development economists shared certain traits with the other principal schools of the postwar era, including those associated with central planning and modernization theory, their understanding was distinct. And as individual development economists put forward unique but related theories that turned on sovereignty-driven notions of economic justice, the basic assumptions of the doctrine of unequal exchange became so influential that most anticolonial elites accepted it as a universal truth by the mid-1950s. Its content and its context together provide an interesting map of how anticolonial elites understood the past and the present of international capitalism at mid-century.

Development economists shared some terrain, for example, with Marxist critics of imperialism who had long built bridges between the extraction of raw materials, territorial conquest, and imperial rivalry. Indeed, unequal exchange would become associated intimately with a global Marxist critique by the mid-1960s to form a crucial plank of popular calls against "neo-colonialism." But Prebisch and most other development economists were not Marxists. For one, they did not believe in a historical dialectic

---

[33] Prebisch, *The Economic Development of Latin America*, 11.

dominated by class warfare. Neither did they find capitalism to contain the seeds of its own destruction; Prebisch sought rather to enlarge and rework the international market while redistributing power within it. Furthermore, most cared little for the ideological debate between communism and capitalism and even less for the Cold War. They looked at the past with a different tradition in mind: the powerful and expanding desire of imperialists to exploit the resources of others.[34]

Development economists also shared some traits with what one historian has called the "court vernacular" of capitalist development in the West, modernization theory. Like modernization theorists, they sought a transition to a better life through development – what Albert O. Hirschman, who moved between these schools of thought, called "the process of *change* of one type of economy *into* some other more advanced type." Like modernization theorists, development economists saw increased capital accumulation as the motor of that progress. Like modernization theorists, most did not doubt the desirability of development of a Western variety – they believed that the overall effect of development would be to multiply the opportunities for mutually profitable exchange among people. Hirschman in particular found elegant Walt Rostow's analogy of "take-off" to describe that process.[35]

But Prebisch, Hirschman, and other development economists differed from the mandarins of modernization on two principal questions. First, what caused Third World poverty? Second, from where would new capital to alleviate poverty come? Most modernization theorists placed the onus for poverty on the "backwards cultures" of "traditional societies." In emphasizing the difference as societal, they tended to banish the histories of colonialism, unequal exchange, and other exploitation from their economic analysis. Development economists found those histories central and held that the challenge confronting the Third World was intractable without acknowledging the vestigial impacts of colonial rule.

---

[34] For an intellectual summary, see: Patrick Wolfe, "History and Imperialism: A Century of Theory, from Marx to Postcolonialism," *The American Historical Review* (1997), 388–420.

[35] Nick Cullather, "Development? It's History," *Diplomatic History* 24: 4 (2000), 641; Albert O. Hirschman, *The Strategy of Economic Development* (New Haven, CT: Yale University Press, 1958), 45–52, emphasis in original. Prime examples are the American sponsorship of Prebisch's most popular policy program, import substitution, as well as the Rockefeller Foundation's support of the Economic Commission of Latin America: Sylvia Maxfield and James H. Nolt, "Protectionism and the Internationalization of Capital: US Sponsorship of Import Substitution Industrialization in the Philippines, Turkey and Argentina," *International Studies Quarterly* 34: 1 (March 1990), 49–81.

The first question, on the causes of poverty, shaped the development of economists' understanding of the second, the source of capital for development. Hans Singer, who put forward a nearly identical thesis of unequal exchange at the same time as Prebisch, felt strongly about both points. From his position at the United Nations, he disagreed with the American and Western European emphasis on foreign aid and investment. There existed "a gathering conviction ... that things cannot be allowed to go on as they are," he said. It did not make sense to "help the underdeveloped countries along while at the same time they are allowed to lose on the swings of trade." The dispute about the source of capital was a difference of quality, then, not degree. The argument for nationalist policies to create indigenous capital was a position steeped in the experience and the interest of the periphery.[36]

Yet, although important, these differences should not be overstated. While it is true that development economists put forward a distinct view from that of their Marxist and modernizing counterparts, it is also important to note that rapid and often bewildering political change characterized the era of decolonization. It was a transformative time and different ideas battled for primacy. Thus, economists from different schools often coopted each other's insights. It would be too simple to say that sovereign rights economists navigated a middle course between Cold War maxims. The web was more densely woven; no aspect of development economics could claim an uncluttered pedigree or influence.

One distinctive feature is that the development economists turned their attention to decolonization and its effects on international capitalism more intently. For them, US-Soviet tensions had little bearing on the important questions they asked. Instead, they were interested mostly in the ongoing split between former colonizers and former colonies. Within that focus, the idea that low raw material prices meant to benefit imperial power was shared by many experts. In fact, it had been put forward by influential theorists of imperialism for half a century. They all gave different amounts of weight to trade balances, but John Hobson, Joseph Schumpeter, Leonard Woolf, and John Maynard Keynes each took into consideration what Keith Hancock described in his 1950 Marshall Lectures as the relationship between "the trappings of sovereignty" and "the wealth of colonies." In one of the earliest examinations of the new concept of "economic development," Schumpeter linked empires' wealth

---

[36] Cited in Toye and Toye, *The UN and the Global Political Economy*, 179.

to their ability to undertake "the conquest of a new source of supply of raw materials." His 1946 obituary of Keynes emphasized the connection Keynes drew between profitable capital investment and the "conquests of new sources of food and raw materials." The historians Ronald Robinson and John Gallagher built on those positions in their influential 1953 article, "The Imperialism of Free Trade," in which they argued that commercial control had long been an alternative to formal colonial power. Their new categories, formal and informal empire, covered the same physical and cognitive space as Prebisch's periphery.[37]

Scholars from the United States formed part of the consensus that linked political conquest, formal or informal, to economic subordination. Thorstein Veblen, for example, keyed in on "the handsome margin of profit" from advancing "the frontiers of the pecuniary culture among the backward populations" as proof of his larger thesis about predation in modern society. Parker Thomas Moon, a Columbia University professor who advised Woodrow Wilson at the Paris Peace Conference, also emphasized industrial demand for low-priced raw materials as the driving force of imperialism. The Harvard economist John H. Williams used "uneven development," a phrase central to Lenin's theory of imperialist rivalry, to describe the effects of international trade in 1929. Eugene Staley, an economist at the Council on Foreign Relations, recommended policies in the 1930s and 1940s that reflected the confluence of interests between the industrialization of the "underdeveloped countries" and the projected US need for raw materials. Historians William Appleman Williams and William Leuchtenberg had also begun to point to the similarities between American commercial diplomacy and European imperialism by the early 1950s.[38]

---

[37] William Keith Hancock, *Wealth of Colonies* (Cambridge University Press, 2012 [1950]), 5; Leonard Woolf, *Economic Imperialism* (New York: Harcourt, Brace & Howe, 1920), 33, 51; John A. Hobson, *Imperialism: A Study* (London: Nisbet, 1902), 76–9; Edward B. Barbier, *Natural Resources and Economic Development* (New York: Cambridge University Press, 2007), 52; Joseph A. Schumpeter, "John Maynard Keynes, 1883–1946," *The American Economic Review* 36: 4 (September 1946), 500–1; John Gallagher and Ronald Robinson, "The Imperialism of Free Trade," *Economic History Review* 6 (1953), 1–15.

[38] Thorstein Veblen, *The Theory of the Business Enterprise* (New York: Scribner's Sons, 1904), 295; Parker Thomas Moon, "Raw Materials and Imperialism," *Proceedings of the Academy of Political Science in the City of New York*, 12: 1, International Problems and Relations (July 1926), 180–7; Parker Thomas Moon, *Syllabus on International Relations* (New York: MacMillan, 1926), 38–45; John H. Williams, "The Theory of International Trade Reconsidered," *The Economic Journal* 39: 154 (1929), 195–209; Tyler Priest, *Global Gambits: Big Steel and the US Quest for Manganese* (New York: Praeger, 2003), 230–1; William E. Leuchtenburg, "Progressivism and Imperialism: The Progressive

A number of economists also preceded Prebisch in making international economic inequality their primary concern. The work of Romanian economist Mihail Manoilescu on what he called "unequal exchange," which he associated with protective measures for national manufacturing sectors, and the "backwards economies" of Eastern Europe influenced Prebisch and other Latin American theorists of inequality. In the early 1940s, too, the Austrian economist Paul Rosenstein-Rodan and the American historical economist Charles Kindelberger laid more groundwork for unequal exchange in the field of statistical analysis, in this case through close examinations of short-term capital movements in and out of "the economically backward areas." If Prebisch took a divided world as his sphere, these economists already had begun to attach importance to his center-periphery formula, even if it was not identified as such.[39]

In the sense that unequal exchange built off the momentum of decolonization, it was similar to permanent sovereignty. The gravamen of Prebisch's analysis was as much about the political moment as it was about its intellectual context. In any case, it immediately struck a chord with other professional economists, including those who disagreed. "At no previous period in history have such large regions and vast populations found themselves drawn irresistibly into new orbits of economic activity," the first professor of Colonial Economic Affairs at Oxford, S. Herbert Frankel, told students in 1952. Frankel, who would later become a founding member of the free-market Mount Pelerin Society, nonetheless accepted the central premise of development economists. He explained his rationale for doing so vividly. "The great disintegrating process" of decolonization had begun to erase old economic patterns, he said. A close reading of the recent past pointed to the shortcomings of a definition of decolonization "based mainly on political criteria." Rather, its unfolding was a "seed-bed of change" that augured economic adaptation.[40]

Movement and American Foreign Policy, 1898–1916," *The Mississippi Valley Historical Review* 39: 3 (1952), 483–504; William Appleman Williams, "The Frontier Thesis and American Foreign Policy," *Pacific Historical Review* 24: 4 (1955), 379–95.

[39] For a detailed exploration of Prebisch's influences and context, see: Joseph Love, *Crafting the Third World: Theorizing Underdevelopment in Rumania and Brazil* (Palo Alto, CA: Stanford University Press, 1996), 119–42; H. W. Arndt, "Development Economics before 1945," in J. Bhagwati and R. S. Eckhaus, eds., *Development and Planning: Essays in Honour of Paul Rosenstein-Rodan* (London: Allen & Unwin, 1972), 24–9.

[40] Herbert Frankel, *The Economic Impact on Underdeveloped Societies* (Cambridge, MA: Harvard University Press, 1953), 1, 4, 14. On Frankel, see: John Toye, "Herbert Frankel: From Colonial Economics to Development Economics," *Oxford Development Studies*

Frankel became a critic of unequal exchange. But many other development economists agreed with Prebisch and put forward similar or related
theories in the 1950s. Like Frankel, Columbia University professor Ragnar
Nurkse set the "underdeveloped" periphery against the "developed"
center. Unlike Frankel, the Estonian-born economist agreed with Prebisch
that the historical relationship between the center and the periphery
preserved the poor nations in what he called "the underdevelopment
equilibrium." The wealth created by international trade in the
nineteenth-century world economy "was partly due to the fact that there
was a periphery—and a vacuum beyond," he wrote in 1953.[41]

Like others had, Nurkse also downplayed the ideological differences of
the Cold War. The "much-debated issue" of whether the forces of economic progress should be deliberately organized by states or left to
private enterprise was "essentially a question of method," he said, and
was less important than "the economic nature of the solution." What he
meant was that his underdevelopment equilibrium was not a decree of
fate. Nations could escape endemic poverty if they could increase the
amount of capital available to their economies.[42]

One of the more philosophical economists who joined Prebisch and
Nurkse in questioning the "classical theory" of international trade was
Hla Myint. The Rangoon University professor, who received his PhD in
welfare economics at the London School of Economics, thoroughly scru-
tinized the gains promised by international trade to "backward countries." For him, the problem was the disjuncture between the niceties of
trade theory and "the process by which some of the backward countries
were opened up." Economists would do well to decouple "backward"
human resources from "under-developed" natural resources in their

---

37: 2 (2009), 171–82. At the same time, unequal exchange did not hold a universal
appeal and sharpened the dichotomy between early neoliberals and the rest of the field.
Jacob Viner, Simon Kuznets, and Gottfried Haberler all questioned the empirical validity
of the doctrine of unequal exchange. Viner went so far as to dismiss Prebisch's work as a
"manifesto"—a set of "malignant fantasies, distorted historical conjecture and simplistic
hypotheses." See: Haberler, "Integration and Growth of the World Economy in Historical Perspective," *The American Economic Review* 54: 2, Part 1 (March 1964), 1–22;
Viner, *International Trade and Economic Development* (London: Clarendon, 1953);
Kuznets, *Economic Growth of Nations: Total Output and Production Structure* (Cambridge, MA.: Harvard University Press, 1971).

[41] Frankel, *The Economic Impact on Underdeveloped Societies*, 70–81; Ragnar Nurkse,
Problems of Capital Formation in Underdeveloped Countries (New York: Oxford University Press, 1953), 10.

[42] Frankel, *The Economic Impact on Underdeveloped Societies*, 70–81; Nurkse, *Problems
of Capital Formation*, 10–16, 22–3.

discussions of "the nature of economic backwardness," Myint added in a lecture written for the *Oxford Economic Papers*. His intent focus on raw materials, free of what he considered the racist assumptions underlying the "phenomenon of backwardness," led him to two important conclusions. First, the "economic struggle" faced by the poor nations was part of the deliberate concentration of power "in relation to the world at large." Second, the "mutual interaction" between poverty and resource control was "an essentially dynamic and historical process taking place over a period of time." A knavish injustice dominated that history, Myint believed, by which poverty came from the "artificial" and "disequalizing" obstacles to development put in place by colonial powers.[43]

By the late 1950s, the consensus on international economic inequality had become so thick that even economic historians such as Karl Polanyi and Bernard Semmel had begun to look for the political roots of mid-nineteenth-century classical trade theory and the context of calls among the European ruling classes for reviving "the lost art of colonization." The problem, they and all the rest accepted as given, was that the price of primary commodities had been determined as part of a material relationship between rulers and subjects. This idea was persuasive and popular. It was held widely in the 1950s, including by the three men who, along with Prebisch, were arguably the most influential development economists of the era: Albert O. Hirschman, William Arthur Lewis, and Gunnar Myrdal.[44]

Like Mexican Ambassador Ramón Beteta, Hirschman described early in his career the ways that a perceived need for raw materials drove Italian fascist expansionism into Africa in the 1930s. In 1957, as he began to establish himself as an expert in the field, he wrote about the "dualism" within the underdeveloped countries, the separation between industry and raw material production on a regional level, as a reflection of the broader "uneven development" of the international system. A year later he wrote about the corrosive problems that could stunt economic growth at the earliest, most fragile moments of statehood. Of the utmost

---

[43] Hla Myint, "The Gains from International Trade and the Backward Countries," *The Review of Economic Studies* 22: 2 (1954), 129–42; Hla Myint, "The 'Classical Theory' of International Trade and the Underdeveloped Countries," *The Economic Journal* 68: 270 (1958), 317–37; Hla Myint, "An Interpretation of Economic Backwardness," *Oxford Economic Papers* 6 (June 1954), 132–5, 144.

[44] K. Polanyi, C. M. Arensberg, and H. W. Pearson, eds. *Trade and Markets in the Early Empires* (Glencoe, IL: Free Press, 1957); Bernard Semmel, "The Philosophic Radicals and Colonialism," *The Journal of Economic History* 21: 4 (1961), 513–25.

importance to safely navigate the path of independence to development was the improvement of a nation's "ability to invest." Crucially, what he described as "viable political forces" could set policies to "help narrow the gap between the developed and the underdeveloped countries." Those forces, in turn, needed to retain the "developmental advantages of sovereignty" granted by decolonization.[45]

Lewis, who arrived at the London School of Economics in the 1930s from the British colony of St. Lucia, ran in the same Pan-Africanist circles as George Padmore, C. L. R. James, and Paul Robeson. His first major work ascribed the "harvest of vice and woe" in Africa and the West Indies to the "reckless quest for wealth" by British imperialists, a pursuit that ultimately led to the slashing of prices for sugar and banana exports. In 1949 he published a survey of the international economy between the two world wars that, unlike other contemporary textbooks, focused on the declining prices of raw materials as a factor in global depression. "The changing trends in the demand and supply of primary products" were crucial, he said, because the less developed economies had become important consumers of the goods manufactured in Europe and the United States. For him, the terms of trade had moved against primary products consistently after 1883, mostly as a result of the "opening up of new countries."[46]

As they did for Prebisch, Lewis, and Hirschman, the assumptions of classical economists also formed a target for Gunnar Myrdal. The Swedish economist had spent the decade after his career-making 1944 analysis of US race relations, *An American Dilemma*, studying the forces underlying international inequality. (He was not alone among development economists in drawing the connection between American segregation and the economics of imperialism. Nurkse found the moment to link in one phrase the lag between economic theory and "the actual course of events" to the history of US race relations. "John Brown's body lies a-molding in the grave," the Estonian emigré wrote, "but his soul goes marching on.") Like Prebisch, Myrdal attacked the belief in comparative

---

[45] Albert O. Hirschman, *A Bias for Hope: Essays on the Development of Latin America* (New Haven, CT: Yale University Press, 1971), 277–9; Albert O. Hirschman, "Investment Policies and 'Dualism' in Underdeveloped Countries," *The American Economic Review* 47: 5 (1957), 550–70; Albert O. Hirschman, *The Strategy of Economic Development* (New Haven, CT: Yale University Press, 1958), 49, 187, 200–1.

[46] Robert Tignor, *W. Arthur Lewis and the Birth of Development Economics* (Princeton University Press, 2006), 33–5, 45; W. A. Lewis, *Economic Survey, 1919–1939* (London: Tinling and Co., 1949), 149–56, 178, 195.

advantage as a "scientific law" that existed above "the political element" of international society. He elaborated on that point in his popular 1956 textbook, *An International Economy*. The appearance of "economic development of underdeveloped countries" as a banner phrase in international debate symbolized the arrival of a new set of interests, he wrote. Their international influence reaffirmed his belief that it was misguided to pretend that the study of economics could be "objective" or "purely scientific."[47]

Myrdal believed this critique was especially pertinent to neoclassical theories of the perfect market. In *Rich Lands and Poor*, written in 1957 for a Harper & Row series aimed at the general public, he used the doctrine of unequal exchange to explain how "the backwash effect" in the international economy disproved the idea of the perfect market. It was, in fact, the very real play of political forces in the market, he argued, that tended to increase the inequalities between regions.[48]

He linked the influence of that economic belief to what he called the "Great Awakening" of decolonization in a speech the same year: "All international relations" shivered under the reverberations of that "political avalanche," the repercussions of which he expected would "fill the history of the rest of the century." From that perspective, he predicted that the Cold War would be reduced to an "unpleasant nuance or perverted modality" of history. The more important issues of world affairs would revolve around the "many things in common" held by the poor nations: their skin colors were darker, they carried resentful memories of imperial rule and personal discrimination, and they were poor. Above all, he intoned, they were "conscious of it."[49]

That mindfulness, often expressed in terms of rebirth or awakening, was the supreme common denominator of the elites who would connect unequal exchange to permanent sovereignty. The notion of a self-conscious awakening was central to the formation of a cohesive school of thought among the anticolonial elites: they regarded themselves, and

[47] Nurkse, *Problems of Capital Formation*, Preface, 120; Gunnar Myrdal, *The Political Element in the Development of Economic Theory* (London: Routledge & Paul, 1953); Gunnar Myrdal, *An International Economy: Problems and Prospects* (New York: Harper and Brothers, 1956), 9–16, 336–7.

[48] Gunnar Myrdal, *Rich Lands and Poor: The Road to World Prosperity* (New York: Harper and Brothers, 1957), 26–9.

[49] Gunnar Myrdal, "Economic Nationalism in Underdeveloped Countries," in *The Dyason Lectures: Economic Nationalism and Internationalism* (Canberra: The Australian Institute of International Affairs, 1957), 19, 24, 29.

were regarded by their closest observers, through their similarities. The prime similarity, their mobilizing root, was this stirring sense of becoming conscious to the possibilities of decolonization. An alert and progressive synthesis thus defined their character and, as Myrdal noted, led to higher expectations. The anticolonial elites he observed would discuss their dissatisfaction with political independence at length. Myrdal's arguments about the newly political nature of economics – along with the doctrine of unequal exchange, Hirschman's uneven distribution, Lewis's dual economies, and so on – built on the same core belief.

The actual concrete policies to redistribute wealth varied in these and other assessments, but the basic assumption remained: an unjust past bequeathed an international economy stacked against the periphery. For the development economists, as for so many other intellectuals in the 1950s, the imperial past was part of a symmetry of belief about what Hans Singer called the "interlocking vicious circles" of poverty.[50]

The Oxford historian Albert Hourani summarized the emerging consensus in 1953: "[T]he essence of imperialism" was less in the official legal and diplomatic controls of colonial rule than in its "material consequences" and subsequent "moral relationship ... of power and powerlessness." In a 1955 lecture at the National Bank of Egypt, Myrdal also turned his gaze upon "the very large and steadily increasing economic inequalities between the developed and underdeveloped countries." The many deviations within and across that great division did not invalidate its generalization about the inequality between the rich and the poor nations, he continued. Besides, it was completely natural that the leaders of the poor nations "put part of the blame" on the "world economic system which keeps them so poor while other nations are so rich and becoming richer."[51]

The meetings of the Third Committee of the UN General Assembly in 1955 validated that sort of observation. Delegates there – in particular the permanent representative of Saudi Arabia to the United Nations, the Lebanese anticolonial elite Jamil Baroody – acted to clinch the link between permanent sovereignty and unequal exchange.

---

[50] Hans W. Singer, "Economic Progress in Underdeveloped Countries," *Social Research* 16 (March 1949), 5.
[51] Albert Hourani, "The Decline of the West in the Middle East," *International Affairs* 7: 2 (January 1953), 31; Gunnar Myrdal, *Economic Theory and Under-Developed Regions* (London: Duckworth, 1957), vi, 6–7.

The immediate political context of the discussions between Baroody and his counterparts was the ongoing debate over the Suez Canal. As with the Iran oil crisis, international discussions again provide new insight into perceptions of the nationalization and the way it affected notions of international economic justice. In fact, the disputes over Iranian oil and the Suez Canal were closely linked in the minds of anticolonial elites. Mohammed Mossadegh had visited Egypt in 1951, directly after his trip to the United States, and had been welcomed as a nationalist hero. The two nations even signed a treaty against British imperialism before his departure. "[T]he Iranian move for the nationalization of oil induced extremists in Egypt to demand ... the nationalization of the Suez Canal" even before Gamal Abdel Nasser took power, the professor of Middle East Studies at Johns Hopkins, Majid Khadduri, explained to his colleagues in late 1951.[52]

But the connection was greater than one of regional nationalism. For one, the discussions at the United Nations reveal that the doctrine of unequal exchange was becoming standard fare for discussions about inequality among diplomats who were not professional economists. The United Nations again had played a central role in this. The UN Department of Economic Affairs, for example, made Prebisch's critique readily available to the leaders of anticolonial movements, new nations, and the other members of his periphery. Mimeographs of the analysis were translated into English and French, reprinted in journals, and distributed as pamphlets. The department also published and distributed another widely-read essay by Prebisch, "Some Theoretical and Practical Problems of Economic Growth," in 1951.[53]

---

[52] Majid Khadduri "The Anglo-Egyptian Controversy," *Proceedings of the Academy of Political Science* 24: 4 (January 1952), 96. Recently, see: Lior Sternfeld, "Iran Days in Egypt: Mosaddeq's Visit to Cairo in 1951," *British Journal of Middle Eastern Studies* 43: 1 (2016), 1–20. On Suez, see: Guy Laron, *Origins of the Suez Crisis: Postwar Development Diplomacy and the Struggle over Third World Industrialization, 1945–1956* (Washington, DC: Woodrow Wilson Center Press, 2013); Diane B. Kunz, *The Economic Diplomacy of the Suez Crisis* (Chapel Hill: University of North Carolina Press, 1991); Peter Hahn, *The United States, Great Britain, and Egypt, 1945–1956: Strategy and Diplomacy in the Early Cold War* (Chapel Hill: University of North Carolina Press, 1991).

[53] Raúl Prebisch, *The Economic Development of Latin America and Its Principal Problems* (Lake Success, NY: United Nations Dept. of Economic Affairs, 1950), UNA; Raúl Prebisch, *Le Développement de l'Amérique Latine et ses Principaux Problèmes* (Commission Economique des Nations-Unies pour l'Amerique Latine, 1950); Raúl Prebisch, "Theoretical and Practical Problems of Economic Growth," ECLA, Official Records, E/CN.12/221. On the broad applicability and movement of the argument, see: Packenham,

The economic argument of unequal exchange had also begun to fuse with the legal question of permanent sovereignty. When Djalal Abdoh and the Latin American delegates contemplated permanent sovereignty as a means to protect the rights of poor nations in 1952, the Latin Americans had used the doctrine of unequal exchange to explain the need for new international laws. Uruguayan ambassador Cusano, for example, described "the catastrophic balances of trade for raw materials" in his call for the resolution. And when Bolivian ambassador Siles compared the corporate exploitation of tin resources with those of oil, he argued that foreign companies involved in each had amassed "tremendous wealth" by manipulating the "terms of trade" for raw materials.[54]

Unequal exchange and permanent sovereignty came even closer together in the 1955 meetings, where delegates again discussed permanent sovereignty. The committee had been assigned the broad question of social and humanitarian affairs, but its anticolonial elites devoted considerable time to the discussion of what they called "economic self-determination." A division over the link between natural resources and self-determination pitted the United States, the United Kingdom, and the Netherlands against an "Asian-African-Arab group" led by Baroody and Abdul Rahman Pazhwak, a diplomat from Afghanistan. Like other UN diplomats and the development economists, both men connected national law and the international economy with the greater process of decolonization.[55]

The renewed emphasis on permanent sovereignty revealed another key operating idea of the sovereign rights program. No state could "exercise the right of political self-determination" if it were not "the master of its own resources," Baroody said. Widespread economic inequality meant that problem was not strictly a "colonial issue," Pazhwak added. Instead it reflected the need to act on the universal right to self-determination, a right that "had in our age acquired a compelling moral force." To codify permanent sovereignty in international law, he continued, was an attempt "to spare the future the calamities of the past." What anchored their view of permanent sovereignty was their broad conception of colonial legacy. They contrasted the bitter past with a better present endowed with

The Dependency Movement, 16–19; Johan Galtung, "A Structural Theory of Imperialism," *Journal of Peace Research* 8: 2 (1971), 81–117.
[54] UNGA, Official Records, Seventh Session, Second Committee, December 11, 1952, A/C.2/SR.232.
[55] Shrijver, *Sovereignty over Natural Resources*, 49–56; UNGA, Official Records, Report of the Third Committee on Draft International Covenants on Human Rights, A/3077.

democratic qualities at the same time as they noted the powerful legacy of imperialism.[56]

Like other anticolonial elites, both men came to this position from a combination of national and international experience. For Pazhwak, who had just returned from the Afro-Asian summit in Bandung, this had to do with the writing of history itself – five years earlier he wrote a pamphlet that decried the "distorted" depiction of Afghanistan as a passive "buffer state" at the expense of its own rich history.[57]

For Baroody, the legal struggle to negate the economic past also carried on as part of a longer history. The Saudi ambassador received his under-graduate degree from the American University of Beirut in 1926. Before joining the Saudi UN delegation in 1945, he had written a collection of well-received poems, represented Lebanon at the 1939 World's Fair in New York, advised the editors of *Reader's Digest* on their new Arabic edition, and taught Arabic at Princeton. A 1949 debate about world government, sponsored by the American Academy of Political and Social Science, revealed the nature of his political-historical views. Baroody placed Soviet and American policies of "modern expansion" – the race of the "big powers" to extend "their economic frontiers" outside their territorial limits – within a thousand-year history of colonialism for economic gain that dated back to the beginning of the Crusades in 1095. The scramble for "the abundant but slightly developed natural resources" of the Middle East represented a new stage in that history of "power politics at its worst." Tellingly, both American and Soviet diplomats had "little regard to the welfare and aspirations of the people caught between the titanic blocs." To reverse the trend toward imperial continuity within the Cold War, Baroody urged the leaders of the poor nations to forge a "collective foreign policy toward the outside world."[58]

Both Baroody and Pazhwak wove their fabric of explanation out of the skein of a vast but precisely interpreted history. They were also

---

[56] UNGA, Official Records, 10th Session, Third Committee, October 18, 1955, A/C.3/SR.638; UNGA, Official Records, 10th Session, Third Committee, October 28, 1955, Provisional A/C.3/SR.644.

[57] Rahman Pazhwak, *Aryana: Ancient Afghanistan* (London: Key Press, 1950), 5–6; Mohamed Abdel Khalek Hassouna, *The First Asian-African Conference Held at Bandung Indonesia* (League of Arab States, 1955), 181.

[58] Kurt Waldheim, et al, *Jamil M. Baroody, 1905–1979* (New York: Arab Information Center, 1980), 3; Jamil M. Baroody, "Middle East–Balance of Power versus World Government," *Annals of the American Academy of Political and Social Science*, 264, World Government (July, 1949), 46, 48, 50–1.

forward-looking. The era had passed, they said, when gunboats and soldiers, traders and investors, civil servants and diplomats could bring to heel
noncompliant nationalists. The political climate of decolonization did not
permit it. "The right of peoples to self-determination was an accepted axiom
of modern thought," Baroody told Pazhwak and the other UN delegates in
1955. A new resolution on permanent sovereignty was necessary "to prevent
what had been a frequent occurrence in the nineteenth century, namely that a
weak and penniless government should seriously compromise a country's
future by granting concessions in the economic sphere."[59]

These discussions reveal that permanent sovereignty over natural
resources was beginning to be described as an inalienable right of nations.
In formulating the legal principle and the economic problem it sought to
resolve, the anticolonial elites at the United Nations continued to make
the national international: they turned the unique experience of individual
nations into a metonym for international suffering under colonialism. The
trope whereby national experiences personified greater injustice in the
international economy was a common feature of the economic culture of
decolonization thereafter. Added to that was the argument that political
freedom without economic power was inconsistent.

For the anticolonial elites, the standards governing international trade
and foreign investments in raw materials were unnatural holdovers of a
bygone age, concocted by the more powerful states and enforced unilaterally against the weak. In turn, permanent sovereignty and unequal
exchange became shorthand for discussions about the global economy
in which all poor nations took part. More than that, the economic frame
made more tangible the important gravitational pull of Third World
likeness—an underlying sense of affinity based in mutual history and
the common drive to overcome that history. That consensus on international asymmetry favored the birth of the economic culture of decolonization and the sovereign rights program in the 1950s.

The new consensus also led to the rise of sovereign rights as a legitimate
force in international politics. So appealing was the message of economic
inequality and a legal solution that even an arch-antagonist like George
Kennan conceded its influence. At a calmer moment, he struck a more
earnest tone in his Latin America journal. Regarding US relations with

---

[59] UNGA, Official Records, 10th Session, Third Committee, November 30, 1955, A/C.3/
SR.677; UNGA, Official Records, Third Committee, 10th Session, November 25, 1955,
A/C.3/SR.672.

Venezuela, he lamented "this unhappy relationship in which each country was beholden to the other in a manner slightly disgraceful." He hoped that the international community could find "some better answer" to the problem, a way to balance "the needs of those economies which are capable of developing the natural resources of this earth and those other peoples who have been permitted to extend over those resources the delicate fiction of modern sovereignty."[60]

The self-aware unity of the anticolonial elites, based on Kennan's delicate fiction, was in its origins an outward-looking strategy, and anticolonial elites increasingly endeavored to conceive of it as such. The sovereign rights program thus stood somewhere between social-scientific theory and moral ethos. It was at the same time an attempt to identify the meaning of decolonization for international capitalism and to transform any given event into an exercise of the interpretation of its underlying meaning. Gunnar Myrdal published a lecture on "Economic Nationalism and Internationalism" a half-decade after Kennan pondered the future of sovereignty. It may be the most profound short analysis of the effects of decolonization on international economic thought ever written. For him, it was impossible to deny the feedback loop between decolonization and the new economic arguments. "Intensified economic nationalism in all countries are interrelated in a circular fashion, each change being at the same time the cause and effect of the other changes, with the result that the changes cumulate," he wrote.[61]

But for all his insight, Myrdal overlooked one crucial characteristic of the moment. Permanent sovereignty and unequal exchange caught on together because each connected people with their circumstances in ways they found valuable. The intimate relationship between anticolonial law and international capitalism, in other words, was that the circumstances of life on the periphery endowed that vision with a peculiar force. Albert O. Hirschman may have come closest to capturing the moment when he wrote that anticolonial elites such as Djalal Abdoh, Jamil Baroody, and Rahman Pazhwak arrived at their similar conclusions through an "elucidation of immediate experience" that pointed to "variations upon a common theme."[62]

Again, true enough. But still too simple. It is more accurate to say that unequal exchange and permanent sovereignty fit so logically into the patterns of thought of elites, echoed so lucidly their realities of life and

---

[60] George Kennan, Diary Notes of Trip to South America, February 28, 1950, George F. Kennan Papers, Seeley Mudd Manuscript Library.
[61] Myrdal, *The Dyason Lectures*, 4.
[62] Hirschman, *The Strategy of Economic Development*, v.

emergent codes of behavior, that the ideas could mean something very real to a wide variety of actors. The link between economic inequality and its legal remedy loomed large because the two positions made sense together to so many people. That is, the combination of anticolonial law with development economics was an argument that had the virtue of portraying a position that a variety elites could accept as a foregone conclusion.

Permanent sovereignty and unequal exchange overlapped naturally. The anticolonial elites came to understand that proposition of mutual recognition through a process that emphasized ideas and politics, thoughts and actions. When a small group of Arab experts turned their gaze on what Myrdal called the "closely controlled enclaves for exploiting oil" in the second half of the 1950s, they ensured that this culture of decolonization would generate far more than a tempest in a UN teapot.[63]

---

[63] Myrdal, "Economic Nationalism in Underdeveloped Countries," 18–19.

2

Past Concessions

The Arab League, Sovereign Rights, and OPEC, 1955–1960

Rarely if ever, has the development of economics by its own force blazed the way to new perspectives.... The major recastings of economic thought...were all responses to changing political conditions and opportunities.[1]
Gunnar Myrdal, 1957

A concession deals with a developing situation and it has to develop and grow to meet changing circumstances.[2]
Anes Qasem, 1959

In his welcome speech to the delegates from twenty-nine nations at the momentous 1955 Afro-Asian summit in Bandung, Indonesian President Sukarno decried "the modern dress" of colonialism "in the form of economic control, intellectual control and actual physical control." The speech, accompanied by many others, represented part of what Indian Prime Minister Jawaharlal Nehru called at a banquet held in the honor of Saudi Prime Minister Faisal in Rangoon a week later, "the sentiment, desire and demands of the Asian-African people." The universal condemnation of colonialism at the conference was telling, Egyptian President Gamal Abdel Nasser told a mass rally in Cairo afterwards. "The major achievement of the conference was the unanimous agreement on the major issues put forward," he said. King Faisal agreed, telling reporters

---

[1] Gunnar Myrdal, *Asian Drama: An Enquiry into the Poverty of Nations*, vol. I (London: Pantheon, 1968), 9.
[2] Petroleum Commission, *Petroleum Development in Libya, 1954 through Mid-1960* (Tripoli: Government Press, n.d. [1960]), 7.

that "the conference had proven that the Asian-African people universally had national consciousness."[3]

Elites that cohered around decolonization had begun to systematically articulate sovereign rights in the early 1950s at the United Nations. The reach of their viewpoint afterward relied on its powerful language of overlaid physical, political, and temporal boundaries. These boundaries extended to include Sukarno, Nehru, Nasser, Faisal, and other national leaders. The arguments for sovereignty over resources also made sense to Abdel Khalek Hassouna, the Secretary General of the Arab League, who attended the Afro-Asian conference as a member of Gamal Abdel Nasser's delegation from Egypt. Inspired by his experience on the Economic Committee at Bandung, particularly the discussions of matters relating to oil, Hassouna directed the Petroleum Bureau of the Arab League to study the oil concessions of Iraq, Saudi Arabia, Iran, Kuwait, the Trucial States, and Libya. As this chapter relates, the oil elites in the Petroleum Bureau concluded that the concessions were essentially leonine treaties wherein weaker peoples had delivered up their natural wealth on imposed terms. The oil elites then convened an Arab Petroleum Congress in 1959, where they began to apply the sovereign rights thesis to the oil concessions of the Middle East. This ultimately led to the founding of the Organization of Petroleum Exporting Countries (OPEC) in 1960. All the while, a new UN Commission on Permanent Sovereignty interpreted and shaped the broader Third World drive to control natural resources.

The shared mindfulness evident in this set of events reveals that the early days of the anticolonial elite and their conception of a public weal is a story that moved between states as much as within them. The founding of the First Arab Petroleum Congress in 1959 and OPEC in 1960 as international interest groups was awash in the broader program of sovereign rights. The ideas of the oil elites, in particular, the application of sovereignty by Libyan oil official Anes Qasem, also bring to light a shift in the tenor of sovereign rights: if more and more elites branded the international economy as imperialistic, it was because they developed new expectations. In this period, anticolonial elites looked at sovereign rights as an order of magnitude greater than political independence. It was not just a right but the foundation for policy.

---

[3] Bradley R. Simpson, *Economists with Guns: Authoritarian Development and U.S.-Indonesian Relations, 1960–1968* (Stanford University Press, 2008), 18; Report from the Chinese Ministry, "Comments on the Asian-African Conference from the Participating Countries after the Conference," May 10, 1955, History and Public Policy Program, Digital Archive, CWIHP.

For Gunnar Myrdal, this vision reached across the globe. The international economic inequality that "the poorer nations ... brought to world attention" through the United Nations and now at Bandung, was for him the "major economic fact in the world today."[4] The story recounted here reveals that the sovereign rights program was not a simple negative device or quarrel with the past. Rather, it was a language of moral action that empowered anticolonial oil elites. The idea that new nations had the natural right of their own to control their resources became, as a consequence, a proposition of great validity. For the most faithful, the right to sovereignty elevated the problem of deeply rooted imperial economics from a political-economic interpretation of the past to a regenerative vision of the future.

When Abdel Khalek Hassouna joined other anticolonial elites in Bandung in April 1955, the early sovereign rights program had already run into diplomatic opposition. The anticolonial elites who deliberately asserted the right to permanent sovereignty in the United Nations in 1952 and 1955 witnessed bitter arguments against it. An American corporate lawyer who observed the 1952 meetings derided the outcome. "[T]he capital-importing countries were able to inject the principle of permanent sovereignty over natural wealth," he wrote. "In the jargon of the Human Rights Commission, this principle came to be known as economic self-determination." The *New Republic* also lamented the trend in language reminiscent of the Victorian-era argument about whether or not certain people were "fit" for self-government: "It is the sudden appearance on the stage of scores of new nations, most of them inadequately and some completely unequipped for the exercise of total sovereignty, and this at a moment when such sovereignty is both more complete and more dangerous than at any time in modern history."[5]

That interpretation depicted the process of decolonization as something like a marauding horde. Like the economic culture of decolonization, it also built on a longer tradition. Many others joined George Kennan in the belief that Western resource control was justified by global utility. This was an old colonial argument. For example, when nationalist movements began to critique oil concessions at the Permanent Mandates Commission of the League of Nations, imperial officials had already begun to characterize their mineral resources as belonging to humanity as a whole. Lord Lugard, the famous British explorer and colonial

---

[4] Myrdal, "Economic Nationalism in Underdeveloped Countries," 18–19.
[5] Hyde, "Permanent Sovereignty," 855; "The Post-Imperial Age," *The New Republic* 135: 25 (December 17, 1956), 10.

administrator, described the resources of the British colonies in 1922 as "the heritage of mankind," to be developed "in the interests of ... the world at large." Major statements from the United States and Western European countries followed that position during and after World War II – the Atlantic Charter of 1941, for example, discussed the need for "access, on equal terms, to the trade and to the raw materials of the world."[6]

American diplomats rejected the sovereign rights argument in the United Nations in the 1950s in similar terms. Mary Pillsbury Lord, the flour heiress and Eisenhower fundraiser who replaced Eleanor Roosevelt as US representative to the UN Human Rights Commission, disputed the notion of permanent sovereignty itself in the 1955 meetings with Jamil Baroody and Abdul Rahman Pazhwak. "The political principle of self-determination does not have clear economic applications," she said. "No state could be economically independent." For good measure, she also called the 1952 permanent sovereignty resolution an "unfortunate history."[7]

Baroody responded to Lord that such a separation of decolonization and the international economy did not line up with his and others' experiences. "The overwhelming fact of modern times ... was the growth of nationalism in Asia and Africa," he said. The refusal to let the "yoke" of colonialism continue to upset nations' independence through continued economic control was not a misdirected application of self-determination. It was "the acid test of political maturity." He added that the arguments he and others had made about the cascading process of decolonization were widely accepted. The recognition of the "economic aspect of self-determination" was so prevalent, in fact, that it was "identical with the resolution on self-determination adopted unanimously ... at the Bandung conference."[8]

---

[6] F. D. Lugard, *The Dual Mandate in British Tropical Africa* (London: Blackwood and Sons, 1922), 60–1; Antony Anghie, *Imperialism, Sovereignty, and the Making of International Law* (Cambridge University Press, 2005), 158–61, 211–12; Sundhya Pahuja, *Decolonising International Law: Development, Economic Growth, and the Politics of Universality* (New York: Cambridge University Press, 2011), 132, 138–9.

[7] UNGA, Official Records, Third Committee, 10th Session, October 31, 1955, A/C.3/SR.646.

[8] UNGA, Official Records, Third Committee, 10th Session, November 3, 1955, A/C.3/SR.648. For early discussions on Bandung: Richard Wright, *The Color Curtain: A Report on the Bandung Conference* (New York: World Publishing, 1956); George McT. Kahin, *The Asian-African Conference: Bandung, Indonesia, April 1955* (Ithaca, NY: 1956); Carlos Romulo, *The Meaning of Bandung* (Chapel Hill, NC: University of North Carolina Press, 1956); G. H. Jansen, *Afro-Asia and Non-Alignment* (London: Faber, 1966). Important recent appraisals include: Christopher J. Lee, ed. *Making a World after Empire: The Bandung Moment and Its Political Afterlives* (Columbus: Ohio University Press, 2010); Jason Parker, "Cold War II: The Eisenhower Administration, the Bandung Conference, and the Reperiodization of the Postwar Era," *Diplomatic History* 30: 5 (November 2006):

Decolonization was important, in other words, because Baroody and other anticolonial elites wished it so. It is interesting, too, that he invoked the 1955 Afro-Asian summit in Bandung, which his UN colleague Abdul Rahman Pazhwak attended as a member of the Afghani delegation, as confirmation of the legitimacy of permanent sovereignty. He did so because the conference, which was a crucial event in his and others' minds, incorporated the concept into its proceedings.

In a coordinated effort, the meeting had even been promoted as a landmark moment before it occurred. Paul Robeson, speaking for the Council on African Affairs weeks before, stated his "profound conviction" that the convening of the conference "in itself will be recorded as a historic turning point in all world affairs." Eric Kwame Heymann, the editor of the *Ghana Evening News*, quoted the famous dictum of W. E. B. Du Bois in his preconference salute: "The problem of the Twentieth Century is the problem of the color-line." For Heymann this meant that "the epochal embrace of two continents at Bandung" would "buttress inter-racial solidarity and the cause of freedom from poverty, oppression, war, ignorance, disease, and capitalist greed."[9]

The message spread far and wide. Four months after the Afro-Asian summit, in the first meeting between the sovereigns of Saudi Arabia and Iran in a generation, King Saud and the Shah announced the installation of the first direct phone line between their palaces. They also took the moment to express their shared "respect for the United Nations and support for the Bandoeng [sic] resolutions." The confluence of the oil monarchs, who fell within the American bloc in the Cold War, with the others, many of whom did not, reminds us that the economic culture of decolonization demanded the attention of a range of actors. The conference was also, of course, riddled with disagreements, including the famous debate over whether the delegates should also categorize the Soviet Union as an empire.[10]

But Abdel Khalek Hassouna's detailed coverage of the meeting is a trove of detail on what a number of delegates actually agreed upon: the residual landscape of imperialism. The more general momentum and

---

867–92; Pang Yang Huei, "The Four Faces of Bandung: Detainees, Soldiers, Revolutionaries and Statesmen," *Journal of Contemporary Asia* 39: 1 (2009): 63–86; Robert Vitalis, "The Midnight Ride of Kwame Nkrumah and Other Fables of Bandung (Ban-doong)," *Humanity* 4: 2 (2013).

[9] *Spotlight on Africa*, Special Issue 14: 4 (April 1955): 10, 16–17, Reference Center for Marxist Studies, Pamphlet Collection, folder 2, Tamiment Library.

[10] "The King Visits the Shah," *Arab Information: Newsletter of the Arab Information Center* 1: 6 (September 1955): 12.

clutch of the economic culture of decolonization was evident in the introductory remarks of the delegation heads, which Hassouna reproduced. In particular, the speeches consistently invoked both the parallels of national economic experience and the rearguard argument for permanent sovereignty. "We ... whatever be our languages, whatever be our faiths, whatever be our forms of government, whatever be the color of our skins ... have one thing in common," Sir John Kotelawala of Ceylon said, in one of Bandung's many ecumenical moments. "Centuries of servitude and stagnation have left their mark." National independence could not "naturally be maintained unless economic independence [was] also preserved," Foreign Minister Aklilou Habte-Wold of Ethiopia added. Freedom from oppression in the realm of the international economy was necessary to protect hard-won statehood. The leader of Abdul Rahman Pazhwak's delegation, Afghan prince Mohamed Naim Khan, saw the same degradation and possibility, and used Raúl Prebisch's theory to explain it: "The producers of raw materials are confronted with obstacles in the way of promoting commercial relations and trade."[11]

Chinese Prime Minister Zhou Enlai chose permanent sovereignty as the vehicle in which to seek common ground across Cold War boundaries. The Iranian struggle for the "restoration of sovereignty ... over their petroleum resources" had "won the support of all righteous people in the Asian-African region," he said. This statement indicates another aspect of the sovereign rights mind-set. Mohammed Mossadegh was an illustrative figure for Zhou, but the case of Iran was certainly not determinative of his anticolonialism. Rather, in Bandung, the shared notions of sovereign rights ignited a discussion about the international economy that reached beyond the specific time and place of any one event. The gathered elites understood the effect of thinking in such inclusive terms. Their individual cases multiplied the power of their broader concepts, which in turn became prominent because individual leaders presented their histories as representative of a familiar principle.[12]

The principle also led to more specific discussions about policy. Hassouna volunteered for the Economic Committee when the conferees split into working groups because he believed they would cover "the most difficult topics" of the conference. The discussions of the small group revolved around the same themes as the conversations in the United Nations. The line of reasoning made sense to Hassouna. "Since economic sovereignty is

---

[11] Mohamed Abdel Khalek Hassouna, *The First Asian-African Conference Held at Bandung Indonesia* (League of Arab States, 1955), 58, 65, 80, 84.
[12] Hassouna, *The First Asian-African Conference*, 84.

the basis of political sovereignty," he explained, it was normal that the subject of raw materials dominated the proceedings. It also made sense that permanent sovereignty was posed as a collective means to overturn unequal exchange for a number of commodities. Permanent sovereignty was key because it was a means to control supply, he added: the nations represented at Bandung produced "a great—if not the greatest—proportion of the world's petroleum products, raw cotton and rubber," he reasoned, and they could force price increases if they applied their sovereignty collectively. Hassouna also clipped an article by an Indonesian journalist who covered the committee hearings. "There is no denying that Asia and Africa are the richest regions of the world. They abound in untapped natural resources," the journalist wrote. "This enormous national wealth should drive the Asian and African countries to concentrate their efforts on cooperation."[13]

The final communiqué of Bandung – signed by Gamal Abdel Nasser, Nehru, Sukarno, and Prince Faisal of Saudi Arabia, as well as representatives from oil-producing Iran, Iraq, and Libya – made "Economic Cooperation" its first line item. Sovereign rights was its primary concept. For the signatories, "respect for national sovereignty" in the economic sphere was central to Third World development. Following the recommendation of the Economic Committee, they also suggested "collective action" to increase the prices for raw materials. Furthermore, they added that "the exchange of information on matters relating [to] oil" was of particular interest in the "formulation of common policies."[14]

Phrases such as "collective action," "economic sovereignty," and "economic independence" rang through the Afro-Asian conference and other new arenas in which Third World diplomats encouraged each other to make truth claims about the meaning of decolonization. The meeting at Bandung was designed to find points of cohesion within the emergent international community of anticolonial elites. More than that, the meeting helped lead to an enduring formulation of the concepts of unequal exchange and permanent sovereignty for the oil producers. The final recommendation of information sharing and collective action also raised the essential question of strategy: how could anticolonial elites, including those concerned with oil matters, construct a firmer strategic base? How could they extend and make best use of their increasingly regular exchanges of ideas, politics, and policies?

---

[13] Hassouna, *The First Asian-African Conference*, 42, 149.
[14] Romulo, *The Meaning of Bandung*, 93–4; "Asian-African Conference: Communiqué, Bandung," April 24, 1955, *NIEO: SD*, vol. 1, 2–4.

To begin to answer that question, more information was crucial. Hassouna's report also served as a point of departure for him, and afterward the insertion of the oil industry into the sovereign rights program became an important project to Arab oil elites. When he returned to Cairo, he discussed oil and sovereignty with Mohammed Salman, the Iraqi engineer who was the Arab League's Director for Petroleum Affairs. Salman would spend the better part of the following two years traveling between Cairo and the capitals of "all the Arab countries" to collect information on the oil industry from company executives, national leaders, and Western diplomats. Before he embarked on his first trip in November 1955, he convened the League's self-titled Oil Experts Committee – including the "Red Sheikh" from Saudi Arabia, Abdullah al-Tariki, and the Palestinian lawyer who directed Libyan oil affairs, Anes Qasem. The committee's first institutional venture had been the Israeli boycott. Now they set out on a different path. Qasem and Tariki agreed with Salman that greater knowledge about the terms of oil concessions of each nation, which had been kept a closely guarded secret until that point, would protect "oil wealth" and safeguard their "combined rights."[15]

Collective knowledge, most importantly about the production, price, and profit provisions of each oil concession, was vital to asserting their sovereignty, the men believed. They designed a four-page questionnaire for Salman to travel with. Its questions about the terms by which oil was produced made clear the impulse toward greater information. If the companies held a "unified policy," Salman wrote in his notes, so should the countries. The best way to begin to take steps toward that goal, at this point, was to collect as much information as possible.[16]

Salman, Tariki, Qasem, and Iraqi oil minister Nadim Pachachi discussed the responses to the questionnaires for ten days in April 1957. At the same time, new information on the oil concessions in Saudi Arabia, Iraq, and Kuwait had also begun to seep out, often from industry sources. With that information, the men had enough in hand to confirm what they already assumed: the terms of the concessionary contracts in the Middle East, while not entirely uniform, had remarkable similarities. Each concession was of long duration, covered huge amounts of territory, and

---

[15] "New Approach to Arab Oil," *Arab World: A Monthly Review of Progress in the Arab Countries* 4: 9 (September 1958): 10; "Recommendations of the Oil Experts Committee Held between November 5–24, 1955," *OPEC: Origins and Strategy*, vol. I, 144–5.

[16] Arab League, General Secretariat, Public Relations Department, May 24, 1956, *OPEC: Origins and Strategy*, vol. I, 163; "Recommendations of the Oil Experts Committee Held between November 5–24, 1955," *OPEC: Origins and Strategy*, vol. I, 146.

FIGURE 2.1 Heads of Delegation at the Fourth OPEC Conference, Geneva, 1962. Mohammed Salman, who led the initial Arab League push for an international petroleum conference, is the head of the Iraqi delegation, wearing the white coat and black tie. Ibnu Sutowo of Indonesia is on the far left.
Source: OPEC Information Center, P-1962.

contained clauses that disallowed its revision. Furthermore, the concessions allowed the multinational companies to control the amount of oil produced and its price. That information provided a base of shared knowledge with which to work, and the oil experts voted to form a preparatory committee that would convoke an "Arab Petroleum Congress" to discuss the problems with the concessions and possible solutions.[17]

Salman planned for an unprecedented meeting that would both embrace functionaries from the oil nations and gather a corps of anticolonial international lawyers into one room, all to discuss the potential of "national oil legislation" in the context of "world and social conditions relating to the oil industry." He was also keen for the Congress to play an effective public relations role. An "Oil Brains Trust" would be formed to discuss and review the problems of the industry on Radio Cairo and films on the oil industry would be shown in various Arab countries during the

[17] Arab League, Secretariat-General, Permanent Petroleum Bureau, "Report of the Commission of the Arab Oil Experts, April 15 to 25, 1957," *OPEC: Origins and Strategy*, vol. I, 178–80, 183; Simon Siksek, "Oil Concessions – An Arab View," *Middle East Forum* (July 1960): 36–8; J. C. Hurewitz, *Diplomacy in the Near and Middle East, A Documentary Record: 1914–1956*, vol. II (Princeton University Press, 1956); David H. Finnie, *Desert Enterprise* (Cambridge, MA: Harvard University Press, 1958); Gordon H. Barrows, *Middle East Basic Oil Laws and Concession Contracts: Original Texts* (New York: Petroleum Legislation, 1959).

meeting. "Like Aladdin's lamp, the present and potential oil resources of the Middle East offer miraculous opportunities to transform the current landscape," wrote the editors of the Arab League's official newsletter when they first announced the plans for the Congress.[18]

The Saudi delegation to the United Nations revealed the likely political tone of the Congress when it leaked a position paper to the *New York Times* in 1958. The paper groomed the same points of contrast as the broader sovereign rights program. Foreign companies had engrossed national wealth through a series of unfair contracts, it said. The terms of the concessions continued past the expiration date set by the decolonization of international opinion. To remedy the situation, the oil producers needed to take collective steps toward "transforming their oil into a national occupation." A Standard Oil employee wrote that the paper resembled Hitler's *Mein Kampf* "in foreshadowing all the problems the oil companies are likely to be confronted with."[19]

He exaggerated. But still the anticolonial oil elites had begun to make the forceful argument that in the oil concessions the multinational companies retained a powerful lien on their national economies. The oil elites also had begun to frame their inquiry into the oil concessions as representative of systemic circumstances of global inequality. Their experience led them to see the oil concessions as a linked set of problems both among the oil nations and within the existing parameters of a decolonizing international society.

Hassouna gave the opening address when the Congress met in Cairo in April 1959. He first tipped his hat to the internationalism of sovereign rights, which he described as "the common good" sought by the oil producers and "foreign friendly states." He then discussed the primary objective of "drawing up one general petroleum policy." The Committee of Petroleum Economics and Legislation, organized by the Libyan official Anes Qasem and the Saudi official Abdullah al-Tariki, was the centerpiece of the Congress. The delegates heard three papers on the laws governing the relationships between states and companies. Each turned to a basic question: Could national sovereignty be invoked to abrogate the old oil concessions?[20]

---

[18] "First Oil Congress of Arab States," *MEED* 1: 23 (August 30, 1957): 1; "Oil in the Arab World," *Arab World: A Monthly Review of Progress in the Arab Countries* 3: 6–7 (November 1957): 31.

[19] Grove to Stevens, November 5, 1958, *OPEC: Origins and Strategy*, vol. I, 227, 239–40.

[20] "Address of Sayyed Abdel Khalek Hassouna," April 16, 1959, League of Arab States, The Secretariat General, Department of Petroleum Affairs, *PFAPC*; Committee of Petroleum Economics and Legislation, Minutes of the First Session, no. 39, *PFAPC*.

That question had driven Tariki, who had worked closely with Salman to plan the conference since 1957, for over a decade. Like many anticolonial elites, he began his career abroad, taking degrees in geology at the University of Cairo and then at the University of Texas at Austin in the 1940s. (One wonders if his experience as a minority in Texas, where he was sometimes mistaken for Mexican and denied entry into bars and restaurants, affected his understanding of international politics.) He worked for Texaco in 1947 and then in 1948 joined the staff of the Texas Railroad Commission, which regulated production in the United States to maintain domestic prices. Then he returned to Saudi Arabia as an in-house oil expert for the Ministry of Finance. He rapidly became the main force in oil policy and was by then a vocal critic of colonialism and its legacies. In 1952 he advocated that the oil producers who benefited by expanding production during the Iranian boycott should compensate Iran for their "unjust revenue." In 1954 he pushed for a contract with the Greek magnate Aristotle Onassis that would allow Onassis to replace Aramco as the primary shipper of Saudi oil, in an attempt to break the concessionaire's monopoly on downstream activities. When the US troops landed in Lebanon in 1958, he described the Eisenhower administration as "an imperialist aggressor supporting reactionary governments to cloak western exploitation of Arabs." *Fortune* magazine described him as "a fanatical nationalist" the same year.[21]

Now he hired an American lawyer, Frank Hendryx, to present a paper to the Congress entitled "A Sovereign Nation's Legal Ability to Make and Abide by a Petroleum Concession Contract." Hendryx argued that the "the buildup of sentiment, belief, and finally of trends" in the international community had brought about a consensus that "independent sovereign governments" should exercise greater resource control. As importantly – drawing from the legal work of Alexander Fachiri, J. Lassa Oppenheim, and Henry Bonfils – he found legal precedent for the right to

---

[21] Robert Vitalis, *America's Kingdom: Mythmaking on the Saudi Oil Frontier* (Stanford University Press, 2007), 194–227; Robert Bryce, *Cronies: Oil, the Bushes, and the Rise of Texas* (New York: PublicAffairs, 2005), 34–5; Muhamad Mughraby, *Permanent Sovereignty over Oil Resources: A Study of Middle East Oil Concessions and Legal Change*, Middle East Oil Monographs No. 5 (Beirut: The Middle East Research and Publishing Center, 1966), 131; Nathan J. Citino, "Defending the 'Postwar Petroleum Order': The US, Britain, and the 1954 Saudi-Onassis Tanker Deal," *Diplomacy and Statecraft* 11 (July 2000): 137–60; "OCB Intelligence Notes: Reactions to US Intervention in Lebanon," July 8, 1958, doc. CK3100199891, *DDRS*.

"modify or eliminate provisions of an existing petroleum concession" in American, British, and French law.[22]

But that intellectual history of sovereign rights hardly mattered, said Hendryx. The source of the right to permanent sovereignty was as moral as it was historical in the age of decolonization. Calls to sovereignty did not need extensive legal precedent because they asserted "the nation's economic independence, prosperity, and sole hope for the future." If an oil concession did not yield equitable terms, if the well-being of the nation was threatened, that was enough of a proper motive for contravening it, he argued. The reevaluation of concessions required "no torturous or fine-spun reasoning." Sovereignty was a basic right of "unimpeded freedom." It followed that the oil producers needed to take measure of existing concessions to protect their sovereignty. To do so was both morally correct and legally justifiable. "The legal rights and moral duties of the nation must prevail," Hendryx concluded.[23]

Farouk Muhamed El-Bakkary – the Egyptian Secretary General of Mines, Quarries and Petroleum – followed Hendryx with a dry but precise paper that traced the evolution of what he called "the principle of state ownership" over mineral wealth. But where Hendryx found the right in Western European law, Bakkary explained it through Latin American and Islamic legal traditions. His evidence, though, served the same broader argument about decolonization as an advancing force. Foreign capitalists coveted oil alone, he said. Independent governments, on the other hand, recognized their public responsibility. Any number of examples of the poor countries' constitutions and mining codes revealed this to be true, he continued, citing reports by the new UN Commission on Permanent Sovereignty. That sort of formal guarantee needed to shape future oil contracts "with a view to realizing the nation's control."[24]

Anes Qasem, the Palestinian lawyer who directed Libyan petroleum affairs, chaired the session. Like other anticolonial elites, his early

---

[22] The paper does not have citations, but Hendryx appears to have drawn heavily from Alexander P. Fachiri, "Expropriation and International Law," *British Yearbook of International Law* 6 (1925): 159–70. In this, Fachiri cited several authorities and cases to argue for the formation of a new "law of nations" in the mid-nineteenth century that protected states from "gross injustice" at the hands of another state.

[23] Frank Hendryx, "A Sovereign Nation's Legal Ability to Make and Abide by a Petroleum Concession Contract," *PFAPC*.

[24] Farouk Muhamed El-Bakkary, "A Treatise (Submitted to the Conference) on the Legal, Economic and Political Effects resulting from the Principle of the State Ownership of the Mineral Wealth in its Territory," *PFAPC*.

professional work underpinned his arguments about international economic justice. He graduated from the law school at the University of London in 1949 with a thesis on personal freedom under British laws of habeas corpus. It was especially notable to him that the system was designed to protect "the free movement of the individual," which he considered central to the functioning of societies "where human dignity is upheld." His history – which began with sixteenth-century common law and proceeded through the 1679 and 1816 Habeas Corpus Acts – emphasized the rights of prisoners to challenge "illegal detention."[25]

Much of the 131-page paper was a technical analysis debates in the House of Lords about legal jurisdiction, but Qasem examined British abolitionist arguments in the late eighteenth and early nineteenth centuries in his most interesting case studies. Two stand out. First, in the well-known 1772 Somerset versus Stewart case, the "negro slave" Somerset refused to work without being paid after being brought by Stewart from the United States to England. "The negro thereupon was seized and forcibly carried on board a ship bound to Jamaica," Qasem wrote. But English lawyers intervened and, upon successfully arguing the case, secured Somerset's freedom. The second case was that of the famous Hottentot Venus, who Qasem described as "a female native of South Africa" who was brought to London and placed on exhibition in the Egyptian Hall of Piccadilly Circus. He explained how the antislavery African Association put forward a writ of habeas corpus against the men who "appeared to have the custody of her, and who received money for such exhibition." But when she and her promoters proved that she was "exhibited with her consent and that she shared the proceeds," the writ was rescinded.[26]

The point in these cases, Qasem wrote after several other examples, was that the legal system was designed to "keep check ... on acts which deprive the individual of his freedom." In a phrase, Qasem had written a history of laws designed "to safeguard personal liberty against arbitrary use of power." He attended the 1959 Arab Petroleum Congress with that notion of protecting liberty from power. He also arrived with the express blessing of his boss at the Libyan Ministry of National Economy, Regeb Ben Katu, who wrote beforehand that Qasem and the other oil elites sought to "bring about a proper petroleum awakening in the Arab world." The trope of awakening had appeared again, and as before it

[25] Anes Mustafa Qasem, *Habeas Corpus* (University of London, 1949), 1, 8–10.
[26] Qasem, *Habeas Corpus*, 37–9.

placed emphasis on the process of articulating the nature of the problem and becoming critically aware of its potential solutions.[27]

As it had been for others, the collection and sharing of information and experience was crucial to the spirit of petroleum awakening for Qasem. He used his comments on the Petroleum and Economics panel to illustrate how national law could limit foreign infringements upon sovereignty. He set the specific example of the 1955 Petroleum Law of Libya, which he wrote as a policy model for other nations. The Libyan law responded to each of the main problems of the old concessions, he said. First, it claimed as national property all oil found "in its natural state in the layers of the earth." Second, it imposed strict limits on concession sizes – a "checkerboard division" that barred the "retention of large areas" by individual companies. The rectangular grid Qasem drew over the national map was thus a physical expression of the sovereignty of Libya over its land and its oil. Third, the law established regulations for the forcible surrender of untapped concessions. The "ghost of an approaching deadline" increased competition, Qasem said, and thus improved the government's negotiating position.[28]

As important for Qasem was the belief that no contract between a nation and a private company could be permanent. On this point more than any other, the old concessions were fundamentally flawed. In 1957, just two years after writing the Petroleum Law, he had begun to feel that the terms had been "too generous and that something had to be done to raise the stake." Concession terms should never become "fossilized," he wrote in a memorandum. In an argument that seems likely to have been drawn from Hersch Lauterpacht's recent interpretations for the UN International Law Commission, Qasem argued that "a concession deals with a developing situation and it has to develop and grow to meet changing circumstances."[29]

Lauterpacht, an Austrian jurist who was a member of the UN International Law Commission and a judge for the International Court of

---

[27] Qasem, *Habeas Corpus*, 14–16; *Petroleum Development in Libya: 1954 through 1958* (Tripoli: Government Press, 1958), 4.

[28] "The Petroleum Law No. 25 of 21st April, 1955," OPEC, *SDIPI: Socialist People's Libyan Arab Jamahiriya and Qatar, Pre-1966*, OIC; Anis Qasem, "Petroleum Legislation in Libya," Appendix 15, PFAPC; *Petroleum Development in Libya, 1954 through Mid-1960*, 5, 7.

[29] Petroleum Commission, *Petroleum Development in Libya, 1954 through Mid-1960*, 7. See also: Hersch Lauterpacht, "Codification and Development of International Law," *AJIL* 49 (1955): 16–43.

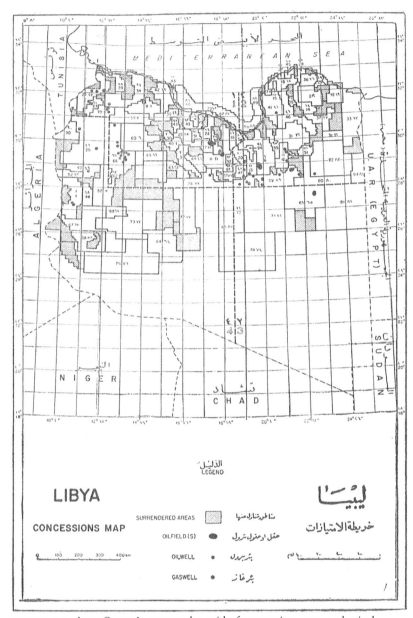

FIGURE 2.2 Anes Qasem's rectangular grid of concessions was a physical expression of Libya's sovereignty over its oil. This and other concepts were widely applied by other oil producing nations in the following decade.
Source: Abdul Amir Q. Kubbah, *OPEC, Past and Present* (Vienna: Petro-Economic Research Centre, 1974), 103.

Justice in the 1950s, had argued forcefully that the changing circumstances of international life required changes to old treaties, in particular, those that were imposed under some sort of duress. The term "changing circumstances" would be used again and again by oil elites in the following years. Qasem argued that it was particularly meaningful because it perpetually extended sovereignty. Sovereignty thus meant more than simply asserting the right to national control. It also meant that nations had the right to find policies, each progressively better than the previous, that would put more power in government hands. In turn, more capital would flow into the nation. In other words, old signposts no longer served as useful guides.

Like permanent sovereignty and unequal exchange, changing circumstances would have great staying power because it drew on the egalitarian morality of decolonization. Like the other ideas, too, it emerged out of both a rich tradition and a specific moment that was characterized above all by a belief in the transformative impact of decolonization. What the terms bundled together – a belief that international law had the power and the right to constantly reevaluate and change economic relations – constituted a political mind-set of consequence.

That common mentality of self-assertion knit the oil elites together. When Salman moved from the Arab League to the Iraqi petroleum ministry the next year, American analysts labeled him "a moderate counterpart" to the "radical" Tariki. But he echoed the Congress consensus in Cairo. The standard narrative of the economic culture of decolonization – recrimination and resurgence – bathed his opening and closing addresses. He first discussed his 1956 and 1957 surveys of "the history of the relationship" that led to the old concessions. The stipulations in the concessions that limited sovereignty arose from that history. But in an era marked by decolonization, they clashed with "international developments in law and justice," he said. The revision of the "outmoded" contracts was thus necessary. Until their concessions were modified, the "stench of exploitation" would continue to emanate from them.[30]

The delegates to the 1959 Congress also sought to take action. They issued a declaration that urged the oil-producing countries to establish "a joint advisory board" to discuss common problems. They hoped this would form the basis for them to continue to wrestle with the

---

[30] Wolf-Hunnicut, *The Concessionary Regime*, 69; "Opening Address by Mohammed Salman," April 16, 1959, *PFAPC*; "Closing Address by Mohammed Salman," April 16, 1959, *PFAPC*.

applicability of Hendryx's moral-legal junction, Qasem's "changing circumstances," and Salman's "international developments in law and justice." A decision by the multinational oil companies to lower oil prices in 1960 would prompt them to move more quickly than they might have otherwise.[31]

The 1960 price decision and the response to it revealed that the Arab oil elites had not conducted their half-decade project in a vacuum. Key to understanding the international lean to the Arab oil elites is the fact that Salman, Tariki, and Qasem had agreed at the earliest stages of planning the Arab Petroleum Congress to invite "the non-Arab oil-producing countries whose conditions are similar." This included Venezuela. The Director of Mines and Hydrocarbons of that nation, Juan Pablo Pérez Alfonso accepted the Arab League's invitation. He went to Cairo as an observer only, but the Latin American connection proved as invaluable in the founding of OPEC in 1960 as it had in the UN discussions in the 1950s. Latin American actors continued to be, in a sense, valuable translators of anticolonial ideas and policies.[32]

Pérez Alfonso was a second-generation oil elite from Venezuela, which had been the most important oil exporting country in the world since the 1920s – around the time that Pérez Alfonso left Johns Hopkins medical school to study law and political science at Universidad Central de Venezuela. As the Minister of Mines and Hydrocarbons, he built on the work of the founder of the ministry, Manuel Egaña, who took advantage of Franklin Delano Roosevelt's Good Neighbor policy to hammer out new concession agreements with US corporations in the 1930s and 1940s, in which the concessionaires agreed with a number of conditions, the most important of which was their unconditional acceptance of the sovereign right of Venezuela to levy income taxes on their activities.[33]

Egaña was, in short, the author of the "delicate fiction" of sovereignty that George Kennan had disparaged on his Latin America excursion in 1950. He also took an increasingly international outlook around that time. In 1949, after Chase Manhattan published a study that pointed to Venezuela's competitive disadvantage vis-à-vis their oil-producing counterparts in the Middle East, Egaña had Venezuelan oil legislation translated into English and Arabic and sent a delegation to Iran, Saudi Arabia, Kuwait,

---

[31] "Resolutions of the First Arab Oil Congress," April 23, 1959, *Venezuela and OPEC* (Caracas: General Secretariat of the Presidency of the Republic, 1961), 105.
[32] "First Oil Congress of Arab States," *MEED* 1: 23 (August 30, 1957): 1.
[33] Manuel Egaña, *Tres Décadas de Producción Petrolera* (Caracas: Venezuela, 1947).

Iraq, Egypt, and Syria. To be sure, he acted out of national interest. He
feared more than anything that competition from cheaper Middle Eastern
oil would undercut Venezuelan market control. But he also believed in a
strategy that would emphasize the oil-producing nations' shared interests,
and that the "invaluable social and economic conquests" of the Venezuelan government could be of use to the Middle Eastern producers in
their own negotiations with the multinational companies and Western
governments. "Direct relations of friendship with governments in the
Middle East" would allow the oil producers to "seek a way to reach a
price equilibrium for oils from both origins," he remembered later.[34]

The 1949 Venezuelan mission also extended invitations to a Venezuelan National Petroleum Congress, which Abdullah al-Tariki and
Manucher Farmanfarmaian, who would sit on Mossadegh's Oil Committee and also observe the 1959 Arab Petroleum Congress, attended. Tariki,
who had just moved back to Saudi Arabia from Texas only to return to
South America, told Venezuelan reporters then that he hoped "to study in
depth the technical and economic structure of the Venezuelan oil industry,
as well as the Law that governs the relationship between the State and the
concessionaires."[35]

These talks amounted to little and were tabled for almost a decade. But
Egaña attended the First Arab Petroleum Congress as a member of the
Venezuelan delegation, where either he or the journalist Wanda Joblanski
introduced Pérez Alfonso to Tariki. The two men discussed their mutual
agreement in the possibilities of the world's largest oil producers entering
into a pro-rationing agreement – a collective decision to produce less oil,
modeled on Tariki's experience with the Texas Railroad Commission. If
they did, they could reset the terms of trade for petroleum. Supply-side
control could bring a "fair" price that took into account "the intrinsic
value of oil," they believed. The day after the meeting of the Committee
on Petroleum Economics and Legislation, the two met again at a yacht
club in Maadi, a southern suburb of Cairo. They were joined by Farmanfarmaian, Mohamed Salman, who represented Iraq, and a Kuwaiti
representative. The men agreed to a series of measures including the
defense of oil prices and the establishment of national oil companies.[36]

---

[34] OPEC, *Information Booklet*, January 1973, OIC.
[35] Juan Carlos Boué, "OPEC at (More Than) Fifty: The Long Road to Baghdad, and
     Beyond," *Oxford Energy Forum* 83 (2011): 16–18.
[36] Francisco Parra, *Oil Politics: A Modern History of Petroleum* (London: I. B. Tauris,
     2004), 92–3; Skeet, *OPEC*, 16–17; Manucher Farmanfarmaian and Roxane Farmanfar-
     maian, *Blood and Oil: A Prince's Memoir of Iran, from the Shah to the*

In October 1959, four months after the Congress, Tariki hosted Salman and Qasem in Saudi Arabia for a meeting of the Arab oil experts. They recommended the formulation of a "unified Arab petroleum law" built on the economic, legal, and historical notions of sovereign rights. They also began to agree on means to do so. Prices could be increased, they hoped, through different mechanisms of national supply control. Such moves would in turn help each nation alter the terms of its concessions, which the men again described as "out of tune" with the reality of decolonization. Salman and Tariki then visited Pérez Alfonso in Caracas, where they began to work out a plan for production control. This culminated in a draft of the "World Proration Proposal" that was circled among anticolonial elites and oil industry experts in late 1959 and early 1960.[37]

At the same time, calls for greater national control over oil were not allowed to dissipate. In particular, many Arab elites began to discuss the kind of company-country relationships they envisioned for the future. For example, Ashraf Lufti, a Palestinian lawyer employed by the Kuwaiti government who would later become Secretary General of OPEC, evoked the broad potential of permanent sovereignty in a book inspired by the First Arab Petroleum Congress. To seek a remedy for low prices, petroleum ministers needed to engage in a dialogue similar to that occurring in the UN General Assembly subcommittees, he said. Now that the mystery shrouding the oil concessions of the imperial era had been unveiled, the producers could benefit from their shared knowledge through "a concrete plan of action."[38]

That general proposal received a fillip when oil prices began to drop in 1960. Prices had remained stable throughout the 1950s. The guaranteed

Ayatollah (New York: Random House, 2005), 339–42. On Joblanski, see: Daniel Yergin, *The Prize: The Epic Quest for Oil, Money and Power* (New York: The Free Press, 2008), 516–18; Anna Rubino, *The Queen of the Oil Club : The Intrepid Wanda Jablonski and the Power of Information* (Boston: Beacon Press, 2008), 165–98. Who made the introduction, in the end, is less important than the relationships that it developed out of, as well as those that developed out of it.

37 Simon G. Siksek, *The Legal Framework for Oil Concessions in the Arab World*, Middle East Oil Monographs No. 2 (Beirut: The Middle East Research and Publishing Center, 1960), 13–14; Tariki and Pérez Alfonzo, "World Proration Proposals," 1959–1960, box 4Jc66, Texas Independent Producers and Royalty Owners Association Records, Dolph Briscoe Center for American History, Austin, TX.

38 Ashraf Lufti, *Arab Oil: A Plan for the Future*, Middle East Monographs No. 3 (Beirut: The Middle East Research and Publishing Center, 1960 [1959]), viii, 1, 29–30, 55–8. On Lufti, see: OPEC, *Secretaries General of OPEC, 1961–2008*, OIC.

income, along with the chilling example of Mossadegh, had discouraged action by the oil producers. But increased production among the largest companies, new production from smaller ones, and the entry of the Soviet Union into the world market as an oil exporter had caused a glut by 1959. Furthermore, the Eisenhower administration had formalized US import quotas, closing off the lucrative American market to many sources of foreign oil. The largest oil companies decided then to maintain their profits by reducing their tax commitments to the producing countries. They did so by lowering the posted prices for crude oil, which were the prices used to calculate taxes. The move was unilateral, taken without consulting the oil officials.[39]

Tariki telegraphed Pérez Alfonso, and then the revolutionary Iraqi government invited the members of the Maadi agreement to Baghdad. There, representatives from Saudi Arabia, Venezuela, Iran, Kuwait, and Iraq announced the creation of the OPEC on September 14, 1960. The first communiqué of OPEC read much like the Arab League, Bandung, and UN documents that preceded it. The principal aim of the organization was "the unification of petroleum policies for the Member Countries and the determination of the best means for safeguarding the interests of the Member Countries individually and collectively." The oil elites also insisted that they be consulted on pricing matters and called for a system for "the regulation of production."[40]

Tariki considered the OPEC communiqué an "instrument for economic emancipation." He believed that the first decade of decolonization – in particular, the meetings of anticolonial elites in New York, Bandung, Caracas, Cairo, and Baghdad – marked the emergence of a dramatic new mode of international politics. In a sense, he was right. The engagement of the major oil producers with the nascent sovereign rights program in the second half of the 1950s stoked the creation of a new collective of commodity producers. The individual interests of each oil nation, not to mention those within each nation, cannot be discounted – compelling evidence exists, for example, that the Saudi faction that eventually ousted Tariki hoped OPEC would provide a conservative shield against Nasserism. Yet Tariki's basic assumption, and his emphasis on the

[39] Yergin, *The Prize*, 512–16; Richard H. K. Vietor, *Energy Policy in America since 1945: A Study of Business-Government Relations* (New York: Cambridge University Press, 1984), 129–38.

[40] Abdul Amir Q. Kubbah, *OPEC, Past and Present* (Vienna: Petro-Economic Research Centre, 1974), 21–2.

economic possibilities of decolonization, was shared among oil elites and anticolonial elites more broadly. Fuad Rouhani, the Iranian official who became the first Secretary General of OPEC, described the organization's goal in these terms: "to impress public opinion in all the important oil-exporting countries and to unite these countries in a common front."[41]

OPEC formed part of a broader culture on the international periphery that by 1960 had been shaped for a decade by the general agreement about permanent sovereignty, unequal exchange, and the changing circumstances of global capitalism. By nature ecumenical in its rhetoric of common plight, its universal condemnation of classical terms of trade, and its internationalist belief in a curative sovereignty, the culture of decolonization provided a *lingua franca* that diverse voices could employ to justify their defiance. Decolonization was marked by the emergence of an international consciousness. The concepts of permanent sovereignty, unequal exchange, and changing circumstances resonated through the Third World. The founding of OPEC was steeped in that remarkable development because the oil elites believed in the same abiding argument that highly asymmetrical power relations endured into the era of decolonization, even if an increasing number of nations were formally equivalent in terms of juridical sovereignty. Indeed, the oil elites found the concessions to be a keen example of the trend and sought to use their "collective sovereignty" to alter them.

The UN Commission on Permanent Sovereignty over Natural Resources also formed part of that world. Their meetings overlapped exactly with those of the Arab League Petroleum Bureau. The meetings and work of the Commission lay bare cognitive, legal, and economic links that made welcome the peregrinations of the oil producers into the sovereign rights program. The history of the UN Permanent Sovereignty Commission from 1958 to 1961 also reveals that, when set on the big backcloth of sovereign rights, OPEC was less an extraordinary union than an ordinary one.

But at the time the members of the Permanent Sovereignty Commission, including Rahman Pazhwak, found the moment itself extraordinary. The Commission was formed in 1958 when the General Assembly took

---

[41] Abbas Alnasrawi, *Arab Nationalism, Oil, and the Political Economy of Dependency* (Westport, CT: 1991), 118; "Press Communique – Tehran," July 2, 1962, *OPEC: Official Resolutions and Press Releases, 1960–1983*, OIC. For a sharp description of the differences between OPEC members, see: Nathan J. Citino, *From Arab Nationalism to OPEC: Eisenhower, King Saud, and the Making of U.S.-Saudi Relations*, 2nd edn (Bloomington: Indiana University Press, 2005), 150–6.

up the recommendations he, Baroody, and the other members of the Economic and Social Council made in 1955. It had a straightforward objective: to examine the international status of permanent sovereignty, which the General Assembly resolution had described as a "basic constituent ... of the right to self-determination." After a survey of the mechanisms of permanent sovereignty in every nation, colony, and territory and more than thirty meetings, the commission members wrote their first official report. The conclusion was as forthright as their instructions: anticolonial elites of all stripes had employed the language of sovereign rights when writing national laws regulating the actions of foreign companies. What a disparate array of actors had called the awakening of consciousness had become central to the use of permanent sovereignty to redistribute wealth in specific cases.

The chairman of the Commission was Oscar Schachter, an American lawyer who headed the General Legal Division of the UN Secretariat. Schachter shared important assumptions with Pazhwak, Qasem, and other anticolonial lawyers. International law, he wrote in 1954, could not be conceived of as "a body of existing and fairly precise rules." Rather, international law was better understood as encompassing the process in which usage and precedent developed into legal rules. Because of the great changes that occurred with decolonization, international society was at a moment in which precedent mattered less than ever before. He described this as a sort of extenuated rebirth, the generation of a new "body of law" through which "slowly, in some cases imperceptibly, practice was developing into norms."[42]

Schachter applied that theme of change to the question of permanent sovereignty in the earliest commission report, drafted in December 1959. The range of new measures adopted by states to "exercise their sovereignty" was astonishing, he wrote. In particular, he and the commission members had collected a huge corpus of "official codification efforts" in the Third World. Constitutional and legislative conditions everywhere, it seemed, now protected "sovereign rights and the national interest." Nationalism in the oil industry was one example of that postwar trend for the commission members, as Iranian, Libyan, Venezuelan, and Mexican laws revealed. Those governments had begun to give themselves

---

[42] Oscar Schachter, "The Role of International Law in the Practice of the United Nations," UN, Official Records, General Legal Division, December 11, 1954. See also: Oscar Schachter, "The Development of International Law through the Legal Opinions of the United Nations Secretariat," *British Yearbook of International Law* 25 (1948): 91–132.

maximum discretion and "wide latitude for terms more favorable to the nation." In addition, Bolivia, Brazil, Burma, Cambodia, Chile, Guatemala, India, Indonesia, Liberia, Pakistan, Paraguay, Peru, the Philippines, Thailand, Tunisia, and Turkey had all passed new laws in the previous decade tightening the regulations on foreign investment in natural resource extraction.[43]

It was notable to the commission members that this trend had largely passed over the territories that remained under some form of official colonialism. The rulers of African colonies, for example, had made some concessions to nationalist and internationalist pressure, namely emphasizing that mineral rights were vested in the "indigenous state." But those rights were still ceded to private or semi-public companies and the indigenous populations in these areas were thoroughly "alienated" from the land; that is, the local ruling bodies of colonies and trusteeships in Africa had not established effective legal protection of permanent sovereignty. That alienation also extended into the old Middle East petroleum concessions, according to the commission.[44]

The report was a signature example of the decolonization-era efforts to collect information to which the United Nations and other international bodies dedicated great energy. In turn, this and other information strategies also contributed substantially to the fortunes of the sovereign rights program. In general, their findings reinforced the belief that political liberation could lead to faster changes in the economic relationship between the poor and rich nations. In the specific case of the first permanent sovereignty study, Pazhwak and other delegates argued that the report, while momentous, did not capture "the real situation in the field of exploitation by foreigners and their companies of natural wealth and resources of non-self-governing territories, trust territories and less developed countries." After all, the Commission had also been charged

---

[43] Annex, UN Commission on Permanent Sovereignty over Natural Resources, Official Records, Second Session, Preliminary Study by the Secretariat, December 15, 1959, A/AC.97/5.

[44] UN Commission on Permanent Sovereignty over Natural Resources, Official Records, Second Session, Preliminary Study by the Secretariat, December 15, 1959, A/AC.97/5. A follow-up report in 1962 placed considerable emphasis on laws passed in the "States which have attained their independence in the most recent past," including the republics of Chad, Congo (Brazzaville), Dahomey, Ivory Coast, Mali, Senegal, and the Central African Republic. These governments had taken small steps exercising legislative rule, but the report found that much of their raw material wealth remained under foreign control. See: UN Commission on Permanent Sovereignty over Natural Resources, Official Records, Second Session, Preliminary Study by the Secretariat, November 28, 1962, A/AC.97/5/Rev.2, E/3511.

FIGURE 2.3 Abdul Rahman Pazhwak, Oscar Schachter, the Chilean delegate
Daniel Schweitzer, and the Filipino delegate Melquiades Gamboa meet before the
second session of the Permanent Sovereignty Commission, February 16, 1960.
Source: UN Photo/MB. Courtesy of the United Nations Photo Library, Photo No. 169052.

with making recommendations to strengthen permanent sovereignty, to
be passed by the General Assembly as a resolution. To do so, they told
Schachter, the commission needed more detailed comparative information on particular violations of sovereignty. They focused in particular on
the contractual clauses and profits of foreign businesses in the natural-
resources sectors. Building on that point in the Commission meetings in
1959 and 1960, Pazhwak and the Chilean delegate Daniel Schweitzer
successfully pressed for a strong resolution that fully supported nations'
application of permanent sovereignty and moved jurisdiction into
national courts. In the larger meeting of the Economic and Social Council,
referring to the Calvo Doctrine and the UN Charter as parts of an
unfinished story, Pazhwak justified his support for a more detailed
appraisal by stating that "political and economic self-determination
were indivisible."[45]

---

[45] Schrijver, *Sovereignty over Natural Resources*, 66–70.

Schachter followed this advice and produced a second report, which led to another UN resolution on permanent sovereignty in 1962. More importantly, it was clear that permanent sovereignty had struck a responsive chord. In a common front, Third World leaders insisted that the economic structure and performance of their countries had been shaped decisively by their lack of sovereignty under colonialism. That interpretation was radical in the hands of some but was closer to the mainstream than many historians have accepted. Pazhwak's arguments about the indivisibility of political and economic self-determination, in particular, captured a view that was common among anticolonial elites, who also as a rule perceived permanent sovereignty as a basis for the redistribution of wealth in the international economy.

In the first half of the 1960s, the Non-Aligned Movement, the UN General Assembly, the Afro-Asian Peoples Solidarity Organization, and many other groups, including OPEC and Raúl Prebisch's UN Conference on Trade and Development would adopt similar resolutions calling for permanent sovereignty. For oil elites, this increasingly firm model of dissent turned out to be the ground upon which they would fabricate a position of international influence.

The vocal calls for economic emancipation and early policy outlines of permanent sovereignty formed part of an economic culture of decolonization that was becoming more influential in international society. It was both a broad movement and intensely personal. Jammed in among the men at the First Arab Petroleum Congress was Simon Siksek, a Jerusalem-born lawyer who studied at Cambridge and Princeton. He remembered looking across the assembly hall and seeing the delegates listen intently to Hendryx, Qasem, Salman, and the others. The event made an impression: "For the first time in the Arab world, matters that had hitherto been the exclusive domain of international lawyers ... were brought up for discussion before 500 delegates," he wrote. In his emotive engagement with the moment and its possibilities, Siksek was typical of the anticolonial elite class. His professional experience also encapsulates two other important characteristics of the rise of sovereign rights during decolonization: the impulse toward gathering information and the use of that information to make an argument about inequality in international society. When he attended the First Arab Petroleum Congress, he and a colleague at the American University of Beirut, Albert Badre, were in the midst of completing a demographic study of oil labor in Saudi Arabia, Kuwait, and Iraq , a project that was part of a Princeton Economics Department study funded by the Ford Foundation.

They initially set out to analyze the "human resources infrastructure" in the oil fields and refineries of Kuwait, Saudi Arabia, and Iraq. But from their first interview, Siksek and Badre began to note how international politics affected their understanding of what had at first been a technical premise. To gain "proper perspective" on labor issues in their local contexts, they wrote, it was necessary to understand that "Arab popular belief holds that the oil deals have not been fair." It was uniformly supposed among Arab oil workers and government officials that the concessions were not "faithful representations of national interest" because the governments that signed them were under foreign domination.[46]

Siksek and Badre labeled that belief "the unfair thesis." They likened the relationship between that belief and any social-scientific analysis related to the oil sector to the parable of the elephant and the blind men. One could not grasp manpower problems without observing at a distance "the elephant ... in its essence," they wrote. This was as true of what they described as the new Arab managerial class as it was of the average worker. The oil elites cultivated the same terrain of the mind as "the tremendous rise of the Afro-Asian masses," the two men wrote. What kept "Arabs awake nights with worry" was the burning fact that their nations and their nations' oil concessions were "still subject to various shades of colonialism."[47]

The unfair thesis, shades of colonialism, petroleum awakening, economic self-determination, changing circumstances, unequal exchange, permanent sovereignty – different phrases expressed the problems and objectives of the oil elites. These particular ideas and their meanings imprinted themselves in the economic culture of decolonization. The move to control oil had a space in that culture, according to the vision of the oil elites. The parallel tracks of oil politics and decolonization in their understanding of historical trends were also clear enough to them: the owners of the oil concessions had purloined the wealth of others. That seizure of oil wealth was indicative of two broader truths. First, the great awakening of decolonization, although monumental, left other types of

---

[46] Siksek, *The Legal Framework for Oil Concessions*, 2; Albert Y. Badre and Simon G. Siksek, *Manpower and Oil in Arab Countries* (Economic Research Department, American University Beirut, 1959), v, 8, 17. The project was part of the Ford Foundation's Inter-University Study of Labor Problems in Economic Development. Siksek and Badre depended on assistance from Harvard economist John Thomas Dunlop and fieldwork from a young Princeton graduate student who would later become U.S. Secretary of the Treasury, Michael Blumenthal.

[47] Badre and Siksek, *Manpower and Oil*, 11–16.

exploitation in its wake. Second, and more optimistic, decolonization provided a premise in permanent sovereignty that could take postcolonial exploitation the way formal colonialism had gone.

The spread of the sovereign rights movement created a common climate of enthusiasm. Its conceptual and political breakthrough was evident in its high profile in the contemporary mind-set. As political self-determination was achieved, economic emancipation became the chief cause of the internationalist anticolonial struggle. The oil elites tapped into that broader understanding of the age. Imperialism was fundamentally anachronistic, W. E. B. Du Bois told his readers in one example from around the same time. But that did not mean it could be denied that "the present plight of the world is a direct outgrowth of the past." Siksek and Badre echoed those sentiments. Oil exploration had grown "at a juncture when politically the various countries in it were beginning, after centuries of foreign domination, to assume responsibility for their own destiny," they wrote.[48]

That understanding pointed toward increased activity. The elites in the oil world – including Hassouna, Salman, Tariki, Egaña, Pérez Alfonso, and Qasem – were in fact already innovative users of that transnational perspective. And they believed that the identification of the problem and the sharing of information were only the first steps. But even as oil elites began to meet in greater numbers and more often than ever before, even as they began to use their collective knowledge to formulate more detailed strategies, a large gap separated the blossoming of interest in sovereignty from the reality of practice. The Eisenhower administration, for one, expressed little concern about the formation of OPEC. "Anyone could break up the Organization "by offering five cents more per barrel [to] one of the countries," the president said in a January 1960 meeting of the National Security Council (NSC). That view had remarkable continuity. "The blow of Mossadegh Madness to the Iranian treasury in 1951–1954 has not been forgotten," a State Department official advised in 1967.[49]

---

[48] W. E. B. Du Bois, *The World and Africa* (New York: International Publishers, 1968), 2; Badre and Siksek, *Manpower and Oil*, 236.

[49] Memorandum of Discussion at the 460th Meeting of the National Security Council, September 21, 1960, *FRUS 1958–60*, vol. IV, doc. 309; Paper Prepared in the Department of State, February 8, 1967, *FRUS 1964–68*, vol. XXXIV, doc. 19. Allen Dulles expressed greater concern than the others in 1960, but he appears to have been in a small minority.

The persistence with which efforts to assert sovereignty over oil were discarded in the 1960s spoke a truth that anticolonial oil elites, who were still scarred by the Iranian failure, knew all too well. The idea that permanent sovereignty was a right may have moved into the mainstream of international thought, but attempts at economic emancipation would only come at a price.

3

Histories of Petroleum Colonization

Oil Elites and Sovereign Rights, 1960–1967

Among these shifting sands, the need for flexibility over the terms of these new oil-producing rights is paramount.[1]
Francisco Parra, 1964

What can be achieved today may have appeared impossible ten years ago and may appear almost a "sell-out" ten years hence.[2]
Nadim al-Pachachi, 1965

A panoply of illustrious radicals added their voices to the chorus that branded the international economy as heir to a criminal colonial past. One was the 91-year-old W. E. B. Du Bois, who made economic inequality the driving rhetorical force of his final American speeches before leaving the United States to live out his life in Ghana. "While the political control of colonies has greatly decreased, large parts of the world and its people remain under imperialism by economic power," he told audiences. "We might then regard the world outside Europe and the United States as still colonial."[3]

Another purveyor of anticolonial economics was Ernesto "Che" Guevara. When the president of the Inter-American Bank invoked José Marti's desire for foreign investment at the 1961 meeting of the

---

[1] Francisco Parra, "The Development of Petroleum Resources under the Concession System in Non-Industrialized Countries," doc. EC/64/III, OIC.
[2] Nadim al-Pachachi, "Development of Oil Concessions in the Middle East," *ROAPE* 1: 4 (May 1965), 24.
[3] W. E. B. Du Bois, "But a Few Years: Africa in Battle against Colonialism, Racialism, Imperialism," Afro-American Heritage Association, 1960, Reference Center for Marxist Studies, Pamphlet Collection, folder 2, Tamiment Library.

Inter-American Economic and Social Council, Guevara responded by quoting a letter Marti wrote in 1891. Marti had tempered his financial internationalism with a stern nationalist warning, said Guevara: "The country that buys, commands; the country that sells serves; commerce must be balanced to protect liberty. A country that would be free must be free in commerce."[4]

Guevara presented Raúl Prebisch a copy of his treatise on guerilla warfare at that meeting – with the dedication "a means for economic development." When he spoke at the UN General Assembly three years later, just months before leading his ill-fated guerilla excursion into the Congo, he reframed his anticolonialism in Prebisch's language. "The so-called deterioration of the terms of trade is nothing less than the result of the unequal exchange between countries producing raw materials and industrial countries," he said. Like Du Bois, he also identified national sovereignty as the most promising retaliation against the bygone yet unremitting injuries of imperialism. If the poor nations could use their sovereignty to forge "new terms of trade between the exploited and the exploiters," they could get out from under the "political domination of the imperialists and the colonialists."[5]

The statements of these and other well-known figures reveal the currency of the basic insights of the development economists and the international lawyers who took the measure of decolonization during the previous decade. Du Bois, Guevara, and others wrote and spoke about redistribution, price readjustments, and permanent sovereignty not in the dispassionate language of social science but in the flesh and blood politics of subjugation and liberation. They saw in the international economy a metaphysic of repression that was both cause and effect, what dependency and world-systems theorists Celso Furtado and André Gunder Frank had begun by then to call "the dialectic of development" or "the development of underdevelopment." Their urgency was reinforced by the recognition, or hope, that the political breakup of colonial rule might extend to the international economy.[6]

[4] "Che Guevara at Punta Del Este," New York: World View Publishers, 1961, Reference Center for Marxist Studies, Pamphlet Collection, folder 46, Tamiment Library.
[5] Garavini, *After Empires*, 88; Ernesto Guevara, "Colonialism Is Doomed." December 11, 1964, Republic of Cuba, Ministry of External Relations, Information Department, Reference Center for Marxist Studies, Pamphlet Collection, folder 46, Tamiment Library.
[6] Celso Furtado, *Dialectica do Desenvolviminto* (Rio de Janeiro: Fundo de Cultura, 1964); André Gunder Frank, "The Development of Underdevelopment," *Monthly Review* 18 (September 1966), 17–30.

This sweeping arc of interpretation was not limited to the most famous, scholarly, or eloquent radicals of the era. The conviction that the international economy remained a colonial perversion, propped up by what Du Bois referred to as "the dying Ricardian economics," was also pervasive among the less well-known organizations that were bursting into being across the Third World. The Afro-Asian People's Solidarity Organization, for instance, collapsed the sovereign rights argument into a single statement in 1960. Drawing from an economic report commissioned at their inaugural meeting in 1958, the delegates held that an "archaic feudal exploitation" continued to limit the rehabilitation of economies "ravaged by imperialist plunder." The Indian representative to the group's Permanent Secretariat, H. D. Malaviya, presented the report's findings. First, he said, calls for economic emancipation were a natural outgrowth of political decolonization. Second, economic development would prove a "mirage" unless the nations could work together to achieve the "permanent parity of prices for raw materials." The assembled heads of state agreed. To fight poverty meant the introduction of "fair prices on raw materials," which in turn necessitated concerted action to "restore full mastery over their wealth and resources."[7]

AAPSO joined several groups in the 1960s – including the Organization of African Unity, the Non-Aligned Movement, the UN Conferences on Human Rights, and the UN Conference on Trade and Development – that followed the UN meetings, the Afro-Asian summit in Bandung, the First Arab Petroleum Congress, and OPEC in laying emphasis on the effect of decolonization on international law and the international economy. The ideas at the base of the economic culture of decolonization and the sovereign rights program gained power in part because they spoke directly to the condition elites perceived across the decolonizing world and in part because they reflected the rising power of the new states in the international community. As they sensed the power of those concepts, many different types of people began to experiment with the claims of solidarity that echoed across international society.[8]

---

[7] David Levering Lewis, *W. E. B. Du Bois: Biography of a Race, 1868–1919* (New York: Henry Holt, 1993), 85; "Resolution on Economic Policy adopted by Conakry Conference," in H. D. Malaviya, *Report on Problems of Economic Development of Afro-Asian Countries* (Cairo: Dar el Hana Press, April 1960), 1–2, 12–15, 27, 70–80.

[8] Y. Etinger, *African Solidarity and Neo-Colonialism* (Moscow: Novartis, 1969), Reference Center for Marxist Studies, Pamphlet Collection, folder 2, Tamiment Library; Organization of African Unity, "Resolutions of the Summit Conference," May 25, 1963, *ISIL* 1965, 46–7.

This chapter reveals how oil elites in particular interpreted their world through an increasingly standard "history of petroleum colonization," as Abdullah al-Tariki called it. But the experience of the oil elites also brings to light that, even if there was consensus on the problems of the past, writing the end of the narrative was fraught with difficulties. Defining practical means to economic emancipation was harder than talking about past subjugation. Consensus among the oil elites on the policies needed to achieve their shared objectives did not exist and, despite attempts to make sovereign rights a mechanism of cohesion in the fight for better concessionary terms, fragmentation was the norm.

The friction among oil elites representing different nations became outright hostility during the royalty negotiations conducted by OPEC between 1962 and 1965. Gradualist and insurrectionist factions disagreed about the extent to which sovereignty could transform the oil concessions. The infighting among the OPEC nations and individual elites was so rife that many observers, including those who wished it well, doubted the organization's very survival. The divergent interests posed difficult questions for the oil elites: What were to be the immediate aims of their collective action? How could they overturn the terms of trade? What were the limits of permanent sovereignty as economic diplomacy?

As they considered these questions, the awareness of the potential of joint action seemed to heighten the points of division that drove oil elites apart; their deep desire to bring together disparate interests under the banner of economic emancipation thus had its costs. There was something elusive, then, about oil elites' calls for sovereign rights and the way in which it caused its members to grapple with the shifting, overlapping, and often contradictory identities that formed the economic culture of decolonization.

But sovereign rights also worked through, not despite, contradictions. If the oil elites inhabited a complex and often contentious universe, to understand their disagreements is not to say that the new internationalist language of sovereign rights was without power. Rather, sovereign rights was a sticky concept, as the new histories of petroleum colonization reveal. By the mid-1960s, the success of the sovereign rights program built on the growing self-awareness and accumulated experience of the anticolonial elite class. The program moved into the mainstream of the international community and forever shifted the terms of international debate about oil control.

The emphasis on the rupture of colonial deference, and the insurgency of that attitude, was part of a concerted public relations and policy campaign by oil elites. They interpreted their emergence as part of the awakening of decolonization and frequently colluded in the saturnalia of the sovereign rights program among themselves and within other groups. Three examples of the oil elites' experiences in the early 1960s reveal how, in that context, the new history of petroleum colonization hardened into a widespread and unshakable belief.

The first is the Second Arab Petroleum Congress, which took place in Beirut in October 1960. Mohammed Salman opened the meeting by criticizing "the attitude of the petroleum companies" during the recent price reductions. The companies' unilateralism, he said, was contrary to "the trends and hopes of Arab public opinion." The future of the oil industry should be based not on that sort of imperious behavior, but on the principle of "economic equity." The delegation heads then divided into two groups, the first of which would again discuss "petroleum economics and legislation." As before, the oil elites' discussions seemed inherently reasonable to them. In the wake of the establishment of OPEC, "it was natural" that the question of sovereignty over oil would occupy the "foremost place" in their meetings, wrote Farouk Muhamed El-Bakkary, the Egyptian official who had presented on the panel with Tariki, Anes Qasem, and Frank Hendryx the previous year, and now took the minutes.[9]

This time the law and economics group elected Tariki as chair. The Saudi oil director also presented a paper in which he reviewed the history of oil prices culminating in the companies' price cuts in 1959 and 1960. To make his argument that company control over price and production was inconsistent and discriminatory, he turned to development economists' arguments about the historical underpricing of raw materials. The companies failed to take into consideration the "basic value of oil" for modern industry, he said. A "new formula" that would do so would link the Middle East posted price to the price of oil produced near the Gulf of Mexico and factor in transportation costs. This was one possible step toward eliminating "the mystery and inequities—with the resulting ill will—which have existed in the past." Tariki added in his comments that the oil elites still suffered from a lack of information, a problem he no doubt hoped OPEC would address. The producing governments needed

---

[9] Al Sayyed Farouk Mohamed al Bakkary, "Report on the Activity of the First Group," n.d. (October 1960), vol. I, League of Arab States, *PSAPC*.

to "scrutinize such data and figures carefully," he said, especially because of the "discrepancy" between the numbers declared by companies to the host governments and to their home governments for tax purposes.[10]

More broadly, Tariki believed it was crucial that the oil producers use their collective sovereignty to press their own agenda with greater force. He invited Frank Hendryx, who was still under contract with the Saudi government, to present another paper on the rights of sovereign states. The shift in tone between 1959 and 1960 was sharp. Hendryx attacked the companies' history of exploitation with greater vigor. He zeroed in on the companies' legal stance that the long-term concession agreements were frozen at the date of their conception. By framing that argument as one of the "sanctity of contracts," company lawyers were attempting to foist "an atmosphere of law and legal morality" on the producing nations that had no valid legal or moral basis, Hendryx said. Given the transformative character of decolonization, the argument for stasis could only be considered a fantasy. It was "founded on a premise that the world in which this relationship was born and continues to exist is not alone unchanging but is also, for the purpose, the best of all worlds." The changing circumstances for the oil concessions, owing to the "economic and political coming of age" of the producers, meant that this "self-created shadow zone must vanish."[11]

A second example of the influence of the new histories of petroleum colonization comes from the relationship between Nadim Pachachi and Anes Qasem, whose concept of "changing circumstances" was developing into an explicit doctrine for oil elites. In 1960 Qasem hired Nadim Pachachi as a consultant to study "at close range" his Libyan petroleum laws.

Pachachi, an Iraqi who earned a PhD in petroleum technology from the University of London in 1938, had represented his country on several rounds of negotiations with its major concessionaire between 1954 and the 1958 Iraqi revolution. Pachachi summed up his overall strategy in a 1958 pamphlet. It began with a description of the internationalism of Iraqi oil nationalism. Oil was not only the "nerve center of the national economy," he wrote, it was closely linked to "international developments." He also used the pamphlet to criticize the old concessions. They had been

---

[10] Abdullah Tariki, "The Pricing of Crude Oil and Refined Products," October 1960, vol. I, *PSAPC*; Al Sayyed Farouk Mohamed al Bakkary, "Report on the Activity of the First Group," vol. I, *PSAPC*.

[11] Frank Hendryx, "The Same World," October 1960, vol. I, *PSAPC*.

signed in the late 1920s and early 1930s under conditions that "compelled the Iraqi negotiator to be lenient with the oil companies." His history continued into the following decades as other circumstances, in particular, the failure of Mohammed Mossadegh, similarly limited the possibility of imposing Iraqi sovereignty. It was too bad that, in that bleak environment, he had only been able to address minor issues like the renegotiation of discount rates, the closer evaluation of costs of production, and the reform of national tax laws. But Pachachi believed the time for leniency had ended. "So much depends on the circumstances," he wrote. "What seemed possible" by the end of the 1950s, for example, would not even have been conceivable when the last Iraqi concession was negotiated in 1932.[12]

Pachachi wrote the pamphlet amid the brewing revolutionary tumult that had seized the country, and he was on the defensive. He further justified his policies, against accusations that they were too piecemeal, in a 1958 speech to the Iraq Senate. His small victories served as a means to a greater end, he told the legislators: "I do not wish it to be thought ... that we should be content with what we have achieved so far." For him, the new wave of activity in the Arab League Petroleum Bureau – led by Mohammed Salman, who would soon take Pachachi's position in the new government – opened up new horizons. "We must advance with the times, seize opportunities and watch those developments abroad which have a bearing on the relation between the Government and Oil Companies operating in Iraq," he said. "What may be difficult to obtain today may be easy tomorrow, what one fails to accomplish in 1954 may succeed in doing in 1960."[13]

The power of the concept of changing circumstances was clear. Pachachi repeated the argument again in 1965 in a brief "history of the development of oil concessions in the Middle East" for a Baghdad journal. Like other histories of petroleum colonization, this one began with the inequity of the old concessions. The 1925 "negotiations" in Iraq, for example, had not been negotiations at all. A British threat to cleave oil-rich Mosul from the rest of the country poisoned that concession and the ones that followed from their birth, he wrote. Continued control of national oil production by the Iraq Petroleum Company into the 1950s and 1960s flew in the face of decolonization. But the "new environment"

---

[12] Nadim al-Pachachi, *Iraqi Oil Policy: August 1954–December 1957* (Beirut: The Research and Translation Office, 1958), 1–2.
[13] Nadim al-Pachachi, "Text of the Speech," *Iraqi Oil Policy: August 1954–December 1957*, 6–7.

that grew out of decolonization had changed the climate. "What can be achieved today may have appeared impossible ten years ago and may appear almost a 'sell-out' ten years hence," he wrote again. In other words, "the growing influence in world affairs of the emerging Afro-Asian bloc" continued to complement "the establishment of a unified front" of oil elites. That change was especially evident in how he and other elites understood recent history, he continued. "The nationalization of . . . Dr. Mossadegh" was still his primary point of reference, but it was no longer considered a total failure. From the changing perspective of the present, it was instead a necessary step in a longer process.[14]

The shifting image of Mossadegh pointed to a new chapter in the history of petroleum colonization, Pachachi believed. More subtly, it also indicated the ongoing role of Iran in the sovereign rights program. Pachachi noted that the Shah's government had begun to lead the way again in the late 1950s, this time with the 1957 agreement between the National Iranian Oil Company and the Italian national oil company, ENI. In return for providing a share of the capital for oil exploration and production, the National Iranian Oil Company would receive 75 percent of the total profit, through the 50 percent that accrued directly to the government in income taxes and royalties and an even split in the remaining profits. The deal, which covered the development of three oil fields, promised what one commentator called "a new pattern for Middle East oil agreements." Its ratification in the Majlis set off "the twentieth-century equivalent of a gold rush" in Iran, according to one industry journal. Company officials from the United States, Great Britain, the Netherlands, Italy, West Germany, and Japan crammed into Tehran hotels to negotiate similar small-scale production contracts, and the director of the National Company, Abdullah Entezam, announced that a Qasem-like "division of Iran into oil areas had begun."[15]

Mossadegh's old Oil Committee had also reasserted itself, now with the support of the Shah. The committee recommended a new "Oil Exploration Bill," which the Majlis passed in July 1957. The legislation stipulated that the National Company would have at least a 30 percent holding in all new joint operations. It also gave the Majlis the right to veto any

---

[14] Nadim al-Pachachi, "Development of Oil Concessions in the Middle East," *ROAPE* 1: 4 (May 1965), 13–15, 24.

[15] "Iran," *MEED* 1: 4 (March 29, 1957), 3–4; "Iran: Discussions with Foreign Oil Interests," *MEED* 1: 6 (April 12, 1957), 6; "Iran: The Oil Agreement with AGIP Mineraria," *MEED* 1: 24 (September 6, 1957), 4–5; "Iran: Other Foreign Oil Interests," *MEED* 1: 24 (September 6, 1957), 5.

contracts that it considered an affront to Iranian state power, a clause that Entezam said "respected in every way the spirit" of constitutional provisions designed to "retain" sovereignty. To celebrate the passing of the bill, the Shah invited members of the Oil Committee to his summer palace on the Caspian Sea. He announced at the party that it was his aim to make the National Company "the largest of its kind in the world."[16]

Pachachi followed those developments closely, and he visited Italy while the ink on the Iran contract was still drying. "All Middle East oil producing countries, including Iraq, are studying with keen interest the new allocation of oil royalties under this new agreement," he wrote then. And, although he found the going rough with the Iraq concessionaires, he knew that Tariki had been able to use the Iranian success to extract favorable terms from a Japanese company later in 1957. The powerful Japanese Ministry of International Trade and Industry at first opposed Tariki's terms, which they found "progressively harsher" after the Iranian-Italian deal. But when he refused to budge, they nevertheless approved an offshore concession that gave Saudi Arabia ownership of 56 percent of sales and the right to purchase another 20 percent of the oil produced at a discount.[17]

For Pachachi, the concept of changing circumstances became a sort of self-fulfilling prophecy. He understood the actions of Entezam and Tariki as an opportunity for Iraq. Two weeks later, he asserted national rights to offshore oil in a public statement: "all natural resources of the submarine area" were the property of the nation, he said, employing the language of permanent sovereignty. "New factors" had arisen as a result of the Iranian and Saudi agreements, he continued. Iraq would "take advantage" of those and other "rapid oil developments."[18]

He was unable to lead that effort personally because of the 1958 revolution in Iraq. But an opportunity soon emerged in Libya. Anes Qasem, who knew Pachachi from the planning sessions for the First Arab

[16] "Iran: Oil Exploration Bill," *MEED* 1: 12 (May 31, 1957), 3–4; "Iran: The Iranian Oil Exploration Bill," *MEED* 1: 17 (July 5, 1957), 6–7; "Iran: Iranian Oil Exploration Bill," *MEED* 1: 19 (July 19, 1957), 4; "Iran: Oil Exploration Law," *MEED* 1: 21 (August 2, 1957), 7; "Iran: Oil Developments," *MEED* 1: 48 (February 28, 1958), 2.

[17] "Iraq: Negotiations with the Iraq Petroleum Company," *MEED* 1: 25 (September 13, 1957), 6; "Iraq: Oil Royalties," *MEED* 1: 39 (December 20, 1957, 5–6; "Saudi Arabia: Offshore Oil Production," *MEED* 1: 7 (April 19, 1957), 8; "Saudi Arabia: Japanese Oil Agreement," *MEED* 1: 34 (November 15, 1957), 10.

[18] "Iraq: Offshore Oil Exploration Rights," *MEED* 1: 36 (November 29, 1957), 4; "Iraq," *MEED* 1: 48 (February 28, 1958), 3.

Petroleum Congress, asked for his help on rewriting the Libyan Petroleum Law in 1960. Pachachi was more than happy to oblige. After several weeks reviewing Libyan petroleum laws in Tripoli, he suggested that the government increase competition in the bidding system, tighten control over the concession relinquishment process, and revise upward the fees and royalty payments of new and old concessions. Qasem added that any companies that refused to acquiesce to the new terms would not receive consideration for new concessions. The two men had essentially applied the doctrine of changing circumstances to Qasem's 1955 law, making it stricter and more favorable for Libya. Their amendments were issued by Royal Decree in July 1961. That personal interaction was also part of a broader effort of the Libyan Petroleum Commission. The government had "benefitted from the experience of other countries in the petroleum industry" in the past, one member of the commission wrote in 1961. Like others, he emphasized the international traits of the national project. The advice from Pachachi bore out the importance of discussions with elites from "other countries which own petroleum and which are going through the same phase."[19]

A third and final example of the growing appeal of the sovereign rights argument for oil elites is the intervention of Feisal al-Mazidi, a Kuwaiti official, at the Non-Aligned Movement's Conference on the Problems of Economic Development in 1962. A number of officials from the OPEC nations had joined their co-denominationalists in Belgrade in 1961 at the conference that founded the Non-Aligned Movement. Historians have tended to emphasize the disjuncture between that meeting and the 1955 Bandung summit, as well as the many schisms that typified early Third Worldism – between and within nations and transnational alliances, over definitions of nonalignment and neutrality, and ultimately around how competing visions of identity affected particular political projects. But important similarities also link Bandung to Belgrade and tied the participating nations together. In addition to their stance apart from the Cold War, the economic and legal language of the nonaligned delegates stands out. "All peoples may, for their own ends, freely dispose of their natural wealth and resources without prejudice," they agreed. "[E]fforts should be made to remove [the] economic imbalance inherited from

---

[19] "Regional Developments: 1. Oil Policy," *MEED* 1: 13 (June 7, 1957), 1; Petroleum Commission, *Petroleum Development in Libya: 1954 through Mid 1961* (Tripoli: Petroleum Commission, 1961), 8; Abdul Amir Q. Kubbah, *Libya: Its Oil Industry and Economic System* (Baghdad: The Arab Petro-Economic Research Centre, 1965), 78–97; "Petroleum Regulation No. 6 of 3rd December, 1961," OPEC, *SDIPI: Socialist People's Libyan Arab Jamahiriya and Qatar, Pre-1966*, OIC.

colonialism and imperialism." The delegates also invoked the doctrine of unequal exchange when they called for "just terms of trade" for the poor nations.[20]

The first specialized meeting that occurred under the auspices of the Non-Aligned Movement was a 1962 economic development conference at the Nile Hilton. There, Mazidi joined officials from other nonaligned nations, the oil-producing nations of Algeria, Libya, Saudi Arabia, and Venezuela, and the leadership of the Arab League and the Organization of Afro-Asian Economic Cooperation. The sovereign rights program loomed large when a number of the representatives expressed their wish to use their nations' right to sovereignty to overturn unequal exchange. Behind their design of legal and economic cooperation lay "a common political consciousness and a common political will," the Algerian ambassador to Egypt said. The Libyan delegate agreed in his summary of the meeting: "All developing countries facing common trade problems should adopt a common policy in production," he said.[21]

Mazidi cited the doctrine of unequal exchange in his speech. The problem of achieving economic development was "connected with terms of trade," he said. In case his counterparts doubted his understanding of the concept, he explained it: The low prices of primary goods caused a "score of subsumed problems," which in turn led to "the enormous gap that separates standards of living in developing and developed countries." Importantly, his argument drew not just on the growing consensus, but directly from a 1961 report commissioned by the OPEC Secretariat with the Arthur D. Little firm. In part a statistical comparison of oil prices and the United Nations index for export prices of manufactured goods, the

[20] "Belgrade Declaration of Non-Aligned Countries," September 6, 1961, *NIEO: SD*, vol. I. On the Non-Aligned Movement, see: G. H. Janson, *Nonalignment and the Afro-Asian States* (New York: Praeger, 1966); Peter Willetts, *The Non-Aligned Movement: The Origins of a Third World Alliance* (New York: Pinter Publishing, 1978); H. W. Brands, *The Specter of Neutralism: The United States and the Emergence of the Third World, 1947–1960* (New York: Columbia University Press, 1989); Rob Rakove, *Kennedy, Johnson, and the Nonaligned World* (Cambridge University Press, 2012). For recent takes on division within the movement: Itty Abraham, "From Bandung to NAM: Non-Alignment and Indian Foreign Policy, 1947–65," *Commonwealth and Comparative Politics* 46: 2 (April 2008), 195–219; Svetozar Rajak, "No Bargaining Chips, No Spheres of Interest: The Yugoslav Origins of Cold War Non-Alignment," *Journal of Cold War Studies* 16: 1 (2014), 146–79.

[21] "The Speech Delivered by H. E. Mr. Hadi Ghani," *The Conference on the Problems of Economic Development* (Cairo: United Arab Republic, 1962), 85; "The Speech Delivered by H. E. Mr. Shamsuldin Arabi," *The Conference on the Problems of Economic Development*, 236.

Little report found that "the posted oil prices ... are today lower than they have been at any time since mid-1953."[22]

That the well-heeled Kuwaiti could use a report from the prominent Boston consulting firm to accuse others of monopolizing wealth and privilege reveals the influence of sovereign rights as an analytical abstraction for concrete historical conditions. Mazidi was a bright-eyed undergraduate at Keele University in London in the mid-1950s when Salman, Qasem, Tariki, and Pachachi had begun to plan the First Arab Petroleum Congress. (He drove a powder white Jaguar and threw parties at his rooms at the opulent Dorchester hotel.) A 1957 photo, taken around the same time the others met to discuss Salman's surveys of the petroleum industry, shows the future Kuwaiti official and his mates lampooning the British fear of Nasserism in the university's annual RAG parade. Playing Gamal Abdel Nasser, Mazidi mock-salutes his crowd of admirers as eight British students dressed as bankers with arm bands, brief cases, and bowler or top hats carry him on a litter – as much an image of what a number of sane people believed as a caricature.[23]

When assigned to sentinel duty as a young government economic official a half decade later, he turned to the problem of petroleum colonization by using language other elites understood. The law and economics group of the Second Arab Petroleum Congress, the Qasem-Pachachi collaboration, and the Mazidi intervention were not independent points on a chart. Rather, they were representative of a broader pattern that developed in the early 1960s. The oil elites joined others at international meetings to invoke sovereign rights and develop its legal, economic, historical, and ultimately cultural terms of reference. The final communiqué of the 1962 Non-Aligned meeting in Cairo, signed by Mazidi and the delegation leaders of thirty-one nations, broadcast the extent to which the sovereign rights program informed discussions about international capitalism on the periphery. The conferees agreed that "the terms of trade" continued to operate to the "disadvantage of the developing countries." National independence had been an important step in the right direction, but "complete decolonization" would not be possible without the exercise of "sovereign rights over national resources."[24]

---

[22] "The Speech Delivered by H. E. Feisal Mazidi," *The Conference on the Problems of Economic Development*, 279–83; OPEC, "Explanatory Memoranda on the OPEC Resolutions of the Fourth Conference Held in Geneva, April–June, 1962" (Geneva, 1967), OIC.

[23] Keelites of Colour, The Keele Oral History Project, Keele University.

[24] Cairo Declaration of Developing Countries, Approved at the Conference on the Problems of Economic Development, July 18, 1962, *NIEO: SD*, vol. I.

FIGURE 3.1 Feisal al-Mazidi at Keele University's 1957 RAG Parade.
Source: Christopher Hayhurst, courtesy of Keele University.

The sovereign rights program also continued to gain momentum in the United Nations. By the end of 1962, the UN Permanent Sovereignty Commission's efforts came to fruition when the General Assembly passed a stronger resolution on "Permanent Sovereignty over Natural Resources." The resolution, which built on the discussions of the mid-1950s and the work of the Permanent Sovereignty Commission, was hailed as the "economic pendant" to the 1960 UN Declaration on the Granting of Independence to Colonial Territories. The extensive employment of unequal exchange and permanent sovereignty inside and outside the UN reveals that those ideas had become *a priori* for anticolonial elites. Expressions of the economic culture of decolonization, in other words, represented nontheoretical facts reaffirmed again and again by discovery. General truth arose from widespread experience.[25]

Similarly, the new histories of petroleum colonization were histories in which the meaning the elites attributed to the oil concessions was shaped

[25] Nico Schrijver, *Development without Destruction: The UN and Global Resource Management* (Bloomington: Indiana University Press, 2010), 43.

out of their understanding of imperialism and decolonization. OPEC and the Arab League's Petroleum Congress held several meetings in the first half of the 1960s, in which expressions of the shared history and object-ives were ubiquitous. In one example, delegations from Saudi Arabia, Iraq, Libya, Venezuela, and Kuwait descended upon Geneva for an OPEC ministerial summit that lasted from April until June 1962. They began their meetings on a positive note, expressing the common belief that their work lay within the larger anticolonial context. Their first item of busi-ness, discussion of the report from the Arthur D. Little firm, tended toward consensus. The Little report was rooted in the economic culture of decolonization, in particular, the questions of permanent sovereignty and unequal exchange. It is still unpublished, but the conclusions the OPEC officials drew from it are telling. The ministers discussed in par-ticular the historical relationship of oil prices with the prices of different manufactured goods. The obvious "damage" to their purchasing power in the 1950s revealed the truth to the assertions that the price of oil simply did not reflect its importance as the main source of energy for modern economic growth. The rich countries of the industrialized world depended on the regular flow of oil for "every phase of their life," yet they were not prepared to give "in return for it a *quid pro quo* which would be fair and reasonable in all the circumstances."[26]

The OPEC ministers also took careful note of Cold War politics in their attempt to craft a sense of camaraderie around the pursuit of "fair and reasonable" prices. They did not wish to impugn the "competitive system . . . in the international economy," they said. But it would be the "height of irresponsibility" if they "were to sit by with arms folded" as low prices destroyed their nations' "chances for the future." The ministers then depicted themselves as part and parcel of a broader problem for commodity producers. The problem of unjust prices was not peculiar to petroleum, as the Little report revealed, but faced "many of the under-developed countries which are exporters of primary commodities." They concluded their meeting summary with a desultory illustration of a world still caught in the past: "[I]t is no longer possible to live at peace in a world where the rich are getting richer and the poor poorer." They not only criticized the global hierarchy of wealth and power, but also gave privilege to the growing emphasis on the use of sovereignty to prevent further losses. "Somewhere a full stop must be put to the deterioration in

[26] OPEC, "Explanatory Memoranda," Geneva, 1967, OIC.

the position of the petroleum exporters vis-à-vis the highly industrialized nations," they believed.[27]

The collection of information was again crucial. The Little report itself became a means of cohesion because its confidential findings again nurtured a sense of sameness, just as Salman's surveys of the oil concessions had done a half-decade earlier. In addition to analyzing UN reports on the prices of oil and different baskets of manufactured goods, the report also suggested the risks but ultimate benefits of joint supply control, which aligned with the Tariki-Pérez Alfonso plan of pro-rationing. It also estimated that the companies operating in the Middle East realized huge average returns on their assets, an average of 66 percent per year between 1956 and 1960. Perhaps most importantly, the report confirmed the importance of information gathering and prompted the OPEC Secretariat to commission further studies, including a highly regarded one on "taxation economics" at the 1965 Arab Petroleum Congress, by then in its fifth iteration.[28]

It also motivated OPEC to further develop in-house expertise. As before, the experience of a Latin American elite played a decisive role. Francisco Parra, a Venezuelan economist, wrote the Little report and became the *de facto* spokesperson for OPEC when he left the firm to become economic adviser to OPEC's first Secretary General, an Iranian official named Fuad Rouhani, in 1962. By 1964 he was the director of OPEC's Economics Department and in 1968 he became the organization's Secretary General. A close reading of his public speeches from the early 1960s reveals that he found the sovereign rights line of thought significant. He was particularly interested in the idea of OPEC as a collective experiment in sovereign rights. The 1959 Arab Petroleum Congress had begun to form "a center where ideas of a broader scope were exchanged," he told a group at Johns Hopkins University in 1962. OPEC was an iteration of the same "growing determination of its Member Countries to take a hand ... in the shaping of events in an industry in which they are so dependent."[29]

---

[27] OPEC, "Explanatory Memoranda," Geneva, 1967, OIC.

[28] Francisco Parra, *Oil Politics*, 100; OPEC Secretariat, "Taxation Economics in Crude Production," Papers of the Fifth Arab Petroleum Congress, Cairo, March 1965, OIC; Shell International Petroleum Company, *Current International Oil Pricing Problems* (London, 1963); George Polanyi, "The Taxation of Profits from Middle East Oil Production: Some Implications for Oil Prices and Taxation Policy," *The Economic Journal* 76 (December 1966), 770–1.

[29] Francisco Parra, "OPEC and the Oil Industry in the Middle East," October 22, 1962, OIC.

For Parra, it was essential that the elites in OPEC remembered their broad objective of gaining "a better appreciation of the general conditions and the state of development" of their own and other oil-producing nations. This was difficult, as the group's early information-gathering attempts revealed. Indeed, in the earliest days of the organization, the oil producers were linked as much by what the Beirut-based journalist Ian Seymour called "a lack of relevant information" as they were by their dependency on oil revenues. Parra emphasized this in the first edition of the *Inter-OPEC Newsletter*, a new internal project he created as soon as he was hired. "The real facts about the oil industry" were notoriously hard to come by, he wrote in a plea to the OPEC member nations to share information with each other. The disclosure of national information to the international group was necessary, Parra explained, because "the history of the oil negotiations and the experience of all the producing countries have shown us that" the questions of revenue and development were "seldom solved by the unilateral magnanimity of the companies." Without information, in other words, the countries stood no chance of extracting better terms for their oil production.[30]

The oil elites responsible for their nations' policies agreed. Mohammed Salman, now the Oil Minister of Iraq, told the other delegates in 1962 that he hoped that the founding of OPEC would bring the issue from "the phase of studies into that of action and execution." He and others hoped that the upcoming royalty negotiations, in particular, would help increase the producers' share of oil revenue. Moreover, the Iraqi oil minister believed that raising the issues collectively would help shift the oil prices to a "just basis." Ahmed Zaki Yamani, who had recently replaced Abdullah al-Tariki at the helm of Saudi oil policy, also made the link between anticolonial economic thought and OPEC explicit in the 1962 meetings: "The problem of prices is a historical problem. In this subject, we want nothing more than justice." He continued: "If we desire to ensure our revenues from petroleum, or even their increase, we cannot be blamed, since we are the owners of this natural wealth." The new contracts signed by Iran, Libya, and Saudi Arabia since 1957 revealed to him that "the times have changed."[31]

---

[30] "Introduction," *ION* 1: 1 (April 1962), OIC.

[31] *ION* 1: 4 (July 1962), OIC. One of those reports, commissioned to the Italian economist Giorgia Fua, examined the profitability of the international oil companies. Wanda Joblanski, the influential editor at *Petroleum Intelligence Weekly*, "conveniently ignored" the independence of this report, according to Parra. Instead, she linked the report to the Italian oil magnate Enrico Mattei, with the intention of connecting the new organization

Salman supported his arguments through the doctrine of unequal exchange, again citing the secret Little report. He wrote that it was "most unjust that they should see the price of oil steadily go down while the prices of necessary imports steadily go up." Parra also linked these statements, which he republished in an early edition of the *Inter-OPEC Newsletter* in 1962, to "one of the fundamental grievances of the under-developed nations—that their terms of trade were out of their control."[32]

Parra himself was well-versed in the arguments of the sovereign rights program. He also became a keen publicist of that view. He spent most of November and December in 1963, for example, traveling in the Middle East, where he gave several public lectures. To business students at the American University of Beirut, he emphasized the concept of changing circumstances. The oil concessions had been "overly generous" in their discharge of sovereign rights, he began. Furthermore, the duration of the old concessionary agreements had "unfortunately" been applied to the precise conditions under which the companies extracted oil. The old concessions even included language calling for the nations "to abstain from formulating laws which would be applicable to the concessionaire companies." Even though the nation was officially the landowner and held title to its resources, such clauses limited governmental freedom of action, Parra continued. This was a problem because it meant that when governments did act, it was as mere advisers "rather than by virtue of their sovereign powers."[33]

The rise of sovereignty was a tributary of the stream of decolonization for Parra. He turned repeatedly to the argument of the equivalency of experience of the oil elites and other anticolonial elites. As seen "in the light of changing circumstances elsewhere," it was time to create "a little elbow-room" for governments to "jostle along more comfortably with the general current of events," he said. "We share in common with other underdeveloped countries throughout the world problems which must be overcome."[34]

Parra then attended the Fourth Arab Petroleum Congress, also in Beirut, where he delivered a paper entitled "Radical Changes in the

---

to "the twin bogies of government control and Communist infiltration," Parra wrote, so the report would be "damned as a menace to freedom, the Western Alliance, and World Peace." See: *ION* 1: 2 (May 1962), OIC.

[32] *ION* 1: 5 (August 1962), OIC; *ION* 1: 4 (July 1962), OIC.

[33] Francisco Parra, "The Oil Industry's Organization in the Middle East and Some of Its Fiscal Consequences," November 13, 1963, OIC.

[34] Parra, "The Oil Industry's Organization in the Middle East," November 13, 1963, OIC.

International Oil Industry during the Past Decade." He began with a historical discussion of the old concessions, again stressing that the concessions were of extraordinary long duration. He then hit on the theme of changing circumstances again. The right to exploit oil had been granted "with reference to the prevailing circumstances at the time, when those circumstances have everywhere changed," he said. The concessions were anachronistic. They needed "to adapt themselves to the time."[35]

He reworked the themes of changing circumstances and petroleum colonization the next week, this time as the guest of a group of Arab petroleum engineers in Baghdad. For this audience the tone was more militant. "The fundamental question of equity" in the oil concessions was a question of whether or not the producing countries could "optimize their revenues," he said. There was no doubt in his mind that the OPEC nations had a right to put their concessions under continuous review until equity was achieved. This was a "modern" vision that drew its legitimacy from the attempts by the underdeveloped nations "to close their ranks" vis-à-vis the industrialized nations at the United Nations. "Among these shifting sands, the need for flexibility over the terms of these new oil-producing rights is paramount," Parra said.[36]

The first Secretary General of OPEC, Fuad Rouhani, who hired Parra away from Arthur D. Little, was of a voice with him in this public offensive. The Iranian lawyer, who earned two degrees at the University of London in the 1930s, was invited to give a lecture series on "the various points of contact of oil with law" to a UN seminar for international lawyers in January 1962. His arguments were illustrative. The history of the oil industry provided "food for the intellect and the emotions" of international lawyers, he began. He then captured the most striking theme in the histories of petroleum colonization in dramatic language:

"Black gold" is the term with which petroleum is hailed each time a political visionary or a poet lets his imagination run on the force with which this commodity has, in the course of recent history, attracted the greed of the avaricious or the dark machinations of politicians. On the other hand, a thirteenth century Persian mystic invoked the sanctity of oil, in a moment of ecstasy, as the means by which he would attain ultimate union with the Divinity, for it would, and did, consume him at the stake of martyrdom.

---

[35] OPEC, "Radical Changes in the International Oil Industry during the Past Decade," Paper No. 58 (A-1), *Papers of the Fourth Arab Petroleum Conference.*

[36] Francisco Parra, "The Development of Petroleum Resources under the Concession System in Non-Industrialized Countries," EC/64/III, OIC.

FIGURE 3.2 1st OPEC Board of Governors, May 3, 1961, Geneva, Switzerland. Fuad Rouhani is seated at the head of the table. Two seats to his right, in the light jacket, is Francisco Parra.
Source: OPEC Information Center, OPEC P-1961 1BOG (1).

Oil, then, was both the source of "dark machinations" of foreign control and the divine "ecstasy" of liberation. But Rouhani would not stop at the symbolic. His speech was also a searching examination of the origins and crucial role of sovereign rights in international law and, consequently, in the international political economy.[37]

The more immediate history of the modern oil industry was one of voluminous legislation, Rouhani continued. But the germ of the history of all those laws was the same: the simple "question of ownership." The debate over sovereign control was "necessarily international" because of the simple fact that oil as a commodity moved to and from the "remotest corners of the world." But the discovery of oil and the writing of the oil concessions in the previous, imperial age meant that the old concessions also existed under a divided legal regime. Rouhani explained what he understood as two opposing traditions of ownership: First was the

---

[37] Fuad Rouhani, "International Agreements and Contracts in the Field of Petroleum," Seminar Paper No. 26, UN Inter-Regional Seminar on Techniques of Petroleum Development, January 23, 1962, OIC; Kubbah, *OPEC, Past and Present*, 12.

Spanish "Royalty Doctrine," which had recognized the State as the owner of petroleum deposits since the Spanish Mining Ordinance of 1783. In line with this tradition, although Rouhani noted that some jurists disagreed, was "Mohammadan law." The "prevailing view" for both was that sovereigns granted the right to mine subsurface mineral deposits, but that the right did not bestow ownership to its taker. The title to crude and gas passed at the well-head, not beneath it.[38]

The oil concessions in the Middle East had not followed that concept, according to Rouhani. They instead adhered to the competing tradition of English common law, which granted subsoil ownership to the individual that occupied the land. That definition of ownership was "archaic," he continued. Most people he knew, in fact, disliked the very term "concession" for two reasons: its content and its connotation. "As to substance," the concessions were transactions in which a "pre-Constitution sovereign, unmindful of the interests of his people, gave too much for too little." Casting an even darker pall was the way the term captured the gist of the relationship between the oil nations and the companies. As Rouhani put it, the problem was simple. A concession was by definition "a giving of the weak to the strong."[39]

He then turned to the key question of how decolonization would change international capitalism. "The important awakening" of the oil producers in the 1950s was transformative, he said. As they grew "more conscious of their rights and interests, a movement arose for radically improving" their positions. Moreover, that rise to self-assertion had been necessarily collective because the oppression it responded to had been systematic. Here the "excellent study" by the UN Commission on Permanent Sovereignty spurred on Rouhani. The Commission's discovery of a "similarity of treatment in analogous situations" led him to believe that the continued comparative legal study of the old and newer oil concessions was crucial. In fact the shared conditions and consciousness of the oil producers, "a corollary of national sovereignty," had already begun to make such a project possible. For him it was the very "growing realization" of their common national interests that brought OPEC into being.[40]

---

[38] Fuad Rouhani, "International Agreements and Contracts in the Field of Petroleum," January 23, 1962, OIC.
[39] Fuad Rouhani, "International Agreements and Contracts in the Field of Petroleum," January 23, 1962, OIC.
[40] Fuad Rouhani, "International Agreements and Contracts in the Field of Petroleum," January 23, 1962, OIC.

Rouhani summarized this set of beliefs for delegates from the OPEC nations and invited guests of other oil-producing nations at a meeting in July 1963. The existence of OPEC was proof that the oil-producing nations were no longer content to be treated as mere collectors of royalties, he said. Dissatisfaction had led the nations to adopt "sovereign measures," including the acquisition of "expert knowledge of the international conditions which govern the industry." He then compared the problems of the OPEC nations to those of other raw material producers. Like producers of coffee or copper, he said, the economic problems of the oil nations derived from the fact that there was not "a fair return for the primary commodities which the countries in question supply to the world." This understanding was part of a broader joint effort related to decolonization: "In this new orientation and awareness lay already the germ of our association of today, for different nations with the same interests achieving individual consciousness are bound to realize in time that the defense of their rights needs the most valuable power of collectivity."[41]

Arguments like these had begun to follow the learned formulas of the economic culture of decolonization, and were remarkably similar in tone and content to the hundreds of discussions held in meetings across the global periphery in the early 1960s. Rouhani turned in his UN speech to what he described as the moral contributions of "the great international jurist" J. Lassa Oppenheim, in particular, his comment in the first volume of *Public International Law* that "vital changes of circumstances may be of such a kind as to justify a party in demanding to be released from the obligations of an unnotifiable treaty." Here was the intellectual rationale for a movement that was already well underway. Following Anes Qasem, Frank Hendryx, Parra, and others, Rouhani argued that the changing circumstances of decolonization made the revision of the concessions a moral obligation.[42]

But if the oil elites joined the legions who supported sovereign rights in the early 1960s, their verbal commitments to an idea did not oblige national acts of solidarity. Disagreement also ran rampant. OPEC officials could discuss what Rouhani called the "reawakening of the national spirit," but actual advances were partial. Parra admitted in 1963 that the

---

[41] OPEC, "Speech Delivered by Mr. Fuad Rouhani, Secretary General, at II Consultative Meeting," Geneva, July 1, 1963, OIC.
[42] Fuad Rouhani, "International Agreements and Contracts in the Field of Petroleum," January 23, 1962, OIC.

earliest negotiations between the oil nations and the companies, on royalty expensing, followed less from decolonization than "the niceties" of
the colonial era. Writing in retrospect, Francisco Parra criticized the early
frailty of OPEC more harshly. "The united needle-workers' trade unions
of greater Manchester would have produced something with more red
blood in it," he wrote. (It was not for nothing that he often described
OPEC's primary goal in defensive terms, as the prevention of further
price cuts.)[43]

The disjuncture Parra and Rouhani identified between form and substance revealed a crucial weakness in OPEC's first attempt to bargain with
the multinational oil companies as a group. An important gulf opened
between two groups, the gradualists and the insurrectionists, over the
contentious issue of royalty expensing between 1962 and 1965. The
royalties paid under what Rouhani called "the earliest traditional concessions" were the principal source of income for the OPEC members. The
problem was that, although royalties had increased slightly, their contribution to national income remained at levels considered insufficient by the
OPEC members. In 1962 Iran, Kuwait, Libya, and Qatar were entitled to
12.5 percent of the value of the oil produced; Saudi Arabia received 22
cents per barrel, which was roughly equivalent to 12.5 percent; and
Venezuela earned 16.67 percent. But whereas the Venezuelan royalty
was paid to the government in addition to their income tax, the contracts
of the Middle Eastern countries allowed the companies to deduct their
royalty payments from their income taxes. Royalty was thus "a term
without substance," Rouhani wrote.[44]

Each member nation initially sought to negotiate the royalty expensing
issue on an individual basis. But soon the nations empowered Rouhani to
conduct collective discussions on their behalf. All eight members sent
identical letters notifying the companies that they should negotiate directly with OPEC, as well as noting that each nation would undertake
unilateral action if their "equitable and reasonable" demands were not
met. For the new OPEC public relations department, this step was proof
of "the long road OPEC [had] travelled." It was also evidence of the fact
"that OPEC stood for something solid and understandable." It was
important to the oil elites that OPEC now held an official negotiating
function in addition to its consultative and advisory positions. In this

---

[43] Parra, "The Oil Industry's Organization in the Middle East and Some of Its Fiscal
    Consequences," November 13, 1963, OIC; Parra, *Oil Politics*, 99.
[44] Fuad Rouhani, *A History of O.P.E.C.* (New York: Praeger, 1971), 217–20.

interpretation, the first steps toward joint action pointed to a broader historical change: "It is a long way back, in terms of history and feasibility, to the days when the gunboat was the ultimate arbiter in commercial disputes with the backward nations."[45]

Rouhani pressed the oil ministers to adopt a resolution on royalties at their April 1962 summit in Geneva. Because oil was "a wasting asset," the companies needed to conform themselves with the "practice observed generally in the world" and compensate the OPEC nations for "the intrinsic value of petroleum," the resolution declared. If the companies did not, the nations would pass laws that amended the royalty clauses of the concessions to prohibit the companies from crediting their royalty expenses against income tax. That this was their right was "incontestable," according to the ministers. The OPEC public relations office further explained that position. There was no justification for "the fusion" of royalty payments into income tax "in such a manner that royalty becomes entirely unreal." The practice actually left "the country poorer to the extent of the taking."[46]

Meanwhile, more new contracts also continued to point toward the injustice of the old concessions. In particular, a series of new concession agreements were signed between the United Arab Republic (UAR) and oil companies in September 1963. All contained highly favorable provisions for the host country, including relinquishment provisions along Libyan lines and stipulations that the "national sector" would receive 75 percent of all profits from the operations. The OPEC Secretariat noted that these agreements were made despite the fact that the costs of production in the UAR were much higher than elsewhere and the possibility of making a strike of the magnitude of the OPEC producers was remote. This gave the lie to a basic position of the multinational oil companies: that "they cannot afford to pay more." The company position, which consistently labeled host government intervention as "the intrinsic malevolence of the economically immature," in Parra's words, was even less tenable given those successes. Such arguments had lost their validity for a simple reason: "The twentieth century is not the nineteenth." Indeed, according to the OPEC negotiating position, ongoing company procrastination on the royalty expensing issue had arrived at a moment "where the patience

---

[45] *ION* 2: 8 (August 1963), OIC; "Three Years of OPEC," *ION* 2: 9 (September 1963), OIC.
[46] OPEC, "Explanatory Memoranda," Geneva, 1967, OIC.

of OPEC and public opinion in the countries it represents has reached the breaking point."[47]

In that context, the leaders of Iran, Iraq, and Saudi Arabia supported Rouhani in the early stages of the negotiations. Amman Radio released a statement from Saudi Crown Prince Faisal that warned the multinationals to accept the "just solution" proposed by Rouhani. If not, OPEC would "prove its effectiveness by other means than negotiations." Similarly, the Shah of Iran gave an interview to *Kayhan International* in which he expressed his confidence in Rouhani. The companies needed to realize that "OPEC is an organization they must recognize and of whose strength, and even necessity, they must be aware." In response to questions from the Iraq News Agency, Prime Minister Ahmed Hassan al-Bakr also advocated the joint position. In addition, the OPEC Secretariat pointed at Argentina's renegotiation of its oil contracts in 1963, in particular, Argentinian President Illia's description of its policies as the fulfillment of "the sovereign and irrevocable decision of the Argentine people."[48]

But in the end the royalty negotiations yielded little more than disappointment and exasperation. The multinational companies, who Rouhani described as "reticent and unaccommodating," responded to the initial OPEC member letters by stating their willingness in principle to expense royalties instead of crediting them, but on the condition that the countries would grant an equivalent discount on prices. Company lawyers again put forward the legal argument for the sanctity of contracts, that "contractual obligations must be respected." Rouhani responded that a revision of the royalty clauses was fully justified, given the "inequitable" difference among the OPEC members. After several rounds of negotiations the companies proposed a compromise in November 1963. They would admit in principle the practice of expensing royalties on the condition that the producing countries would grant a smaller discount of 8.5 percent off prices. The proposal thus gave little on the question of royalties. It also contained a number of stipulations that aimed to strengthen the juridical position of the old concessions. The ministers rejected it, and the companies offered another slight improvement in their terms the following year, this time through a regressive discount.[49]

---

[47] *ION* 2: 10 (October 1963), OIC.
[48] *ION* 2: 10 (October 1963), OIC; *ION* 2: 11 (November 1963), OIC.
[49] Rouhani, *A History of O.P.E.C.*, 225–9.

At this point, the rift opened in OPEC. The division first became apparent in a November 1964 meeting in Djakarta. On one side there was a gradualist faction: Iran, Kuwait, Qatar, Libya, and Saudi Arabia all took the position that the revised offer was the best they could get without recourse to national legislation. On the other side, Iraqi oil minister Sayid Abdul Aziz al-Wattari publicly rejected the company offer as "prejudicial to the interests of OPEC members and incompatible with their sovereignty." He was joined in this insurrectionist position by his Venezuelan and Indonesian counterparts Manuel Pérez-Guerrero and Ibn Sutowo. Importantly for them, the company offers contained a stipulation that would move all disputes into international arbitration, a condition that Mossadegh had refused in 1951. That condition was considered as "humiliating and incompatible with the concept of state sovereignty," the Iraqi oil journalist Abdul Amir Kubbah wrote. Of even greater offense, the corporate counteroffer included a "most-favored company" clause, which stipulated that companies would not be required to make total payments on crude oil greater than if the most favorable existing arrangement were applied. This was not only backwards to the widely diffused belief in an economic equivalent to decolonization, it was also a backhand slap in the face of the oil elites. The clause meant that governments could not "use their sovereign powers" to grant concessions that were more favorable than the existing ones, Kubbah explained to his readers. "This is a ridiculous condition to attach to an offer made in good faith."[50]

The offer also raised eyebrows in the gradualist nations whose leaders had elected to accept the company offer. The Kuwaiti parliament voted it down, for example, and one deputy described it as "a threat laced with a bribe." The open disagreement irritated the insurrectionist oil elites. OPEC might have been successful in creating "practical oil consciousness," Wattari told Francisco Parra and others at the Fifth Arab Petroleum Congress, held in Beirut in 1965. But the royalty negotiations had not really changed the concessionary agreements, which Wattari reminded them had been signed "at a time when Arab Governments did not possess full sovereignty but were under foreign domination."[51]

---

[50] "Resolutions of OPEC's Seventh Conference held in Jakarta, November 1964," *ROAPE* 1: 1 (February 1965), 32–3; Abdul Amir Q. Kubbah, "OPEC's Highest Common Denominator," *ROAPE* 1: 1 (February 1965), 17–20.

[51] "No Rubber Stamp," *ROAPE* 1: 2 (March 1965), 19; "Wattari Comments on the Resolutions of the Fifth Arab Oil Congress," *ROAPE* 1: 3 (April 1965), 31.

Francisco Parra tried to look on the bright side at the 1965 Congress. The royalty negotiations were at least an example of a "new element" of collective bargaining, he said. Moreover, the companies had accepted OPEC as a transnational representative of its member nations' interest: "Through OPEC, the exporting countries could, for the first time, face the international major oil companies as a team." That view whitewashed severe friction in the ranks. OPEC had been forced to leave acceptance or rejection of the royalty settlement to its member countries, a decision that was followed by a lame injunction in the group's next public statement, in which its members "declare[d] ... once again their solidarity to each other." Key to that *espirit de corps* would be their joint goal of ending the "further deterioration of their terms of trade."[52]

But even if the oil elites believed in unequal exchange, the royalty expensing case reflected indecisiveness, not strength in numbers. The OPEC Secretariat's injunction of Prebisch's doctrine rang hollow for Abdullah al-Tariki, who had become the most vocal critic of gradualism among the oil elites. The Red Sheikh had been sacked as the director of oil policy and exiled from Saudi Arabia in 1962. He then moved to Beirut, where he founded the Arab Petroleum Research Bureau with the Lebanese lawyer Nicolas Sarkis. In 1964 the US State Department reported on the rumbling disturbances his views posed, particularly in Iraq. "Other producing governments could draw the same conclusions" if Wattari followed Tariki's admonitions that he press for greater national control, the Department told its ambassador in Baghdad. "[The] concept of unilateral change of agreements which already has its adherents, e.g. Tariki, would be markedly strengthened."[53]

Tariki argued that the gradualist faction's acceptance of the royalty offer was conformist. He blamed Iran for the failure in an interview for Abdul Amir Kubbah's journal, the Baghdad-based *Review of Arab Petroleum Economics*. The Shah considered "the appeasement of the monopolistic companies and of the imperialist governments behind them as a *quid pro quo* for past favors," he claimed. He also contended that the Iranian foreign minister had visited the Arab gradualists before the 1964 OPEC summit in Djakarta to convince them to abandon Iraq, Venezuela, and Indonesia. That was just at the minor end of the scale. Iranian

---

[52] "OPEC and the Principle of Negotiation," *SFAPC*, 22–4; "Resolutions of OPEC's Seventh Conference held in Jakarta, November 1964," *ROAPE* 1: 1 (February 1965), 32–3.
[53] DOS to Iraq Embassy, April 13, 1964, *FRUS 1964–68*, vol. XXXIV, doc. 179.

reactionary influence reflected a broader problem with gradualism, Tariki said. If the companies continued to reward Iran with greater production, they could split the organization. "OPEC will become a toy in the hands of the companies," he predicted darkly.[54]

That frustration was vividly conveyed by Kubbah, an Iraqi journalist who observed the petroleum industry from his office in the Pachachi building in downtown Baghdad. Kubbah was born in that city, studied at American University of Beirut, and then enrolled in the PhD program in economics at New York University in 1951. He completed his coursework and qualifying exams, and then left to join the Iraqi Ministry of Economics in 1954. After the Iraqi revolution of 1958, he joined Pachachi and Qasem in Libya, where he eventually became the director of the Economic Department in the Ministry of Petroleum Affairs. He returned home to Baghdad in 1964 to found and edit the monthly petroleum journal. He explained its purpose in the first issue. Modern technology had turned oil into a source of "fabulous material wealth," but despite the work of the Arab Petroleum Congress and OPEC not enough had been done to promote "petroleum consciousness." By this he meant the creation of an international "'climate of opinion' that would support the oil-producing governments in their dealings with the oil companies." The bargaining position of governments would remain weak "without such a guiding light."[55]

Kubbah interviewed Tariki and Abdel Khalek Hassouna, who remained at the head of the Arab League, for his first issue. His first question for the two men cut to the nub of the division between the gradualists and the insurrectionists. If it became possible for the producing countries to agree on a common oil policy, what obstacles stood in the way of "a collective action aiming at the nationalization of oil production facilities?" Hassouna responded by urging caution. He admitted that nationalization was indeed "related to the sovereignty of the state." But it was not the "only way open to ... oil producing and exporting countries to control prices." More moderate options existed, most importantly the old pro-rationing blueprint. Collective control over supply would allow the oil producers "to achieve the same end" as nationalization, but within a "framework of unification and coordination of oil legislation and policies."[56]

[54] "Tariki Speaks His Mind," *ROAPE* 1: 1 (February 1965), 14–16.
[55] "About the Author," Kubbah, *OPEC: Past and Present*, front and back flap; "Editorial: The Ideals We Intend to Serve," *ROAPE* 1: 1 (February 1965), 2.
[56] "Arab League Thinking on Vital Issues," *ROAPE* 1: 1 (February 1965), 4–5.

Tariki refused to speak against nationalization as a possibility. It would be "easy and practicable" for the Arab producers to nationalize, he said, if the nations could "harmonize the oil policies." But he agreed with Hassouna that mass nationalization was unlikely under present circumstances. To take such a step required a series of smaller ones among the producers, most importantly production agreements along the lines Hassouna suggested. Each producer needed to prorate supply and "thus strengthen the structure of prices."[57]

Months later, though, Tariki described the nationalization of Arab oil as a "national necessity" at the 1965 Arab Petroleum Congress. He did so on the last day of the conference before "a packed auditorium," which promised papers from Tariki and Francisco Parra, but transformed into a public debate on Tariki's paper.[58]

Tariki did not stick to his precirculated paper, but delivered a largely extemporaneous speech that defended his stance in favor of nationalization. He began by invoking the motto of his alma mater, the University of Texas at Austin – "Know the truth and it shall make you free." His freedom-inducing truth was that the oil producers no longer needed to fear "the bold idea" of nationalization, as they had since the days of Mossadegh. His belief in the plausibility of nationalization derived from the basic idea that the framework "imposed on us during the era of imperialism" had run its course. The scaffolding of petroleum colonization was "rotten," and it was widely accepted that oil prices were "a political matter, entirely unrelated to supply and demand." Furthermore, even if the royalty negotiations had been degrading – "what a humiliation for the companies to dictate to a group of sovereign governments in this way" – it was nonetheless true that the prime position of OPEC oil in the world market held out the possibility for radical action. "If we cannot nationalize today, let us at least prepare ourselves to do so later," he said.[59]

The official Congress record called Tariki "a vanguard figure," and noted that at this point he spoke "in the midst of" raucous applause. He built on that "certain animation" by turning again to the standard history of petroleum colonization. This time he began in Iran in 1901. But as with the other histories, the actual date or specific details of the contract mattered less than the fact that it was a symbol of the concessions being

[57] "Tariki Speaks His Mind," *ROAPE* 1: 1 (February 1965), 14–16.
[58] "Sunday 21 March," *MEES* 8: 21 (March 26, 1965), 20–32.
[59] "Sunday 21 March," *MEES* 8: 21 (March 26, 1965), 24–6.

"outdated" writ large. Tariki then rehearsed the conventional catalog of contrasts between the past and the present to ruthlessly criticize the actions taken by OPEC in its first five years.[60]

Tariki argued that the crux of the matter was perception. The tragedy of the royalty negotiations, for him, was that the gradualists assumed weakness when, in fact, the position of the countries was strong. Tariki used statistics to support his call for more effective action. The ultimate measures for him were the price of oil, which was used to calculate income, and the concentration of its supply. When compared to the global concentration of oil within the OPEC member nations, low prices became representative of two trends for Tariki: the strength of the forces of petroleum colonization to lower potential income and the potential of the oil nations' collective pursuit of nationalism to change those forces. The low price of oil was the monetized equivalent of the tensions of sovereign rights; this for Tariki illustrated the distance between the past, present, and possible conditions of things. Government income from oil in the Arab countries had increased, he conceded. But this was because production, not prices or the resulting government take, had risen sharply. Income per barrel had not risen since the late 1940s and early 1950s, when the "fifty-fifty" profit-sharing deals came into effect. Since then, according to Tariki, income had leveled off.

The quantitative metrics thus became a proxy for a foregone opportunity with the royalty negotiations, allowing him to present his statistics as a form in miniature of a history of continued petroleum colonization. The ability of the oil companies to fix prices was "colonialism in its worst form," he said.[61]

Against that backdrop, the combination of internationalism and particularity of Tariki's paper also merits a close look. "Exporting raw materials from a certain country implies an intention to deprive that country of its natural right in industrializing itself and raising the standard of living of its population," he wrote. "[T]he present status of the oil industry in the Arab countries is a perfect example of economic colonialism. The foreign companies have full control over the destiny of the Arab nation and realize tremendous profits out of the Arab

---

[60] Abdullah el Hammoud el Tariki, "Nationalization of Arab Petroleum Industry Is a National Necessity," *Papers of the Fifth Arab Petroleum Congress*; "Tariki's Study," *SFAPC*, 10.

[61] Abdullah el Hammoud el-Tariki, "Nationalization of Arab Petroleum Industry Is a National Necessity," *Papers of the Fifth Arab Petroleum Congress*.

TABLE 3.1 *Abdullah al-Tariki, "Exports of the Main Producing Areas, 1963," from "Nationalization of Arab Petroleum Industry Is a National Necessity," March 1965*

Regions	Quantity exported in thousands of barrels per day	Percentage to the world exports of oil
Caribbean Zone	3,055	25.0
Southeast Asia	340	2.8
Soviet Union, Eastern Europe, and China	740	6.1
Iran	1,342	11.0
Arab countries of the Arabian Gulf	4,813	39.4
Arab countries of North Africa	1,045	8.6
Total of the Arab countries	5,858	48.0
Total of the world exports of oil and its products	12,205	100

Source: Fifth Arab Petroleum Congress, Cairo, Papers and Discussions, vol. I, Economics.

national wealth." The oil concessions had been dictated upon the Arab people, he said. In the light of nearly two decades of decolonization, they were "primitive." But the problem of continued economic colonialism extended well beyond the Middle East. Citing the 1955 Afro-Asian summit in Bandung, the meetings of the Non-Aligned Movement since 1961, and the June 1964 meeting of the UN Conference on Trade and Development, he repeated that call for an increase in the "share of the developing countries' governments in their exported wealth."[62]

Many in the crowd voiced their approval of this interpretation. But many did not. Sayyid Abdelrahman al-Bazzaz, an Iraqi lawyer who had just finished his term as OPEC Secretary General, rose in response. Bazzaz had spoken with representatives of the oil companies in a meeting on royalties in Geneva just two months earlier. Men like Tariki did not represent OPEC, he began. They wrongfully viewed the companies as "nothing but a modern means of imperialism." Nevertheless Bazzaz's

---

[62] Abdullah el Hammoud el-Tariki, "Nationalization of Arab Petroleum Industry Is a National Necessity," *Papers of the Fifth Arab Petroleum Congress.*

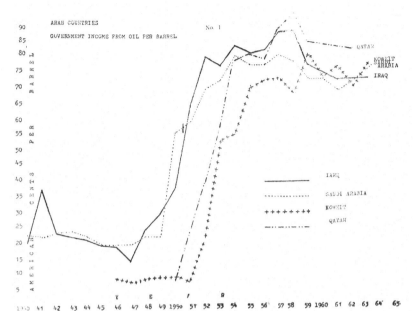

GRAPH 3.1 Abdullah al-Tariki, "Arab Countries: Government Income from Oil Per Barrel," from "Nationalization of Arab Petroleum Industry Is a National Necessity," March 1965.
Source: Fifth Arab Petroleum Congress, Cairo, Papers and Discussions, vol. I, Economics.

final arguments for a revision to the royalty expensing problem, which he inherited from Rouhani, actually showed a great deal of common ground with Tariki, even if he was not willing to risk national legislation. Bazzaz's description of what he described as a better middle course actually showed common ground with Tariki. A new understanding of "international fairness" – that "when the rules of Law and the rules of equity are in conflict, the rules of equity must prevail" – was essential to a fair debate between the countries and the companies, he said. The companies needed to accept that oil production now existed in "a changing world," of "changing circumstances ... changing ideals and principles."[63]

Now he attacked Tariki for "provoking emotional reaction rather than addressing reason." So did Feisal Mazidi, who attended the meeting as a

---

[63] "Speech Delivered by Al-Bazzaz, OPEC's Secretary General," *ROAPE* 1: 2 (March 1965), 37–9.

member of the Kuwaiti delegation. That afternoon, he languished on the speaker's list for over two hours. When he finally had his chance, he also scolded Tariki for slipping into demagoguery: he was speaking to "a thousand experts here in the Congress, not to the man in the street."[64]

But then, like Bazzaz, he agreed with Tariki's basic premise. "Further negotiations would be futile. Now we must legislate and use our sovereign powers," he said. Instead of nationalization, however, he suggested that governments use their taxation rights. In short, he agreed with the prepared remarks Parra was to give. He even suggested that taxation might serve the same purpose as nationalization: "We should tax the companies to the limit and then beyond the limit – but fast – to the extent where it would no longer be profitable for them to stay. Then they would say goodbye and get out of their own accord." "I am not opposed to nationalization; eventually it will have to come," he concluded.[65]

Francisco Parra also criticized Tariki in impromptu remarks, given before he read parts of his original paper on national taxation of foreign enterprises. "Cold calculation will serve the interests of the producing countries better than red-hot emotion," he said. But when Parra turned to his prepared paper, which held that taxation could increase the host governments' share of profits without reducing the incentive of the companies to continue investing in production, his broad assumptions again mirrored those of Tariki.[66]

The heated discussions on the last day of the 1965 Arab Petroleum Congress provided a searching analysis of both the possibilities and the defects of the sovereign rights program. As Tariki's critics noted, the positions of the gradualists and insurrectionists were not mutually exclusive. The oil elites agreed that they had gotten a bad bargain from the foreign oil companies. Moreover, they agreed that it was the responsibility of the oil-producing nations and of OPEC to continue to change the climate to a point where better agreements became possible.

At the same time, the failure of the royalty negotiations revealed that changing the old concessions was a difficult prospect. A week after the 1965 Congress, the Cairo newspaper *al-Akhbar* sponsored a debate

[64] "Tariki's Study," *SFAPC*, 10–11.
[65] "Discussion on the Tariki Paper," *MEES* 8: 21 (March 26, 1965), 31. In the Fourth Congress, Mazidi won a prize for his paper on the natural gas in Kuwait. See: Prize Winning Papers, November 1963 *Papers of the Fourth Arab Petroleum Congress*.
[66] "Afternoon Session," *MEES* 8: 21 (March 26, 1965), 32–3.

between Tariki and Iraq's oil minister, Sayid Abdul Aziz al-Wattari, on "the future of Arab oil." Things again turned tense when the moderator, the Egyptian economist Fawzi Mansur, asked if "a single country, such as Iraq" could take on the oil companies alone. Tariki lashed out. The failure to negotiate royalty expensing, "where the right was clear," proved that any measures short of nationalization were "sterile methods." Furthermore, he said, it was not necessary to start from a position of unanimous agreement. Supply cuts from any two producers in the same region, for example Iraq and Kuwait, could "serve as a beginning." Likewise, if monarchical Libya stopped "slaying" Algerian attempts to "preserve its rights" by increasing production, the two North African countries could stand up to the "oil monopolies" that brought their supply to the growing Western European markets.[67]

Wattari agreed in principle: to accept the companies' offer had been to exchange one yoke for a new, not necessarily less crushing one. But when pressed by Mansur he found himself in greater sympathy with the gradualists. The gradualist efforts to indicate attainable policies were more practical than Tariki's call for nationalization, he said. Nationalization was ultimately desirable, of course, but its "risk factor" was too great. The experience of Mossadegh had proven that. Even small changes, like the problem of royalty expensing, caused great discord. There was thus "no visible road" for Tariki's scenario. Insurrectionism was, unfortunately, less a representation of existing sovereignty than a hope of mustering one into being.

Wattari's dampened enthusiasm pointed to the deeper weakness of sovereign rights as a common denominator for diplomacy. Francisco Parra, writing on behalf of the OPEC Secretariat, had already held that Tariki's ideas fell short of "the supreme test of politics." Was the simultaneous enactment of national legislation, in a word, practical? It was not, according to Parra: "We are only harming ourselves if we think that eight sovereign states, with interests which are not always compatible, will immediately set out on any radical course without due deliberation," he said in 1964.[68]

It was a candid dispute in which Tariki and the other insurrectionists found themselves shunted to the margins of the new history they sought to forge. That was unfortunate, Amir Kubbah wrote in the *Review of Arab Petroleum Economics*. The gradualist faction had hamstrung OPEC

---

[67] "Debate on the Future of Arab Oil," *ROAPE* 1: 3 (April 1965), 33–4.
[68] *ION* 3: 7 (July 1964), OIC.

and turned it into a "sick colossus in Geneva." Their lack of vision, he believed, made it impossible to escape "the rapacious clutch" of the old concessions. If the OPEC members could not be "sensible enough" to agree on Tariki's plans for pro-rationing, at the very least, future generations would "curse our politicians for failure to clip the power of companies to decide our fate."[69]

Still, even given OPEC's lethargy, many outside observers saw the organization and its driving ideas as a threat. American officials "pointed up [their] concern" again in 1965 again "that the ideas of Abdullah Tariki still have considerable popular appeal in the Arab world." They also argued that the influence of Tariki also had kinder face: "Faisal Mazidi in Kuwait, who, while not in favor of immediate nationalization, still advocates eventual government control of the oil industry." This contrast of Tariki and Mazidi by US officials, like that of Tariki and Mohammed Salman a half decade earlier, calls into question the common branding of Tariki as lonely radical. His ideas should not be so easily severed from their larger political and intellectual context. Although his rhetoric was uncompromising and Parra, Mazidi, and others found nationalization impractical, the arguments they shared were more mainstream than radical.[70]

Parra summarized that set of beliefs in the *Inter-OPEC Newsletter* in 1963. The member countries of OPEC could not "overlook the fact that the terms of trade have been, and continue to be, steadily worsening against them," he wrote. According to this position, the OPEC nations were not so much underdeveloped as underpaid nations. OPEC was for him a means to use sovereignty collectively to right that problem. It was "a gathering of countries with the same problems and the same aspirations: to exchange information and plan the future, to strive toward a unified policy and, most important to support each other in the common struggle." For him, the lesson was clear: "When a country is a member of OPEC, it can no longer be isolated." Emphasizing the rise of anticolonial elites in international society, an article in the industry journal *Petroleum Press Service* made the same point more succinctly: Owing to the work of "new professionals" in the oil-producing countries, "the missionary work of OPEC has not been wasted."[71]

[69] "The Sick Colossus," *ROAPE* 1: 4 (May 1965), 2.
[70] Circular Airgram, December 22, 1965, *FRUS 1964–68*, vol. XXXIV, doc. 186.
[71] *ION* 2: 6 (June 1963), OIC; "The New Professionals," *Petroleum Press Service* (December 1963).

Gradualists and insurrectionists alike were swept up in the anticolonial elite wave, which Kubbah joined others in calling "the petroleum awakening." This was because the histories of petroleum colonization – like the arguments about unequal exchange, permanent sovereignty, economic self-determination, and changing circumstances – transformed the concrete experiences of people and nations into a set of abstract propositions about the natural course of decolonization. In turn, that shared economic culture also gave meaning to those specific experiences. The argument was thus about specific instances and about the character of the historical process itself. The histories told and retold among the oil elites revealed one vast assumption: that once the reign of colonial inequality was consumed by the fires of sovereignty, however quickly or slowly, there would arise out of its ashes a more natural and just international economic order. The sense was that time was speeding up and that the old concessions would inevitably dissolve into the past.

That vision influenced the oil elites more than any other single set of ideas. If the division between gradualists and insurrectionists revealed that anticolonial elites could not agree on their answers to specific problems, this was a chaos of vitality rather than lassitude. A submerged culture ran beneath the sectarian divides over strategy. As the histories of petroleum colonization and the constant invocations of "petroleum awakenings" and "oil consciousness" revealed, the heart of that view resided in its pattern of past sin and present and future resurrection.

Yet the royalty negotiations exposed a real problem: it was difficult to see where the articulation of diverse interests stopped and their aggregation into a common policy began. That soft spot of decolonization and its economic culture would continue to plague the oil-producing nations in the second half of the 1960s.

4

Rights and Failure

The 1967 Arab Oil Embargo

Nobody denied the right of permanent sovereignty ... Sovereignty itself is of a permanent nature.[1]
> Muhammad Mughraby, 1966

It will not be possible to present the American action to the Arab world (nor probably to most of the Third World) as simply an assertion of a recognized international right.[2]
> Eugene Rostow, 1967

At the moment when Radio Cairo charged US and British aircraft with participating in the first Israeli attack of the June 1967 Arab–Israeli War, the oil consciousness developed during the previous two decades became more closely attuned to regional politics than ever before. The insurrectionists in Iraq stopped oil shipments to the United States and Great Britain because of their "military assistance to the enemy" on June 6 and the other Arab producers followed suit within the day. Observers in Saudi Arabia, Kuwait, Iraq, and Libya documented what one US official called the "continued polarization ... of the political scene." The International Confederation of Arab Trade Unions urged workers to sabotage pipelines and oil rigs, and workers walked off their sites from Algiers to Jidda. In one meaning-laden moment, Algerian military officers

---

[1] Muhamad Mughraby, *Permanent Sovereignty over Oil Resources: A Study of Middle East Oil Concessions and Legal Change*, Middle East Oil Monographs No. 5 (Beirut: The Middle East Research and Publishing Center, 1966), 38.
[2] Eugene Rostow, "Agenda for Control Group Meeting," June 1, 1967, National Security Files, box 106, LBJL.

repainted the offices of Standard Oil in the orange and black of Sonatrach, the new state-owned company.[3]

For the rest of the summer, pronouncements of solidarity among the Arab oil elites accompanied the decisions to stop the flow of oil. Saudi Oil Minister Ahmed Zaki Yamani, for example, told Aramco executives that he would hold them "gravely responsible if any drop of our oil" reached the United States.[4] But Yamani, who had replaced Abdullah al-Tariki as the director of Saudi oil policy in 1962, also worked to limit the intensity of the cut-off. Like his predecessor, he was trained in the United States, where he received degrees from Harvard and New York University. Unlike Tariki, Yamani had gained a reputation as a friend of the West. He sided with the gradualists in the royalty negotiations and sought a close and cordial working relationship with oil companies and other US businesses in general, to such an extent that in 1974 Emma Rothschild would describe him in the *New York Review of Books* as "bullish on America."[5]

His actions during the 1967 oil embargo point to the complex contours of the economic culture of decolonization and the sovereign rights program. He met with an executive of Aramco, the Saudi concessionaire, on June 10, 1967. A visiting Iraqi delegation had urged "vigorous measures," including nationalization, Yamani said. But he had a plan to forestall the Iraqis. He had scheduled a meeting with them for the

---

[3] Embassy Iraq to DOS, June 6, 1967, *FRUS 1964–68*, vol. XXXIV, doc. 232; Information Memorandum from Battle to Katzenbach, June 19, 1967, *FRUS 1964–68*, vol. XXI, doc. 98; Embassy Iraq to DOS, June 8, 1967, *FRUS 1964–68*, vol. XXI, doc. 195; Embassy Kuwait to DOS, June 7, 1967, *FRUS 1964–68*, vol. XXI, doc. 210; Embassy Saudi Arabia to DOS, June 9, 1967, *FRUS 1964–68*, vol. XXI, doc. 291; Embassy Libya to DOS, June 11, 1967, *FRUS 1964–68*, vol. XXXIV, doc. 243; Editorial note citing Telegram 1305, June 11, 1967, *FRUS 1964–68*, vol. XXXIV, doc. 240; Embassy Algeria to DOS, June 9, 1967, *FRUS 1964–68*, vol. XXXIV, doc. 237. On the origins of the Six-Day War, see: Douglas Little, "Nasser Delenda Est: Lyndon Johnson, the Arabs, and the 1967 Six-Day War," in H. W. Brands, ed., *The Foreign Policies of Lyndon Johnson: Beyond Vietnam* (College Station: Texas A&M University Press, 1999); Roland Popp, "Stumbling Decidedly into the Six-Day War," *Middle East Journal* 60: 2 (Spring 2006), 281–309; Galia Golan, "The Soviet Union and the Outbreak of the June 1967 Six-Day War," *Journal of Cold War Studies*, 8: 1 (2006), 3–19.

[4] Riyadh to DOS, June 7, 1967, National Security Files, box 107, LBJL.

[5] Emma Rothschild, "Where the Energy Crisis is Pushing Us," *New York Review of Books*, January 24, 1974. At the former, he studied international disputes over private capital investments. When he returned to Saudi Arabia in 1956, he first joined the Ministry of Finance but soon began to work under Tariki in the Office of Petroleum and Minerals. See: Vitalis, *America's Kingdom*, 233–4; Citino, *From Arab Nationalism to OPEC*, 152–60; Jeffrey Robinson, *Yamani: The Untold Story* (London: Simon and Schuster, 1988), 42–4, 50–2.

following day, in which the executive would defend Aramco and the other oil concessionaires as conduits between the Western and Arab governments in the postwar negotiations. The executive would tell the Iraqi delegation that his company would urge the Johnson administration to make "their best efforts" to pressure Israel to draw back from any territorial gains, Yamani instructed. "I know your government [is] willing to give this assurance," he said. The State Department was willing indeed. Former National Security Council Adviser McGeorge Bundy, on loan from the Ford Foundation to lead an emergency committee on the crisis, advised Johnson to give oil companies "some US statement or action for which they can claim partial credit," a message that had already been passed on to Yamani.[6]

More important was the fact that the meeting, three days after the start of the Six-Day War and 1967 Arab oil embargo, began a three-month search for what one journalist called a "face-saving formula" through which Saudi Arabia and the other gradualist Arab producers could renege on the embargo. When Yamani began to remonstrate openly against the embargo in late June, it led to a public quarrel with Iraqi officials. He told the *Financial Times* that if the embargo continued the Arab world "stood to lose as much economically as they had already lost territorially." US Secretary of State Dean Rusk welcomed this as evidence of "enlightened self-interest." The *New York Times* reported that "[t]he Arabs, as usual, had a proverb to fit the situation. *Rahet al-sakra; waijit al-fakra.*" The newspaper slickly translated the couplet: "Gone the wine fumes; thinking resumes."[7]

A different rhyme applied in insurrectionist Iraq, whose successive governments had consulted Abdullah al-Tariki on oil matters since 1963. Prime Minister Tahir Yahya accused Yamani and the Saudis of deserting the Arab cause and announced through the Iraq News Agency that Iraq's embargo would continue indefinitely, notwithstanding the "losses we suffer for the sake of the Arab nation." Those losses, Yamani responded, would translate into a new balance of power among the oil-producing nations. Iran was of particular concern. The Shah smelled

---

[6] Aramco cable PC 683, June 10, 1967, *FRUS 1964–68*, vol. XXXIV, doc. 238 (editorial note); Memorandum to Johnson, July 10, 1967, *FRUS 1964–68*, vol. XXXIV, doc. 256.

[7] Robert C. Toth, "Arab States Seen Seeking Accord with West," *Los Angeles Times*, July 28, 1967; "Saudi Minister Urges Arabs to Reconsider," *Financial Times*, July 1, 1967; Nicholas Herbert, "More Moderation on Arab Oil," *The Times* (London), July 1, 1967; DOS to Embassy Saudi Arabia, July 11, 1967, *FRUS 1964–68*, vol. XXIV, doc. 257; "Mideast Arabs," *New York Times*, July 2, 1967.

blood, he continued. If the Arabs did not resume their production, Iran would "become the largest oil-producing state in the Middle East and probably the world."[8]

The mutual recriminations were loaded with drama, but with meaning too. If the history of oil concessions was for some a well poisoned by the imperial past, for Yamani the threat of competition among oil producers was more ominous. Others agreed. The Shah himself disparaged the embargo in sentiments that echoed those of the Saudi oil elite. "[I]t was ridiculous for any Arab to believe that the West could really be hurt by an Arab oil embargo," he told one US official. His evidence was compelling: production from Venezuela, Iran, and the United States could easily cover the Arab gap. Indeed, in a raw display of the internecine tensions that had plagued OPEC since its inception, Iran and Venezuela took advantage of the Arab production cuts to increase their market shares. Kuwait and Libya also joined Saudi Arabia in breaking the embargo in 1967.[9]

Those too were sovereign acts. When placed into the context of decolonization and the sovereign rights program, the story of the 1967 Arab oil embargo suggests the durability of the sovereign rights program's fundamental paradox: national interest often dictated a path that moved against the collective solidarity of sovereign rights. There existed effective limits to collective action as an operative strategy for the oil elites.

Yamani's policies hewed close to this reality of weakness. But the deep rifts among the Arab producers and within OPEC occurred at a time in which sovereign rights continued to gain international purchase, as meetings of the UN Economic and Social Council, OPEC, and the UN Conference on Trade and Development reveal. Anticolonial elites communed more than ever in the mid-1960s. International lawyers and development economists continued to express a profound desire to overturn the colonial economic injustice they saw continuing far into the age of decolonization.

Through their conversations about the politics, economics, and histories of independence, anticolonial elites forged and reinforced connections to one another, shared useful knowledge, grouped themselves according

---

[8] "Saudi Call to Resume Oil Supplies," *The Times* (London), July 8, 1967; "Soviet Warships to Visit 2 Egyptian Ports Today," *New York Times*, July 10, 1967; *MEED* 11: 27 (July 13, 1967), 481–2; Wolfe-Hunicutt, *The End of the Concessionary Regime*, 153–4, 172; *MEED* 11: 26 (July 6, 1967), 478.

[9] Memorandum of Conversation, August 23, 1967, *FRUS 1964–68*, vol. XXII, doc. 231.

to expertise, and tracked their progress over time. The new UN Conference on Trade and Development, founded in 1964 under the leadership of Raúl Prebisch as an incubator of nationalist economic policies, soon became the most influential organization in which anticolonial elites advanced sovereign rights.

The doctrine of unequal exchange commanded an unparalleled influence when UN officials first began to imagine the birth of UNCTAD in 1962 and 1963. Reports asserting the deleterious effects of unequal exchange flooded the offices of scores of international organizations and national governments. In 1962, the same year that OPEC received the Little report and employed Francisco Parra, the UN *World Economic Survey* held that "developing primary producing countries" had suffered "the long-term deterioration of [their] terms of trade" at an annual rate of 10 percent between 1950 and 1960. The annual reports of UN regional economic commissions confirm how rampant this perception was. Reports by the member-states of the Economic Commission for Africa and to the Economic Commission for Asia and the Far East led the second to declare that unequal exchange painted a "clear picture" of their shared problems. Even economists at the General Agreement on Tariffs and Trade, hardly anticolonial in their politics, unearthed statistics demonstrating that the volume of exports of industrial countries had increased at nearly double the rate of those from the developing world between 1928 and 1955.[10]

This was not a set of isolated voices, but a chorus. The 1963 meeting of the Economic Commission of the Organization of African Unity, held in Naimey, Niger, illustrates the allure of this economic brand of anticolonial internationalism. Kifle Wodajo, the acting president of the organization, was delayed along with other delegates by runway problems at the Naimey airport. Wodajo, who would soon lead UN investigations into the status of South West Africa, by then had grown accustomed to the pitfalls of international travel. He had represented Ethiopia at

---

[10] UNCTAD, Official Records, First Committee, Summary Record, Fourth Meeting, April 17, 1964, E/Conf.46/C.1/SR.4; ECOSOC, Official Records, Thirty-Sixth Session, July 2, 1963, E/SR.1265; ECOSOC, Official Records, Thirty-Fifth Session, April 18, 1963, E/SR.1262; ECOSOC, Official Records, Annual Report of the Economic Commission for Asia and the Far East, E/3735; ECOSOC, Official Records, Annual Report of the Economic Commission for Africa, E/3727/Rev.1; UNCTAD, Official Records, First Committee, Summary Record, Fourth Meeting, April 17, 1964, E/Conf.46/C.1/SR.4; *Helping Economic Development in Asia and the Far East: The Work of ECAFE* (United Nations: Office of Public Information, 1964).

international conferences since earning an MA in political science at the University of Wisconsin four years earlier. His thesis, on Ethiopia's foreign relations between the culmination of the Scramble for Africa in 1884 and the outbreak of World War I, was emblematic of the commonly held views among anticolonial elites that linked the experiences of formal colonialism and informal economic domination. He argued that the turn-of-the-century treaties guaranteeing Ethiopian national independence were "meaningless and unintelligible" unless they were regarded together with the "bird's-eye view" of the period's official colonial assumptions. European administrators had only "grudgingly accepted" independence after the weak Ethiopian government guaranteed European commercial influence. The economic problems that ensued for Ethiopia because of that unequal relationship were not much different from the problems of formally colonized nations, Wodajo concluded. Moreover, the experience of Ethiopia was shared by "the few independent countries in Africa and Asia when European colonialism was at its highest pitch." None were free from economic domination.[11]

Wodajo set the tone of the 1963 OAU meeting with a speech that was soaked through with sovereign rights. "Most of us are today so much disposed as a matter of habit to think of African Unity in terms of political ideals," he said. That political awareness was crucial, but should not overshadow "the imperative of economic necessities." Independence was not the end goal of decolonization, he continued. Development was. This was a problem because the contrast between that political change and the continuity of international economic inequality was stark. The problems of Africa were "similar to those which confront the majority of mankind."[12]

His host, Niger President Hamani Diori, was also concerned about the economic problems that had continued past political independence. His nationalism had changed upon independence, he told Wodajo, as he became "fully aware of the primary importance of economic factors." He then explained the internationalist logic of national economic sameness, which Wodajo had just mentioned, through an image of concentric circles of oppression and identity. "Virtually all the African states" shared

---

[11] Kifle Wodajo, *Ethiopia's Treaty Relations with Britain, France and Italy, 1884–1914* (MA, University of Wisconsin – Madison, 1959), 1, 13–15, 114–17; Kifle Wodajo, Rapporteur, *Question of South West Africa: Report of the Ad Hoc Committee for South West Africa* (New York: United Nations, 1967).

[12] "Statement by the Acting Secretary-General," December 10, 1963, ECOSOC, Official Records, ECOS/3.

the concerns and hopes of Niger. In turn, the African stance on inequality reflected "the present position of the Third World in the economic field." That shared position itself resulted from a deeper problem of bias within Western economic thought, he added. "The strict law of supply and demand" in the international economy was no such thing, he said, in a direct echo of Raúl Prebisch. Comparative advantage resulted from a particular imperial moment in history, and imperial interpretation of economic growth. Trade was wrapped up in domination and its unfair terms led to a "binding economic dependence."[13]

Reports and discussions from the UN Economic Commissions and the OAU thus joined those from OPEC, the Permanent Sovereignty Commission, and the Non-Aligned Movement in the early 1960s. Together these arguments present a wide-angle photograph of a shared belief about international economic inequality. The scholarly geneses of sovereign rights, in turn, became less important than the fact that some form of economic emancipation had become a prevalent expectation. Sovereign rights was, at the same time, more than a theory of the causes of inequality or a call to use the power of national law to solve the problem. It also encompassed a set of beliefs about the endurance of inequality.

The UN Economic and Social Council picked up that thread again when its delegates began to consider a permanent Conference on Trade and Development in 1963. The planning committee asked Prebisch, who continued to lead the Economic Commission for Latin America, to prepare a report to justify the creation of a global group dedicated to trade reform. He used the report to reemphasize the shared problem of unequal exchange on the periphery. He also pointed toward a complex ecology of possibilities to move beyond the "division of a world into areas of poverty and plenty," including compensatory financing for industrial development, the transfer of technology, diversification of industry, and modernization of agriculture. But all of his recommendations boiled down to what the delegates at the inaugural UNCTAD meeting called "the essential element" of sovereignty. Respect for sovereign control of their

---

[13] "Statement Delivered by H. E. Mr. Diori Hammani," December 10, 1963, ECOSOC, Official Records, ECOS/10/SR.2/Apx.1. Diori – like the first presidents of the Ivory Coast, Dehomey, and Mali – attended the École William Ponty, a teacher's college that occupied a former slave-trading post on the island of Gorée. On the social politics of that school, see: Tony Chafer, "Education and Political Socialisation of a National-Colonial Political Elite in French West Africa, 1936–47," *The Journal of Imperial and Commonwealth History* 35: 3 (September 2007), 440–3.

economic resources was necessary for the poor nations to create policies to gain a greater share of international wealth.[14]

The truth of unequal exchange and its relation to decolonization seemed verifiable to Prebisch when he presented his report to the UN Economic and Social Council in July 1963. Somewhat iconoclastically, he told the group that in 1948 he originally declined the offer to direct the Economic Commission for Latin America because of his "conviction that the economic thinking of the day was not in line with the realities of the situation." He had feared that "any action taken ... might be undermined or thwarted by the predominance of Anglo-Saxon economic ideas." But something had changed in the ensuing fifteen years. The arguments that radiated from his and other institutions had traversed the periphery and become a potent force. Once considered "explosive and revolutionary," his theory of economic inequality now seemed "a mere statement of the obvious."[15]

One might condemn Prebisch for overstating the popularity of his argument if numerous members of the council did not also agree. Among them was Kifle Wodajo, who headed the Ethiopian delegation. He hoped aloud that the new body that the Economic and Social Council proposed could become a forum to "discuss primarily the trade relations between the developing countries and the industrial countries in order to provide the former with remunerative prices for their exports." The Indian ambassador to the United Nations, R. K. Nehru, agreed. "In spite of the progress of decolonization, the gap between the developed and less developed nations of the world – the rich and the poor – had not yet closed and in many ways had widened," he said. Like Wodajo and many others, Nehru emphasized "the important problem of improving the terms of trade for producers of primary commodities."[16]

Unequal exchange was also the prevalent argument at the inaugural meeting of UNCTAD in March 1964. Prebisch privately expressed his "marked desire" before the conference that the delegates avoid "political controversy." That proved impossible. UN Secretary General U Thant opened the proceedings by describing what he called "the dilemma of our times" – the "universal understanding" that political emancipation had not been accompanied by a

---

[14] Final Act of the United Nations Conference on Trade and Development, June 16, 1964, *ISIL* 1970, 83–4.

[15] ECOSOC, Official Records, Thirty-Sixth Session, July 2, 1963, E/SR.1265.

[16] ECOSOC, Official Records, Thirty-Fifth Session, April 18, 1963, E/SR.1262; ECOSOC, Official Records, Thirty-Sixth Session, July 3, 1963, E/SR.1266. As Secretary of External Affairs of India in the late 1940s, Nehru had taken an uncompromising stance toward continued imperial influence in border areas. See: Simon Smith, "French Imperial Outposts in Post-Imperial India, 1947–54," *European History Review* 3: 2 (1996), 187–97.

FIGURE 4.1 Raúl Prebisch delivers the opening statement of the UN Conference
on Trade and Development, March 24, 1964. Seated to his left is Philippe de
Seynes, the UN Under-Secretary of Economic and Social Affairs. To his right is
Abdel Moneim El Kaissouni, the President of the Conference.
Source: UN Photo. Courtesy of the United Nations Photo Library, Photo No. 368107.

"concomitant and desirable rate of economic progress." A slew of anticolonial elites seconded him, including many from the oil-exporting nations.
By the time the Iranian delegate stood to express his support, he could note
that similar views had been expressed by the representatives from Iraq, Saudi
Arabia, and Venezuela. So he kept his statement short: "The fact was that the
terms of trade of the primary exporting countries had been deteriorating."[17]

---

[17] Comgen 226 for Narasimhan from Prebisch, June 27, 1963, doc. S-0858-0003-03, UNA-
NY; "Opening Statement by Secretary General to Trade Conference," March 23, 1964,
SG/SM/41, doc. S-0084-0007-05, UNA-NY; UNCTAD, Official Records, First Commit-
tee, Summary Record, Sixth Meeting, April 20, 1964, E/Conf.46/C.1/SR.6; UNCTAD,
Official Records, First Committee, Summary Record, Seventh Meeting, May 1, 1964, E/
Conf.46/C.1/SR.7.

The meaning of the moment was just as clear to Prebisch. "The developing countries are determined to interpret current economic and social phenomena in their own way, and provide the solutions which seemed appropriate to them," he wrote in his report of the meeting to the Economic and Social Council. In his report, U Thant wrote that Prebisch's interpretation had accumulated a seemingly endless number of adherents. The new assertiveness of "the South," he hoped, would be "a turning-point in the history of international economic relations." He added a month later that the conference had "shown the way toward a more just and rational international economic order."[18]

The founding meeting of UNCTAD, held in Geneva, reveals that sovereign rights involved the development of a new understanding of processes existing on an international canvas, concerning a multitude of actors, and occurring over the long term. The understanding was widespread in the mid-1960s. The forty-seven heads of state of the Non-Aligned Movement held their second summit later the same year in Cairo. They expressed their support of the UNCTAD mission in language that emphasized economic violations of the hard-won political sovereignty that came with decolonization. "Colonialist attempts to maintain unequal relationships, particularly in the economic field, constitute serious dangers," they wrote in their final communiqué. Another assertion of the "right of sovereign disposal in regard to their natural resources" appeared in that document alongside references to "external intervention" in the Congo and the Portuguese colonies and the rule of "minority regimes" in South Africa, Southern Rhodesia, and Palestine.[19]

In 1964, when Jean-Paul Sartre wrote in his introduction to Franz Fanon's *Wretched of the Earth* that many nations had only achieved "a simulacrum of phony independence," his statement was less an innovation than a pithy expression of a consensus. What he and others had begun to label "neo-colonialism" had already developed as a shared set of beliefs across the periphery. The rise of sovereign rights was a

---

[18] ECOSOC, Official Records, Thirty-Seventh Session, July 16, 1964, E/SR.1320; U Thant, "Preface," n.d. (September 1964), doc. S-0084-0007-05, UNA-NY. Such statements are consistent with his earlier views on decolonization. See: U Thant, "A Burmese View of World Tensions," *Annals of the American Academy of Political and Social Science*, vol. 318, Asia and Future World Leadership (July 1958), 34–42.

[19] "Conference of Heads of State or Government of Non-Aligned Countries," October 1964, *ISIL 1970*, 19–20.

deliberate process of interpreting the meaning of the imperial past and justifying state power as a means to international economic justice. "Economic emancipation [was] the essential element in the struggle for the elimination of political domination," the heads of the Non-Aligned Movement wrote. The first UNCTAD delegates defended every nation's "sovereign right ... freely to dispose of its natural resources" the same year. As economic, legal, and historical thought nurtured a sense of solidarity, oil elites participated actively in that front, inside and outside of OPEC.[20]

There are a number of examples of how oil elites deliberately positioned themselves as part of the rise of sovereign rights. One comes directly from the OPEC Secretariat, whose officials closely followed the developments of UNCTAD. "The eyes of the world are focused on Geneva this month, and on the conference taking place their under the auspices of the United Nations," Francisco Parra wrote in the *Inter-OPEC Newsletter* in March 1964. "There is no more important problem facing the world than the question of the emergence of the former colonies and mandates as free members of the community of nations." The meeting was important for the oil producers, Parra said, because of the similarity between the oil concessions, their price problems, and the greater issue of "the downward trend" of commodity prices. "The barrel of exported oil will no longer buy what it used to buy," he wrote. Furthermore, the problem was also "far deeper than simple economics" shared across the Third World. It was a question of sovereign nations pressing "just demands" for a fundamental change to the international economy.[21]

Another example emerges from the minutes of the UNCTAD planning sessions in the UN Economic and Social Council in 1963. The Iraqi delegate discussed the "unfair contracts" between the oil companies and producing nations and linked them to the problem of unequal exchange. When a US delegate suggested that the conferees consider adopting resolutions that would protect the "sanctity of contracts," the Iraqi responded

---

[20] "Introduction," in Franz Fanon, *The Wretched of the Earth* (New York: Penguin, 1969), 9; "Conference of Heads of State or Government of Non-Aligned Countries," October 1964, *ISIL* 1970, 34; Daniel J. Whelan, "Under the Aegis of Man": The Right to Development and the Origins of the New International Economic Order," *Humanity: An International Journal of Human Rights, Humanitarianism, and Development*, 6: 1 (2015), 102.

[21] *ION* 3: 3 (March 1964), OIC; *ION* 3: 4 (April 1964), OIC.

that it was "illogical" for a UN body to do preserve such raw deals. The organization had been proposed in part to emphasize "the inalienable right of sovereign states" to take any measures to ensure "complete sovereignty over anything which is theirs," he continued. Delegates from Iran, Saudi Arabia, Indonesia, and Libya joined Iraq in voting against the sanctity clause and other American provisions that sought to ensure extra-national legal jurisdiction.[22]

The Fifth Arab Petroleum Congress in 1965 gives another example of the functional link between oil elites and the broader economic culture of decolonization. The Arab League produced an official history of the Petroleum Congresses and OPEC for the meeting. That history – which emphasized the roles of Tariki, Pérez Alfonso, and to a lesser extent Salman – again connected the recent events of oil politics to decolonization. The official history also duly stressed that the old oil concessions were part of the greater problem of inequality in postwar international capitalism. The Arab oil elites' shared interest in overturning their concessions formed a link in a global chain of dissent against policies that had been fixed "without taking into account . . . the interests of the producing countries."[23]

The official statements by OPEC at the 1965 Congress, written and presented by Francisco Parra, drew the same picture. Parra began with what he considered a telltale history of petroleum colonization. In this version, the "first concession" that granted a foreign company the right to exploit national oil had been written in Sumatra in 1890. The rules of that concession, "by a Dutch company over a Dutch-dominated territory," became typical of the concessions granted under similar conditions in the Middle East thereafter. He expanded on that position in a second paper, which again held that the advent of decolonization had been a crucial change in perception, in particular, of the conscious need for more laws asserting sovereign control. The oil concessions were, to be sure, in some ways different from other questions of economic dominance, Parra said. But OPEC's desire to change the concessions represented more than a unique critique of the particular "economic and political structure" of the concessions. They also were part of a more

---

[22] Karol N. Gess, "Permanent Sovereignty Over Natural Resources: An Analytical Review of the United Nations Declaration and Its Genesis," *International and Comparative Law Quarterly* 13: 2 (January 1964), 442. For the broader debate, see Rodman, *Sanctity vs. Sovereignty.*

[23] League of Arab States, "History of the Arab Petroleum Congresses and the Creation of the Organisation of Petroleum Exporting Countries," *SFAPC.*

general preoccupation with "ideals and principles." The credibility of this belief emerged from a shared history – the most important oil concessions had been signed at a time when the nations concerned "were politically subordinated, directly or indirectly, to foreign powers." Concessions had been made absent the "real and free will" of the nations.[24]

Parra's nod to Indonesia indicated another aspect of the formative influence of that interpretation: the growth of OPEC membership. Along with Libya, Indonesia had joined the organization in 1962. Membership, in turn, had another effect. Now an Indonesian delegation regularly accompanied the Venezuelans and the Iranians as observers at the Arab Petroleum Congress. When he attended his first Congress in 1965 as Parra's guest, the Indonesian Minister of Basic Industry and Mines, Chairul Saleh, had already conducted arduous negotiations with foreign oil companies in his country in what one historian calls the attempt to "extirpate the legacy of Dutch colonialism by rewriting the laws governing exploitation of the country's resources."[25]

In fact, the Indonesian example captures both the force and the tensions of sovereign rights in the mid-1960s. The Indonesian project was also an international one, Saleh told OPEC ministers gathered in Djakarta in 1964. But even though he sided with the insurrectionists in the royalty negotiations, he also understood the international push for justice through oil control could not be too bold. OPEC was "still an infant," Saleh said, that needed to take baby steps before it could walk. But it was also true for him that the maturing relationship could not continue to be characterized by gross inequity. "For this we have a saying in our language: *duduk sama rendah berdiri sama tinggi*," he continued. "We need them as partners not as leeches." The local adage applied to the aggregate situation. At the 1965 Arab Petroleum Congress he came to the same conclusion but phrased it more comprehensively and with greater militancy: "It is high time for oil to become a weapon in the hands of developing Countries in their various battles."[26]

Saleh believed that discrete national histories were lumped together in a larger trajectory at the same time as he hoped that oil could be used in "various battles." This cumulative view was shared by other Indonesian

---

[24] OPEC, "OPEC and the Principle of Negotiation," *SFAPC*; OPEC, "From Concessions to Contracts," *SFAPC*.
[25] Simpson, *Economists with Guns*, 101–9.
[26] "Negotiation or Legislation," November 1964, in Kubbah, *OPEC, Past and Present*, 105; "An Indonesian Declaration," *SFAPC*.

leaders. After meeting with Mohammed Salman in 1962, for example, Indonesian Prime Minister Ibn Sutowo had told the *Iraq Times* it was "clear that we have identical views on a number of issues." OPEC had been formed for that reason, he said, "to look after the affairs of the oil producing countries and protect their rights."[27]

It was against this background that OPEC established official relations with the UN Economic and Social Council in 1965. Oil elites were pleased to link themselves to the group that had written the first permanent sovereignty resolution and established both the Permanent Sovereignty Commission and UNCTAD. Iraq's foreign minister, Adnan al-Pachachi, cousin of Nadim al-Pachachi, was on hand for the announcement. "Such relations would be fruitful both for the United Nations and for OPEC," he said. Majid Rahnema, the Under-Secretary of State for Economic and International Affairs of Iran, also welcomed the agreement. His language echoed the ringing interpretation of the worldwide intellectual shift put forward by U Thant and Raúl Prebisch at the UN Conference on Trade and Development. "Ideas which had seemed unpalatable only ten years before were now generally accepted," he said, in a statement that placed the past on the far side of a pivot. "It might therefore be said that a turning point had been reached in the evolution of economic thought."[28]

Ashraf Lufti, now the OPEC Secretary General, wrote to Prebisch in 1966 to express similar sentiments. "[L]ike the rest of the primary-commodity producers," the OPEC nations found themselves suffering from a lack of control over production and from low prices. The objectives of OPEC were in "complete conformity" with the founding principles of UNCTAD, Lufti continued. Of signal importance in changing that global inequality was the shared goal of taking collective action "to provide to developing countries producing minerals and fuels an appreciable increase in the revenues which accrue to them." The oil producers faced the rigidity and duration of the oil concessions, he wrote. These encroached upon "the sovereignty of the state" in the same general way as unfair prices for other commodities. All this occurred in the same international and historical context. What Lufti called the "oligopolistic pattern" of the past continued to limit "the most basic functions of a modern state."[29]

[27] *ION* 1: 8 (November 1962), OIC.
[28] ECOSOC, Official Records, Thirty-Ninth Session, June 30, 1965, E/SR.1365; ECOSOC, Official Records, Thirty-Ninth Session, July 8, 1965, E/SR.1373.
[29] Lufti to Prebisch, April 11, 1966, ARR 40/1842, box 80, TDO 321/3 (1st), UNA-G; "OPEC and International Petroleum," n.d. (April 1966), ARR 40/1842, box 80, TDO 321/3 (1st), UNA-G.

Whether from Iran or Iraq, Venezuela or Indonesia, Kuwait or Saudi Arabia, whether working for international organizations, their home governments, or independently, oil elites understood fully the logic of opposition of the sovereign rights program. The currency of that view was impressive. The UN General Assembly adopted a stronger resolution on permanent sovereignty the same year Lufti wrote Prebisch. The anticolonial elite delegates there pressed the legal agenda further than ever before when they called for the creation of new "mutually acceptable contractual practices" that would increase the share of Third World governments in "the administration of enterprises which are fully or partially operated by foreign capital." With six abstentions, including the United States, the resolution entitled "Permanent Sovereignty over Natural Resources" passed 104 to 0. A writer for the journal *World Petroleum*, who followed the debate closely, described the outcome as "the pragmatic consequence of the age of equality among countries."[30]

The events that led to the June 1967 war and the Arab oil embargo are part of a longer history of the Arab-Israeli conflict. But they also seemed at first to confirm the anticipated arrival of sovereign rights. Gamal Abdel Nasser linked oil to the Arab–Israeli dispute on May 22, 1967, when he declared the Gulf of Aqaba an Arab *mare clausem*. He ordered the removal of UN peacekeepers from Sharm el Sheikh on the strategic promontory overlooking Aqaba's only entrance, the Straits of Tiran, and declared a blockade on Israel-bound vessels carrying "strategic cargoes." Nasser's term, "strategic," pointed to the five Liberian-flag tankers that went back and forth from Iran to Israel, transporting 300 million tons of oil per year. Israeli Prime Minister Levi Eshkol told US President Lyndon Johnson that the blockade formed the final link of an Arab chain of "stranglish encirclement" that threatened his nation's existence. "To open the Gulf of Aqaba to at least oil for Israel," US National Security Adviser Walt Rostow wrote, "will be the test of who wins this trial of will and nerve."[31]

Here it makes sense to turn to the US response to the Aqaba blockade for two reasons. First, US policy toward the sovereign rights program would become more important in the following years. Second, in May

---

[30] Charles Heller, "Oil at the United Nations: Permanent Sovereignty – Phase II," *World Petroleum* 28: 2 (February 1967), 46.

[31] CIA Intelligence Information Cable, June 4, 1967, National Security Files, box 106, LBJL; Tel Aviv to White House, June 5, 1967, National Security Files, box 107, LBJL; Rostow to Johnson, Rusk, and McNamara, June 4, 1967, National Security Files, box 107, LBJL.

1967 discussions at the United Nations and in the upper echelons of the Johnson administration reinforced the sense that decolonization had reshaped global politics in profound ways. In this case, the sovereign rights program stood out in its relation to the domain of maritime law. Johnson lay down the legal principle that underpinned US policy on May 23 when he accused Nasser of blocking "free and innocent" passage through Aqaba. This appeal to what the United States depicted as a basic principle of the Law of the Sea provoked a fierce debate over its historical precedents. Under close international scrutiny in particular was the 1958 UN Convention on the Territorial Sea, which governed the legality of blockades.[32]

Johnson's statement meant that the United States had formally accused Nasser as a lawbreaker under Article Fourteen of the 1958 law, which defined innocent passage as "not prejudicial to the peace, good order or security of the coastal State." But Article Sixteen, which Nasser cited, gave coastal states the right "to prevent passage which is not innocent." The law was roomy enough for opposing interpretations. The reading of the State Department's legal branch was that innocent passage was "determined objectively according to the conduct of a transiting vessel, not by the character of its cargo." That interpretation evaded Nasser's assertion that merchant oil tankers were nonetheless "prejudicial." Morocco's UN ambassador explained this in an emergency meeting of the Security Council: Nasser sought only to bar cargoes that strengthened "Israel's aggressive potential." US officials accepted that stance internally. Oil was "prejudicial" because it supplied Israel's military. Nasser also had remarked, correctly, that oil was on American "strategic" embargo lists for Cuba and China.[33]

Innocent passage fell on stony soil on the level of recent history too. Israeli access to Aqaba had been sown in the aftermath of the 1956 Suez crisis, a fact that Arab leaders had not forgotten. Egypt had maintained

---

[32] "Statement by the President on Rising Tensions in the Near East," May 23, 1967, *PPPUS*.

[33] Leo Gross, "Passage through the Strait of Tiran and in the Gulf of Aqaba," in *The Middle East Crisis: Test of International Law*, ed. John W. Halderman (Dobbs Ferry, NY: Oceana Publications, 1969), 141; M. McDougal and W. Burke, *The Public Order of the Oceans* (New Haven, CT: Yale University Press, 1962), 258; Meeker to Rusk, May 27, 1967, "Legal Status of the Strait of Tiran and the Gulf of Aqaba," National Security Files, box 106, LBJL; UNSC, Official Record, Security Council Minutes, June, 1 1967, S/PV.1346; Nathaniel Davis, Memorandum, May 26, 1967, National Security Files, box 106, LBJL; "Contingency Paper: Immediate Arab–Israeli War," May 28, 1967, National Security Files, box 107, LBJL.

an Aqaba blockade on Israel since 1948, and one main objective of
Moshe Dayan's Sinai military operation in 1956 was to break it. This
was successful. The oil lifeline to Iran sprang into life when US Secretary of State John Foster Dulles agreed to support Aqaba's international character in return for the Israeli withdrawal from the
strategic cliffs above the Straits of Tiran. An American tanker contracted by a South African marketing company carried the first Iranian
petroleum consignment to the Israeli deep-water port of Eilat on April
22, 1957.[34]

Great Britain, the Netherlands, and Portugal maneuvered to enshrine
Dulles's promise in maritime law at the 1958 conference, when they
submitted a last-minute revision to Article 16 in a subcommittee. Quickly
dubbed the Aqaba Clause but written in generic geographic terms, the
revision would protect passage not only through straits connecting two
parts of the high seas but also between "the high seas and territorial
waters." The subcommittee adopted the change after contentious debate
by a margin of thirty-one votes to thirty, the closest roll call of the two-
month conference. Jamil Baroody spoke for the Arab delegations in the
final plenary session when he said Aqaba Clause "had nothing to do with
the principle of freedom of navigation" but rather had been "carefully
tailored to promote the claims of one state." The Arab participants –
including Baroody and Francisco Parra's future selection to direct the
OPEC Legal Department, Iraqi delegate Hasan Zakariya – withdrew
from the conference in protest.[35]

The history of what Baroody called in the 1958 conference "a muti-
lation of international law" was a direct factor in the denunciation of
Johnson's 1967 conception of innocent passage. This ran counter to the
expectations of some US officials, who hoped the appeal to innocent

---

[34] Robert Bowie, *Suez 1956: International Crises and the Role of Law* (New York: Oxford
University Press, 1974), 10; *American Foreign Policy, Current Documents* (Washington,
DC: Historical Division, Bureau of Public Affairs, 1957), 975–6; "Iran: Israel and Persian
Oil," *MEED* 1: 8 (May 3, 1957), 7; "Israel: Oil Supplies," *MEED* 1: 8 (May 3, 1957), 9.
[35] UNCLS, Official Records, vol. III, A/CONF.13/C.1/L.71; UNCLS, Official Records, vol.
II, Annex I, DHL; UNCLS, OR, vol. III, A/3519; UNCLS, Official Records, vol. II, A/
CONF.13/38; Ali El-Hakim, *The Middle Eastern States and the Law of the Sea* (Syracuse
University Press, 1979), 156; D. H. N. Johnson, "Some Legal Problems of International
Waterways, with Particular Reference to the Straits of Tiran and the Suez Canal,"
Modern Law Review 31 (1968), 157; Hasan S. Zakariya, "The Impact of Changing
Circumstances on the Revision of Petroleum Contracts," OPEC Seminar, July 1969, OIC;
Arthur Dean, "The Geneva Conference on the Law of the Sea: What Was Accom-
plished," *AJIL* 52 (1958), 607.

passage would alleviate the pressure Nasser had placed on the Arab oil producers. Johnson's statement was designed, one wrote, to give "the producing countries the best possible excuse for moderation by presenting a plausible image of evenhandedness." But the seemingly impartial vehicle of international law did not conceal the partisanship underlying its construction or application. Reports from the US mission to the United Nations led Eugene Rostow, the State Department's contact point with New York, to advise that it would "not be possible to present the American action to the Arab world (nor probably to most of the Third World) as simply an assertion of a recognized international right."[36]

Arguments in the Security Council bore out Rostow's prediction when Third World delegates reacted viscerally to US efforts to orchestrate an official declaration on innocent passage. Importantly, the declaration also quickly became identified with rumors of American naval movements. The Indian ambassador berated "the repressive measures being adopted by colonial powers." The delegate from Cairo likened US naval policy to "nineteenth century of warship diplomacy." The State Department found the situation even less tractable because the nonaligned members in the Security Council that "Nasser might listen to," Yugoslavia and India, "had already declared for the UAR." Jamil Baroody, still the Saudi permanent representative in 1967, then labeled US policy "a new form of colonialism" in the General Assembly.[37]

Such statements – echoed by Baroody's Iraqi, Algerian, Libyan, and Kuwaiti counterparts in the General Assembly – grabbed the attention of oil-consuming nations and undermined support for the US-led declaration on innocent passage. Potential signatories from Western Europe and East Asia had begun "to believe that even such a declaration on their part would lead to serious discrimination against their Middle Eastern interests," the Pentagon reported. That failure confirmed for American policymakers not only the weakness of the legal argument but also the growing power of the Arab oil producers in international society. The Johnson administration's support of innocent passage had become bracketed into

---

[36] "Chairman of the Task Force: The Working Group on Economic Vulnerabilities," National Security Files, box 106, LBJL; Eugene Rostow, "Agenda for Control Group Meeting," June 1, 1967, National Security Files, box 106, LBJL.

[37] UNSC, Official Records, Twenty-Second Year: Supplement for April, May, and June 1967, S/7925; Intelligence Note, June 2, 1967, National Security Files, box 107, LBJL; UNGA, Official Records, Fifth Emergency Session, Verbatim Records of Meetings 17 June–18 September 1967, A/PV.1526.

a larger conversation about the growing importance of Arab oil production to the international economy.[38]

The United States could do nothing to unseal Aqaba. Meanwhile, Nasser
continued to tighten the link between the Arab–Israeli problem and the
question of resource ownership. A Kuwaiti correspondent asked him
about the use of "Arab oil as a weapon in battle" at a press conference
in Cairo on May 25, 1967. He responded with verve. "I believe that all
weapons must be used in this battle, whether by governments or by the
people," he said in a scarcely veiled warning of popular action to the
leaders of the oil-producing nations. The American ambassador in Cairo
reported afterwards that "any Arab leader who refused" to link oil supply
to the battle against Israel "would risk literal as well as political assassination." Failure to support Nasser, State Department intelligence analysts
agreed, would expose "every regime" in the Arab world to "the revenge
of the aroused masses."[39]

The threat of popular action was enough to bring the oil ministers of
the Arab nations to Baghdad on June 4. They linked the broader question
of sovereignty in the oil industry to maritime law and the dispute with
Israel. The oil producers would cut off any countries that "took part in
aggression against the sovereignty or territory or territorial waters of any
Arab state, with particular reference to the Gulf of Aqaba." They also
said that oil would be denied to all countries supporting Israel in case of
war.[40]

In a meeting with Nasser at the Kubeh Palace in Cairo two months later,
with the embargo still in effect, Yugoslav President Josef Brop Tito analyzed the situation. Oil also stood front and center in his mind. "We know
that the imperialists are very interested in the region of the Middle East
because they have very strong interests in oil," he said. Tito's handle
materialized at a critical juncture between the ongoing regional conflict,
the question of sovereign rights in the oil industry, and the Cold War in the
Middle East. For the US government, which would pay closer attention to
the international politics of oil control after 1967, the strategic position of

[38] Principle Deputy, June 2, 1967, National Security Files, box 107, LBJL.
[39] Davis memorandum, May 26, 1967, National Security Files, box 106, LBJL; CIA Intelli-
     gence Information Cable, June 4, 1967, National Security Files, box 106, LBJL; Nolte to
     DOS, June 2, 1967, National Security Files, box 106, LBJL; Intelligence Note, June 2,
     1967, National Security Files, box 107, LBJL.
[40] McCloy to Rusk, June 5, 1967, *FRUS 1964–68*, vol. XXXIV, doc. 229.

Arab production introduced a serious challenge to the vision of national security that had predominated since the end of World War II.[41]

All this was wrapped up with the ongoing American support of Israel. For many, this strengthened the bond between the Soviet Union and the Arab states. Soviet foreign minister Andrei Gromyko explained his understanding of the Middle East to Eastern European foreign ministers later that year. "Although it is still quite loose, an anti-imperialistic coalition of Arab states is emerging," he said. This was a pattern upon which Soviet officials hoped they could capitalize. The conclusion of the CIA was similar. The support of innocent passage in late May had the "obvious effect" of strengthening "the Soviet position as friend and protector of all Arabs against their imperialist foes," analysts concluded.[42]

The Cold War in the Middle East also turned on an understanding of the place of energy supplies, especially oil, in American national security thought. The industrial strength, economic productivity, and the generation of wealth in the West had been primary components of the American strategy of containment in the Cold War since the late 1940s, as discussed earlier. Energy-intensive industrial production was central to the process of postwar recovery and Cold War economic growth. The place of oil in that framework only grew in importance in the 1950s and 1960s. The industrialized member states of the Organization of Economic Cooperation and Development consumed 60 percent of the world's energy by 1966, for example. When the 1967 embargo began, the Middle East provided Western Europe with almost two-thirds and Japan with over 90 percent of total oil imports.[43]

The political-economic value of oil led to concern within the US government. The Department of the Interior concluded in May 1967 that, in the case of punitive Arab oil diplomacy, the extended loss of Kuwaiti and Saudi Arabian production would cause "serious disturbances" in the national and international economies. CIA analysts predicted that the impact of a full embargo would be severe. Within six months, "there would be a decline of perhaps twenty percent in the industrial

---

[41] Notes Regarding Yugoslav-Egyptian Talks, Tito Presidential Material Archives, August 11, 1967, Cold War in the Middle East, Digital Archive, CWIHP.

[42] "Report by the Bulgarian Foreign Minister on the Ministerial Meeting in Warsaw Regarding the Situation in the Middle East, 9–21 December 1967," History and Public Policy Program, Digital Archive, CWIHP; National Intelligence Estimate, "The Middle Eastern Crisis," May 26, 1967, National Security Files, box 106, LBJL.

[43] *Petroleum: Journal of the European Oil Industry* 29: 6 (1966), 258; *Petroleum: Journal of the European Oil Industry* 31: 1 (1968), 295.

consumption of primary energy, which would cause a sharp decline in production," one official fretted. In late June 1967, CIA Director John McCone told the National Security Council that oil could no longer be "dismissed as purely a commercial and vested interest" by policymakers. Such a perspective was obtuse, he believed. Oil reserves in Western Europe had dropped so quickly by then that, if production did not resume to pre-1967 levels immediately, the loss would pose "all kinds of trouble" for the international economy.[44]

The embargo called into question something more fundamental than the physical security of oil, then. It loomed over the postwar formula of high growth, high consumption, and low unemployment that had come to define American and, increasingly, global capitalist culture.

Evidence of the general problem was unmistakable in the most immediate area of concern for many American policymakers in June 1967: Vietnam. Middle East production provided 75 percent of monthly requirements in Southeast Asia, including all aviation fuel. In the case of an extended embargo, State Department officials believed, military supply would need to be rerouted from the Western hemisphere. Such a deviation would "probably require production controls and product allocations in the United States." As the specter of wartime-like rationing implied, the possible effects of the Arab embargo were not secondary concerns.[45]

To add to US concerns, the embargo threatened to do more than derail Southeast Asian supply lines or even undermine two decades of economic growth. Arab oil power also had an unsettling effect on relations within the North Atlantic alliance. Much to the chagrin of the Johnson administration, the French government began to encourage bilateral diplomacy between producing and consuming nations. American policymakers argued that bilateral deals would create nationalistic competition among consumers, undermine the price benefits of the privately controlled international oil market, and prevent a rapid solution to the potential supply

---

[44] Memorandum from the Director of the Office of Fuels and Energy, May 23, 1967, *FRUS 1964–68*, vol. XXXIV, doc. 228; Directorate of Intelligence, "Intelligence Memorandum: Impact on Western Europe and Japan of a Denial of Arab Oil, June 1967," National Security Files, box 107, LBJL; Memorandum of a Briefing by Director of Central Intelligence McCone, June 29, 1967, *FRUS 1964–68*, vol. XXXIV, doc. 252.

[45] "Official Report of Proceedings before the US Department of the Interior, March 31, 1965," White House Central Files, EX TA 6/Oil, box 19, LBJL; CSM-310-67, Appendix E, June 2, 1967, National Security Files, box 107, LBJL; "The Working Group on Economic Vulnerabilities," May 20, 1967, National Security Files, box 106, LBJL.

crisis. Instead, the United States believed the members of the NATO alliance should work directly with each other and with the private companies to overcome the embargo.

The dispute over the relative merits of Western cohesion came to a head at a June 1967 meeting of the OECD Oil Committee. On the table was an American proposal to declare the embargo an emergency. Doing so meant the Johnson administration could authorize a temporary suspension of US antitrust legislation, which in turn would allow American oil companies to work with each other and with European companies and governments to solve supply problems. The meeting began with a French objection to the "provocative" nature of a united consumer effort. Anything but a quiet Western front would further galvanize the oil producers, the French delegates argued. But after the French delegation withdrew, the other nations forged a plan to circumvent the embargo by taking advantage of the oil producers' difficulty of detecting shipments on the high seas.[46]

Still, American concern grew when West Germany leaned toward French policy in mid-June 1967. In a conversation with the German economic minister Karl Schiller, Eugene Rostow emphasized the necessity of NATO-member cooperation to minimize the embargo's impact. Schiller responded with "a lengthy diatribe" about American companies' domination of the German consumer market. He would follow French advice and initiate a national energy policy should it become necessary. Rostow responded that this idea was short-sighted. "Western cohesion would have a beneficial effect on conservative oil producers since it would strengthen their hand in arguing that Nasser was damaging Arab interests," he said. "On the other hand, if we do not have a common stand, we will be picked off one by one."[47]

French and German obduracy owed in part to initially favorable prospects for continued supply. But their attitudes toward cooperation began to change when leaders realized that exports might not promptly resume from Iraq, Libya, or Algeria. France at last acquiesced in the Oil Committee in July, enabling the emergency statement. The resultant cooperation between the industrial nations and the multinational oil

---

[46] Letter from Finlay to Moore, June 8. 1967, *FRUS 1964–68*, vol. XXXIV, doc. 234; Rusk to Udall, June 8, 1967, *FRUS 1964–68*, vol. XXXIV, doc. 235; DOS to the Embassy France, June 17, 1967, *FRUS 1964–68*, vol. XXXIV, doc. 245; Mission to OECD to DOS, June 12, 1967, *FRUS 1964–68*, vol. XXXIV, doc. 241.

[47] DOS to Embassy Germany, June 19, 1967, *FRUS 1964–68*, vol. XXXIV, doc. 246.

companies allowed the companies to meet the European shortage through increased Venezuelan, Iranian, and US exports.[48]

Arab oil also filled the shortage. The nations described in the State Department as "conservative," "moderate," or "pro-American" only grudgingly had been dragooned into collaboration by Nasser. In Saudi Arabia, for example, King Faisal faced a dilemma. His smoldering abhorrence of Nasserism, owing largely to Nasser's stoking of conflict in South Arabia, was well-known. Still, the State Department reported that "at present he knows he must . . . live down the accusation of being a Western stooge." CIA operative Kermit Roosevelt, Jr. organized a lunch between an NSC official and Saudi Prince Mohammed in late May 1967. "Where Israel is involved, no Arab government has any choice but to rally to the common cause," the prince explained. In the case of war, Saudi Arabia would take precautionary measures to deprive "extremists" of a reason for sabotage, including "closing oil installations indefinitely."[49]

But this was a public policy, designed for public consumption. When Ahmed Zaki Yamani began working to circumvent the embargo in the first week of June, officials from Kuwait and Libya joined him. Two days after the embargo began, the Kuwaiti government approached the US ambassador about secretly contravening the embargo by using the "bedu chicanery" of changing tanker manifests. In Libya, King Idris initially told the US ambassador that, although the oil stoppage was regrettable, he needed to maintain it "for appearances' sake." But by late July, his government also was breaking the embargo through direct exports to West Germany and indirect shipments via Canada and Ireland to the United States and the United Kingdom. Kuwaiti and Libyan diplomats also supported Yamani in his arguments to the Iraqis that the loss of oil receipts had become a serious problem. The nations

---

[48] Ethan Kapstein, *The Insecure Alliance: Energy Crises and Western Politics since 1944* (Oxford University Press, 1990), 146–8; Embassy France to DOS, June 27, 1967, *FRUS 1964–68*, vol. XXXIV, doc. 250; Mission to OECD to DOS, June 30, 1967, *FRUS 1964–68*, vol. XXXIV, doc. 254; Mission to OECD to DOS, July 21, 1967, *FRUS 1964–68*, vol. XXXIV, doc. 259. On Iranian and Venezuelan policy, see: DOS to Embassy Iran, August 23, 1967, *FRUS 1964–68*, vol. XII, doc. 229; Embassy Venezuela to DOS, June 7, 1967, *FRUS 1964–68*, vol. XXXI, doc. 542; Memorandum from Rostow to Johnson, July 28, 1967, *FRUS 1964–68*, vol. XXXI, doc. 543.

[49] "The Working Group on Economic Vulnerabilities," National Security Files, box 106, LBJL; Saunders, "Memorandum for the Record," May 31, 1967, National Security Files, box 106, LBJL.

announced in July 1967 that the embargo had cost Kuwait approximately £1 million and Libya $1.5 million per day.[50]

The Arab heads of state met in Khartoum on August 29, 1967. It was evident by this time that the embargo was not functional. The Khartoum communiqué is most famous for Nasser's promise to remove Egyptian troops from Yemen and its "three no's" – no peace, no recognition, and no negotiation with Israel. But the meeting had other consequences too. Saudi Arabia, Libya, and Kuwait would pay approximately $378 million a year of "reconstruction aid" to Egypt and Jordan, payments that would extend into the following decade and soon become a central means of financial support for Palestinian "front-line" organizations. In return, the producers received approval to resume full oil shipments to the West without accusations of betrayal. All three nations openly resumed full production the same morning the resolution was adopted.[51]

By the fall of 1967, the possibility of a unified policy among the Arab oil producers had caused some consternation among Western policymakers. The basic assumptions of sovereign rights, which had become pervasive on the global periphery, were part of that story. The Khartoum communiqué, for example, employed the program's language: "Arab oil ... is an Arab asset which can be put to use in the service of Arab aims." Likewise, the Aqaba crisis recast international maritime law and, as policy options for the United States narrowed, the embargo aroused fears about the potential of national oil control to subvert international economic stability and traditional US national security strategies.[52]

---

[50] CIA Intelligence Information Cable, June 8, 1967, National Security Files, box 107, LBJL; Embassy Kuwait to DOS, June 10, 1967, *FRUS 1964–68*, vol. XXXIV, doc. 238; Telegram 212867 to Tripoli, June 20, 1967, *FRUS 1964–68*, vol. XXXIV, doc. 247; Telegram 568 from Tripoli, August 10, 1967, RG 59, Central Foreign Policy File, 1967–69, PET 17–1 LIBYA, NARA, cited in *FRUS 1964–68*, vol. XXXIV, doc. 263. See also: DOS to Embassy Libya, June 16, 1967, *FRUS 1964–68*, vol. XXXIV, doc. 244; Embassy Libya to DOS, June 30, 1967, *FRUS 1964–68*, vol. XXXIV, doc. 253. Here it is better to report each earnings loss as reported by the governments, given instability in the currency rates between May and November 1967. See: Michael Bordo, Michael Oliver, and Ronald MacDonald, "Sterling in Crisis: 1964–1967," *NBER Working Paper Series* 14657 (January 2009), 8–10.

[51] Embassy Saudi Arabia to DOS, *FRUS 1964–68*, vol. XXI, doc. 300; Intelligence Note from Hughes to Rusk, September 1, 1967, *FRUS 1964–68*, vol. XXI, doc. 458; National Intelligence Estimate, "The Outlook on Saudi Arabia," April 7, 1970, *FRUS 1969–76*, vol. XXIV, doc. 14; Telegram 941 from Tripoli, September 5, 1967, RG 59, Central Foreign Policy File, 1967–69, PET 17–1 ARAB, NARA, cited in *FRUS*, vol. XXXIV, doc. 263.

[52] Kapstein, *The Insecure Alliance*, 125.

But for all the ink spilled on the embargo, its outcome made the concerns seem overhyped. Robert Dunlop, the president of Sun Oil Company and sometimes government consultant, wrote a morality tale to this effect in *Oil* magazine. "A friend" had embarked on that classic American vacation, the road trip, in the summer of 1967 and had been blissfully unaware of the embargo throughout his 2000-mile drive. "It surely did not occur to him that shortly after he started his trip, the most massive disruption of Free World petroleum supplies in history occurred," Dunlop wrote. More to the point, "his fellow-Americans, going about their normal business at work or at play, were untouched too."[53]

Other Western policymakers and intellectuals also wrote the Arab embargo off as sophistry. Richard Nixon would restate the most common stereotype three years later: "The Arab oil producers cannot drink their oil." This was the ultimate refinement of the common dismissal of Arab oil power. It was also a statement about the weakness of collective solidarity among the oil producers. In other words, the 1967 Arab oil embargo was a failure not only in the immediate sense that it did not affect American support of Israel. It was also a failure in collective action. Sovereign rights, then, was a formula for fear as much as faith: faith in a reading of history and a vision of international justice, trumped in this case by fear that the absence of cohesion would prevent anything remotely approaching economic emancipation or even effective economic diplomacy.[54]

Comments from anticolonial oil elites reinforced the cumulative weight of that judgment. The Sixth Arab Petroleum Congress, for example, officially supported the "right of the Arab people of Palestine to return freely and honorably to their usurped homeland" in 1967, and the delegates even passed a resolution that "stressed the importance of oil in the battle for Palestine." In its first official publication in 1968, the OPEC Secretariat tied together the resolutions of the congress, the June 4 meeting of the Arab producers in Baghdad, and the Khartoum resolutions. Together, the statements of mutual support were a new "stage in the thinking of the Arab Countries with regard to the use of their most important resource as a weapon for the protection of their national interest."[55]

---

[53] Robert G. Dunlop, "The Inside Story," *Oil* 28: 3 (April 1968), 7.
[54] Memorandum of Conversation, June 5, 1970, *FRUS 1969–76*, vol. XXIV, doc. 23.
[55] "Sixth Arab Petroleum Congress," *SDIPI 1967*, OIC; Introduction to Chapter 5, *SDIPI 1967*, OIC.

But the course plotted was not the one followed. At the Sixth Arab Petroleum Congress, other Arab oil ministers hedged uncomfortably when Iraq espoused its hard line. OPEC then postponed its summer ministerial summit, planned for June, until September, to avoid meeting during the embargo. At the September 1967 meeting, the oil elites preferred to ignore the embargo altogether. Instead, they focused on demands by Libya and Iraq that the oil companies increase prices "as justified by prevailing economic conditions in the international oil industry."[56]

This was in part because oil elites from the gradualist nations and the functionaries of OPEC felt that a heavy emphasis on what they considered the uniquely Arab problem of Palestine would be counterproductive for the group of the whole. This reflected a strain of conservatism within the organization. Francisco Parra, for example, had argued at the Fifth Arab Petroleum Congress in 1965 that, although differences on tactics separated the more "militant" elites from other members of the organization, the "rightness of its cause" was a common denominator. Yet he also said the oil producers needed to play a "patient" role that reflected the expertise of its elites. Only in this way could the organization "symbolize the common cause of the oil-exporting nations" and represent "their legitimate interests." He described the 1967 Arab oil embargo more pointedly in retrospect: The Six-Day War had "simply washed over OPEC as though nothing had happened." This was a note of relief. Indeed, he and others were thankful that OPEC had not "allowed itself to be dragged into the Arab–Israeli conflict" because they believed such a contentious issue would likely split the organization apart.[57]

Parra may have been right. But the failure of the Arab embargo also reinforced the oil producers' international reputation as ineffective actors, renowned above all for their mutual mistrust. That conclusion led to others, namely that the conscious sense of disappointment in late 1967 worked to further open the fissure between the abstract objective of economic emancipation and the reality of limited sovereignty. At a deeper level, then, the failure of the embargo was another reminder that sovereignty was in many ways ill-adjusted to be an effective instrument of anticolonial elites' economic demands.

Even Parra later felt that "OPEC accomplished little during its early years." Sure, he searched for a silver lining: the royalty expensing

[56] "Resolutions of the Thirteenth Conference," *SDIPI* 1967, OIC.
[57] "OPEC and the Principle of Negotiation," *SFAPC*; Francisco Parra, *Oil Politics: A Modern History of Petroleum* (London: I. B. Tauris, 2004), 107.

negotiations had at least brought in extra income, and the companies had not lowered prices since 1960. But given the revolutionary bent of anticolonial law and economics, the *ennui* was off. "The trouble was, it didn't *feel* good," he wrote. "The protracted negotiations and the tiny concessions, tea spooned out by the companies, cent by cent, did not smack of victory to the member countries. No one at this point was proud of OPEC."[58]

But even if the situation didn't feel good, even if Arabs couldn't drink their oil, sovereign rights still remained pervasive for a number of anticolonial elites. The program grew in strength in the mid-1960s with a tendency toward self-perpetuation. This is evident in the work of a number of young Arab lawyers, including two of the most analytically rigorous: Muhammad Mughraby and Mohammed Bedjaoui.

Mughraby was a Lebanese lawyer whose Columbia University dissertation was published in English by the same Beirut press – managed by the editors of the *Middle East Economic Survey*, Ian Seymour and Fuad Itayim – that printed books by Simon Siksek and Ashraf Lufti. When Mughraby left Beirut to attend Columbia University Law School in 1962, he was drawn to the seminars of Philip Jessup and Wolfgang Friedmann, both of whom had already begun to examine the stirrings of what the first called "transnational law."[59]

By the time Mughraby matriculated, the two professors had dedicated their careers to testing the traditional concepts of international law against the new realities of the decolonizing world. Friedmann had concluded that the existing rules of international law had been "overwhelmingly developed by the nations that today are in the position of the 'haves.'"[60] Jessup, a well-known legal expert since the 1930s, agreed. He took great issue with the assertions by Hans Morgenthau, George

---

[58] Parra, *Oil Politics*, 107.

[59] Mughraby, *Permanent Sovereignty over Oil Resources*, xv–xvi. Itayim would later describe the "self-styled defenders of Western civilization" as maintaining an "arrogance matched only by their duplicity." See: Faud Itayim, "Arab Oil – The Political Dimension, *Journal of Palestine Studies* 3: 2 (Winter 1974), 84. On "transnational law," see: Philip C. Jessup, *Transnational Law* (New Haven, CT: Yale University Press, 1956). For new historical interpretations, see: Arnulf Becker Lorca, "Sovereignty Beyond the West: The End of Classical International Law," *Journal of the History of International Law* 13: 1 (2011), 7–73; Benjamin Coates, *Transatlantic Advocates: American International Law and US Foreign Relations* (PhD Thesis, Columbia University, 2011), 93–9.

[60] Wolfgang Friedmann, " The Position of Underdeveloped Countries and the Universality of International Law," *Columbia Journal of Transnational Law* (1963), 76– 86.

Kennan, and others that the new rules put forward at the United Nations and elsewhere formed "a primitive type of law resembling the kind ... that prevails in certain preliterate societies." Jessup believed it was international law before decolonization that was "provincial." By the early 1960s, he wrote, it faced a collective countercheck by the "global membership" of the "international community."[61]

Mughraby built on the two men's basic ideas, but in his final analysis mostly drew from the global membership to which Jessup referred. The Latin American experience was again crucial, as Mughraby's interest in the work of Jorge Castañeda reveals. Castañeda, who studied law at the National Autonomous University of Mexico in the 1940s, joined the Mexican foreign service in 1950. In 1955 he won a grant from the Carnegie Endowment for International Peace to study Mexico's UN policy. Like other elites from nations that had long been independent, his study found the rise of decolonization crucial to understanding new trends in international politics: the "common goals of the small powers" were inseparable from the greater "colonial problem," he wrote. The essential truth that linked the nations together was "the preservation of their independence in the face of the external influences which prevent self-determination." For this reason, the United Nations had passed resolutions on permanent sovereignty and the related principles of nonintervention and domestic jurisdiction. That "intensified rhythm," for Castañeda, represented "a new stage in the history of movements for national freedom."[62]

Castañeda was invited to join the UN International Law Commission in 1959, where he worked with Oscar Schachter and Rahman Pazhwak. He summarized his experience for a Mexican audience the next year. Through the Commission, the United Nations had moved past its "traditional" function of affirming treaties into the more important one of "the

---

[61] Philip C. Jessup, *The Use of International Law* (Thomas M. Cooley Lectures, University of Michigan Law School, 1959), 1, 4, 9–10, 20–2.

[62] Mughraby, *Permanent Sovereignty*, 170–201; Jorge Castañeda, *Mexico and the United Nations* (New York: Manhattan Publishing Company, 1958), 4, 10–11, 14, 62–8, 197–8. See also: Wolfgang Friedmann, *The Changing Structure of International Law* (New York: Columbia University Press, 1962); Jorge Castañeda, "The Underdeveloped Nations and the Development of International Law," *International Organization* 38 (1961); and, earlier still, Norman Bentwich, et. al., *Justice and Equity in the International Sphere* (London: New Commonwealth Institute, 1936). Bentwich, a noted expert on colonialism and international law, collaborated with the young William Arthur Lewis in 1942. See: Rita Hinden, William Arthur Lewis, Norman De Mattos Bentwich, and A. Creech Jones, *Freedom for Colonial Peoples* (London: National Peace Council, 1942).

creation of international law." This was a natural development because inequality had driven discrimination in terms of the application of legal rights in the imperial era, he said. Before decolonization, international law had been created "not only behind the backs of the small states, but also against them." It was precisely because the new nations had been "passive objects" of international law that they began to "rebel against its application." The momentum of that rebellion proved that old international laws had begun to "decay." Here, Castañeda used the adjective *periclitada*. By invoking Thucydides' famous interpretation that the death of Pericles triggered a fast demise of Athenian grandeur, he suggested a rapid fall after a durable apogee.[63]

Mughraby found that interpretation appealing, and his 1966 doctoral thesis applied the "newly-emerging branch" of international law, in particular the subfield of permanent sovereignty, to the oil industry. The efforts in the United Nations had led anticolonial legal thought to "express itself in the form of the right of permanent sovereignty over natural resources," Mughraby wrote. The concept had made an indelible scratch on his mind and furnished the lens through which he would interpret the reams of material published on the oil industry since Salman conducted his first surveys after Bandung. The 1964 founding of the Conference on Trade and Development, the 1962 report of the UN Commission on Permanent Sovereignty, and the arguments at the UN committees in 1952 and 1956 had transferred the discussion of decolonization from a political to an economic plane, he believed. A new phrase – "economic sovereignty" – meant that decolonization and the push for justice in global capitalism "were so interrelated" to many elites "that they conceived of them as one."[64]

Mughraby was indebted to Raúl Prebisch as well. In fact, he built his argument for the new international law of national oil control on assumptions that began with unequal exchange. That concept had remarkable purchase, he wrote, because it captured a sort of ultimate validity in its dismissal of comparative advantage for raw material producers. A multitude of studies proved Ricardo's theory "inadequate and unrealistic," he wrote. "Underdeveloped countries are increasingly being faced with disadvantageous terms of trade." Like comparative advantage on the intellectual plane, this was a material inheritance of the colonial era.

[63] Oscar Schachter, "Questions of Treaty Reservations at the 1959 General Assembly," *AJIL* 54: 2 (April 1960), 374, 377; Jorge Castañeda, "Naciones Unidas y Derecho Internacional," *Foro Internacional* 1: 2 (October–December 1960), 223–6.
[64] Mughraby, *Permanent Sovereignty*, 13–14, 17, 20–6, 162.

Prebisch's doctrine thus captured the great gap between "the two classes of nations, the rich and the poor."[65]

Mughraby then made explicit a point many of his counterparts assumed but left unsaid. The oil companies' failure to recognize the national right to revise contracts was akin to maintaining the validity of colonialism. He continued: sovereignty was inherent to human existence peoples and, therefore, nations could not lose it during their time under colonial rule. That innate human quality had never been absent, just suppressed. The return of sovereignty thus required national leaders to reexamine any agreements made while under colonial or otherwise unequal status. The poor nations sought to "reestablish [their] economic equality ... in the community of nations," he wrote. To do so meant the end of "generally old and inequitable agreements," including the oil concessions.[66]

The growing alliance that cohered around sovereign rights mattered more and more to greater and greater numbers of anticolonial elites. Joining Mughraby was the better known Algerian lawyer, Mohammed Bedjaoui, who picked up the sovereign rights argument in 1968. He began his career in international law a decade earlier, when his doctoral dissertation at the French *Centre National de la Recherche Scientifique* won the annual Carnegie Endowment competition for best European manuscript. In it, he identified the dilemma between nationalism and internationalism through an analysis of the experiences of "international officials" since World War II, most pointedly the belittling and harassment of UN officials during the American Red Scare. For the technocratic utopia of world government to have any bearing, international civil servants needed to become a class unto themselves.[67]

But if Bedjaoui was an internationalist, he was also a nationalist. Indeed, like most anticolonial elites, he saw nationalism and internationalism as complementary. He left Paris soon after receiving his award to join the Algerian revolution. He published his next book, *Law and the Algerian Revolution*, three years later. "Written in the midst of action, for action," the book scuttled his previous tone of scholarly detachment. At the base of Bedjaoui's well-received analysis stood a deceptively simple

---

[65] Mughraby, *Permanent Sovereignty*, 3–6, 13.
[66] Mughraby, *Permanent Sovereignty*, 15, 39.
[67] Mohammed Bedjaoui, *Fonction Publique Internationale et Influences Nationales*, Dotation Carnegie pour la Paix Internationale, Centre Européen (Paris: A. Pedone, 1958). On Bedhaoui, see: Umut Özsu, "In the Interests of Mankind as a Whole: Mohammed Bedjaoui's New International Economic Order," *Humanity: An International Journal of Human Rights, Humanitarianism, and Development* 6: 1 (2015): 129–143.

argument about decolonization and international law. "A new system of law, adapted to the needs of an inexorable process of decolonization, has sprung up in the minds of the people and become a fact through the actions of their leaders," Bedjaoui wrote. This new international law included the doctrine of permanent sovereignty. Because of the work of the UN delegates, "free disposal of their mineral resources" was the goal of revolutionary governments everywhere.[68]

Serious scholarship had become a form of advocacy for Bedjaoui. In 1968, the International Law Commission of the United Nations hired him to update the work of Oscar Schachter's Permanent Sovereignty Commission. His first report emphasized the need to continue "the progressive development of international law" to take into consideration "the phenomenon of decolonization." Decolonization was not a spent force, Bedjaoui theorized. If emancipation constituted "a break in continuity" and decolonization dissolved traditional relationships "based on domination," then the components of the former order that reflected that hierarchy also should be eliminated. This was especially true for relations in the international economy, because "*the marks of domination are less quickly erased from economic than from political relations.*" For Bedjaoui, that domination meant that the UN should continue to give priority to "the new concept of the sovereignty of States over their natural wealth."[69]

The Algerian jurist went into greater detail on the relationship between decolonization, international law, and the international economy in his second report. Decolonization was an important historical rupture because it created "a completely different context" for world affairs. A set of "fundamental movements sweeping the world" had gradually destroyed certain types of relationships based on subordination, including those that existed within international capitalism and international law. Building on the insights of the French economist François Perroux and his unified theory of wealth, power, and "poles of development," Bedjaoui held that the "reversing function" of decolonization did more than destroy the "colonial compact." It also presented an opportunity to create new egalitarian structures. Within that framework of opportunity, foremost among the legal and economic consequences to the equality of states was "the right

---

[68] Mohammed Bedjaoui, *Law and the Algerian Revolution* (Brussels: International Association of Democratic Lawyers, 1962), 3–11, 240.

[69] Mohammed Bedjaoui, "First Report on Succession of States in Respect of Rights and Duties Resulting from Sources Other Than Treaties" (1968), UNGA, Official Records, International Law Commission, 12–3, 20–4, 32–42, 60, emphasis in original.

FIGURE 4.2 Mohammed Bedjaoui at the Twenty-Seventh Session of the International Law Commission, May 5, 1975. Bedjaoui is the third person to the right. To his left are Alfredo Martinez-Moreno, the Rapporteur of the Drafting Committee and Robert Quentin-Baxter, the committee chairman.
Source: UN Photo. Courtesy of the United Nations Photo Library, Photo No. 178542.

of peoples to dispose of their natural resources." That right was not just limited to the times, he continued, but was part of a universal struggle. Decolonization had opened, on a larger scale than ever before, a struggle "as old as the world, constantly occurring and reoccurring," he wrote. That repeating struggle inevitably occurred after every upheaval between the old structures, which resisted change with waning strength, and new structures, which asserted themselves with increasing vigor.[70]

Bedjaoui also noted that the rise of sovereign rights did not exist in a vacuum –"any more than it [came] from outer space to lodge in a corner of the earth." The fact was that new states could not disengage entirely from preexisting situations, what he called "the flagrant iniquities" of the

---

[70] Mohammed Bedjaoui, "Second Report on Succession of States in Respect of Matters Other Than Treaties; Economic and Financial Acquired Rights" (1969), UNGA, Official Records, International Law Commission, A/CN.4/216, 8–11, 56–8.

imperial past. This made even more pressing the establishment of international laws protecting nations' "changes in sovereignty." The UN resolutions on permanent sovereignty and the work of groups such as OPEC and the UN Conference on Trade and Development thus formed something that was both a new international law and much more: "a charter of combat of the poor against the rich." If sovereignty were an "absolute, inalienable, and permanent right," it followed that the continuity of contracts signed in the distinct, imperial era were "more and more out of place in the contemporary age."[71]

Muhammad Mughraby agreed. As he saw it, the debate was thus no longer about whether there was cause for change. The "manifestos of economic nationalism in [a] more legalistic form" had changed the base line of the crucial question of sovereignty. "Nobody denied the right of permanent sovereignty. Sovereignty itself is of a permanent nature," he wrote.[72]

Noun and adjective carried freight in that reading. Permanent sovereignty symbolized the elites' determination to redefine decolonization toward a reading that used international law to challenge the exploitative nature of the international economy. Mughraby's and Bedjaoui's works were at the same time ones of original interpretation and of emulation. Anticolonial elites produced innumerable speeches, pamphlets, articles, reports, theses, and books on this and related topics in the mid-1960s. There is no want of material for historians, and the two lawyers took up economic and legal threads that were entangled in many minds. They were products of an ambitious group effort to shape the possibilities and rights of decolonization.

Their work was also a testament to the fact that the program for sovereign rights had become a powerful intellectual and political structure, simultaneously a construct of the culture of decolonization *and* a major tenet of postwar oil politics. The oil elites' desire to change the terms of the old concessions presented "a prime example of the striving of developing countries to achieve economic sovereignty," Mughraby wrote. OPEC had placed the issue of permanent sovereignty "on a transnational level ... by pooling the strength of individually weak oil producing countries." But in the end Mughraby was forced to admit that his work was more about the recent development of a new international law than it

---

[71] Bedjaoui, "Second Report," UNGA, Official Records, International Law Commission, A/CN.4/216, 16–17, 59–60, emphasis in original.
[72] Mughraby, *Permanent Sovereignty*, 35–8, 119.

was about the way that law could change international society. The success of the oil producers depended too much on collective action – "power from without," as he styled it.[73]

On that point, both Mughraby and Bedjaoui fretted that the oil producers were forced into what Mughraby called a "middle-of-the-road" position. Here they ran into the same problem of practice that bedeviled sovereign rights advocates in the oil industry, the problem that enraged Tariki and put Parra on the defensive: in a way, the arguments for economic emancipation through international law reiterated the problem rather than solved it. As a joint endeavor to resolve disputes about the direction of wealth and power in international society, sovereign rights had always been shot through with profound ambivalences that rendered it unstable and contradictory in practice. The oil producers had not responded with "power from without." Instead, their experience exposed a number of weaknesses from within.[74]

Nevertheless, building on the identification of the fundamental problem and the potential solution in the 1950s, the actions of the second decade of decolonization assumed vast importance for oil elites. The vision of international law as a driving force of producer empowerment would continue to resonate, and individual OPEC members would continue to flirt with the idea of power from without. As they did so, oil politics became a site of opportunity for the insurrectionists. Once adopted, their beliefs could not be easily dispelled.

The early failures of the oil elites, from that perspective, reveal that sovereign rights and the economic culture of decolonization incubated in, even if it remained at the margins of, the oil marketplace. And if elites faced a world changing in ways that they could neither direct nor predict in the late 1960s, a number of factors began to shift in their favor.

---

[73] Mughraby, *Permanent Sovereignty*, 31–45.

[74] For a similar argument about international law and human rights, see: Elizabeth Borgwardt, *A New Deal for the World: America's Vision for Human Rights* (Cambridge, MA: Belknap Press, 2005), 318n32. Perhaps this is a universal truth, best expressed by the historian Arthur Lovejoy when he said that human life most often is characterized by hopeful attempts to create harmonious agreement where no basis for accord exists. See: *The Great Chain of Being: The History of an Idea* (Cambridge, MA: Harvard University Press, 1936), 183–207.

5

Nationalist Heroes

Imperial Withdrawal, the Cold War, and Oil Control, 1967–1970

In Iran's dealings with the Western oil consortium, the Shah has cultivated an image of a nationalist hero fighting against foreign exploitation. He has striven to succeed the late Mossadegh in that role.[1]
State Department Report, 1968

In accordance with principles established by the United Nations, the companies cannot ... prevent exploitation of Iran's natural resources.[2]
The Shah of Iran, 1970

On October 31, 1967, US ambassador Armin Meyer joined the Shah of Iran, Mohamed Reza Pahlavi, in the royal box for a concert of the Los Angeles Philharmonic at the new Roudaki Hall performing arts complex in Tehran. Designed with the *fin-de-siècle* opulence of Vienna in mind and pitched as the pinnacle of the accomplishments of Iranian modernization, Roudaki Hall had been inaugurated just days before on the occasion of the Shah's elaborate self-coronation as emperor. At intermission Meyer mentioned the Iranian windfall from the Arab oil embargo and noted in particular "how poorly Iraq has been doing as a result of its excesses." Unlike the gradualist producers, Iraq had not recommenced supply to its prewar markets. Furthermore, the government was engaged in a bitter struggle with its long-time concessionaire, the Iraq Petroleum Company. The Shah responded that the Iraqis were "totally irrational." Their

---

[1] Research Memorandum, Hughes to Rusk, "The Shah of Iran as a Nationalist," March 27, 1968, *FRUS 1964–68*, vol. XXII, doc. 274.
[2] Memorandum of Conversation, "Iranian Oil Matters," April 1, 1969, National Security Files, box 601, LBJL.

misdirected nationalism was taking "the poor Iraqi people down the same catastrophic road as Mossadegh."[3]

But when the Shah summoned up the former Iranian prime minister to Meyer again two months later, he meant to leave an entirely different impression. He had just learned that the oil companies that operated the Iran Consortium, four of which were also party to the Aramco concession in Saudi Arabia, had maintained secret agreements since the early 1950s to limit Iranian and Saudi production. He used such terms as "robbery, thieves, and some unprintable epithets" to describe the companies to Meyer, who called the meeting as "the most unpleasant on my tour here." "If the companies wanted war, they could have it," the Shah fumed. "This time it would not be with a Mossadegh, but with a united Iran behind the Shah himself."[4]

Why did the Shah turn to Mossadegh, who had died months earlier after fourteen years under house arrest, first as a punching bag and then to take on his mantle? Conjuring him up was a polemical contrivance, to be sure, and the Shah's admixture of scorn and grudging admiration suggests a slew of Freudian pathologies. But it is also unremarkable that he turned to Mossadegh as a benchmark, because Mossadegh had come to mean many things to many people since 1951. For most, his was a cautionary tale. Oil elites had found permanent sovereignty a clumsy policy instrument and, indeed, the recurrent theme of undrinkable oil pinpointed a fray in the practice of sovereign rights and cast doubt on the internationalist ethos that supported the program. But the example of Mossadegh also looked to the recent past as a significant overture to what many had begun to describe as a new era for the oil industry. When the Shah claimed he would improve upon the past, he also worked consciously within the nationalist sentiment and language of the former prime minister. His statement assumed certain beliefs had persisted and had even increased their purchase.

In this he came closer to those insurrectionists who viewed Mossadegh as a martyr to a cause. In fact, the revelation of the secret company agreements markedly changed the tone of the annual revenue negotiations between Iran and the oil consortium, and the Shah aggressively pressed the companies for more revenue in 1968 and after. As he became more

---

[3] Telegram, AmEmbassy Iran to DOS, October 31, 1967, *FRUS 1964–68*, vol. XXII, doc. 213.
[4] Telegram, Amembassy Iran to SecState, December 26, 1967, *FRUS 1964–68*, vol. XXII, doc. 255.

truculent, he became more successful. And as he became more successful, he increasingly couched his accomplishments in the internationalist program of sovereign rights. The Shah thus built on the same questions of decolonization and statehood that anticolonial elites had incorporated into their intellectual and political programs. "In Iran's dealings with the Western oil consortium, the Shah has cultivated an image of a nationalist hero fighting against foreign exploitation," one State Department official reported soon after. "He has striven to succeed the late Mossadegh in that role."[5]

If the companies did not acquiesce to increased production, the Shah said again and again in 1968 and 1969, he would push through national legislation to take control of oil production. When threatening to legislate oil control, the Shah told Meyer that Iraq had "long since found companies submissive to such measures." Like the invocations of Mossadegh, this reappraisal of Iraqi policy is telling. In a story of closing margins between gradualists and insurrectionists, elites of all stripes came together to depict the old oil concessions as an affront to their sovereignty, a right that was increasingly held to be sacrosanct. This conviction shaped the Shah's and others' interpretation of the pivotal events of the era and the language in which they expressed aspirations for redistributive justice.[6]

The international experience of decolonization was carved into the collective politics of sovereign rights. Other international factors also influenced Iran's oil policy and point to the ways that the growing legitimacy of sovereign rights formed its context. In addition to explaining the history of closing margins among the most influential oil elites, this chapter and those that follow deal with sovereign rights and US diplomacy together, in large part because the Cold War helped to abet the convergence toward the economic culture of decolonization. Of crucial importance was the British announcement in January 1968 that it would decolonize the Trucial States and remove the British Navy from the Persian Gulf by 1971. This led the administrations of Lyndon Johnson and Richard Nixon to a policy of building up Iranian power and encouraging Iranian–Saudi cooperation. This in turn granted the Shah a new strategic advantage, which he used as a lever in the annual earnings

---

[5] Research Memorandum, Hughes to Rusk, "The Shah of Iran as a Nationalist," March 27, 1968, *FRUS 1964–68*, vol. XXII, doc. 274.

[6] Solomon to Rostow, "Status of Iranian-Consortium Negotiations," December 11, 1967, *FRUS 1964–68*, vol. XXII, doc. 252.

negotiations with the multinational oil companies. Nixon himself intervened on behalf of Iran in those negotiations in early 1970, a decision that further strengthened the sovereign rights program.

To understand those complex series of events, the intersection of anticolonial thought and geopolitics, and the meaning of Nixon's decision, it helps to remember that sovereign rights was more mainstream than radical by the late 1960s. Anticolonial elites persisted in their assumption that international law could open the door to the collective action that could transform the trade relationships they thought characterized global capitalism. It was within that larger circle that smaller ones nested. The meetings of the regional economic commissions of the United Nations in September 1967, a month after the Arab summit in Khartoum, provide an understanding of that context.

For the ministerial meeting of the UN Economic Commission for Asia and the Far East, delegates from forty nations flew into Bangkok. The conference presented Thai Minister of Foreign Affairs Thanat Khoman, who *Time* magazine had described as "a staunch, cheerleading, on-the-field friend" of the United States, a chance to buoy his Third World credentials. To do so, he joined the other delegates in emphasizing the "deep-seated problems" of colonial continuity in the international economy and "the basic identity of interests and problems of the developing countries of various regimes," including the Asians' counterparts in "the developing countries of Africa and Latin America."[7]

In a coordinated effort, Latin American officials met in Bogota the same weekend. They also discussed the unfairness of the international economy and the need for higher foreign earnings for commodity producers. Two weeks later in Algiers, ministers from the member states of the Organization of African Unity and the Economic Commission for Africa also adopted a series of resolutions "on the need for a reform of the international commodity trade system in favor of the exports of developing countries." To prevent the deterioration of the terms of trade, they suggested the formulation of "an objective basis of remunerative prices for primary commodities."[8]

---

[7] "Cheers from a Cheerleader," *Time* 85: 21 (1965), 36; Bangkok Declaration by the Asian Group of the Group of 77, September 27, 1967, *NIEO: SD*, vol. I.

[8] Charter of Tequendama, Adopted at the Special Committee on Latin American Coordination, Bogota, September 29, 1967, *NIEO: SD*, vol. I; African Declaration of Algiers, October 15, 1967, *NIEO: SD*, vol. I.

The regional economic summits were a carefully choreographed exercise prepared to "conceive a common course of action" on the problem of unequal exchange. The Asian and Latin American ministers repaired from their antipodes to join the Africans in Algiers. After noting the similarities of their economic experience and their groups' declarations, the co-denominationalists invoked the morality of economic liberation. "The lot of more than a billion people of the developing world continues to deteriorate as a result of the trends in international economic relations," they wrote. They also gave greater urgency to their desire to move from the stage of deliberation to that of action. The delegates discussed a number of policies, including programs of diversification, industrialization, trade liberalization, and market preference. At the root of each resided the belief that the producers of raw materials should "cooperate among themselves in order to defend and improve their terms of trade."[9]

Permanent sovereignty and unequal exchange now passed as axiomatic truths. Elites that worked for OPEC – including the Iraqi director of its Legal Department, Hasan Zakariya – were caught up in that trend. Like other anticolonial jurists, Zakariya was educated in the West. Like others, his academic work took on the basic questions of inequality and power. His doctoral thesis at Harvard examined the fall of "sovereign immunity" in the national tort law of the United States, Great Britain, and France. He argued that sovereign immunity had survived into the twentieth century in spite of the disappearance of its subject matter: the royal ruler. The indivisible and absolute sovereignty of kings, which should have fallen to the wayside with "the stricken head of Louis the 18th," had been passed on to the national state. Wronged citizens thus had little recourse when the state acted against their property, he wrote. Yet power slowly had begun to shift toward the citizenry in the early twentieth century. This forced all three Western governments to begin "a constant adaptation of the law to the rising needs of the community."[10]

The cognitive overlap between this and the anticolonial oil elites' arguments for "changing circumstances" is striking. For Zakariya, the

---

[9] Charter of Algiers, Adopted at the Ministerial Meeting of the Group of 77, October 24, 1967, *NIEO: SD*, vol. I; Comparison of the African Declaration of Algiers, the Bangkok Declaration, the Charter of Tequendama, and the reference document of the Coordinating Committee of the Group of 77, October 1967, UN, Official Records, DOC MM.77/I/10 and Corr. 1.

[10] Hasan S. Zakariyya, "State Liability in Tort: A Comparative Study of the Development of Its Theory and Practice in the Anglo-American and French Laws," S.J.D. Thesis, Harvard Law School (1954), 44–5, 100–1.

historical shift toward legal adaption to contemporary needs proved that law was a more successful arbiter of justice when the "boundary" between law and society became more permeable. He concluded that law left "in a somewhat shifting and fluid form" was more readily adaptable to "the changing needs of social life." Attempts to depict law as natural – "a simple matter of logic" or "established principles ... which need not be explained or justified" – were to be treated with skepticism. Influenced above all by the work of Harold Laski, Zakariya attacked that position as a "slavish adherence to precedent."[11]

His incipient thought paralleled that of other anticolonial lawyers, including Djalal Abdoh, Anes Qasem, Muhammad Mughraby, Mohammed Bedjaoui, and Jorge Castañeda. How so? In their attraction to the profession, all avoided grandiloquence but were drawn to grand theories. All understood law as fluid, driven by a universalist sense of justice that itself arose from what Zakariya called developments in "historical and other extra-legal considerations." This academic under-standing of international law in context, which formed the basis for later arguments about oil control, shaped the content of their individual academic work, just as it would provide a basis for their collective political program. It is also telling that they all chose, at a young age, case studies that involved what Abdoh had called in 1938 "the right of the victim" to protection from a more powerful entity.[12]

They not only repeatedly raised the same sort of questions but also created a coherent set of arguments that rested on the ideal of reparative justice. That a dominant group remained largely immune from legal jurisdiction was perceived as the main problem to be wrestled with. The anticolonial elites' early academic work, in other words, was born as much of their pursuit for serviceable knowledge as of a love of learning for its own sake. It followed that their approaches, though thorough and logical, were as much about moral passion as cool detachment. They wished not to just understand the world but to change it. It was this quality, among others, that the anticolonial lawyers shared and gave them their common character.

The implication is not far to seek in the career of Zakariya. In identifying sovereign rule over citizens as a feudal relic, he foreshadowed the logic of his interpretation of the oil concessions' rule over sovereign nations. He

[11] Zakariyya, "State Liability in Tort," 158, 280–9.
[12] Zakariyya, "State Liability in Tort," 44; Abdoh, "L'élément psychologique," 219.

was in this way predisposed to envisage a more just international community when Francisco Parra hired him to direct OPEC legal matters in late 1967. His work for OPEC can be understood as an extension of his early studies – a sort of compound interest on youthful idealism.

His position also built on the circumstances at hand. In particular, the letdown of the 1967 Arab embargo was fresh on his mind. He and Parra responded to that failure by reinvigorating OPEC's commitment to sovereign rights through a new Declaratory Statement of Petroleum Policy. The statement also built on Zakariya's analysis of recent oil contracts. Between 1966 and 1968, for example, Abu Dhabi signed new contracts designed "to incorporate 'OPEC terms'" that allowed for the exploitation of areas relinquished by the previous concessionaires. Likewise in Saudi Arabia, Ahmed Zaki Yamani had pressed Italian oil executives to sign a deal that was "one of the most advanced signed in the Middle East in recent years," for its detailed provisions granting a high percentage of national ownership in the integrated operations. The Indonesian national oil company, Pertamina, concluded so many new contracts with foreign companies in 1968 that it published "a typical Indonesian production sharing contract." Each section was built on the first clause: "all mineral and gas existing within the statutory mining territory of Indonesia are national riches controlled by the State." The Libyan and Iraqi governments also signed a number of new contracts that incorporated similar language – the contracts for Libya noted that oil production was meant to serve "the national interest of the people of Libya which has a sovereign right to its natural resources."[13]

This panoply of heartening information was assembled by the OPEC Information Department, which under Parra's direction had begun to identify broader shifts in national oil policy through annual reports. These were the products of the comparative analysis former Secretary General Fuad Rouhani had deemed necessary after reading the reports of the UN Permanent Sovereignty Commission and hiring Parra. This project carried an understanding, born of experience and observation, that the production of knowledge continued to be important. The 1967 report emphasized "the growing awareness of governments throughout the world of the need to tap the valuable resources under their subsoil ... and an increasing tendency for governments to play a more active part in the control and management of their mineral resources." Parra described the publication as being of "key importance" in the "dissemination of

---

[13] *SDIPI 1966*, 67, 135, OIC; *SDIPI 1968*, 45–81, 81–82, 107, 197–199, OIC.

FIGURE 5.1 Francisco Parra as OPEC Secretary General in 1968.
Source: OPEC Information Center, OPEC PICL-1968 (1).

information." Since his days at Arthur D. Little, the gathering of dispersed legal and economic data had been central to the attempts to "consolidate and unify" national oil policies.[14]

[14] *SDIPI 1967*, 11, OIC; Francisco Parra, "Preface," *SDIPI 1967*, OIC.

Speaking to the oil ministers in his final speech as Secretary General in November 1968, Parra further described OPEC as "a reflection and crystallization of several trends in the world economy." Yet OPEC was more than that for him. The organization was proof that the global "forces at work" that had begun with decolonization had created an economic dynamic of their own. The institutionalization of the "aspirations of the producers" let them act "jointly in self-defense" against a market that had been "structured so as to favor" the rich nations and the multinational corporations. The efforts of the OPEC Secretariat, he hoped, had laid sufficient "ground work ... for the unification of policy toward those international problems." The growth of the "intergovernmental" OPEC itself – comprised as it was of specialists in "economics, law, and technical matters" – made him confident that the organization would play a role in shaping future policies.[15]

There is no missing the alert internationalist edge to the politics of the OPEC Secretariat. This is evident again in Zakariya's other major undertaking – the 1968 OPEC Declaratory Statement. OPEC already had followed closely the meetings of the UN Conference on Trade and Development, the 1966 debates over the new UN resolution on permanent sovereignty, and the meetings of the regional economic commissions in 1967. Zakariya built on those meetings and placed anticolonial law at the vital center in June 1968 when he drafted the Declaratory Statement of Petroleum Policy. The statement called upon the member nations to use national legislation to bring about several explicit changes to the old concessions. If implemented, these would bring the concessions into line with the "inalienable right of all countries to exercise permanent sovereignty over their natural resources," which he described as "a universally recognized principle" that had been reaffirmed repeatedly. He insisted, moreover, the concessions were subject to revision "as justified by changing circumstances."[16]

Like his predecessors and contemporaries, Zakariya sought to close the breach between the right to sovereignty and its practice. He thus placed great stress on the notion of "changing circumstances" as a strategy to

---

[15] "OPEC and Oil Companies," November 9, 1968, in Kubbah, *OPEC, Past and Present*, 134.
[16] "The United Nations Resolution on Permanent Sovereignty over Natural Resources," *OPEC Bulletin*, January 1967, OIC; Resolution No. 90, XVI Conference of OPEC, June 1968, Resolutions Adopted at the Conferences of OPEC, OIC; Hasan S. Zakariya, "OPEC Resolution XVI.90: Its Background and Some Analytical Comments," January 1969, OIC.

strengthen the group's claims. He not only included the concept as a rationale in the Declaratory Statement, but presented a rousing defense of its "legal validity" a year later. As a doctrine, changing circumstances was key to the development of international law, he said. In fact, it was so "deeply steeped in philosophy and ethics" that many jurists believed it "owed its existence to the moral conscience rather than the legal one." The right of nations to invoke their sovereignty to change the terms of production contracts, according to the changing circumstances of decolonization, constituted "a clear and unequivocal testimony as to the trend of thought on this matter in the world community as a whole."[17]

Parra also described the Declaratory Statement as constructed upon the previous base created by OPEC, the United Nations, and other institutions of decolonization. Through their support of permanent sovereignty, these groups had made sovereign rights the "fundamental criterion for the justification of revision of contract in accordance with the principle of changing circumstances," he said. That moral certainty and its spirit of action were deeply bound up with a way of historical thinking that was meant to legitimize policy action. It was, in other words, the future as much as the past that was at stake in the endless working over of sovereign rights. For Zakariya and Parra, the easy sympathy for national power was not necessarily limiting. In fact, they believed that the international acceptance of sovereignty left the door open for accommodation between OPEC members. They hoped that the universal acceptance of sovereign rights could weave together the endeavors of the gradualists and the insurrectionists among the oil elites.[18]

That school of thought received a remarkable and unexpected boost in January 1968 when the British government announced its phased withdrawal from the sheikhdoms in the southeastern Persian Gulf, which had been protectorates of Great Britain since the 1820s. The causes and effects of that decision reveal that sovereign rights was never just a simple creed. Nor was the diffusion of its economic culture among oil elites an empty rhetorical conveyance of anticolonial categories. The sovereign rights program arose in particular contexts, and it was in this new one that it would be put to more effective use.

[17] Hasan S. Zakariya, "The Impact of Changing Circumstances on the Revision of Petroleum Contracts," OPEC Seminar, July 1969, OIC.

[18] "Statement of the Secretary General," *OPEC Bulletin*, August 1968, OIC; Francisco Parra, "OPEC: Recent Developments and Future Directions," *OPEC Bulletin*, September–October 1968, OIC.

The program for greater sovereignty among oil elites, despite its ideological momentum, had been disappointing in the 1960s, as the cases of royalty expensing and the Arab oil embargo revealed. But new potential arose, in part, from the most recent failure in collective action. How did the 1967 embargo turn from failure to success? In a three-part story, the financial power of the Arab oil producers, regarded by most as stillborn during the 1967 embargo, played a crucial role in the January 1968 British announcement that it would withdraw its last imperial commitments in the Persian Gulf by 1971. The so-called Gulf Scuttle in turn led a Cold War–minded US government to a regional policy designed to strengthen Iran, after which the Shah used his new influence with the Johnson administration and then the Nixon administration to extract concessions from the oil companies.

The rising importance of Middle Eastern oil in the international economy and the American understanding of the international economy drove that story forward. By virtue of its massive oil deposits, the Persian Gulf was fundamental to capitalist world stability and of great significance in the Cold War for US officials. Policymakers estimated that the oil from there provided over half of European and 90 percent of Japanese energy requirements by 1970. Because of technological advances, the influence of oil also had begun to be felt in economic sectors outside of production, consumption, and transportation. Of special interest was the new financial wealth of certain producers. Saudi Arabia and Iran together provided the United States with an annual net inflow of over $1.5 billion, more than 60 percent of the national trade surplus, one 1970 report reminded Henry Kissinger. It was thus crucial that these two "moderate regimes" remained pro-American. Their vital significance was further heightened by the perceived need to balance the "nationalist elements of radical bent" that ruled Iraq.[19]

American policymakers also put a premium on regional stability because it made the unchecked flow of oil possible. Stability and, more to the point, the secure flow of cheap oil had been a national security imperative since the early Cold War. It had been briefly cast into doubt during the Six-Day War. But the celebratory accounts of beating the Arab embargo in the late summer of 1967 were far from the final word. One major outcome of the war, despite the renewal of confidence in oil supply immediately afterward, was the Gulf Scuttle. The Labour

---

[19] IG Near East and South Asia, "US Policy on the Persian Gulf," March 12, 1970, NSC Files, Institutional Files, folder H-156, RNL.

government of Harold Wilson, which had been in office since 1964, did not make its decision to remove troops lightly. At the center of the internal debate was a question of priorities: Was the maintenance of British power abroad worth its cost? For a long time, the Wilson government believed it was. "The shadow of economic pressure," Wilson told Dean Rusk in 1964 and Lyndon Johnson in 1965, did not bring into question the British imperial commitment to remain on the Arabian Peninsula. Actions supported words until June 1967: When beleaguered British rulers recognized the National Liberation Front in the Aden Protectorate earlier that year, for example, the British government transferred those forces to the Trucial States and Bahrain. Foreign Secretary Michael Stewart told Wilson that the transfer would help "reassure the Shah of Iran and the King of Saudi Arabia about our intentions to maintain and reinforce our position."[20]

A rapid sequence of events in the summer of 1967 softened British resolve. Grave economic troubles already gripped the nation. Then the European Economic Community rejected the British bid for entry for the second time in five years two weeks before the Tiran crisis began, and sterling reserves fell by over $300 million. That rampant monetary speculation increased pressure to devalue the pound. It also called attention to the large financial holdings of the Arab oil-producing countries in Great Britain. Kuwait and Saudi Arabia now held two-thirds of the remaining sterling reserve, approximately $2 billion. Nasser's wartime policy of "inducing the Arab nations to move out of sterling" increased pressure on the British, as Libya and Kuwait withdrew a total of 41 official funds from British banks operating in the sterling area in June 1967. The British Treasury noted that the effects of these

[20] Galpern, *Money, Oil, and Empire in the Middle East*, 264; Telegram, Cairo to DOS, "South Arabia," April 15, 1967, RG 59, Central Foreign Policy File 1967–69, POL 23 ADEN, NARA; Stewart to Wilson, "The Persian Gulf," January 25, 1966, Prime Minister's Office: Correspondence and Papers, 1964–70, folder 2209, UKNA. For other narratives that take into account the relationship between oil and the pound, see: D. C. Watt, "The Decision to Withdraw from the Gulf," *Political Quarterly* 39: 3 (1968), 310–21; William Roger Louis, "The British Withdrawal from the Gulf, 1967–71," *Journal of Imperial and Commonwealth History*, 31: 1 (2003), 83–108. More broadly, see: Simon C. Smith, *Britain's Revival and Fall in the Gulf: Kuwait, Qatar, and the Trucial States* (New York: Routledge, 2004); Phuong Pham, *Ending "East of Suez": The British Decision to Withdraw from Malaysia and Singapore, 1964–1968* (Oxford University Press, 2010); Helene von Bismarck, *British Policy in the Persian Gulf, 1961–1968: Conceptions of Informal Empire* (London: Palgrave Macmillan, 2013); Shohei Sato, *Britain and the Formation of the Gulf States: Embers of Empire* (Manchester University Press, 2016).

"abnormal" movements could not "be at all precise," but by September 1967 the Bank of England attributed a net loss of £80 ($224) million to Arab actions.[21]

American policymakers followed the situation closely. "The Arabs could precipitate a run on the sterling that could literally almost bankrupt the British," analysts in the State Department reported. London's financial infirmity compounded a more profound unease in Washington, where policymakers knew the dollar would not be spared the monetary consequences of a run on the sterling. To make matters worse, the American defensive gold stock was "virtually exhausted," thus increasing the likelihood that the Arab financial diplomacy could further weaken the dollar. All this left the Johnson administration in a no-win situation. The US Treasury could respond to the petro-pound withdrawal by selling large amounts of gold, which would hold the dollar's price in the London market, but further gut its value. Alternatively, the Treasury could let the price of the dollar float, with the attendant risks for world economic stability. This left the United States with little diplomatic wiggle room in the run-up to the Six-Day War. In fact, the Johnson administration considered denying of the oil producers' access to finance capital as a countermeasure to the embargo. But given "the powerful economic weapons" the producers could "use against the Atlantic nations," the State Department concluded that such a bold option was "more a gun at our head than at theirs."[22]

Meanwhile in London, the economic effects of the petro-pound withdrawal, reflationary measures, and a dockworkers' strike had coalesced to drain over £500 million ($1.4 billion) from the British monetary reserve by the end of the summer. The empty coffers led officials at Whitehall to devalue the pound sterling from $2.80 to $2.40 on November 18, 1967. Officials in London and Washington, as well as elsewhere, believed the ramifications for the dollar and, more broadly, the international financial system in place since the 1944 Bretton Woods conference, would be great.

---

[21] Galpern, *Money, Oil, and Empire in the Middle East*, 255–67; Baldwin, "Kuwait Sterling Balances," June 26, 1967, Prime Minister's Office: Correspondence and Papers, 1964–70, folder 1628, UKNA; Bank of England to Rickett, July 10, 1967, Prime Minister's Office: Correspondence and Papers, 1964–70, folder 1628, UKNA; Lavelle to Le Cheminant, "Arab Sterling Balances," September 21, 1967, Prime Minister's Office: Correspondence and Papers, 1964–70, folder 1628, UKNA.

[22] Battle, "Memo to Secretary of State and the Secretary of Defense," May 31, 1967, National Security Files, box 106, LBJL; "Chairman of the Task Force: The Working Group on Economic Vulnerabilities," National Security Files, box 106, LBJL.

It was important, too, that the sterling devaluation strengthened the hand of a faction within the British cabinet that sought to cut military expenditures. One means of doing so was to end the British commitment to its last imperial outposts east of the Suez Canal, including the long-running commitment to the Trucial States in the Persian Gulf. The Johnson administration vehemently opposed the decision to remove troops from the Persian Gulf. "For God's sake act like Britain!" the normally imperturbable Secretary of State, Dean Rusk, roared at British Foreign Secretary George Brown when Brown revealed the plan in January 1968. In that "disturbing and distasteful" meeting, Brown wrote, Rusk accused Britain of "opting out of our world responsibilities."[23]

Beneath Rusk's rant rested a serious concern over the future of a strategic region in which the United States had long relied on British imperialism to defend Western interests. When Brown broke the news to Rusk, nobody knew that by 1971 the United Arab Emirates and an independent Bahrain would come into being with Saudi and Iranian support, an event that ensured stability in the lower Arabian Peninsula. Rather, policymakers feared that the Trucial States and Bahrain would join Kuwait, Qatar, Oman, and the Yemens as new, weak states. Rusk cabled Brown soon after the announcement that the imperial pullout would "feed instability in the region."[24]

The British decision could not have come at a worse time for the United States. The Six-Day War had already revealed serious vulnerabilities to US power in the Persian Gulf. In fact, military weakness during the Aqaba crisis had been a mirror image of the political and economic obstacles. When the Johnson administration began its failed effort to sweeten international opinion through the language of maritime law in May 1967, the

---

[23] Rostow to Johnson, November 13, 1968, *FRUS 1964–68,* vol. XII, doc. 278; DOS to All Posts, November 18, 1968, *FRUS 1964–68,* vol. XII, doc. 279; John Springhall, *Decolonization since 1945* (London: Palgrave, 2001), 94. Domestic social expenditures took the brunt of spending cuts. See: Glen Balfour-Paul, *The End of Empire in the Middle East: Britain's Relinquishment of Power in Her Last Three Arab Dependencies* (New York: Cambridge University Press, 2004), 122–5. For more detail on the US perspective, see: Daniel Sargent, "Lyndon Johnson and the Challenge of Economic Globalization," in *The United States and the Dawn of the Post-Cold War World,* eds. Francis Gavin and Mark Lawrence (New York: Oxford, 2015); Francis J. Gavin, *Gold, Dollars, and Power: The Politics of International Monetary Relations* (Chapel Hill: University of North Carolina Press, 2004), 176–82.

[24] Telno. 184, Foreign Office to Washington, January 6, 1968, Prime Minister's Office: Correspondence and Papers, 1964–70, folder 2209, UKNA.

Pentagon had already begun to work on the bitter pill of military tactics. But the Joint Chiefs of Staff were forced to conclude that they could not break Nasser's blockade by force. One difficulty concerned Israeli demands. In a "somber" message to Rusk, Levi Eshkol explained that the detention of any ship or strategic cargo bound for Eilat would be cause for war. The political geography of the Gulf of Aqaba posed another hitch. The State Department considered passing the convoy through the east channel of the Straits of Tiran, along the Saudi Arabian coast. But this option was discarded because, if King Faisal agreed to the passage, "he would be an almost certain casualty of the current pro-Nasser emotionalism throughout the Arab world."[25]

To make matters even worse, the Pentagon informed Johnson that the transfer of naval forces from the Atlantic Fleet to the Red Sea would take at least a month. Rotation around Africa was necessary because standing East-of-Suez forces would not fare well in an armed conflict. "The capability of these forces to prevail if attacked by major UAR forces is doubtful," wrote the Joint Chiefs. At the grandest strategic level, this was a weakness of priorities: military capital was banked in Vietnam. The Joint Chiefs had noted earlier in the month their "reservations concerning the ability of the United States to meet worldwide military commitments and contingencies beyond the current Southeast Asian conflict." The Pentagon admitted that conventional power could not be decisive in Aqaba, an early hint of the need for a stronger presence in the keystone of what Zbigniew Brzezinski would identify as the "arc of crisis" in 1979.[26]

The failure was nakedly evident on the Cold War stage, a circumstance the British decision exacerbated. The Soviet chargé to the United Nations mocked in late May 1967 the "dissatisfaction of those imperialist circles" that could "no longer deploy their military forces as they wished." Johnson administration officials also tended to worry about regional

[25] Eshkol to Rusk, May 30, 1967, National Security Files, box 106, LBJL; Principle Deputy, Assistant Secretary of Defense to Secretary of Defense, June 2, 1967, National Security Files, box 107, LBJL; DOS, "Agenda for Control Group Meeting," June 1, 1967, National Security Files, box 107, LBJL.

[26] JCSM-310-67, June 2, 1967, National Security Files, box 107, LBJL; JCSM-288-67, May 20, 1967, National Security Files, box 107, LBJL. For the history of US military presence in the region, see William Odom, "The Cold War Origins of the U.S. Central Command," *The Journal of Cold War Studies* 8: 2 (2006), 60; Andrew Bacevich, *America's War for the Greater Middle East: A Military History* (New York: Random House, 2016).

instability in Cold War terms. Rusk wrote at the beginning of the Aqaba crisis that Egypt and the Soviet Union shared the same broad goals: "Nasser's ascendancy in the Arab world and Soviet control of oil and other interests vital to the security of . . . the free world generally." Former Vice President Richard Nixon agreed. If the situation persisted, he warned Rusk in a June 1967 letter, "we will have given the Soviet Union an unparalleled opportunity to extend its influence in the Arab world to the detriment of vastly important United States and free world interests."[27]

There thus existed a coeval sense that the British withdrawal would further break loose regional stability from its traditional moorings. Anticolonial pressure and the ensuing sense of instability, which US policymakers assumed would benefit the Soviet enemy, reached a high pitch in the late 1960s. Radio stations operating out of Cairo, Damascus, and Baghdad – the public voices of those governments – continuously attacked Saudi Arabia, Kuwait, and Iran for their coziness with the West. Moreover, as countless Arab experts had predicted for a generation, US support for Israel also eroded American popularity and led to charges of imperialism. "The Arabs of the Gulf," National Security Council officials wrote grimly in 1970, were "becoming increasingly involved in the Arab/Israeli issue."[28]

The combination of this maelstrom of regional and global politics had the potential to become explosive. The position of the government in Iraq was of immediate concern for the United States, both as a radical regional power and a geopolitical proxy for the Soviet Union. Iraqi actions, steeped in the sovereign rights program but often interpreted in the United States through a Cold War prism, would further justify US support of the Shah in the wake of the Gulf Scuttle. To understand that dynamic, it is useful to first quickly review Iraqi oil insurrection in the previous decade.

---

[27] Meeting Minutes, May 29, 1967, UNSC, Official Records, S/PV.1343; Circular 204952 to All Posts, May 31, 1967, National Security Files, box 107, LBJL; Nixon to Rusk, June 5, 1967, National Security Files, box 107, LBJL.

[28] National Security Council Interdepartmental Group, "Future of U.S. Policy in the Persian Gulf," Presidential Directives II, DNSA. Radio Cairo, Radio Damascus, and Radio Baghdad were accompanied by a number of smaller clandestine stations. On the State Department's concern with anti-Americanism on the Arab Peninsula and radio broadcasts, which one diplomat characterized as "the constant purveyor of claims to the effect that the U.S. is in the midst of dark plots," see: Minutes of Washington Special Actions Group Meeting," October 15, 1973, *FRUS 1969–76*, vol. XXXVI, doc. 215; Kissinger to Nixon, September 8, 1970, *FRUS 1964–68*, vol. XXIV, doc. 209.

Iraq had done more than align itself with the Soviet Union and position itself as a leading anti-Israel voice in the region. The succession of post-1958 governments, including the Ba'athist regime that usurped power in 1968, stood consistently at the vanguard of oil insurrection. Iraqi elites, inside and outside of national government, had long depicted the old concessions as an affront to sovereignty and understood their nationalism as part of a greater international program. In a flurry of activity from 1968 to 1970, the Ba'ath government signed several new contracts for oil from fields nationalized in 1960.[29]

The Ba'athist successes of the late 1960s built on a longer nationalist interpretation of history, which points to a certain continuity between them and their predecessors, as well as the intersection of the geopolitics of oil and the intellectual history of sovereign rights. The history of petroleum colonization in Iraq was widely accepted, and it had been written about by Iraqi oil elites such as Nadim Pachachi, Amir Kubbah, Hasan Zakariya, and others. What they considered the facts of history had been rehearsed again and again: The Iraq Petroleum Company had signed its first concession under formal mandatory control in 1925, and Great Britain granted Iraq independence in 1932 as a means to avoid League of Nations supervision over that and subsequent concessions. The Hashemite monarchy maintained an emphatic pro-Western stance in the following quarter century, despite intermittent nationalist rhetoric and the campaign to increase royalties by Pachachi.[30]

Iraqi oil policy already drew from the economic culture of decolonization and the sovereign rights program under Pachachi's guidance in the 1950s. But nationalism became a more present force after the 1958 revolution. The new government of Abd al-Karim Qasim defiantly confronted the company once it consolidated power. Qasim demanded greater production, increases in Iraq's share of the profits, and the relinquishment of a large portion of the IPC's concession. In response, the IPC offered similar terms to those accepted by Iran after the ouster of Mossadegh and the reinstatement of the Shah in 1953. Qasim refused.[31]

---

[29] See: Samir Saul, "Masterly Inactivity as Brinksmanship: The Iraq Petroleum Company's Road to Nationalization," *International History Review* 29: 4 (2007), 746–92.

[30] For more recent histories of petroleum colonization, see: Pederson, "Getting Out of Iraq – in 1932," 975–1000; Daniel Silverfarb, "The Revision of Iraq's Oil Concessions, 1949–1952," *Middle Eastern Studies* 23 (1996), 69–95.

[31] Wolfe-Hunnicutt, "The End of the Concessionary Regime," 66–72; James H. Bamberg, *British Petroleum and Global Oil, 1950–1975: The Challenge of Nationalism* (Cambridge University Press, 2000), 162–85.

Then in 1960 the major oil companies cut the posted price of crude oil, leading the Qasim government to invite leaders from Iran, Kuwait, Saudi Arabia, Qatar, and Venezuela to Baghdad, where they formed OPEC. Negotiations on Iraqi oil faltered later that year, and Iraq raised Persian Gulf transit rates to Basrah by 1,200 percent. The IPC responded by suspending production for all fields that used the port. In late 1961, the government then passed Public Law 80. Law 80 expropriated all concession areas not under production and can be understood as a step beyond the relinquishment law written by Anes Qasem and Nadim Pachachi for Libya earlier in the year. The law covered 99.58 percent of the 1925 concession, but the principle bone of contention involved the areas in which the IPC had already found oil. The most promising of those surveyed fields was the Rumaila field in southern Iraq. Because it had been surveyed but not tapped, Rumaila existed in a gray area in terms of punitive diplomacy toward sovereign rights. It became a central point of conflict for a decade, but in 1961 its ambiguousness helped Iraq. Because the country had not nationalized any actual production, Western purchasers did not boycott Iraqi oil as they had Iranian oil a decade earlier.[32]

The Iraqi government, however, did not possess the competence to develop the expropriated areas. Realizing this, Mohammed Salman and others began to build up the nation's capacity, which strengthened the government's hand in its ongoing negotiations with its concessionaire. Anticolonial oil elites played a major role. Abdullah al-Tariki, for example, was a key adviser, particularly after Tahir Yahya became prime minister in November 1963. 'Abid al-Jadir, a member of Yahya's Oil Committee who met frequently with Tariki, wrote an article about the "status quo" of Iraqi oil policy in Amir Kubbah's Baghdad journal that reflects the Saudi's influence. The standing relationship between the nation and the company was "intolerable," he said. The government needed to work to increase its capacity to extract oil, which would give it leverage to increase "Iraqi government participation" in the concession and guarantee it a larger portion of the profit.[33]

Given the overall insurrectionist stance in Iraq, Tariki may very well have felt that he was preaching to the choir. Sayid Abdul Aziz al-

[32] National Intelligence Estimate, January 31, 1962, *FRUS 1961–63*, vol. XVII, doc. 183; Talbot to Ball, December 18, 1961, *FRUS 1961–63*, vol. XVII, doc. 150; Komer to Bundy, December 29, 1961, *FRUS 1961–63*, vol. XVII, doc. 156; Bamberg, *British Petroleum and Global Oil*, 141–61; Yergin, *The Prize*, 501–42; J. E. Hartshorn, *Politics and World Oil Economics* (New York: Praeger, 1962), 301.
[33] Wolfe-Hunnicutt, "The End of the Concessionary Regime," 154–5.

Wattari, who received his PhD from Colorado State in petroleum engineering and was just 33 years old when he was appointed to replace Mohammed Salman as the oil minister in 1961, had taken a "not negotiable" position throughout the OPEC royalty expensing negotiations. In fact, he made it official Iraqi policy to follow the prescriptions set out at the 1962 Cairo conference of the Non-Aligned Movement and the 1964 meeting of the UN Conference on Trade and Development. A government spokesperson described OPEC as one of "the most important organizations for collective bargaining ... with a view to securing the legitimate rights of exporting countries." Indeed, the need for that official policy resulted from conditions set by the unequal past: "Under that system of economic tutelage, Iraq was contented with the status of an exporter of raw materials and primary commodities and an importer of finished goods."[34]

But the specific contours of oil consciousness in Iraq also point to the more general overlap of insurrectionism and gradualism. Wattari's lukewarm attitude toward nationalization in his 1965 Cairo debate with Tariki reveal the potential benefits he saw to taking a more accommodating view. His shift was received with open arms by the IPC, and the two parties negotiated a joint agreement to develop production in the Rumaila field in 1965. Internationally, the "Wattari Agreement" was presented by the Iraqi government as a step toward greater collective action among the oil producers, and Wattari called the negotiations with the IPC "a basic element of strength for the removal of the injustice" in the relations between the companies and the producing countries. But the deal upset Tariki, who wrote in the leading Baghdad daily, *Al Thawra*, that it obeyed the arrangements of previous concessions. Not only had it been "concluded by unequal parties," it also made a joke of Iraqi sovereignty. "Governments of civilized countries do not resort to negotiations but to legislation," he said.[35]

In fact, the agreement was decried across the political spectrum in Iraq. Tariki's position and the subsequent failure of the Wattari Agreement

---

[34] "Iraq's Position is Not Negotiable," *ROAPE* 1: 1 (February 1965), 3; Tariq El-Mutwalli, "Iraq's Trade and Economic Relations with the Arab Countries and Outside World," *ROAPE* 1: 1 (February 1965), 10–13. Tariq al-Mutwalli earned a PhD from American University in 1957. See "The Tax System of Iraq: A Study of Taxation in a Developing Country," PhD Dissertation, American University (1957). On Wattari and Jadir, see: Wolf-Hunnicutt, "The End of the Concessionary Regime," 104–13.

[35] "Committee of Arab Oil Experts Meet in Baghdad," *ROAPE* 1: 3 (April 1965), 4; Wolfe-Hunnicutt, "The End of the Concessionary Regime," 171–3.

reflected a shared consensus on, as one historian has put it, "moving forward with an independent oil policy and keeping Rumaila out of the hands of the IPC." Iraqi policy continued to tip toward insurrection in August 1966, when an extreme wing of the Ba'ath Party took control in Syria. The new government in Damascus sought to raise the fees for the Mediterranean-bound crude sent through its pipeline to Banias. The IPC refused to negotiate, and Syria unilaterally increased transit and loading fees. The Syrian Ba'athists declared that their action fell within the broader attempts to use natural resources to "preserve peoples' rights." The company reduced production because of the transit dispute, and the cutback caused revenue losses of approximately 60 percent in Iraq, prompting the finance minister to predict that the clash would "cripple the economy."[36]

The hostility continued when the Iraqi government passed a series of laws that established the Iraq National Oil Company and then extended its powers, the most important of which included the ability to pump oil from, as the OPEC Information Department put it, the "known but undeveloped North Rumaila field."[37]

The adamant refusal to compromise in those new laws reflected the newfound capability of Iraq to develop the disputed field. This important shift was facilitated by Cold War geopolitics, which became more important to the question of Iraq's sovereign rights in the late 1960s. In July 1967, after Soviet President Nikolai Podgorny became the first high-ranking leader to visit Iraq, the director of the new national oil company stated that "[o]ur aim must be the complete control of our oil wealth." A week later Prime Minister Yahya also called for greater governmental control over the oil industry. The two governments signed a protocol setting up an agenda for economic cooperation in December 1967 along those lines. The document emphasized Soviet assistance with technical formation, the drilling of wells in Rumaila, and the transportation and marketing of crude oil. The company director again stressed that Soviet–Iraqi cooperation would "weaken the foreign oil monopolies and strengthen both our countries and our peoples." Yahya used the occasion to denounce the IPC with "the strongest attack … in several years," according to the US ambassador in Beirut. The concessionaires were

---

[36] Wolfe-Hunnicut, "The End of the Concessionary Regime," 173; Embassy Damascus to DOS, "IPC Situation," January 12, 1967, *FRUS 1964–68*, vol. XXXIV, doc. 200; Brown, "Nationalization," 116–7.

[37] "Petroleum Legislation and Related Documents," *SDIPI 1967*, OIC.

"blood suckers," Yahya said, who sought "to prevent us from developing the country's national resources."[38]

There was no break in pressure after the 1968 Ba'athist coup, which lifted Ahmead Hassan al-Bakr and his nephew, Saddam Hussein, to power. After purging its opponents, the Ba'ath government embarked on an autocratic process of economic development that consistently used the concept of permanent sovereignty to support its claims to legitimacy. In one instance, officials told IPC directors that the control of oil profits and production fell within sovereign governments' "generally recognized rights." *Al Thawra*, now an official state news organ, took an identical line about the "battle to extract our rights from the oil companies."[39]

Nothing seemed more illustrative of the role of the Cold War in Iraqi oil policy in the late 1960s than the continued dispute over the Rumaila field. Soviet financial support followed its technical aid in 1969 when the Ba'ath Revolutionary Command Council announced a $140 million Soviet loan for the exploitation of Rumaila. *Izvestia*, the Kremlin news organ, employed a broad brush to paint the implications. The loan represented a "mutually advantageous cooperation between Arab and socialist countries" that was "being extended to an ever-widening range of economic problems, including the problem of creating a national oil industry for the Arabs." Support from the Kremlin undoubtedly strengthened the Iraqi negotiating position. Iraqi exclamations of permanent sovereignty before the 1969 agreement were typically couched in ambiguous terms. The State Department noted, for example, that the 1967 agreement dealt in generalities, giving "no clue to the scope and terms of Soviet assistance." Conversely, the 1969 Iraqi–Soviet agreement called for an expansion of Rumaila production to 100,000 barrels per day by early 1972 and to 360,000 barrels by 1975. Even more importantly, the Soviet Union promised to bring Iraqi crude to market. This made IPC

---

[38] *MEED* 11: 26 (1967), 467; *MEED* 11: 27 (1967), 481–2; A-568, Beirut to DOS, "Petroleum: Iraq," January 4, 1968, RG 59, Central Foreign Policy File 1967–69, PET IRAQ USSR, NARA.

[39] Telegram 829, Baghdad to FCO, "IPC 13," November 26, 1970, Foreign & Commonwealth Office: Commodities and Oil Department, folder 425, UKNA.; British Embassy, "Baghdad Press Extracts," December 30, 1970, Foreign & Commonwealth Office: Commodities and Oil Department, folder 425, UKNA; British Embassy, "Press Reaction to IPC Talks," November 2, 1970, Foreign & Commonwealth Office: Commodities and Oil Department, folder 425, UKNA.

threats of boycott unworkable, the State Department noted. Soviet and Hungarian companies drilled several producing wells in the field in 1970, in spite of British reports of their "antiquated and inefficient" machinery. Iraq received additional loans from Bulgaria, East Germany, and Czechoslovakia in the same year for oil production, all to be repaid in future oil.[40]

Financial backing and technical know-how from the socialist world provided the essential factors in the development of Rumaila. At the same time, though, the Ba'ath and their predecessors also signed oil development contracts with Western companies. Importantly, successive Iraqi governments had also favored development bids and trade agreements with companies and governments on the other side of the iron curtain that were based on payment in future oil in its deals. The uniform stipulation within the future-oil clauses was that oil purchased in return for development capital or projects would be purchased from the Iraq National Oil Company. The result of this series of deals was that nationally controlled oil had a broad backing and diverse markets. The International Monetary Fund even lauded the strategy as "a favorable line of policy to encourage activities of the private sector."[41]

Even so, the right to permanent sovereignty, in this case to Rumaila oil, continued to be an obstacle in Iraq's relationship with the IPC into the following decade. The company proposed substantial production increases and a new agreement on royalty expensing in 1970. The IPC also offered to surrender its claims to the majority of area expropriated in 1961. As *quid pro quo*, though, company executives wanted "exclusive control and marketing of production" from Rumaila. The Ba'athist Revolutionary Command Council, holding the line established since the

---

[40] Oles Smolansky and Bettie Smolansky, *The USSR and Iraq: The Soviet Quest for Influence* (Durham, NC: Duke University Press, 1991), 52; Hughes to the Secretary, "The Soviet Oil Agreement with Iraq," January 15, 1968, RG 59, Central Foreign Policy File 1967–69, PET IRAQ USSR, NARA; "Soviet Oil Activities in Iraq," May 8, 1969, Foreign & Commonwealth Office: Commodities and Oil Department, folder 240, UKNA; "Soviet Drilling Performance," September 25, 1970, Foreign & Commonwealth Office: Commodities and Oil Department, folder 424, UKNA; Jenner, "Iraq/Soviet Oil Developments," November 9, 1970, Foreign & Commonwealth Office: Commodities and Oil Department, folder 425, UKNA; British Embassy, "Development of North Rumaila," October 1, 1970, Foreign & Commonwealth Office: Commodities and Oil Department, folder 425, UKNA; *Petroleum Press Service* (November 1970), 430.

[41] Staff Mission, SM/71/33, Middle Eastern Department, "Iraq: Recent Economic Developments," February 10, 1971, Country Reports, IMFA.

1958 revolution, refused to negotiate "on the grounds that IPC had not really accepted the provisions of Law 80."[42]

The conflict over the ownership of Iraq's petroleum was much more than a two-sided affair between host government and multinational oil consortium. Working within a shared context characterized by as much by decolonization and the rise of sovereign rights as their own thirst for oil, companies and national governments from the Eastern and Western blocs crossed Cold War lines to sign contracts with the Iraq National Oil Company. The burgeoning Iraqi achievement was depicted by the Shah of Iran mostly as a threat but sometimes as a model. The latter depiction was closer to the truth, in the sense that Iraqi advances helped Iran make considerable gains in its relationship with its concessionaire. The Shah's treatment of Iraq as leverage in the negotiations over Iran's oil production was especially effective because it played on American Cold War concerns about Persian Gulf instability. In short, decision makers in the Johnson and Nixon administrations believed that Iran should provide the needed regional security, which the Iraqi–Soviet alliance threatened, upon the British departure.

The policy of "recognizing the preponderance of Iranian power" in the Gulf culminated when Nixon signed National Security Decision Memorandum 92 in November 1970, but it built on a strategy set forth by the Johnson administration. The Johnson administration had anticipated and planned for an eventual British withdrawal, just not so soon. After the British informed the Johnson administration in 1966 of their plan to evacuate the Aden Protectorate by 1968, US officials began to think about what a British-less Persian Gulf would look like, and Johnson discussed with the Shah of Iran and King Faisal of Saudi Arabia different options to "fill the gap the British will leave in South Arabia and the Persian Gulf." The balancing act could be achieved through a simple equation, American officials hoped. First, the United States would accept Iran's assumption of the leading role but urge that the Shah act tactfully. Second, policymakers would encourage Saudi Arabia to play a larger, but supportive, role in Gulf affairs.[43]

---

[42] Oil Department, "Iraq Oil," March 10, 1970, Foreign & Commonwealth Office: Commodities and Oil Department, folder 420, UKNA.

[43] Galpern, *Money, Oil, and Empire in the Middle East*, 266–7. For a perspective that sees more change between the administrations, see: Roham Alvandi, *Nixon, Kissinger, and the Shah: The United States and Iran in the Cold War* (New York: Oxford University Press, 2014), 46–55. For an emphasis on how the Shah's stated views affected US policy, see: Andrew

Fostering goodwill between Iran and Saudi Arabia was key to the strategy. The State Department considered this "sure to be an uphill struggle," for there was no love lost on either side. The Shah constantly reminded US officials that Saudi oil money reached the Arab front-line through the 1967 Khartoum agreement and by other means. In one characteristic instance, he compared "with a sardonic smile" the Saudi oil profits that helped finance "Nasser's campaign of vilification of the US" to American exports in the 1930s of "tremendous amounts of scrap iron to Japan only to have it returned in finished form." For their part, Saudi officials complained consistently of what Foreign Affairs Minister Omar Saqqaf called the Shah's "openly contemptuous" attitude toward Arabs.[44]

Saqqaf – an "avid bridge player" whose "maturity had mellowed his once strident views" as a student at the American University of Beirut, according to one American intelligence report – worried about Iranian ambitions to dominate the Gulf and Arab littoral states." Iranian foreign policy seemed to confirm that concern in 1968 when the Shah resurrected Iran's claim to British-run Bahrain and the Persian Gulf islands of the Tunbs and Abu Musa. Moreover, in a twist of fate, the Gulf Scuttle also coincided with the discovery of large oil reserves on the Saudi side of the Persian Gulf median line, after which the Shah repudiated an earlier agreement and pressed claim to part of the undersea deposits. Saudi Oil Minister Ahmed Zaki Yamani complained of Iranian "deviousness" in those dealings. Detailing Iran's broken promises and Iran's "gunboat diplomacy" against a seaborne Aramco oil rig to US officials, Yamani said the Shah could "out-Machiavelli Machiavelli."[45]

Johns, "The Johnson Administration, the Shah of Iran, and the Changing Pattern of US-Iranian Relations, 1965–1967: 'Tired of Being Treated like a Schoolboy,'" *Journal of Cold War Studies* 9: 2 (Spring 2007), 64–94.

[44] Background Paper, "Visit of Prime Minister Wilson," February 2, 1968, *FRUS 1964–68*, vol. XXI, doc. 132; Embassy Tehran to DOS, "Oil," November 1969, National Security Council Files, box 601, RNL; Embassy Saudi Arabia to DOS, "Saudi-Iranian Relations," April 3, 1969, RG 59, Central Foreign Policy Files 1967–69, POL 7 SAUD, box 2471, NARA.

[45] "Sattid Omar al-Saqqaf," n.d. (1969), RG 59, Central Foreign Policy Files 1967–69, POL 7 SAUD, box 2471, NARA; Telegram, AmConsul Dhahran to SecState, January 31, 1968, RG 59, Central Foreign Policy Files 1967–69, POL 7 SAUD, box 2471, NARA; Memorandum of Conversation, September 13, 1968, *FRUS 1964–68*, vol. XXI, doc. 156. A fourth territorial issue, ownership over the Buraimi oasis, also preoccupied officials. The two countries also had other ongoing diplomatic haggles, including Saudi refusals of Iranian requests to construct a building in Mecca for Shiite pilgrims and to mark the graves of Shiite martyrs near Medina.

But the Americans did not find these challenges insurmountable. This was mostly because the Shah moved along constructive lines, giving up the claim on Bahrain and settling the seabed dispute. Finally, although the sheikh of Sharjah never gave up hope on the Tunbs, the other sheikhs, the Shah, and King Faisal agreed that Iran could station a "token presence" on the islands. Likewise, Saudi Arabia took to conciliation with gusto. Saudi policy in 1968 and 1969 was "one of conscious self-restraint to allow the Shah time to find a solution to the Bahrain problem and cement Saudi–Iranian cooperation," Saqqaf said. By early 1970, relations were so good that Iran agreed to transfer weapons to Saudi Arabia so the monarchy could drive back Yemeni incursions on its southern border.[46]

For the United States, Iranian primacy also had the objective of containing Iraq, whose embrace of sovereign rights and Soviet aid had transformed the nation into what Henry Kissinger called "a geopolitical challenge ... on the way to becoming the principal Soviet ally in the area." In fact, Kissinger used a Cold War rationale in his memoirs to justify the increasingly close relationship with the Shah. Building up Iran would ensure stability in a region "menaced by Soviet intrusion and radical momentum," he wrote.[47]

But it is important to note that other US officials consistently held that the Soviet and radical threats to the strategically significant region were modest at most. The Shah's fear of radical encroachment was, for this group, a manipulative ruse. "The Soviets could get both Iraq and Syria in their clutches," the Shah told the US ambassador in one instance. "Particularly since they are doing so well [in the] triangle of Cairo, Aden-Yemen, and Djibouti this would place them in a dominating position in the Mideast." Noting the weakness of Arab nationalists in the rest of the Persian Gulf, more serene voices contested the outcry. "The well-known themes," the ambassador wrote home after another conversation, "included ... the readiness of Arabs to serve as Commie tools." CIA officials agreed that the Shah's "fear" of the Soviet Union was largely

---

[46] AmEmbassy Iran to SecState, "Gulf Islands," November 15, 1971, National Security Council Files, box 602, RNL; Haig to Nixon, July 14, 1971, *FRUS 1969–76*, vol. XXIV, doc. 102; DOS to Embassy United Kingdom, "Persian Gulf – Talk with British," June 17, 1970, RG 59, Subject Numeric Files 1970–73, POL 33 PERSIAN GULF, box 1994, NARA; Memcon, "US/UK Bilaterals," *FRUS 1969–76*, vol. XXIV, doc. 103; Cabinet Meeting Minutes, "The Persian Gulf," July 22, 1970, Prime Minister's Office: Correspondence and Papers, 1970–74, folder 538, UKNA; Amembassy Tehran to SecState, April 15, 1970, NARA, Subject Numeric Files 1970–73, DEF 1 NEAR E, NARA.

[47] Alvandi, *Nixon, Kissinger, and the Shah*, 55–6.

simulated, concluding that he was not "greatly worried about the Soviet threat."[48]

Calm thus prevailed, at least in most quarters, at the end of the Johnson administration. "While the British announcement will give radical political movements in the Gulf a psychological shot in the arm," the State Department advised, "we do not expect it to lead to any dramatic political future." The Nixon administration also believed that the successful cooperation forged between Saudi Arabia and Iran was enough to prevent meaningful Soviet inroads. As part of Kissinger's overall review of foreign policy in early 1969, an NSC and State Department group undertook a close analysis of Persian Gulf strategy. The review group arrived at the same conclusions as its predecessors – the Soviet threat was unlikely to materialize in any grand way in the Gulf.[49]

All the same, the Cold War and anxiety about Persian Gulf instability remained intractable parts of the official American mind-set on Middle East policy. A number of officials relatedly employed language that was characterized by a sense of impending crisis. The British withdrawal had revived Soviet interest, according to these more anxious appraisals. "Together with the Iranian plateau, the region forms the keystone in an arch of non-Communist countries stretching from Africa to South Asia," wrote the Assistant Secretary of State for Near Eastern Affairs, Luke Battle. The naval command of the US Mideast Forces, just one flagship and two destroyers operating out of Bahrain, would be the only outside military force stationed in the eastern Arab world after the British left. In that context the Soviet Union sought "to take a direct role in Persian Gulf political affairs now that the UK plans to withdraw," another report warned.[50]

The perception of the twin threat of radicalism and Soviet adventurism led first the Johnson and then the Nixon administration to intervene in the annual revenue negotiations between the Iranian government and the Iran Consortium. Each year their intrusions were more decisive.

---

[48] Embassy Iran to DOS, December 29, 1967, *FRUS 1964–68*, vol. XXII, doc. 255; Embassy Iran to DOS, April 8, 1966, *FRUS 1964–68*, vol. XXII, doc. 131; CIA, Board of National Estimates, "The Shah's Increasing Assurance," May 7, 1968, doc. IR00663, DNSA.

[49] Galpern, *Money, Oil, and Empire in the Middle East*, 278–9; NSC Staff, "Persian Gulf," June 4, 1970, National Security File, Institutional Files, box H-111, RNL.

[50] Battle to Rusk, "Outlook in the Persian Gulf States," February 22, 1968, *FRUS 1964–68*, vol. XXI, doc. 138; Hughes to Rusk, "Soviet-US Rivalry in Iran," June 6, 1968, doc. IR00670, DNSA.

Other factors also led American officials toward greater involvement. For one, the growing global importance of Persian Gulf production helped tip the scales. "The simple statistics regarding Middle Eastern oil can only be defined as staggering," the State Department reported in 1967. With production costs roughly a tenth of those of the United States and an annual growth rate of 12 percent since the end of the Second World War, the Middle East provided over a third of "Free World" oil production by the late 1960s. It also contained more than two-thirds of reserves. For another, the British concern over Arab petro-pounds in 1967 was just an early indicator of the oil producers' broader financial clout. The profits from American oil companies had reduced the US deficit by more than 40 percent in the second half of the 1960s, the Senior Interdepartmental Group for National Security Decision Memorandum 92 estimated.[51]

A third factor shaped the oil negotiations more drastically. This was the Shah's discovery of the companies' longstanding collusion to limit production in Saudi Arabia and Iran. After his reinstatement in 1953, the oil companies had used several different means to prevent too much oil from flooding the market. Most important was a secret system of "off-take agreements" that penalized companies for producing more oil than a carefully calculated mean of their total demands from the previous year. The off-take agreements could be effective because the four member companies of Aramco also belonged to the Iran Consortium. For fifteen years, boardroom dealings effectively limited both Iranian and Saudi production to levels that would maintain prices at what the companies considered reasonable levels. The US government learned of the secret agreements as early as 1962, and the oil consultant Walter Levy warned Eugene Rostow in 1966 that "the very fact that a restricted secret agreement exists would be political dynamite in the hands of the Iranians." But soon after, the State Department concluded that the off-take question was "a highly sensitive, inter-company commercial policy matter." As such, it was "desirable for the US government to limit its involvement."[52]

---

[51] "Paper Prepared in the Department of State," February 8, 1967, *FRUS 1964–68*, vol. XXI, doc. 19; NSCIG, NEA, "Future of US Policy in the Persian Gulf," February 5, 1970, doc. PR00508, DNSA.

[52] Thanks to David Painter for the note on US government knowledge of the off-take agreements.

But after the Shah declared the modernizing "White Revolution" in 1963, his country's need for greater oil revenue rose substantially. Iranian revenue demands thus became a driving force in the annual negotiations. By 1966, the Iranian government had begun a press campaign that threatened the Consortium with partial nationalization if production were not drastically increased.[53]

In the face of this pressure, the Johnson administration initially maintained its default position of official neutrality. When Iranian officials urged US Assistant Secretary of State for Economic Affairs Anthony Solomon to pressure the Consortium to meet Iranian revenue requirements in 1967, he refused. The State Department commiserated with Iran's need for capital, he said, but could not "translate this sympathy ... into pressures on the American companies in the Consortium to comply with Iranian wishes." To explain, Solomon reverted to the mantra of business–government separation: In the "free system" of Western capitalism, "companies act according to their commercial interests rather than following instruction from the US Government."[54]

But Solomon did use Mobil Oil's negotiator as a vehicle to recommend that the Consortium agree to one of the Shah's minor demands, that the corporations liberalize their over-lift agreements. That small interference, agreed to by the Consortium members, was designed with the purpose of helping the companies "appreciate the need in making their commercial judgments take into account wider political consideration." From that point on, however, the oil companies found themselves in an increasingly uncomfortable position.[55]

This was because of the Shah's discovery of the Consortium and Aramco off-take collusion in December 1967, which the other companies believed was leaked by the *Compagnie Française des Pétroles*. The new knowledge changed the tone of the revenue negotiations. After one meeting with the Shah, US Ambassador Armin Meyer wondered "whether the time may not have come for the US government to caution the companies against such 'restraint of trade.'" The State Department did not go so far

[53] Hughes to Ball, June 3, 1966, *FRUS 1964–68*, vol. XXII, doc. 147; Intelligence Memorandum, May 6, 1966, *FRUS 1964–68*, vol. XXII, doc. 135; Embassy Iran to DOS, March 2, 1966, *FRUS 1964–68*, vol. XXII, doc 121.

[54] Memcon, November 1, 1967, RG 59, Central Foreign Policy Files, 1967–69, box 1357, PET 6 IRAN, NARA.

[55] Solomon to Rostow, "Status of Iranian-Consortium Negotiations," December 11, 1967, RG 59, Central Foreign Policy Files, 1967–69, PET 6 IRAN, box 1358, NARA; Memcon, "Iran Consortium Exports," March 3, 1967, *FRUS 1964–68*, vol. XXXIV, doc. 203.

but did begin "to urge the companies be as generous as they can in making their next offer to the Iranians." If the Iran Consortium did not do so, one official worried, "we might have to take a more active role in the talks." In a meeting with oil company executives during revenue negotiations the next year, Eugene Rostow told them that the US government "did not wish to take responsibility or become involved in a commercial negotiation." Still, given Iran's new security role, the United States had "a national interest in successful and harmonious resolution of the oil negotiations."[56]

The companies nonetheless resisted the Shah's demands, and Iran eventually accepted production levels that left the country with $40 million less than demanded for 1968. "Although the Shah has backed down, the issue is far from settled," the CIA warned. Officials prepared for another round of negotiations. By mid-1968, the Shah put forth further "incessant demands," according to Ambassador Meyer, who noted that the stipulations came despite the fact that the State Department had "assisted the Shah in satisfactory solution ... in the crisis with the consortium" months earlier. The State Department's in-house oil expert, James Akins, was blunter: "The Shah is an oriental despot and the oil executives are dinosaurs. If they come to blows it could be the battle of the century."[57]

In that battle, the Shah more successfully exploited his Cold War status as an American ally after the British withdrawal announcement. In particular, he used the purchase of military hardware to tilt the oil dialogue in his favor. In 1968, at the same time as he demanded greater oil income from the consortium, he and his military advisers changed their strategy by also requesting a commitment of $600 million in military sales over the following five years. When the Johnson administration hesitated, the Shah

---

[56] Volume 1D, "New Aramco Offtake Agreements and Related Documents," box 2.207/ G138, ExxonMobil Historical Collection, Dolph Briscoe Center for American History, The University of Texas at Austin; Embassy Iran to DOS, February 23, 1968, *FRUS 1964–68*, vol. XXXIV, doc. 217; Solomon to Rostow, "Status of Iranian-Consortium Negotiations," December 11, 1967, RG 59, Central Foreign Policy files, 1967–69, PET 6 IRAN, box 1358, NARA; Memcon, "Iran Oil Situation," March 6, 1968, RG 59, Central Foreign Policy Files 1967–69, PET 6 IRAN, box 1358, NARA.

[57] CIA, Board of National Estimates, "The Shah's Increasing Assurance," May 7, 1968, doc. IR00663, DNSA; Amembassy Iran to SecState, March 5, 1968, RG 59, Central Foreign Policy Files, 1967–69, POL IRAN-US, box 2219, NARA; Airgram 417, Amembassy Iran to SecState, February 10, 1968, RG 59, Central Foreign Policy Files 1967–69, POL 33 PERSIAN GULF, NARA; Letter, Akins to Dowell, March 18, 1968, RG 59, Central Foreign Policy Files 1967–69, PET 6 IRAN, box 1358, NARA.

threatened to turn to the Soviet Union. The regional heads of the State Department, the NSC, the Department of Defense, and the CIA all agreed to increased arms sales as a result. The rationale was simple, according to the final report: "our arms supply relationship has a vital importance in our overall ties with Iran."[58]

The National Security Council built on this report to brief the incoming Richard Nixon that "key to our relations with the Shah and his regime is our assistance for the modernization of Iran's armed forces." The Shah's demands for military equipment, moreover, were "insistent and large, and have increased since the announcement of the British withdrawal from the Gulf." Failure to meet these demands spelled disaster, according to the NSC analysis. Unless the United States remained Iran's principal military supplier, the American position in the Gulf would be seriously weakened.[59]

Arms sales to Iran and oil revenue for Iran thus became a linchpin of the Nixon administration's broader regional strategy. Because Iran's oil revenue would pay for the arms, in short, it became essential to guarantee that revenue. To preserve influence, then, it was crucial to maintain "constructive relations between Iran and the major oil companies," a joint NSC–State Department review group said. "The annual disputes" between the Shah and the Consortium were a matter of considerable concern: "the key question is whether the increase in Iran's income from oil will keep pace with the Shah's demands and Iran's expenditures."[60]

After reading those reports, Henry Kissinger summed up the consensus on the relationship between oil revenue, arms sales, and regional stability to Nixon. "Iran's future financial soundness is still fragile, depending as it still does on the continued flow of oil revenues at a high level," he wrote. "The Shah annually squeezes the American oil companies as hard as he can to maximize those revenues." He added that, if the oil companies did not pay, the Shah's inability to square the credits for the military sales would become a serious domestic burden.[61]

---

[58] IRG for Near East and South Asia, Meeting Record, April 5, 1968, *FRUS 1964–68*, vol. XXII, doc. 277.

[59] "U.S. Relations with Iran," January 1969, National Security Council Files, box 601, RNL.

[60] "US Relations with Iran," January 1969, National Security Council Files, box 601, RNL; Record of National Security Council Interdepartmental Group for Near East and South Asia Meeting, April 3, 1969, *FRUS 1969–76*, vol. E-4, doc. 10.

[61] Kissinger to Nixon, April 29, 1969, *FRUS 1969–76*, vol. E-4, doc. 13.

The Shah's repeated invocations of the Cold War and Nasserist extremism, NSC adviser Peter Flanigan reminded Kissinger, were "colored by the desire to encourage us to give him favorable oil treatment." Kissinger nevertheless pressed for a more explicit government role in the revenue negotiations, despite the fact that Flanigan and other US officials warned that the Shah was using his new position in the Cold War for unprecedented gains in that long-running dispute. Then, in an unrecorded meeting with the Shah in the Oval Office on October 21, 1969, Nixon made a promise to the Shah to lean on the companies to produce and sell more Iranian oil. Afterward he instructed Flanigan to tell the American oil companies that it was in the "US national interest" to "make every effort" to close the gap between the company off-take estimate and Iran's projected governmental requirements.[62]

State Department officials soon reported to Kissinger that the Shah was "counting heavily on alleged Presidential assurances ... given during his October state visit." Flanigan contacted the Iran Consortium members in the following months to impress "the President's desire, on the basis of the national security interest, that the consortium go a long way toward meeting the $155 million gap." In the meantime, the Shah wrote Nixon of his expectations that, based on their conversation, the United States would be "forthcoming in responding to Iran's request regarding oil and also military matters, on which the peace and very future of the Persian Gulf depended."[63]

For their part, the companies protested that Iranian demands were insatiable. Flanigan reported to Nixon in February 1970 that he saw "no prospect of persuading the Consortium" to yield to the Shah. On Flanigan's memo, Nixon wrote in the margin: "Tell them that if they don't help us on this I will redraw the Oil Import Decision. This is an order."[64]

---

[62] Flanigan to Kissinger, January 10, 1970, National Security Council Files, box 601, RNL; Kissinger and Flanigan to Nixon, "Increased Iranian Oil Production through Shipments to Cuba," February 25, 1970, National Security Council Files, box 601, RNL.

[63] Eliot to Kissinger, "Shah of Iran's Expectations," December 1, 1969, National Security Council Files, box 601, RNL; Flanigan to Kissinger, December 17, 1969, National Security Council Files, box 601, RNL; AmEmbassy Tehran to DOS, February 17, 1970, *FRUS 1969–76*, vol. E-4, doc. 46; Kissinger and Flanigan to Nixon, "Increased Iranian Oil Production through Shipments to Cuba," February 25, 1970, National Security Council Files, box 601, RNL.

[64] Kissinger and Flanigan to Nixon, "Increased Iranian Oil Production through Shipments to Cuba," February 25, 1970, National Security Council Files, box 601, RNL.

The threat to the companies' lucrative domestic market appears to have worked. The members of the Iran Consortium agreed on May 7, 1970, to production increases and a loan to be repaid in future oil production. The director of Near East affairs for the National Security Council, Harold Saunders, lavished praise on Flanigan. "Due to your efforts with them, [the Consortium] worked in a more flexible manner this year to bridge the gap between their capabilities and Iran's requirements."[65]

The tracks of sovereignty in the international community were never uniform, as the concurrent negotiations in Iran and Iraq demonstrate. But despite their considerable differences, the oil elites inhabited a maze of mutual dependency, in which the trend of policies and ideas designed to overturn the history of petroleum colonization were general. At the same time as he compared himself to Mossadegh and the insurrectionists in Iraq in his drive to "wage war" with the companies, the Shah also had begun to ground his argument in the same questions of decolonization, sovereignty, and rights that many Third World elites had incorporated into their intellectual and political programs. "The main point," the Shah told Secretary of State Rogers on one representative occasion, "was that, in accordance with principles established by the United Nations, the companies cannot ... prevent exploitation of Iran's natural resources."[66]

As the pulse of activity quickened, the geopolitics of decolonization and the Cold War helped make the sovereign rights program more prominent in world affairs. "The elimination of the UK military position in the Gulf [was] an irreversible decision," a State Department official wrote Dean Rusk in January 1968. He worried it "could be penny-wise, pound-foolish if political changes in the Gulf were to bring about revisions in the terms by which the UK gets its oil." That insight about the terms of oil supply could have been applied more broadly. The forces of change continued to become more intense after Nixon's order. As the Shah's demands increased, the companies reported that they were "hard-pressed" by the leaders of other nations, including Saudi Arabia, who were "anxious to catch up." The rivalries between producers, which

[65] Peter Flanigan, Memorandum for the President, "Information: Oil Consortium," May 8, 1970, National Security Council Files, box 601, RNL; Kissinger to Nixon, "Letter to You from the Shah of Iran," April 13, 1970, National Security Council Files, box 755, RNL; NSC Memorandum, Saunders for Flanigan, "Iranian Consortium Settlement," May 7, 1970, National Security Council Files, box 601, RNL.

[66] Memcon, "Iranian Oil Matters," April 1, 1969, National Security Council Files, box 601, RNL.

doomed the royalty negotiations and the Arab oil embargo in the mid-1960s, were now of a different color.[67]

The sovereign rights program was emblematic of a type of organizational and political endeavor that was new to the twentieth century. As the Shah's symbolic politics of Mossadegh and Iraq made clear, the reform agenda of that program, the individual desires of the oil-producers, and the decisions of American policymakers were not easily unscrambled. The Gulf Scuttle, the rise of Iran as a regional power, and the growing power of nations to control their oil were together definitive proof that "gunboats can no longer 'defend' oil installations as they once did in the heyday of imperialism," one US official wrote. Rather, the question of oil control had become for him and others a more complex "strategic" question, one that different governments could use in different ways.[68]

But to stress the common lineaments of the oil elite and their political program does not mean to reject particularities within it. Quite the opposite. It was through a narrative of parts that sovereign rights in the oil industry began to take on a new trajectory in 1968 and after. As late as 1967, Muhammad Mughraby's theory of "power from without" seemed distant. Sovereign rights, uncertainly poised between nationalism and internationalism, had lurched back and forth in the 1960s. Binding together as it did the interests and experiences of dissimilar groups, the evolving network of oil elites could not overcome that tension.

By 1970, though, the combination of national difference and international solidarity became empowering. This was because sovereign rights could be at once diffuse and, because it was widespread, powerful. It had already had a tremendous impact on a whole generation of lawyers, economists, oil ministers, and even heads of state. Now that it was becoming wound up with other major issues, including Cold War geopolitics, the US government would continue to play an important role.

---

[67] Battle to Rusk, January 9, 1968, *FRUS 1964–68*, vol. XXI, doc. 122; Memcon, "Iran Oil Situation," March 6, 1968, RG 59, Central Foreign Policy Files 1967–69, PET 6 IRAN-box 1358, NARA.

[68] Chester Crocker, "The United States and the Persian Gulf in the Twilight of the Pax Britannica," October 12, 1970, National Security Council Files, Institutional Files, box H-157, RNL.

6

A Turning Point of Our History

The Insurrectionists and Oil, 1970–1971

After political freedom comes the phase of industrial and economic freedom.[1]

Muammar al-Qaddafi, 1970

Over the last twenty years circumstances have changed.[2]

Nadim Pachachi, 1971

A 1970 British intelligence report profiled the new director of oil policy for the Libyan Revolutionary Command Council, Mahmood Maghribi. The profile began with the promise of his early career. Soon after his graduation from the law school at George Washington University in 1966, Maghribi joined Esso Libya as an in-house lawyer. But then his life suddenly changed in June 1967. When he worked with student and labor activists to organize oil and dock worker strikes during the Arab–Israeli war, he was fired, briefly jailed, and finally exiled. He landed in Beirut, where he became active in pro-Palestine politics and even attempted to secure a foreign policy post with the People's Front for the Liberation of Palestine through its Marxist leader and his former school-mate, George Habbash.[3]

---

[1] ME/3349/A/1, "Qadhafi's Bayda Rally Speech," April 8, 1970, Foreign and Commonwealth Office: Commodities and Oil Department, folder 432, UKNA.

[2] *Times* (London), November 9, 1971.

[3] D. K. Haskell, "Call on B.P.," July 7, 1970, Foreign and Commonwealth Office: Commodities and Oil Department, folder 433, UKNA; On Maghribi, see: John K. Cooley, *Libyan Sandstorm* (New York: Holt, Rinehart and Winston, 1982), 17–19; Joe Stork, *Middle East Oil and the Energy Crisis* (New York: Monthly Review Press, 1975), 153–7.

Such information was, if titillating, incomplete. Questions must have abounded for those who read the profile: Was he in contact with those oil elites who made their home in Beirut, including Abdullah al-Tariki? How well did he understand the oil industry and Libya's place in it? And what of his life before joining Esso? A closer look at Maghribi reveals that he believed that international society – including the UN committees and conferences, the Non-Aligned Movement, the Arab Petroleum Congresses, and OPEC – had formed a fertile seedbed for an anticolonial community of learning and debate in the previous quarter century. A closer look also reveals that the economic culture of decolonization provided an intellectual and ideological model in the light of which he hardened his personal defiance.

As a young man, he was also frustrated that, amidst the effervescence of decolonization, the OPEC nations seemed to stagger from crisis to crisis. But in 1970 he was in a position to change all that. A storm of epic proportions had begun to gather in Tripoli, the first rumblings of which were heard upon the reappearance of Maghribi. Oil executives told their counterparts in government that his arrival "constituted a turn for the worse." If vague, that prediction was also correct, for the former Esso employee and political exile quickly remade himself as the most influential radical insurrectionist in the oil industry. Flush with national funds and international support, he launched the first steps of a policy campaign in April 1970 that was to convulse the international economy for the rest of the decade. This chapter tells the story of how the Libyan Revolutionary Command Council attacked its concessionaires with great success under his guidance and, in the process, set off a chain of events that led to OPEC price control in 1971.[4]

Maghribi had doubted the value of oil insurrection in his 1966 dissertation. But by 1970 he believed that the labors of his predecessors and contemporaries would allow him to act without paying the same price Mossadegh had. Three factors stiffened his resolve and helped him succeed. First, Maghribi inherited Anes Qasem's checkerboard division of the nation and, largely because of it, a marvelous strategic position. Second, the oil nations began to take concerted action. The radical governments in Iraq and Algeria continued to develop their national industries and their oil elites worked closely with their Libyan

---

[4] D. K. Haskell, "Call on B.P.," July 7, 1970, Foreign and Commonwealth Office: Commodities and Oil Department, folder 433, UKNA.

counterparts. The nationalism of the moderate producers, with their pragmatic emphasis on self-interest, also bolstered Maghribi's anticolonial internationalism. Third, the Cold War politics of the Nixon administration again encouraged the convergence of the gradualists and the insurrectionists.

Those factors allowed the OPEC nations as a group to swing from price-takers to price-makers by the beginning of 1971, a year of great political, economic, and ideological mobilization. But the meteoric rise of Libyan oil nationalism also reflected and channeled a longer history. Provocative and dramatic as the events of 1970 and 1971 were, they acquired their significance from their connection to the deeper if less conspicuous program of sovereign rights. The program appealed to a large coalition of supporters with intersecting agendas. The commitment to an economic equivalent to decolonization, as well as their self-perception as a forward-looking alliance, enlivened elites across the international community. The success of OPEC in 1970 and after also marked a new psychological era for sovereign rights. Many anticolonial elites felt as if the tide of time was finally turning in their favor. More and more argued that the wave of anticolonial opposition was about to reach a crest. For a moment, it even seemed like the Maghribi and other oil elites would rise above the backbiting whirlpools of different national interests and the undertow of the unequal past.

Maghribi himself believed that he undertook his policies in a conducive context. In 1966 – the same year he finished his dissertation – Josef Brop Tito, Gamal Abdel Nasser, and Indira Gandhi met in New Delhi. They released a joint statement. "Imperialist and neo-colonialist forces" opposed the "achievement of complete political and economic emancipation," they wrote in bold, arresting words. To achieve the economic growth necessary to "break the shackles of poverty," it was important to change the structure of international capitalism, in particular "in relation to the prices of primary products."[5]

Maghribi couldn't have agreed more, and oil emerged as the focus of his studies. He brought the philosophy of the economic culture of decolonization and the aspirations of the sovereign rights program into the heart of his life. As an undergraduate at the University of Damascus in the 1950s, he was exposed to the rising nationalism of the new middle

---

[5] Joint Communique of the Tripartite Meeting, New Delhi, October 24, 1966, *ISIL* (1970).

class, which directed its patriotism not only at the remnants of French rule but also at the colonial system as such. Upon moving to Washington, DC, in the mid-1960s he settled on the research topic of "petroleum legislation in Libya." Like other anticolonial elites, he used the colonial past to cast light on the national present. "The thirty-one years of Italian occupation were the unhappiest in the history of the Libyans," he wrote. Drawing on a close reading of UN meeting minutes, Maghribi then discussed the calls by the Italian, French, and British governments that the nation be placed under a three-party international trusteeship after World War II. An early display of Third World solidarity ended that "whole imperialistic plan" when Haiti voted to reject Italian trusteeship in the UN General Assembly in 1951.[6]

But the political liberation of Libya, while initially and rightfully rejoiced, was only partial for Maghribi. Serious economic problems continued to infringe upon independence; Libya combined "within the borders of one country" all the obstacles to development "that could be found anywhere." But there was hope, and that hope lay in the subsoil. Petroleum production could bring a new day. "All this began to change rapidly with the discovery of oil," he wrote. The cause was clear: the "favorable petroleum law" written by Anes Qasem had allowed for rapid exploration and added over $1 billion to the national economy between 1956 and 1964. Maghribi celebrated the fact that Qasem encouraged the greatest possible number of oil companies to prospect in Libya "as extensively and possible and within the shortest amount of time." Of crucial importance, the 1955 law maintained national ownership of "petroleum in its natural state," a view that Maghribi believed had been inherited from English common law. But, as with the other legal arguments put forward by anticolonial elites, the precedents mattered less than the new context of decolonization. Citing the 1952 UN resolution on permanent sovereignty, Maghribi pointed to the rising universality of the belief in sovereign rights "shared by almost all countries in the world." The resultant collaboration between elites – in particular that of Nadim Pachachi and Qasem in 1960 and 1961 – continued to bring Libyan law "into line with the petroleum laws and the new concessions of other Middle Eastern countries."[7]

---

[6] Christoph Schumann, "The Generation of Broad Expectations: Nationalism, Education, and Autobiography in Syria and Lebanon," *Die Welt des Islams* 41: 2 (July 2001), 174–5, 194–5; Maghribi, *Petroleum Legislation in Libya*, 3–4.

[7] Maghribi, *Petroleum Legislation in Libya*, 10–13, 40–60, 176.

More broadly, Maghribi believed that the "noted difference between old and new concessions" was central to understanding the historical breakthrough that began with Qasem. In that sense, he shared Abdullah al-Tariki's understanding of the history of petroleum colonization, which he also cited favorably. In the act of "acquiring vast areas of a country" for long periods, he wrote, the old concessions allowed the multinational companies to "imprison" the oil nations. That sense of perpetual imprisonment is central to understanding Maghribi's perception of oil politics and its connection to the sovereign rights program. The old concessions had divested the oil-producing nations of their rights as nations, he argued.[8]

Maghribi's devotion to the economic culture of decolonization was characteristic in other ways too. Like other anticolonial lawyers, he drew on the combined nationalism and internationalism inherent in what he called the "new concept of 'transnational law.'" In his hands, transnational law was both a means to challenge the old concessions and, more broadly, representative of the moral force for change that came with decolonization. The incessant calls for "its application to concession agreements is receiving increasing support" because the concept of "changing circumstances" was compelling in the way it shifted the discussion from an examination of the past to "control over this vital resource in the future."[9]

Like other elites, he also believed that the rise of information sharing and technical analysis among anticolonial elites embodied a profound change in international life. His close reading of the papers of the Arab Petroleum Congress, followed by a detailed assessment of new contracts signed after 1960, pointed to the different means that already existed to take control over oil. In particular, the Qasem rule on the relinquishment of untapped areas of the old concessions had been invoked in Iraq through Law 80, in Saudi Arabia and Kuwait by mutual agreement, and in Iran as part of the new offshore concessions. As important, the rejection of the "one-company-monopoly approach" that Qasem imparted was also more and more common.[10]

These change pointed in their sum toward the possibility of the oil nations moving from the role of "an almost bystander" in the oil industry to that of "an active partner," Maghribi hoped. For him and other oil

---

[8] Maghribi, *Petroleum Legislation in Libya*, 88, 98, 50–5, 128–9.
[9] Maghribi, *Petroleum Legislation in Libya*, 72–3, 76.
[10] Maghribi, *Petroleum Legislation in Libya*, 177–8.

elites who surveyed the international landscape in the mid-1960s, a new legal and economic order had begun to cement itself.[11]

If Maghribi's missive looked backward through a winding tangle of older thoughts and actions, it was also more than an endeavor to take stock. First in his political organizing in 1967 and then when he began to work for Muammar al-Qaddafi in 1970, he sought to constitute a close bond between permanent sovereignty, national production control, and the price of oil. But his knowledge of Libyan history, his critique of the old concessions, his expertise on the new ones, and his pouring over of papers by Frank Hendryx, Francisco Parra, Tariki, Qasem, and others did not, of course, mean that he was destined to end the history of petroleum colonization. Even though anticolonial oil elites had always intended their analyses of international society to serve in the efforts to change it, action was not a default position. Neither was success the normal outcome.

It took strategic insight as well as historical imagination to see Libyan oil as a historical pivot. Maghribi's ability to press the issue in 1970 depended as much on Libya's geopolitical and historical advantages as it did on his vision of economic decolonization. These advantages can be measured through two historical developments in the international oil market in the 1960s. First was the change in balance between global supply and demand. Second was the ascendant position of Libya within that shifting market.

The international oil market changed in 1969 from a buyers' to a sellers' market, as contemporary observers noted. This was due to a set of interrelated economic and technological causes. For one, the appetite for oil had grown unabated in the industrialized nations and, increasingly, in the developing world – advertising claims by companies that labeled oil "the world's main source of power" or "the life blood of progress" in the 1960s were hardly exaggerated. Moreover, at the same time as demand outpaced supply, production of oil in the United States reached a peak and US production could no longer provide the spare capacity to offset supply stoppages from other sources.[12]

In short, the international market had become relatively dry. OPEC oil fed that thirst. James Akins, the State Department expert, explained the

---

[11] Maghribi, *Petroleum Legislation in Libya*, 177–82.
[12] "Routes of Progress," *The Arab World: The Journal of the Anglo Arab Association* 27 (July 1956), 19; "Power for Progress," *The Arab World: Journal of the Anglo-Arab Association* 31 (April 1957), 13. For the statistics in context, see: Steven A. Schneider, *The Oil Price Revolution* (Baltimore: Johns Hopkins University Press, 1983), 59–75.

ramifications for the international political economy a few years later: a production loss from any major producer could cause a "temporary but significant world oil shortage." Such a skewed market gave the OPEC members "economic leverage," which he predicted would make it more likely that they would "hold together, to raise prices and conceivably to limit output." This was an early example of what political scientist Joseph Nye in 1980 described as the new "rhetoric of energy security" in the industrialized West, which for him confirmed a collective anxiety about oil supply and prices.[13]

The anticolonial elites in the OPEC Secretariat and the oil nations' governments saw the opportunity. Amir Kubbah, who had closed down his Baghdad journal and joined the OPEC Information Department after the Ba'athist takeover, wrote that 1970 marked a "turning point in the history of the oil industry." The changing market shifted the "balance of bargaining power" from the multinational companies to the oil elites. "Economic and political forces were set in motion, which seem to have put an end to a long era of cheap oil," he believed.[14]

A number of other events related to the broader currents of decolonization further tightened the market and improved Maghribi's bargaining power. For one, civil war had crushed the incipient production of Nigeria. The nation, which would join OPEC in 1972, started to produce oil on a commercial level in the mid-1960s. Inspired by the reports of the UN Permanent Sovereignty Commission and the OPEC Declaratory Statement, the Nigerian military passed laws based on the doctrine of permanent sovereignty, in particular, a 1969 Petroleum Decree that vested the ownership of oil with the national government. But so did the secession government in the oil-rich Eastern region of Biafra. Oil installations became favored military targets, and warfare brought production to a near standstill.[15]

Likewise, oil from Saudi Arabia had been rerouted following the closing of the 750-mile Trans-Arabian Pipeline that supplied a Mediterranean outlet in Syria. After the 1967 war, Saudi Arabia maintained a policy to avoid shipments through the pipeline as long as it ran through Israeli-occupied territory. When Saudi Oil Minister Ahmed Zaki Yamani

---

[13] James E. Akins, "The Oil Crisis: This Time the Wolf Is Here," *Foreign Affairs* 51: 3 (1973), 469; Joseph S. Nye, Jr., "Energy Nightmares," *Foreign Policy* (1980), 132–54.

[14] OPEC, *Annual Review and Record* (1970), OIC.

[15] Chibuike Uche, "Oil, British Interests, and the Nigerian Civil War," *The Journal of African History* 49 (2008), 111–35.

scheduled new deliveries in September 1969, even though Israel still controlled the stretch that traversed the Golan Heights, the pipeline was sabotaged four times between then and December. Syria closed its outlet, and supply would not resume until February 1971. The closure of the Suez Canal, the other major link between Persian Gulf oil and Western European markets in the postwar era, also tightened supply. When Nasser closed the canal to shipping in 1967, companies were forced to "demothball" old tankers and divert carriers from the ore and grain trades.[16]

If the strain in the market was helpful for many oil producers, Libya was the most obvious beneficiary. The nation's "short haul" production, just across the Mediterranean from the markets of Western Europe, was a significant factor in filling the demand for new consumption and offsetting the production problems from other sources. That economic station meant greater freedom of action for Maghribi. "With the present tight – and even dangerous – international supply situation, the Libyans hold all the aces," the British Oil Department lamented in 1970.[17]

The strong hand also had something to do with the recent history of the growth of Libyan oil production in the 1960s. The nation's market position had improved in that decade in large part because most westerners viewed its monarchy as a source of regional stability. That rationale was straightforward in a 1967 policy review by the State Department. First, as the global economy grew, so did petroleum production. Second, the most important new source was Libya. Third, King Idris stood with the United States in the Cold War. "In a trend favorable to European security," Libyan production had "reached the level of a major Persian Gulf producer," the State Department reported.[18]

American officials had presented monarchical Libya as a reliable source of oil since at least May 1959, when the National Security Council (NSC) met to discuss NSC directive 5820, the Eisenhower administration's remarkable reconsideration of policy toward pan-Arab nationalism. In

---

[16] "PFLP Clams Responsibility for Sabotage," *MEES* 13: 3 (November 14, 1969), 17; "Tapline Sabotaged for Third Time," *MEES* 13: 2 (November 7, 1969), 6; CIA Intelligence Memorandum, March 1971, *FRUS 1969–76*, vol. XXIV, doc. 94; Annex 1 to Interagency Oil Task Force, NSSM 114, "World Oil Situation," January 24, 1971, National Security Council Files, Institutional Files, box H-180, RNL.

[17] Memorandum by the Minister of Technology, "The Oil Supply Situation," September 29, 1970, Foreign and Commonwealth Office: Commodities and Oil Department, folder 435, UKNA; Oil Department, "Libyan Oil," September 21, 1970, Foreign and Commonwealth Office: Commodities and Oil Department, folder 435, UKNA.

[18] Paper Prepared in the Department of State, February 8, 1967, *FRUS 1964–68*, vol. XXI, doc. 19.

the wake of the anti-Nasserist Eisenhower Doctrine, cooler heads had convinced the president that Nasser's pan-Arabism was not necessarily incompatible with the primary American objectives in the Middle East: the maintenance of the free flow of oil and the exclusion of Soviet influence. Still, the NSC found reason for concern about the stable supply of cheap oil that was so central to their notion of national security. Persian Gulf oil producers had "too much economic and political leverage." This would tempt the more radical Arab producers, in particular, Iraq, to use oil production "arbitrarily" for political gain.[19]

Libya's newly discovered reserves, on the other hand, were safely within the Western bloc. The only hitch lay with the largest multinational oil companies, whose executives were "loathe to ... jeopardize their position" in Saudi Arabia and Iran. In the meeting, Eisenhower and Vice President Richard Nixon disagreed about how best to pressure the multinationals to increase their Libyan investments. The president held that "under a system of free enterprise" the government's role was to "make certain that there are no obstacles" to "world-wide" oil development, not to encourage a "crash program for ... Libyan fields." Nixon disagreed on pragmatic terms. "The nub of the matter was what to do about Libya," he said. If the oil companies "deliberately retard[ed] the development of the Libyan oil fields," that would weaken the relationship with a key regional ally.[20]

Nixon and Eisenhower failed to realize that the problem of Libyan oil had already been resolved by Anes Qasem. Smaller companies jumped at the chance to enter Libya on his terms, and production grew rapidly in the 1960s. At the same time, the nation remained securely pro-American. In a February 1967 review, the Persian Gulf desk even held up King Idris's "moderation" as a paradigm. More intimate contact along the lines of that achieved with Idris would allow US officials to help other Arab oil producers overcome the ideological ferment of pan-Arabism and become more "interdependent with the West." Officials again categorized Libyan oil a "safe alternative" to the Persian Gulf in the wake of the 1967 embargo.[21]

---

[19] Memorandum of Discussion at the 406th Meeting of the National Security Council, May 13, 1959, *FRUS 1958–60*, vol. IV, doc. 298. On the Eisenhower Doctrine and pan-Arabism, see: Yaqub, *Containing Arab Nationalism*, 237–67.

[20] Memorandum of Discussion at the 406th Meeting of the National Security Council, May 13, 1959, *FRUS 1958–60*, vol. IV, doc. 298.

[21] Paper Prepared in the Department of State, February 8, 1967, *FRUS 1964–68*, vol. XXI, doc. 19; "Western Interests in Arab Oil," December 27, 1967, *FRUS 1964–68*, vol. XXI, doc. 26.

With trust came production. Greater and greater amounts of Libyan oil arrived at new and old networks of refineries and gas stations across Europe. At the time of the 1969 revolution, the country was the fourth largest producer in the world, the second largest exporter, and supplier of a quarter of Western Europe's energy needs. In short, one official at the British Oil Department wrote, Libya had become "a phenomenon of the post-war oil boom."[22]

Then, the Libyan Revolution transformed the international politics of oil. Amir Kubbah, the Iraqi journalist turned OPEC public relations employee, would write four years later that "it took a Muammar al-Qaddafi ... to shake OPEC off its lethargy and to goad it into real constructive action." By then Qaddafi was on his way to becoming an international pariah, but Western diplomats knew little about the leader of the Revolutionary Command Council in the months following the coup. For the State Department, the 27-year-old army captain was a caricature – "a man raised in the desert" with "the virtues and vices of a fundamentalist prophet." American officials understood little more than that the hitherto unknown leader had "a strong sense of mission."[23]

The desert puritan's public statements fast added clarity to how his sense of mission would be applied to oil production. When he ordered the removal of US troops from the Wheelus Air Base in an April 1970 speech, the same month Maghribi took control of the oil negotiations, Qaddafi linked the military decision to "the battle with the foreign oil companies." The end of the US Army presence and the coming end of foreign control over oil were part of a broader understanding of "the political freedom" of Libya, he said. His words then echoed the narrative logic and language of sovereign rights. "After political freedom comes the phase of industrial and economic freedom," he continued. "This poses one of the biggest problems facing the world as a whole and the Islamic States in particular." It was his government's official policy to "recover their full rights from the oil companies."[24]

---

[22] Oil Department, "British Interests in Libyan Oil," May 27, 1970, Foreign and Commonwealth Office: Commodities and Oil Department, folder 432, UKNA.

[23] Kubbah, *OPEC, Past and Present*, 52; Memo for Kissinger, "Qadhafi Resignation Reported in Libya," September 27, 1971, National Security Council Files, box 739, RNL. On Qaddafi, see: Douglas Little, "To the Shores of Tripoli: America, Qaddafi, and Libyan Revolution, 1969–1989," *The International History Review* 35: 1 (2013), 70–99.

[24] Telegram No. 615, Tripoli to FCO, "Libyan Posted Price Negotiations," April 11, 1970, Foreign and Commonwealth Office: Commodities and Oil Department, folder 432, UKNA; ME/3349/A/1, "Qadhafi's Bayda Rally Speech," April 8, 1970, Foreign and Commonwealth Office: Commodities and Oil Department, folder 432, UKNA.

Maghribi knew that narrative like the back of his own hand. His agreement to chair Qaddafi's new committee on oil brought "no comfort to the companies," whose executives complained of his "extremist attitude to Western oil interests" to the British embassy in Tripoli. He showed no signs of letting "the grass grow under his feet" when he used his first public statement to argue that the tight market made Libyan oil more valuable than company pricing policies allowed. The oil companies could not continue "to suck the people's wealth," he said. This was more than just nationalist bravura. His arguments also built on the economic and legal foundations of the sovereign rights program. He told the Libyan News Agency days later that "the committee's basic function is to establish fair prices for Libyan oil." There would be "no limit" to the measures the government would take – including nationalization, he said – in order to assert that right.[25]

The model set by the economic culture of decolonization was influential. Interestingly, Maghribi came to his insurrectionist position in 1970 through gradualism. He had written in 1966 that nationalization, "although a dear desire to many hearts, including the writer's, seems at present to be impracticable." He also concluded that Tariki's arguments for nationalization at the 1965 Arab Petroleum Congress were unfeasible because of the OPEC members' inability to arrive at a consensus. It would be "unwise" for any one country "to embark upon such a step alone," he wrote. The example of Mossadegh was "still too clear to be ignored." To take on an insurrectionist policy required what seemed impossible: "a collective stand from most of the oil exporting countries."[26]

That was then, this was now. In the spring of 1970, Maghribi's sense of violated economic justice and his knowledge of the oil industry allowed him to parlay Libya's strategic advantages into policy. Maghribi had internalized and naturalized the progressive notion of the onward march that drove the economic culture of decolonization among anticolonial elites, and for that reason was able to link the daily

---

[25] Telegram No. 650, Tripoli to FCO, "Libyan Posted Price Negotiations," April 16, 1970, Foreign and Commonwealth Office: Commodities and Oil Department, folder 432, UKNA; Telegram No. 680, Tripoli to FCO, "Posted Price Negotiations," April 21, 1970, Foreign and Commonwealth Office: Commodities and Oil Department, folder 432, UKNA; "Libya Prepares 'Contingency' Plan if Oil Price Talks Fail," *PIW* 13: 27 (April 27, 1970), 2; "Maghribi Warns Oil Companies against Resisting Libya's Price Demands," *PIW* 13: 28 (May 1, 1970), 2–3.

[26] Maghribi, *Petroleum Legislation in Libya*, 180–7.

business of oil negotiations to a larger understanding of the past and the present. If every new Libyan law had helped the country obtain "a larger share of its oil wealth than before," he had written in 1966, the constant changes in circumstances pointed toward greater militancy. Within that vision of unremitting change, Maghribi also made clear he was a dedicated internationalist. He had noted in 1966 that Anes Qasem's laws depended not just on his own insight, but also on "the experience of the Middle Eastern countries which preceded her in developing their oil wealth." That transnational learning process had helped Qasem avoid in Libya "many of the mistakes" of the "old" concessions in Iran, Iraq, and Saudi Arabia.[27]

When looking for ways to shape his policy of pressure, it was thus natural that Maghribi turned to Abdullah al-Tariki. No single person had been more vocal about the history of petroleum colonization or more active in its narration. His 1965 speech on nationalization and petroleum colonization remained the key exposition of the oil elites' potential power, and he had stubbornly resisted the gradualist spirit of the 1960s. He sustained his argument into the 1970s, when he was considered by all both a tremendous authority and an agent provocateur, for his constant arguments for nationalization and his savage criticism of gradualism as soft-minded appeasement.

At Maghribi's invitation, Tariki traveled to Tripoli to advise the Oil Committee in the summer of 1970. He was not alone but came with his business partner at the Arab Oil Research Center, a Lebanese lawyer named Nicolas Sarkis. Like Maghribi, Sarkis was typical of the internationalist class of anticolonial oil elite. In a way, the two men represent a generational shift in the oil elites. The new elites built on but moved beyond the work of their predecessors. They also believed that the changing circumstances would allow them more opportunities to act. Francisco Parra described Sarkis as representative of "a large and constantly growing body of opinion which is impatient of negotiation and compromise" – a stance that had been "nugatory when the concessions were signed," but what was by the late 1960s "the most important force in the world."[28]

Like Maghribi, too, Sarkis was not just a player in that force but also a student of it. He wrote his doctoral thesis for the University of Paris Law Faculty in 1961 on "the petroleum factor" in Middle Eastern

---

[27] Maghribi, *Petroleum Legislation in Libya*, 187, 222.   [28] *ION* 3: 5 (May 1964), OIC.

economic growth. The thesis is a symptomatic and detailed example of the genre of histories of petroleum colonization. Its first section analyzes the historical relationships between producing countries and the oil companies through the lens of "the disadvantages of the current situation." The second discusses the "breakdown of the traditional balance" in the petroleum market in the late 1950s in the broader context of decolonization. The third looks to the "emergent imperatives of the future," in particular, the possibility of a collective oil policy on the part of the Arab producers.[29]

The figure of Mossadegh – which served as an index of the never-ending, ever-changing conversation among the oil elites about sovereign rights – was also crucial to Sarkis. But whereas Maghribi and others took the overthrow of Mossadegh as a warning siren, Sarkis thought of it as a moment in which old ideas clashed with new ones. Like Maghribi, he summarized the Iranian's position on domestic jurisdiction with approval – Mossadegh had not only denied the right of the international court to arbitrate the case but in the process had affirmed "the right of sovereignty." But Sarkis went further. The policies of Iran opened the eyes of all that could see that the oil concessions were "colonial charters," he wrote, not freely-negotiated agreements. Mossadegh, so constantly evoked by the oil elites as a notice of caution, was thus also a beacon from the past. Much more, he was a martyr to an immovable cause.[30]

Sarkis also credited Mossadegh with setting the more comprehensive precedent of "opposing parties explicitly pressing their points of view" in the oil industry. The rise of the new adversarial style was especially important because it forced the oil elites into the realization that information was crucial to sovereign rights, he argued. As the oil elites had found their voice and formed interest groups based on their sovereign rights in the 1950s, one fact emerged that was of principal importance – the "faithful records of oil company transactions" found in their annual reports were anything but, Sarkis said sarcastically. The opacity of company accounting and a lack of collective knowledge about the industry had allowed the multinational oil companies to perpetuate their superior position. For this reason, Tariki and others had accused the companies of

---

[29] Nicolas Sarkis, "Le Pétrole Facteur D'Intégration et de Croissance Économique," Thése pour le Doctorat en Droit, Universite de Paris, Faculte de Droit et des Sciences Economiques (1962), 5.
[30] Sarkis, "Le Pétrole Facteur D'Intégration," 29–32.

"hiding much of the information that would unmask their price maneuvers" in the 1950s and early 1960s.[31]

The expansion of knowledge had been key to the rise of the economic culture of decolonization, Sarkis believed. He thus dedicated his life to a search for information that would help the oil producers confront the companies. He certainly saw his dissertation as part of a longer process. A comparative analysis of the history of imperialism and the old concessions added to that dynamic of past oppression and present liberation for him. The "dismemberment" of the Ottoman empire, the "parceling" of the Middle East into "miniscule States," and the "archaic structure and feudal regime" put in place by the major powers reached a climax when the oil companies generalized "the most unusual type of contract" in the 1920s and 1930s: the oil concession. To examine the "extraordinary extension in time and in space" of the old concessions was thus to understand the substance of past inequality. That inequality persisted not only because of the terms of trade for oil, a concept Sarkis picked up from Gunnar Myrdal. It carried on also because the concessions relegated the oil producers to the status of "quasi-nation," a category that gave the lie to their nominal political independence. He went even further: "the concept of nation in economic thought" contradicted the experience of the producers. Instead, they held a subordinate role in an international economy that was comprised less of sovereign states than of a "hierarchy of powers … a set of relationships and proportions that constituted an economic ensemble."[32]

Like other oil elites, Sarkis also saw progress on the horizon. He had observed in 1961 that the growth in popularity of Qasem's smaller, shorter concessions were becoming a new contractual norm. He also believed the new concessions were but a "transitional phase" between the "traditional regime of the generalized concession and the Arabization of the industry." The sense of momentum was clear to him in the political as well as the contractual realm – the "atmosphere of bonhomie" after the First Arab Petroleum Congress had begun to move price discussions from a "sparse and vague" platform to a more concrete one. For Sarkis, the collective maintenance of a "fair price" through coordinated production policies and improved contractual terms had become the supreme objectives of OPEC. Between 1959, when he

---

[31] Sarkis, "Le Pétrole Facteur D'Intégration," 32.
[32] Sarkis, "Le Pétrole Facteur D'Intégration," 34, 71–3.

started the dissertation, and 1961, when he finished it, the oil producers learned that they held a "common interest."[33]

When Maghribi invited Tariki and Sarkis to Tripoli, all three men already shared a common frame of mind. They also knew a great deal about Libya's place in the international oil industry. Tariki had, of course, worked closely with Anes Qasem in the Arab League Petroleum Bureau and had also discussed Libyan oil with Amir Kubbah when the latter interviewed him in Baghdad in 1965. Sarkis was also familiar with the structure of Libyan oil law, as revealed by his favorable review of Qasem's standard of relinquishment in his doctoral thesis. Their policy suggestions to Maghribi built on the fact that national production still ran along Qasem's initial "checkerboard" scheme. They noted that one effect of the diffusion of power among smaller companies was that many of these companies depended on Libya to supply the majority of their oil.[34]

This was a weakness they could exploit. In April 1970, Maghribi demanded increases in the posted price of 44 cents a barrel with back payments to 1961 and a further back payment of 35 cents a barrel to 1967. The retroactive payments were a "basic matter," he told reporters, "a correction ... for previous underpricing by the companies." The lower prices had been part of a successful attempt to woo investors and gain a foothold in the European market, but Maghribi depicted them as an affront to Libyan sovereignty. In addition, he demanded a new tax rate of 55 percent. The companies refused, and the Revolutionary Command Council forced down production from 3.7 million to 2.9 million barrels per day between April and September 1970 to force the issue. Maghribi and his colleagues in this way said, according to one observer, "you owe us the whole industry."[35]

In four years, Maghribi had gone from law student to Standard Oil employee to deportee to champion of sovereign rights for the new government of Libya. Despite reports questioning whether Qaddafi and other members of the Revolutionary Command Council endorsed his "radical and extremist view of the oil companies' operations," British

---

[33] Sarkis, "Le Pétrole Facteur D'Intégration," 90–1, 104, 131–4, 249.

[34] Sarkis, "Le Pétrole Facteur D'Intégration," 38, 46.

[35] "Price 'Correction' Is What It Wants, Libya Now Says," *PIW* 13: 29 (May 11, 1970), 5; Melhuish to Brant, "Negotiations between the Libyan Government and the Producing Companies," May 19, 1970, Foreign and Commonwealth Office: Commodities and Oil Department, folder 432, UKNA.

policymakers wrote, the "Libyan demands as formulated by Maghribi" gained momentum in the second half of 1970.[36]

At this point, the actions of the Nixon administration began to influence the course of events. In June, the major oil companies requested diplomatic support from the US government in their drive to evade the new Libyan terms. The State Department responded in the negative, suggesting simply that the companies use "every means available to deal imaginatively with the problem of seeking to accommodate themselves with the foreseeable evolution of events in Libya." The government had decided to rebuff the pleas for intervention, although it did encourage the companies to offset Libyan production losses with oil from Iran and Saudi Arabia.[37]

The companies faced mounting pressure that autumn, but the State Department again expressed little concern. Analysts informed Nixon that the celebration of the first anniversary of the Libyan Revolution in September would be "marked by policy announcements affecting the US-dominated oil industry." The Revolutionary Command Council most likely would use the holiday to garner popular support for the imposition of a price increase. Again, the US government was indifferent. Any price hike, the memo offhandedly concluded, would be "something the companies could live with ... by passing it on to the consumers."[38]

These decisions followed a broader strategic decision within the Nixon administration to accommodate individual oil producers, a policy that decision makers believed was the best to serve US interests. Peter Flanigan, who had just concluded his intervention in the Iran revenue negotiations, explained the government position: "The penalties of a break with Libya, in terms of emphasizing the degree to which Russian-controlled Arab states hold Europe and Japan in pawn for energy

---

[36] Tel. 628 to Tripoli, "Libyan Oil," June 2, 1970, Foreign and Commonwealth Office: Commodities and Oil Department, folder 432, UKNA; Oil Department, "British Interests in Libyan Oil," May 27, 1970, Foreign and Commonwealth Office: Commodities and Oil Department, folder 432, UKNA.

[37] Katz to Trezise, "Oil Problems in Libya and the Middle East," July 28, 1970, *FRUS 1969–76*, vol. XXXVI, doc. 51; DOS to Iran Embassy, July 30, 1970, *FRUS 1969–76*, vol. XXXVI, doc. 52; DOS to Certain Diplomatic Posts, "Libyan Oil Negotiations," September 26, 1970, *FRUS 1969–76*, vol. XXXVI, doc. 56.

[38] DOS, Memo for the President, "Libyan Revolutionary Celebrations," August 29, 1970, National Security Council Files, box 739, RNL.

requirements and also as a result of the exacerbation of the existent tanker shortage, were much greater than the negatives which would result from a settlement with Libya." In other words, Cold War considerations trumped the concern about the potential consequences of Libyan policy for the oil industry.[39]

Moreover, the Nixon administration believed that accommodating Libyan demands on taxes and price would set a less toxic precedent than the threatened alternative of nationalization. The State Department's director of the Office of Fuels and Energy, James Akins, told the British ambassador in Washington that the price and tax increases were not "the real danger." Rather, Akins worried that the Libyans might be "contemplating expropriation of some or all US oil interests." Given that more dire threat, yielding to Maghribi's price increase seemed "reasonable" to him.[40]

The policy of accommodation guided the Nixon administration throughout 1970. It irritated multinational oil executives, who believed in the benefits of a unified stand against further sovereign infringements on their oil control. Their opinion was best summarized by Shell's lead negotiator in Tripoli. To yield to Maghribi would "demonstrate to the world" that the oil producers could "dictate the price of oil," he said. Similar demands, already called for by Algeria and Iraq, could swiftly spread to the other members of OPEC.[41]

The chairmen of BP and Shell traveled together to New York in September 1970 to try to convince US officials to back away from the policy of accommodation. They left London with the blessing of the British government, and Foreign Secretary Alec Douglas-Home urged the US undersecretary for political affairs, Alexis Johnson, not to "persuade [the companies] to give way." Johnson demurred. When they arrived in New York, the chairmen found "the US State Department more concerned with the implications ... for the short-term Western supply position than with the world-wide implications." Douglas-Home then ordered the British ambassador in Washington to "urgently" call on Johnson and James Akins to explain "the long-term risks." Douglas-Home also cabled Secretary of State William Rogers to insist that he

[39] Flanigan, "Libyan Oil," September 29, 1970, *FRUS 1969–76*, vol. XXXVI, doc. 57.

[40] Melhuish to Brant, "Negotiations between the Libyan Government and the producing companies on posted prices," May 19, 1970, UKNA, Foreign and Commonwealth Office: Commodities and Oil Department, folder 432, UKNA.

[41] Telegram 1321, Tripoli to FCO, September 21, 1970, Foreign and Commonwealth Office: Commodities and Oil Department, folder 432, UKNA.

"encourage the US majors to maintain a united front." It was to no avail, and State Department policy remained that the companies had "no real option but to settle on the Libyan's terms."[42]

Akins described the New York meeting in detail. The "formidable" chairman of BP – Sir Eric Drake, who had absconded to Iraq with the accounting books of Iran's Abadan refinery in 1951 – argued that the companies should stand firm against Maghribi. The consequences of surrender would be great. Acceptance of Libyan terms would expose the companies "to blackmail all over the world." The world faced "the most important week in the history of the oil industry since Mossadegh," he said. He then turned to the government officials and told them that the fate of the oil industry hung on American diplomatic support for the companies. But Johnson and Akins, unmoved, brushed aside his argument. Akins responded that the hands-off US policy had "the companies' interests at heart." His perception of the threat was different. At its core, accommodation actually protected the companies from their own rigidity. Accommodation prevented the companies from provoking "irreparable action" by Libya.[43]

After Occidental Oil famously assented to Libya's unilateral price hike in September 1970, Maghribi successfully pressured the larger oil companies for an Occidental-equivalent price increase and more beneficial profit-sharing agreements. Before then, the oil producers believed they could ill afford to slow production, because there was enough surplus elsewhere. Now Maghribi could impose his will. By October, the Revolutionary Command Council had extracted agreements from the major oil companies – first from Chevron and Texaco, then from Standard and Mobil, and finally from BP and Shell. The agreements increased the price and

[42] Telegram 2845, Washington to FCO, September 25, 1970, Foreign and Commonwealth Office: Commodities and Oil Department, folder 435, UKNA; Telegram 2081, UK Mission, New York to Washington, September 25, 1970, Foreign and Commonwealth Office: Commodities and Oil Department, folder 435, UKNA; DPO(70)22, Memorandum by the Secretary of State for Foreign and Commonwealth Affairs, September 30, 1970, Foreign and Commonwealth Office: Commodities and Oil Department, folder 435, UKNA; Memorandum of Conversation, October 3, 1970, *FRUS 1969–76*, vol. XXXVI, doc. 58; Telegram 2828, Washington to FCO, September 24, 1970, Foreign and Commonwealth Office: Commodities and Oil Department, folder 435, UKNA.

[43] Wilmott to Ellingworth, "Libyan Oil," October 23, 1970, Foreign and Commonwealth Office: Commodities and Oil Department, folder 435, UKNA; Telegram 2856, Washington to FCO, September 26, 1970, Foreign and Commonwealth Office: Commodities and Oil Department, folder 435, UKNA.

created a new national tax rate of 55 percent, which broke with the 50–50 profit-sharing principle established to amend the old concessions after World War II. Sir Eric Drake blamed the US decision not to stand up for the companies. "With ill-conceived hostility," he told one US official, "it was really the fault of the US Government that oil companies had felt forced to give in to Libyans."[44]

That was one interpretation. The Libyan oil minister, 'Izz al-Din al-Mabruk, painted Maghribi's policy in a different light. "[P]rior to the revolution, there was no one who cared to impose any kind of control on the companies," he told *Al Ahram* in May 1970. This was an overstatement. It is true that the ideological ardor of the new regime helped enable their success, but the specific policies built on those of its predecessors. The link between the anticolonial laws of Anes Qasem and the pressure Maghribi and Mabruk placed on the oil companies a decade and a half later casts doubt on any impenetrable divide drawn between the Libya of Idris and that of Qaddafi.[45]

The evidence of the long-established economic culture of decolonization was also apparent in Mabruk, for he too had developed his political consciousness within it. He had worked for Francisco Parra and Hasan Zakariya in the OPEC Legal Department for the half decade before the Libyan Revolution. At the Fifth Arab Petroleum Congress in 1965, he even presented a paper on how "changing circumstances" in the international economy had affected new oil production contracts. He called then for "a radical new approach to the question of oil concessions" to overturn the "rigid and outdated concession agreements." His main argument was a derivative of Mossadegh's national jurisdiction argument. The old concessions could not be binding because they were contracts of "an administrative nature" and thus fell under national purview. Mabruk also was likely among the men nodding his heads during Tariki's fiery speech on petroleum colonization on the last day of that Congress; his report at the next year's meeting examined potential scenarios for transnational supply control and prices, explicitly following Tariki's arguments about the possibilities of pro-rationing.[46]

---

[44] National Intelligence Estimate 36.5–71, Washington, April 30, 1971, *FRUS 1969–76*, vol. E-5, no. 2, doc. 74; "Majors Capitulate in Libya to New 55% Oil Tax Rate," *PIW* 9: 41 (October 12, 1970); DOS to Embassy United Kingdom, "Middle East Oil," October 14, 1970, *FRUS 1969–76*, vol. XXXVI, doc. 59.

[45] "Libyan Oil Minister Reviews Oil Policy Issues," *MEES* 13: 31 (May 29, 1970), 5–6.

[46] "From Concessions to Contracts," *MEES* 8: 21 (March 26, 1965), 22; "Qadhafi Heads New Libyan Government," *MEES* 13: 13 (January 23, 1970), 3.

Mabruk's message of a great break from the past was thus combined with a deeper awareness of the foundations upon which Libyan policy built and its relation to a broader international movement. He used both motifs in a 1970 meeting with company executives. The men faced each other "at a turning point of our history," he said. The new era would be characterized by two "basic principles" associated with "the change of circumstances" in the world surrounding the industry. First, the Revolutionary Command Council would "safeguard [its] complete right" to oil through national legislation. Second, it would also work to increase prices by "collective action through OPEC." But he didn't stop there. In addition to the OPEC members, Mabruk also called on a broader authority. In their aggregate, Libya's actions were "a most legitimate right" supported by the UN resolutions on "the permanent sovereignty of nations over their natural wealth and resources."[47]

The Libyan oil elites also used the standard economic argument of unequal exchange. The economic argument underpinned their internationalism. In one example, Mabruk added in a different meeting that a recent UN Conference on Trade and Development study noted the rising prices of manufactured industrial goods vis-à-vis the unchanged prices of crude oil. Libya would "not waver as regards our just demands" in that context, he said. "For we see no sense at all in political independence if it is not accompanied by economic liberation."[48]

Decolonization permanently redrew the political map of the world by awakening anticolonial elites' legal and economic sentiment. By late 1970, the internationalism of Libyan policy, historical and contemporary, represented a serious threat to the supply of oil to Europe. The threat was augmented by the fact that other oil elites admired Libyan policy. If the Iraqi government "took sympathetic action," British officials worried, Libyan actions could cause "serious trouble" in the international economy.[49]

Ba'athist Baghdad did not disappoint. Each side in the dispute over the nationalized Rumaila field remained adamantly opposed to compromise. But the negotiations shifted perceptibly in the government's favor during 1970 at the same time as Mabruk and Maghribi pressed their advantage

---

[47] "Address by the Minister of Petroleum and Minerals to Executives of Oil Companies," January 20, 1970, Foreign and Commonwealth Office: Commodities and Oil Department, folder 432, UKNA.

[48] "Libyan Oil Minister Reviews Oil Policy Issues," *MEES* 13: 31 (May 29, 1970), 5–6.

[49] Melhuish to Brant, "Negotiations between the Libyan Government and the Producing Companies," May 19, 1970, Foreign and Commonwealth Office: Commodities and Oil Department, folder 432, UKNA.

in Libya. In February the government passed a new law that revoked an article of the 1961 nationalization decree that allowed the government to increase the consortium's area of production in the future.

The new head of oil affairs for the Ba'ath Revolutionary Command Council, Sa'doun Hammadi, wrote the law because it officially prohibited any growth in the influence of the IPC. Hammadi also situated himself in what by this time was the commonsense history of national economic liberation. Like other oil elites in the second generation, his academic and professional formation was international and his topic of study was national. His arrival to the directorship of the Iraqi oil ministry was first by way of the University of Wisconsin, where he earned a PhD in economics in 1957. In Madison, he analyzed the problem of establishing an agricultural tax regime in Iraq. His thesis shared other attributes with the academic writings of other anticolonial elites. For one, he took a wide-angle approach to the relationship between theory and practice – the tension between what he called "the stock of economic theory at our disposal" and the imperfect conditions of "what really exists." For another, his objective was social change, in this case how to use legal power to redistribute wealth within the nation. This could occur, he believed, only if "the underlying social conditions [were] ripe to bring about that change." He hoped his world was ripe in the 1950s, based his study of Iraqi land law, which was undergoing changes that were very similar to those proposed by anticolonial internationalists in other fields. Iraq had witnessed the same "rise and growth of nationalism" as the rest of the Third World, he wrote, as well as the subsequent "social strife for justice in wealth and income distribution."[50]

Hammadi finished the thesis on the eve of the 1958 Iraqi Revolution, and he saw the land tenancy system as a major cause of injustice in his country. Its reform, in fact, had become a cause of the increasing unrest in the nation. The fear of revolution had forced landed Iraqi elites to consider the desirability of legal change, Hammadi wrote. However, he predicted, their "lack of sincere progressive spirit" did not bode well for their future. But at least Iraqi policymakers (and doctoral students) had examples they could follow. Here he turned to other national cases. Drawing on the work of Ragnar Nurkse on capital formation in developing countries as well as the history of Japanese, Indian, and

---

[50] Sadun Lawlah Hammadi, *Agricultural Taxation in Iraq*, PhD dissertation, University of Wisconsin (1957), 1–4.

Latin American land laws, tax systems, and national development, Hammadi argued that tax reform could spearhead a broader redistributive effort. The greater goal, of which tax reform could just be a part, was to change the "internal mechanics" of society to achieve a "broad, long-run justice." He was particularly interested in the early attempts by Prebisch's Economic Commission for Latin America to measure the impact of new taxes through interviews with farm operators.[51]

The implementation of such a vision in Iraqi oil policy was more likely in 1970 than ever before. The Ba'athist government had supported a radical internationalist oil policy since its 1968 coup, following in the footsteps of their predecessors. In fact, when new Iraqi president Ahmed Hassan al-Bakr gave the opening address to an OPEC Conference meeting in Baghdad in November 1968, just months after taking power, he told the oil ministers that his government – "now, more than [at] any time in the past" – saw the benefit to working with its counterparts to "implement a policy for the direct national exploitation of oil resources." Like so many others, he depicted the history of petroleum colonization as a collective one. "The Organization of Petroleum Exporting Countries did not come into being by accident nor did it come to consider a particular problem," he said. Instead, its *"raison d'être* is the mutual interest of the member countries, the unity of their goals and the similarity of the problems they faced."[52]

Francisco Parra, now OPEC's secretary general, flew from Vienna to Baghdad for the meeting. He agreed with Bakr about "the very essence of our association." The founding of OPEC had been "an historic occasion" because it marked the moment the oil producers had collectively refused to think of themselves "as landlords receiving a rent, the amount of which would be determined by the financial position of the tenant."[53]

Hammadi agreed with Parra and others that OPEC was as much a reflection of world political-economic trends as the originator of them. Like Parra, he also understood that each state had its "special circumstances." For him, Iraqi policy was as much the product of a specific moment in time and a particular combination of economic, political, and technological circumstances as it was a natural progression of anticolonial

---

[51] Hammadi, Agricultural Taxation in Iraq, 5–6, 10, 239–43.

[52] "Opening Address by the President of the Republic of Iraq at the Inauguration of the OPEC XVII Conference," *OPEC Bulletin*, November 1968, OIC.

[53] "Address by the Secretary General at the Inauguration of the OPEC XVII Conference," *OPEC Bulletin*, November 1968, OIC.

history. The recent agreements with the Soviet Union built on "the advanced legal outlines" established in the previous decade, he wrote in 1970. In fact, they had been designed "with the basic aim of developing the national oil industry ... without falling into the traps of foreign interests." (His position regarding the relationship between indigenous capital growth and raw material rents, he added in an official 1970 publication, again drew its understanding from the 1952 work on capital formation by Ragnar Nurkse.)[54]

Hammadi further toughened the Iraqi line in March 1970. He announced a new edict, Law 20, which granted even wider powers to the government, including the right to "fix the price of commodities, e.g. posted prices of oil."[55] The law vested considerable power in the government to "interfere" with company operations, including seizing oil with compensation or taking over operations without compensation. According to the British Oil Department, the law was "one more milestone on the road to state control."[56] Oil executives also reported that Hammadi was watching closely the beginning of negotiations in Tripoli, and believed their negotiations were "mightily hindered by the events in Libya."[57]

Hammadi and Maghribi found support for their policies from Hasan Zakariya, who continued at the helm of the OPEC Legal Department. Days after Hammadi announced Law 20, and days before Sarkis and Tariki would travel to Libya, Zakariya joined the two oil consultants on a panel at the Seventh Arab Petroleum Congress, held in Kuwait in March 1970. Zakariya used the meeting to flesh out Anes Qasem's concept of relinquishment in light of the 1968 OPEC Declaratory Statement. He described the practice as beginning with the discussions over the 1925 Iraqi concession, lamenting that the "embryonic" principle was never really implemented then. Similarly, he said, articles in the 1933 Iranian and Saudi concessions were actually designed to limit relinquishment.

[54] Republic of Iraq, *Oil and Minerals in Iraq* (Baghdad, 1970), 7, 97, 124.
[55] British Embassy, "Law No. 20 of 1970," March 7, 1970, Foreign and Commonwealth Office: Commodities and Oil Department, folder 420, UKNA.
[56] Bryant, "Iraq and the IPC," March 18, 1970, Foreign and Commonwealth Office: Commodities and Oil Department, folder 420, UKNA.
[57] Telegram 2856, Washington to FCO, September 26, 1970, Foreign and Commonwealth Office: Commodities and Oil Department, folder 435, UKNA; C.T. Brant, "Libyan Oil and Iran and Iraq," October 1, 1970, Foreign and Commonwealth Office: Commodities and Oil Department, folder 435, UKNA.

"It was not until the mid-1950s that the application of relinquishment first gathered momentum," he wrote, beginning with the 1955 Libyan petroleum law, its subsequent revisions, and Iraqi Law No. 80 of 1961. Those laws, he believed, had been "significant and far-reaching" in their transformation of the oil agreements "in such a way as to render them more equitable to the host countries." On one level, they represented modifications of existing concessions through national legislation. On a deeper note, relinquishment returned the concessions "over to the state in their entirety." The oil elites of the previous generation – Qasem, Nadim Pachachi, and Mohammed Salman – had thus "helped to publicize and dramatize the issue, to sharpen the general awareness of the inequities from which most petroleum concessions in the area suffered, and to draw attention to the acute need for their revision."[58]

It was not mistake that Zakariya would discuss both Iraq and Libya in 1970. The president of Algeria, Houari Boumedienne, also frequently voiced his support for those nations. In one case, at a June 1970 meeting of OPEC in Algiers, he used the concept of unequal exchange to discuss their position with other oil elites. The work of Hammadi and Maghribi was an attempt to arrest "the constant deterioration in what are known as the terms of trade," he told the assembled oil ministers in his welcome speech. Unequal exchange represented a problem in international economic relations so widespread that "the predominant feature of a colonial relationship still prevails in essence and in effect."[59]

Boumedienne's speech followed an agreement between Algeria and Libya to form a joint oil exploration company, which was patterned after the Iraqi National Oil Company. The decision had been made after visits to Algeria by Qaddafi and, afterward, Mabruk in April 1970. The deal made sense for each nation. Each was anxious to promote direct development of their oil resources on their own account. Algeria had a great deal of geophysical survey and drilling equipment at its disposal, but not enough capital. Libya had capital but was short on technical expertise and equipment. The agreement itself applied well-understood concepts to the particular situation. Cooperation would help each "accelerate their development and eliminate the backwardness inherited from imperialism,

---

[58] Hasan S. Zakariya, "Progressive Relinquishment under OPEC Declaratory Statement of Policy of 1968," March 16–22, 1970, *Seventh Arab Petroleum Congress*, Vol. I: Economics (Papers), Paper No. 30 (A-2), OIC.

[59] "Translation of the Text of President Houari Boumedienne's Speech," *OPEC Bulletin*, August 1970, OIC.

a situation which has created a united front between the two states against all the forces of oppression, monopoly, and exploitation." The agreement constituted "a united front to defend their interests in the face of foreign trusts and monopolies," Algerian Minister of Industry and Energy Belaid Abdessalam told the Algerian News Agency. The meeting between the Algerians and the Libyans reflected "a growing desire on the part of the countries in the Middle East and North Africa to control their own oil industries," the *Economist* reported. British officials agreed – there was an effort among Abdessalam, Hammadi, and Mabruk "to harmonize their oil policies." This sort of coordination had been the objective of the Arab League Petroleum Bureau and OPEC for a decade.[60]

The Libyan, Iraqi, and Algerian negotiations also occurred in another public context that emphasized fraternity: the tenth anniversary of OPEC. Oil continued to be "the precious lifeblood of industry and of human activity in general," read OPEC's official anniversary statement. The oil producers would continue to fight for their "legitimate rights of regulation and control," it continued. They would do so based on the broad concept that the best remedy to the old concessions remained "a unified front of the host countries." The unified front, in turn, relied upon "the extensive inquiries and reliable research" conducted within OPEC in the past decade. The levels of knowledge had come a long way since the four-page surveys Salman traveled with in 1956 and 1957. It now led not only to the "objective and realistic criticism of the old agreements." New knowledge also, as the measures taken by Libya, Iraq, and Algeria revealed, "set the stage for new agreements free from the inequities of the original ones and more in keeping with the spirit of the time."[61]

The perception was that each of the oil insurrectionists had a coherent national purpose. Each was also part of the broader dynamic, grounded in the political-economic ideology of decolonization. The British ambassador in Tripoli came to a similar conclusion as the OPEC anniversary statement, but couched it in less heroic language. The Libyan breakthrough of October 1970 set a precedent to "increase postings all round

---

[60] "Libya and Algeria Agree on Formation of Joint Oil Company," *MEES* 13: 26 (April 24, 1970), 1; "Algeria and Libya to Explore Jointly in Both Countries," *PIW* 13: 27 (April 27, 1970), 2; Cutting, Oil Department, "Algerianisation," April 25, 1970, Foreign and Commonwealth Office: Commodities and Oil Department, folder 432, UKNA; Cabinet Paper, "Libyan Nationalization of Oil Companies," July 7, 1970, Foreign and Commonwealth Office: Commodities and Oil Department, folder 433, UKNA.

[61] "Into the Second Decade, Press Release No. 4–70," September 14, 1970, *OPEC: Official Resolutions and Press Releases, 1960–1983*, OIC.

the Middle East and Africa," he wrote. Maghribi, Mabruk, and the Revolutionary Command Council had "played their hand with remarkable skill," and had reason "for congratulating themselves on having struck a blow for the Arabs and the Third World in general."[62] If oil elites from Algeria and Iraq had read those words, they would likely agree. For the influential journal *Petroleum Intelligence Weekly*, "the big question now" was not whether Libyan policy would be successful. It was how it would change "big concessions around the world."[63]

Arguments that the old oil concessions needed to be overturned had been central to the development of the sovereign rights program. But those arguments had only haunted the margins of the international political economy of the 1950s and 1960s. But after Maghribi "shot his bolt" in September and October 1970, in the words of one observer, the shot turned into a volley.[64] In the following three months, gradualists and insurrectionists would work together through OPEC to overturn key parts of the old concessions. At the same time, the Nixon administration's policy of accommodation would assist them in achieving that goal in February 1971.

The Persian Gulf producers and Venezuela demanded and received what another observer called "the new rules of the oil game" immediately after the oil companies conceded the tax increase in Libya. In one example, oil executives in Iran reported that their official contacts had begun "muttering about the consequential effects for them of the concessions in Libya" whenever they had the opportunity. They believed "the Libyan changes *must* ultimately affect the terms under which the Consortium operate in Iran." The Shah, according to another report, was "clearly scenting blood."[65]

---

[62] Goulding to Brant, "Libyan Oil," October 13, 1970, Foreign and Commonwealth Office: Commodities and Oil Department, folder 435; "Majors Capitulate in Libya to New 55% Oil Tax Rate," *PIW* 9: 41 (October 12, 1970), 1–2.

[63] "Will New Libyan Deals Topple '50–50' around the World?" *PIW* 9: 39 (September 29, 1970), 1.

[64] Hannam, "Libyan Oil and LNG," November 7, 1970, Foreign and Commonwealth Office: Commodities and Oil Department, folder 435, UKNA.

[65] Embassy Libya to DOS, "New Rules for the Oil Game," December 5, 1970, *FRUS 1969–76*, vol. XXXVI, doc. 64; Amembassy Caracas to SecState, December 1, 1970, RG 59, Subject-Numeric Files, 1970–73, PET 3 OPEC, box 1482, NARA; Trezise to Flanigan, December 17, 1970, RG 59, Subject-Numeric Files, 1970–73, PET 3 OPEC, box 1482, NARA; Ellingworth, "Libyan Oil," October 5, 1970, Foreign and Commonwealth Office: Commodities and Oil Department, folder 435, UKNA; C.T. Brant, "Libyan Oil and Iran and Iraq," October 1, 1970, Foreign and Commonwealth Office: Commodities and Oil Department, folder 435, UKNA.

The OPEC oil ministers met in Caracas in December 1970 to decide how to capitalize on the Libyan gains as a group. In that early locus of consistent arguments about sovereign rights and international oil, the delegates placed their meeting in the broader historical current of decolonization. In his opening statement, Algerian oil minister Belaid Abdessalam urged continued action to avoid "a further deterioration of terms of exchange between our countries and the industrialized nations." He expanded on that position: It would be "unjust, to say the least" for the "rich countries" to continue to sell manufactured goods at "cease-lessly increasing prices and, at the same time, to benefit from the use of our oil . . . at less and less remunerative prices." The oil ministers added as a group that they supported the measures that had been taken by Libya, Algeria, and Iraq "to safeguard their legitimate interests with respect to the upward revision of posted or reference prices." Referring back to the 1968 Declaratory Statement and Zakariya's 1969 argument about "changing circumstances," the members then set out standardized new revenue demands, including the 55 percent tax rate and a uniform posted price.[66]

They also informed the companies that they would be required to participate in joint company–cartel negotiations to determine the details of the new stipulations. Here the oil ministers followed the policy outlines that had failed during the royalty negotiations of the early 1960s – namely making the organization, not the individual producers, the official inter-locutor. If the negotiations were not successful, they added, the ministers of each OPEC nation would determine a new procedure to achieve the desired terms for oil "through a concerted and simultaneous action." For the first time, OPEC had issued a communiqué announcing its members' agreement not just on basic principles but also on the formula to achieve them. For Amir Kubbah, who attended the conference, it was "indicative of the mood" of the ministers that the Caracas resolutions incorporated the threat not just of national action but of collaborative nationalist action if the companies failed to respond to their demands.[67]

The Caracas resolutions formed one part of a sophisticated collective strategy for the oil producers in late 1970 and early 1971. So did what

---

[66] "Oil Prices and Manufactured Goods' Prices," December 9, 1970, in Kubbah, *OPEC, Past and Present*, 114–15; "Text of Resolutions of XXI OPEC Conference," *MEES* xiv, no. 10 (1 January 1971), 1–3.

[67] "Text of Resolutions of XXI OPEC Conference," *MEES* xiv, no. 10 (January 1, 1971), 1–3; Kubbah, *OPEC, Past and Present*, 55.

followed, when Mabruk revived Libyan retroactivity demands and called for higher prices for Libyan oil the day after the meeting. This move was designed to force the companies to undertake separate negotiations with the Gulf and Mediterranean producers. Mabruk had already discussed this tactic with the other oil ministers, and they agreed to it. Despite their other misgivings with the Libyans – the Shah and King Faisal, for example, had already lumped Libya into their regional arguments about radical encirclement – the oil ministers approved. The object was to see how far past a Gulf benchmark the Libyans could push the companies. The oil ministers resolved to "support fully" the Libyan demands and, more broadly, the ministers expressed their policy of generalized mutual support, in the light of their belief that the member governments had "the legitimate right to expect concession operators to comply with the highest national interest."[68]

The companies, in an effort to avoid being caught in an upwardly spiraling price war between Libya and the Gulf producers, sought to coordinate what they called "global" negotiations with all of OPEC. The attempt to go global, a last ditch effort, went poorly. American accommodation again affected this outcome. Nixon dispatched Under-secretary of State John Irwin to Iran and Saudi Arabia in January 1971 with the mandate of convincing the Shah and King Faisal to support the OPEC-wide negotiations. Henry Kissinger called Irwin a day before his departure. Days earlier Kissinger told him he was "not on top of" the oil negotiations. Now Kissinger began the conversation by expressing his extreme displeasure that he had only just been informed of the mission. He then gave Irwin new instructions. Above all else, Kissinger valued his recent diplomacy with the Shah. Irwin was to "get out of the line of fire when the firing starts."[69]

Irwin followed Kissinger's instructions in a two-hour meeting with the Shah on January 17, 1971. He began by apologizing for coming on the

---

[68] "Text of Resolutions of XXI OPEC Conference," *MEES* xiv, no. 10 (1 January 1971), 4.
[69] Oil Task Force, Situation Report, January 15, 1971, National Security Council Files, box 1271, RNL; DOS to Certain Diplomatic Posts, "Washington Oil Talks," January 8, 1971, *FRUS 1969–76*, vol. XXXVI, doc. 65; Transcript of a Telephone Conversation between Kissinger and Irwin, January 11, 1970, *FRUS 1969–76*, vol. XXXVI, doc. 67; Telephone Conversation, Kissinger and Irwin, January 15, 1971, Kissinger Transcripts, doc. KA04738, DNSA. On Irwin's mandate, see also: Carter to Stevenson and the Assistant Secretary, January 14, 1971, *FRUS 1969–76*, vol. XXXVI, doc. 68; Bergsten and Saunders to Kissinger, January 14, 1971, *FRUS 1969–76*, vol. XXXVI, doc. 69.

FIGURE 6.1 Libya's 'Izz al-Din al-Mabruk at a two-day extraordinary session of the Organization of the Petroleum Exporting Countries (OPEC) in Vienna, Austria, on September 16, 1973.
Source: OPEC Information Center, OPEC PICL 1973 Portrait (32).

mission in the first place. The United States was not "representing or taking the part" of the oil companies. Instead, he made an argument about economic interdependence and political moderation. A quick, OPEC-wide agreement was in "the greater interest, including that of Iran," he said. Qaddafi's continued threats "that oil would be used as a political weapon" could cause problems not only for Western Europe, but for the global economy. To prevent this, he said, President Nixon followed the companies in insisting on "global talks" between the companies and the producer governments.[70]

The Shah responded that he understood the fear that the companies would be "whip-sawed by *escalation ad seriatim* demands by different producers." Nevertheless, global talks were out of the question because of the December OPEC decision. They were inadvisable anyway because an OPEC-wide discussion would be hijacked by "the extremists," he

[70] Telegram 277, AmEmbassy Iran to DOS, "Under Secretary's Meeting with Shah," January 18, 1971, National Security Council Files, box 602, RNL.

continued. "It was not possible for Iran and the Gulf producers to impose their will on Venezuela or radical Arab producers such as Libya, Algeria, and possibly Iraq," he said. Irwin protested a little but, perhaps mindful of Kissinger's advice, did not press the issue. The Shah, for his part, was implacable. Separate negotiations were, simply, "the facts of life."[71]

Irwin continued his mission the next day when he flew from Tehran to Riyadh to meet with King Faisal and his oil minister, Ahmed Zaki Yamani, the following day. Faisal, who as the Prime Minister and Minister for Foreign Affairs of Saudi Arabia had attended the Bandung Conference in 1955, agreed with the Shah that separate negotiations were best. "[I]ntroducing Algeria and Libya into this negotiation will render agreement impossible or at least result in a settlement which will cost the companies much more heavily," he told Irwin. The Libyans were young army officers ignorant about oil, Yamani added. They were intent on "killing [the] goose that laid the golden eggs." But the Saudi oil minister, who had met with his Iranian counterpart the previous day, held the line. Global talks were not possible and inadvisable. "No one should expect the moderates to be able to influence the radicals in an OPEC negotiation," he added. "Indeed if negotiations are in the OPEC framework, the moderates would probably have to settle for the radicals' demands."[72]

When Nixon dispatched Irwin to Iran and Saudi Arabia this trip, his mission was to deliver an appeal for those nations to stand together against the insurrectionists. But his discussions with the Shah and King Faisal convinced him this was a fool's errand. Over protests from the ambassador in Tripoli, who wrote that the decision would "play right into Libya's hands," he recommended that the US government accede to the separate regional talks, which were slated to begin in Tehran and, after that, in Tripoli. His rationale was steeped in the Shah's "facts of life," which to him boiled down to the incorrect assumptions of his mission. He wrote as much in the report he submitted. There was no chance Saudi Arabia and Iran would "curb the extremists" in global negotiations. "Such a hope was futile," he wrote. Neither the Saudis nor

---

[71] Telegram 277, AmEmbassy Iran to DOS, "Under Secretary's Meeting with Shah," January 18, 1971, National Security Council Files, box 602, RNL.
[72] Hassouna, *The First Asian-African Conference*, 214; Telegram from Irwin to DOS, January 19, 1971, *FRUS 1969–76*, vol. XXXVI, doc. 75.

the Iranians were "willing or perhaps able to play moderating role in OPEC-wide negotiations."[73]

By mid-1972 Irwin would place that interpretation into a larger one. Citing the "law of changing circumstances," he urged other officials to accept the existence of "a new relationship between the oil companies, the producer governments, and the consumers." Nothing could be gained from averting one's face from the iron logic of that inescapable reality, he believed. He was right: The OPEC ministers from the Persian Gulf met in Tehran on February 5, 1971, and adopted a strongly worded resolution. Each nation would introduce "the necessary legal and/or legislative measures" to implement the objectives of the regional negotiation. If the companies refused to send their negotiators to Tehran immediately, they would not be allowed to lift oil. The deadline for company acquiescence was set for February 15, 1971.[74]

The climate in Tehran itself was rife with oil internationalism. The Shah gave a heated speech in the Majlis in advance of the arrival of the oil ministers to Tehran. His factual anchor was a recent UN study on the price of exports. The report proved yet again that unequal exchange plagued the oil producers, the Shah said. Prices for manufactured goods had gone up and the "real income" derived by the OPEC members had fallen, he added. "The old saying that the rich have become richer and the poor poorer, has indeed become a reality during this decade."[75]

The leader of the oil companies' Tehran team, Lord Strathalmond of British Petroleum, briefed Western ambassadors after the negotiations began. Just as the oil elites had planned in Caracas, the major sticking point was his attempt "to negotiate not only a Gulf price but also a Mediterranean crude price" for pipeline oil. If the Mediterranean price could be set, Strathalmond believed, it would "assist their co-negotiators in Libya," led by George Piercy of Exxon. But the Gulf producers would not yield. Yamani, Jamshid Amouzegar of Iran, and the other ministers who welcomed the executives to Tehran indicated that they expected to get the same price for

[73] Embassy Libya to DOS, January 20, 1971 *FRUS 1969–76*, vol. XXXVI, doc. 77; Amembassy London to Amembassy Tunis, January 20, 1971, RG 59, Subject-Numeric Files 1970–73, PET 3 OPEC, box 1483, NARA; Editorial Note, *FRUS 1969–76*, vol. XXXVI, doc. 81; Telegram from Irwin to DOS, January 19, 1971, *FRUS 1969–76*, vol. XXXVI, doc. 76.

[74] Memcon, "Participation and Saudi-U.S. Oil Relations," September 29, 1972, *FRUS 1969–76*, vol. XXIV, doc. 164; OPEC Resolution XXII, February 5, 1971, OIC.

[75] "Erosion of Posted Prices," February 3, 1971, in Kubbah, *OPEC, Past and Present*, 116.

their Mediterranean pipeline outlets as was given to Libya. In the "gloomy" consensus, the companies conceded that it was 'Izz al-Din al-Mabruk with whom they would conduct those discussions. (Mahmood Maghribi had taken up a position as Libya's permanent representative to the United Nations.) Company executives blamed their inability to negotiate on the success of Libyan policy. The Revolutionary Command Council's victory in September 1970 had given all the OPEC nations a new "sense of entitlement," one executive told the State Department.[76]

The Tehran talks concluded on February 15 with a new tax and price agreement. The old oil concessions budged on the crucial question of prices. The oil companies accepted what was considered a substantial price increase – 33 cents per barrel immediately followed by 5 cents more per year until 1975. Officially, the Gulf governments assured the companies that they would not seek to increase their revenues beyond the terms of the agreement for five years. Nor would they support other OPEC governments, "especially Libya," whose demands exceeded their own. The Shah guaranteed this to the US ambassador, who received instructions from the State Department instructing him to thank the Shah for his "categoric [sic] assurances" that the Gulf producers would observe the five-year agreement "regardless of the outcome of negotiations in Libya."[77]

There was little likelihood that these informal promises would be kept. Yamani and Amouzegar had already pressed the companies to include a series of debilitating "escape clauses" that would allow them to further raise prices if Mabruk extracted a better deal in Tripoli. The Iranian and Saudi oil directors also had already voiced their support for a paper circulated by Mabruk and Abdessalam after the Caracas meeting that posited that the company's attempt to keep the negotiations "global" was not only an "infringement on the sovereignty of OPEC member nations" but also a maneuver "to divide OPEC unity."[78]

---

[76] AmEmbassy Tehran to SecState, "Oil Situation: Tehran Negotiations," January 27, 1971, National Security Council Files, box 602, RNL; AmEmbassy Tehran to SecState, "Oil Situation: First Gulf Negotiating Session," January 28, 1971, National Security Council Files, box 602, RNL.

[77] Bergsten to Kissinger, "World Oil Situation," March 9, 1971, National Security Council Files, box 367, RNL; State Department, Bureau of Intelligence and Research, Intelligence Note RECN-3, February 18, 1971, RG 59, Subject-Numeric Files 1970–73, PET 3 OPEC, box 1483, NARA; AmEmbassy Tehran to SecState, "Iranian Assurances re five-year oil agreement," March 11, 1971, National Security Council Files, box 602, RNL.

[78] Telegram, AmEmbassy Tehran to SecState, "Oil Situation," February 3, 1971, National Security Council Files, box 602, RNL.

The Tripoli negotiations began the next week. The group of oil elites led by Mabruk had an overwhelming advantage over the company negotiators. "Libya's overflowing treasury makes it theoretically independent of oil revenues for extended periods," State Department analysts wrote. Mabruk used this leverage to negotiate a higher posted price than that agreed to in Tehran, as well as a freight premium for its Mediterranean crude. The companies also conceded the annual 5-cent increase already in place in the Gulf, plus an additional 2.5 percent.[79]

An intelligence report prepared jointly by the departments of State and Defense, the NSC, and the CIA noted that the Tripoli agreement would wipe out the Tehran one, despite the five-year clause and the personal guarantee of the Shah. The US officials agreed again that the shift had begun in September 1970. Libyan policy had "stimulated regional solidarity," they wrote. The oil producers now showed "a greater degree of unanimity than had been apparent in the past." As a result of OPEC cooperation, in fact, the oil-producing countries held the "dangerous conviction that they held the whip hand."[80]

Anticolonial elites in the UN Economic and Social Council, Permanent Sovereignty Commission, Arab League Petroleum Congresses, and OPEC had argued since the 1950s that the old oil concessions remained largely untouched by the wave of Third World self-assertion. A slew of elites in the 1960s had observed the slow but sure entrenchment of the sovereign rights program. Now Western officials who initially expressed little concern about the appeal and influence of Libyan insurrectionism were cowed. The Revolutionary Command Council would "have to do more than blow outside the walls of the oil companies before they fall down," one British official jauntily reported when Maghribi took over the negotiations. But afterwards the companies found "the going very tough indeed," the British embassy wrote. The Libyans had, in short, been able

---

[79] State Department, Bureau of Intelligence and Research, Intelligence Note RECN-3, February 18, 1971, RG 59, Subject-Numeric Files 1970–73, PET 3 OPEC, box 1483, NARA; Kissinger to Nixon, "International Oil Situation—Libyan Phase," March 27, 1971, National Security Council Files, box 367, RNL; DOS to Certain Diplomatic Posts, April 1, 1971, *FRUS 1969–76*, vol. XXXVI, doc. 88.

[80] National Intelligence Estimate, 30-1-71, "The Persian Gulf after the British Departure," April 1, 1971, National Security Council Files, box 1276, RNL. See also: Embassy Iran to DOS, "Shah's Concern Over Libyan Oil Settlement," April 15, 1971, *FRUS 1969–76*, vol. XXXVI, doc. 89.

to force the companies to "make concessions even greater than those they dismissed as unthinkable" months earlier.[81]

Libyan nationalism became the trigger for a transformation in the impact of oil power and the relevance of sovereign rights in the international economy. Moreover, it generated a great deal of fanfare. Libyan oil policy was depicted – by its makers, supporters, and detractors – as a historical culmination of a much longer process of decolonization. With the arrival of decolonization, so went the narrative, a particular hierarchical ordering of global society as a fact of nature had given way. By 1971, according to this vision, sovereign rights had swung into operation. In doing so, it assumed a mature form among OPEC members – a form related in vision to, yet substantially different in practice from, the cluster of ideas that had shaped the economic culture of decolonization in the previous two decades.

The biggest change was that oil elites could now point to a tangible victory. Anes Qasem, who had returned to the University of London in his twilight years, described the situation. "The difficult question is how far a law can go before reaching the point of being unacceptable or, at least, unattractive," he wrote. Following his greater law of changing circumstances, that question became less difficult for oil elites over time. The acceptability of nationalist oil laws had "passed through a rapid process" of constant change during his long career. At the beginning of his work in the early 1950s, there existed only the vague "thought" that "ways and means would be found to amend both the law and the concession agreements, in the light of developments and changing circumstances." That attitude was now "well vindicated by the history of other countries in the field of petroleum." For him as for the others, the new policies existed on mutually constitutive intellectual and practical planes: "Thus petroleum legislation passed through a process of evolution dictated mainly by petroleum developments and the evolution of petroleum thinking, knowledge, and experience."[82]

Qasem added that the changes in international law and the oil industry were both cause and effect of a broader psychological shift that stemmed from the rising tide of decolonization. "The framework of petroleum thinking" drew sustenance from "the greater emphasis that is being placed

---

[81] M. P. V. Hannam, "Posted Price Negotiations," March 5, 1970, Foreign and Commonwealth Office: Commodities and Oil Department, folder 432, UKNA; Goulding to Brant, "Libyan Oil," October 13, 1970, Foreign and Commonwealth Office: Commodities and Oil Department, folder 435, UKNA.

[82] Anes Mustafa Qasem, "Petroleum Legislation in Libya," PhD dissertation, University of London (1969), 7–8, 11–12.

on the sovereignty of the state over its petroleum resources," he wrote. He found Muhammad Mughraby's work on the United Nations important and agreed that the UN resolutions on permanent sovereignty supported his initial vision that the oil nations were entitled, "in changing circumstances, to take such action and introduce such legislation as be required for the furtherance of its interests." Because permanent sovereignty found its moral basis in the "mutual respect of States based on their sovereign equality," he said, national political and economic goals had always been based on international cooperation. The connection of national policies with international principles – which for him was most evident in the ongoing attempts by his successors in Libya to coordinate policy with Iraq, Algeria, and even Saudi Arabia and Iran – represented the true "spirit" of the program of oil elites for "sovereignty over their petroleum resources."[83]

A student for the second time in his life, Qasem joined the second generation of oil elites in presenting the claim that sovereign rights was codified by the course of history. At the same time, the oil elites remained connected to the greater Third World by the circuits through which their ideas traveled. That international hopscotch was not lost on the shrewdest Western commentators. Joseph Nye, for example, discussed in 1972 the influence of "poor nations over rich nations" in international politics and marveled at Prebisch's success in converting the UN Conference on Trade and Development into "a group of populist pressure."[84]

The circulation of sovereign rights in this specific time and place is also evidence for a shared international culture. A week after the Tehran negotiations ended and the Tripoli ones began, Algerian oil minister Abdessalam granted an interview to the Algiers daily *El-Moudjahid* on the topic of "full sovereignty." He reiterated the link between the oil elites and their anticolonial counterparts: OPEC was "a means of participating in the movement by the underdeveloped countries to pressure the structure of international economic relations into an evolution favorable to the economic emancipation of these countries." Hugo Pérez la Salvia, the Minister of Mines and Hydrocarbons of Venezuela, made a similar point during the 1971 Tehran meeting. Libyan policy fell within the broader OPEC aim "to redress long-standing injustices."[85]

---

[83] Qasem, "Petroleum Legislation in Libya," 13, 17–21.
[84] Joseph S. Nye, "La UNCTAD Bajo Prebisch: La Estructura de Influencia," *Foro Internacional* 12: 3 (January–March 1972), 308, 320.
[85] "Algeria and OPEC," February 23, 1971, in Kubbah, *OPEC, Past and Present*, 117–18; "Opening Speech Delivered by H. E. Dr. Hugo Perez La Salvia," *OPEC Bulletin* 2, 1971, OIC.

FIGURE 6.2 Nadim Pachachi, the OPEC Secretary General, and Ahmed Zaki Yamani, the Saudi oil minister, at the Twenty-Fourth OPEC Conference, held in Vienna in July 1971. Pachachi is at the far right and Yamani is in the middle. To the left is Meshach Otokiti Feyide, the oil minister from Nigeria.
Source: OPEC Information Center, OPEC PICL-1971 24CR.

The oil elites were a self-aware political group with common experiences and a communal sensibility. At the center were men whose careers had been shaped by decolonization. Nadim Pachachi, ten years after working with Qasem to revise Libyan oil law and now the Secretary General of OPEC, also placed Libyan oil policy in that broader context. "We, like they, are raw material producers trying to get an equitable price for the primary product on which our economies depend," he said at the conclusion of the Tehran meeting. This was the great "invisible achievement of OPEC," Qasem wrote. The organization, he said, had been able to use trends in international society to guide its members to a more educated nationalist position. OPEC embodied the unprecedented spirit of international economic activism that had begun with decolonization in the 1950s. The offices in Vienna had become a "forum for raising and discussing problems and exchanging experience."[86]

---

[86] "Interview given in Beirut on February 17, 1971, by OPEC's Secretary General," *OPEC Bulletin* 2, 1971, OIC; Qasem, "Petroleum Legislation in Libya," 23.

But Qasem was not overly triumphalist. He also believed "the main question facing OPEC remains still unanswered." This was whether the organization could succeed in unifying the petroleum policies of its member countries in a way that would militate for the best interests of each. In 1971 and after, claims of success in that realm, as well as of the positive link between that success and the economic culture of decolonization, would grow more forceful. By the middle of 1973 a transnational oil grab would redistribute power across the industry. But even as this avalanche of historic events seemed to promise transformation, it also reanimated the conflicting interests lurking just beneath the surface of the anticolonial effort and exposed the ambiguities within the concept of an economic equivalent of decolonization.[87]

[87] Qasem, "Petroleum Legislation in Libya," 24.

7

A Fact of Life

The Consolidation of Sovereign Rights, 1971–1973

Following along the path laid out by history ... the traditional concession surrendering huge areas to the oil interests now seems a thing of the past.[1]
Journal of World Trade Law, 1971

It could seem alarming for those who wish to cling on to acquired positions and privileges inherited from the past. It remains nonetheless a comfort for those who believe in the irreversible character of the economic liberation of the Arab countries and in the advantages of international cooperation.[2]
Nicolas Sarkis, 1971

The Algerian Bar Association convened an international meeting of fifty lawyers in October 1971. For the Libyan, Iranian, Iraqi, Nigerian, and Venezuelan attendees that converged on Algiers, the physical remnants of imperialism and that nation's war for liberation would have been notable. Bullet marks, scars of the recurrent conflicts between rulers and ruled in the twentieth century, pocked parts of the city, including the walls of the stately Palace of Justice, built by the French in the neoclassical style in 1900. But if the Palace had been a location for the imposition of imperial law, it had become an incubator of anticolonial international law since Algerian independence. As the delegates surely knew when their cars approached the building's entrance, Algerian anticolonialism had always extended to its most important natural resource. One UN diplomat had perfectly summarized the Algerian position on oil and sovereignty in

---

[1] Pierre Barraz, "The Legal Status of Oil Concessions," *Journal of Trade Law* 5: 6 (1971): 630.
[2] Nicolas Sarkis, "Foreword," *AOG* 1: 1 (October 1, 1971): 3–4.

1963. Peoples and nations "who were basically sovereign" could not lose their sovereignty while under colonial rule, he said. If agreements made while under colonial or otherwise subjugated status were found wanting, sovereignty should be "restored to normal."[3]

Algerian decision makers also had professed their belief in the internationalism of the sovereign rights program and the fight to control oil since the 1950s. The nation's first president, Ahmed Ben Bella, in fact, described national control over oil as "the product of a collectivist mentality" that had developed over a century of shared repression and resistance. Nationalist policies continued under Houari Boumedienne, who seized power from Ben Bella in a 1965 coup. Boumedienne summarized the official view in the precise language of sovereign rights in a meeting of OPEC ministers in Algiers in June 1970. The maintenance of the oil nations as "reservoirs of raw materials," along with the "constant deterioration in what are known as the terms of trade," were the characteristic of "the imperialist era." The means the multinational companies used to determine prices, not to mention "the system regulating economic exchanges in the international sphere," had governed relations between "oppressed peoples and the rich imperialist states" for too long. The problem of economic injustice continued "even after the recovery of ... freedom and political independence," he said. Its resolution was a natural step of decolonization, "the same in its form and essence" as the struggles for liberation waged by colonized peoples.[4]

The emancipatory moment of the sovereign rights program and the anticolonial oil elites had arrived, and the set of convictions that made up the economic culture of decolonization shaped anticolonial elites' understanding of the problems they faced and the language they used to voice their aspirations and frame their policies. Like Iraq and Libya, Algeria took action. In February 1971, two weeks after the Tehran negotiations

---

[3] Gess, "Permanent Sovereignty," 443–5. Broadly, see: Zeynep Çelik, *Urban Forms and Colonial Confrontations: Algiers under French Rule* (Berkeley: University of California Press, 1997); Matthew James Connolly, *A Diplomatic Revolution: Algeria's Fight for Independence and the Origins of the Post-Cold War Era* (New York: Oxford University Press, 2002); Jeffrey James Byrne, *Mecca of Revolution: From the Algerian Front of the Third World's Cold War* (New York: Oxford University Press, 2015).

[4] "Documents on Self-Management." Democratic and Popular Algerian Republic, Ministry of Information, Documentation and Publications Department, September 1963, PE.045, box 1, Printed Ephemera Collections, Tamiment Library, New York University; "Algeria and OPEC," June 1970, Kubbah, *OPEC, Past and Present*, 111–12.

were concluded, Algeria became the first OPEC country to nationalize a substantial part of its oil industry. Boumedienne announced to a cheering crowd in Algiers that the nation had made "the historic decision" to take over 51 percent of the French-owned oil and gas industry. The government also made the nationalization an international campaign, and scores of organizations and governments were listed daily in newspapers and on radio as congratulating Boumedienne for "his assertion of Algeria's national rights over her natural resources."[5]

Eight months later, the law conference brought together those intellectual, political, and cultural elements of the sovereign rights program – the internationalism of nationalism, the connection between oil and decolonization, and the emphasis on law as a policy remedy to economic injustice. Its organizer, the bâtonnier of the Algerian Bar, Amar Bentoumi, convened a number of anticolonial oil elites. Nicolas Sarkis, Abdullah al-Tariki, and Hasan Zakariya sat on the opening panel. Zakariya, who would soon leave the OPEC legal department for a position at the United Nations, spoke first. The three years since his authorship of the Declaratory Statement had not diluted his beliefs. If anything, the success of Libya in 1970 had hardened his stance. He had invoked the UN resolutions on permanent sovereignty more and more in the late 1960s, arguing that they held "the true significance and main target" of the Third Worldist narrative of economic liberation. For him, permanent sovereignty had become a "consensus of opinion of the contemporary world community" and "the source of an emerging and progressively developing international law." He now told the lawyers that the oil concessions were "so much of an anomaly" in the age of decolonization that the OPEC members needed to discard them entirely. The Tehran and Tripoli negotiations, which represented the "effectiveness of solidarity and concerted action on the part of the exporting countries," proved that such wholesale change was finally possible.[6]

After Zakariya, Sarkis presented a paper on nationalization. Six years after Tariki's salvo on nationalization at the 1965 Arab Petroleum

---

[5] Henry Giniger, "Algeria Seeking Support over Oil," *New York Times*, March 7, 1971; Giuliano Garavini, "From Boumedienomics to Reaganomics: Algeria, OPEC, and the International Struggle for Economic Equality," *Humanity* 6: 1 (Spring 2015): 85.

[6] Hasan Zakarya, "International Oil and the Energy Policies of the Producing and Consuming Countries," *MEES* 12: 37 (July 11, 1969); Hasan Zakarya, "Sovereignty, State Participation, and the Need to Restructure the Existing Petroleum Regime," *AOG* 1: 4 (November 16, 1971): 21–4.

Congress made for a palpable change in tone, even if the history was familiar. He began with the "trauma created by the Iranian experience in 1951." The experience of Mossadegh had cast "a sort of intellectual terror" over the oil elites, he said. But their fear had dissipated owing to several factors: the Arab Petroleum Congresses, "the bloom of petroleum literature in Arabic," the formation of OPEC, and "most importantly the political upheavals that brought to power a new generation of professionals." That new generation of oil elites could build on the gains of Tehran and Tripoli, which for him were still pegged to the "archaic and absurd system" of the old concessions. (Sarkis also revealed that he had kept up with his reading in development economics. The oil elites would do well to remember, "in the words of A. O. Hirschman," that their efforts should be less "permissive" and more "binding.")[7]

Both Zakariya and Sarkis were pressing the sovereign rights position with more confidence than ever. Tariki, now the senior statesman, spoke in the cleanup position. He began by invoking his experience. For a quarter century he had observed how relations between the nations "that exported oil or other raw materials" and the industrial countries had "remained dominated by economic imperialism or what has been called neo-colonialism." But he did not wish to dwell on the history of petroleum colonization, he told the audience. Instead, he lay down yet another series of broad proposals designed to help the oil nations "establish the rules regarding the cooperation" between themselves and the industrialized nations. In presenting the benefits to be accrued from this collective shift in the power of agenda-setting, he again turned to statistics, this time to a table that traced the growth of OPEC members' revenues since 1961.[8]

It was true, Tariki told the lawyers, that the evolution of total revenue was impressive. But such an analysis depended too much on production increases at stagnant prices. The revenue per barrel of the different oil producers supported the statements by Sarkis that the February 1971 agreements in Tehran and Tripoli were not revolutionary, notwithstanding Zakariya's belief otherwise. "Despite the increase in income for

[7] Nicolas Sarkis, "La nationalisation de l'industrie des hydrocarbures et les imperatifs de developpement economique des pays producteurs," *Le Droit Pétrolier Et La Souveraineté Des Pays Producteurs, Alger, Octobre 1971* (Paris: Librairie Générale de Droit et de Jurisprudence, 1973), 71–2, 75.

[8] Abdullah al-Tariki, "Pour que L'Exploitation Fasse Place a la Cooperation," *Le Droit Pétrolier Et La Souveraineté*, 87–94.

TABLE 7.1 *Oil Revenues of OPEC Member Nations, Cents per Barrel*

Year	Kuwait	Saudi Arabia	Iran	Iraq	Abu Dhabi	Qatar	Libya	Venezuela	Nigeria
1961	74.4	75.5	75.8	76.5	–	83	62.7	93	–
1962	74.8	76.5	74.5	76.7	60.9	82.3	64.7	97.2	–
1963	74.3	78.7	79.7	80.7	36.4	84.2	65.1	98.6	–
1964	76.9	82	80.9	80.1	18.2	84.4	62.9	95.4	–
1965	78.9	83.2	81.1	81.7	32.5	82.2	83.8	95.6	–
1966	78.4	83.5	81.4	81.3	75.3	87.3	87	95.8	–
1967	79.3	84.8	82.5	85.2	76.3	87.2	101.6	102.2	–
1968	80.5	87.8	83.7	90.7	84.5	88.1	100.7	101.4	–
1969	80.8	87.1	81	91.4	87.3	91.9	100	103.5	–
1970	82.9	88.3	80.8	94.2	90.9	91.5	109	109.2	107

Source: Abdullah al-Tariki, "Pour que L'Exploitation Fasse Place a la Cooperation," in *Le Droit Pétrolier Et La Souveraineté Des Pays Producteurs, Alger, Octobre 1971* (Paris: Librairie Générale de Droit et de Jurisprudence, 1973), 97.

the producing countries, they remain in the confines of the role of passive tax collectors," he said. But hope was on the horizon. The 1971 agreements pointed toward a change that would ultimately end with "direct and effective participation in petroleum operations."[9]

The rise in solidarity, the rise in revenue, and the pending rise in control were wound into the same rope, according to the oil elites. The full conference drew a series of conclusions, all based on "the movement of political, economic and social emancipation which has ... been continuously gaining ground in the previously colonized countries." The spirit of emancipation, moreover, extended directly to the "concessionary regime" in the oil nations, which was for the conferees "in fact a remnant of the old colonial ties." In addition, they drew on the more recent history of UN activism. The belief in "sovereignty rights" was universal, they said, citing the series of resolutions and conferences since 1952.[10]

The panel and the conference report were symptomatic of the pervading atmosphere among oil elites in the early 1970s, when control over oil seemed like the most natural thing in the world – a destiny that

---

[9] Abdullah al-Tariki, "Pour que L'Exploitation Fasse Place a la Cooperation," *Le Droit Pétrolier Et La Souveraineté*, 87–94.
[10] Karim El-Khalil, "Proceedings and Conclusions of the Colloquium on 'Petroleum Law and the Sovereignty of Producing Countries,'" *AOG* 1: 3 (November 1, 1971): 22.

the lawyers called a "provisional stage" in the uncoiling of decoloniza-tion. This chapter holds that, at the same time as the language of sovereign rights came fluently to oil elites, the OPEC members' collective diplomacy brought unrelieved turmoil to the old concessions. Libya and Iraq joined Algeria in nationalizing substantial parts of their oil indus-tries in December 1971 and April 1972. By the beginning of 1973, the former factions of the gradualists and insurrectionists came even closer together as Iran and Saudi Arabia squeezed new compromises out of their concessionaires.[11]

Repeated phrases and joint policy planning show how thoroughly the expectation of economic emancipation imbued the culture of decolon-ization and the program of sovereign rights. The ideas and actions of the insurrectionist oil elites in Libya, Iraq, and Algeria were part of a more general sensibility, as the support of their gradualist counterparts reveals. Saudi Oil Minister Ahmed Zaki Yamani "would leave the running to Libya and Iraq," he told the US ambassador in September 1971. If they received better deals, "Saudi Arabia could not be seen to be lagging far behind."[12]

Beneath the explicit sentiment lay a less visible network of intellectual, political, and psychological connections. Like-minded lawyers, diplo-mats, journalists, economists, and officials from Asia, Latin America, the Middle East, and Africa had spun a web across space and time. International conferences, a striking characteristic of the decolonized international community, were the nodes that held that web together. Different groups, large and small, had convened regularly on the topics of sovereign rights for two decades by the early 1970s. The meetings were where their ideas abutted, and are testaments to the depth and perman-ence of the reach of sovereign rights. From a longer perspective, the makeup of international conferences reveals the great cultural transform-ation of international life during the age of decolonization – the shift in the composition from the Congo Conference of Berlin in 1885, to the First Peace Conference in The Hague in 1899, to the Pact of Paris in 1928, to the United Nations in 1945, and finally to the UN Conference on Trade

---

[11] El-Khalil, "Proceedings and Conclusions," 23.
[12] Telegram 745, Jedda to FCO, September 19, 1971, Foreign and Commonwealth Office: Commodities and Oil Department, folder 561, UKNA; "OPEC Countries Plan to Nego-tiate with Oil Companies on Participation and Monetary Changes," *MEES* 14: 48 (1971), 1–7.

and Development in 1964 clearly illustrate the rise of a decolonized international community.

Decolonization witnessed an eruption of institution building. At the same time, as the global meetings took place with greater frequency, smaller conferences within the decolonizing world also became sites at which elites debated the viability of their ideas. In one instance, the economist Edith Penrose used the keynote speech at the 1971 Algerian law conference to cast doubt on sovereign rights as viable economic diplomacy. The American-born British citizen, an economics professor at the School of Oriental and African Studies in London, was a respected academic and political figure. As a young woman, she had publicly defended Owen Lattimore, her colleague at Johns Hopkins University, when he was accused of being a Soviet spy by Joseph McCarthy in 1950. She left the United States soon after and eventually accepted a visiting position at the University of Baghdad, where she began to study the oil industry. She left Iraq just before the 1958 revolution, after which she established herself as an expert on international business through a series of articles that culminated in the now-classic 1970 treatise, *The Large International Firm in Developing Countries: The International Petroleum Industry*. She even made a positive impression on the always critical Amir Kubbah during a return visit to Baghdad in 1965.[13]

But she raised the ire of the oil lawyers in Algiers, especially Nicolas Sarkis, when she told them that their legal arguments had little to do with the economic operations of the oil industry. Yes, the notion of permanent sovereignty had proliferated over time and space, Penrose conceded. Nonetheless, it did not and could never have a free hand. It was "a legal concept ... not a concept used in economic analysis." In other words, if national law reached beyond its economic limits, it would not be enforceable. "Just as economists must work within the legal framework of society, so must lawyers work within the economic framework and within economic realities," she said. The repudiation of the old oil concessions under the banners of permanent sovereignty and changing circumstances might have become a powerful force, but it was "not well worked out, and by no means internationally agreed." This was also because sovereignty was

---

[13] Edith Penrose, *The Large International Firm in Developing Countries: The International Petroleum Industry* (Cambridge, MA: MIT Press, 1970); Clement Levallois, "Why Were Biological Analogies in Economics 'A Bad Thing'? Edith Penrose's Battles against Social Darwinism and McCarthyism," *Science in Context* 24 (2011): 465–85; "Editor's Note," *ROAPE* 1: 5–6 (June–July 1965): 9.

fundamentally a national characteristic, not an international one. "The sovereignty of government forces issues, but it cannot resolve all of them," she said. "No law can decree that water shall run uphill."[14]

The ritual recitations of the economic culture of decolonization held little economic weight for Penrose. She believed that the rise of sovereign rights among the oil producers did not drive the economic power of the OPEC members. Rather, it reflected an economic fact: the shift toward a sellers' market. She ended on a note that questioned the wisdom of a generalized oil insurrection. "Oil is not like any other primary material," she said. It reached too deeply into the basic functioning of the modern world. If the calls of insurrectionists like Tariki, Sarkis, and even Zakariya were ever heeded in full, the international economy "would be strangled." To limit the supply of oil as part of the bargaining process, as the Libyans had done, was little more than a brutal "threat to starve" the global economy. "In international affairs one cannot merely have the law of the jungle," she concluded.[15]

Sarkis was sufficiently stirred to make the Penrose paper the center-piece of the following two issues of *Arab Oil & Gas*, the journal he and Tariki had published out of Beirut since 1964. The journal had developed into a trilingual publication since its inauguration, when it was released only in Arabic and, after 1968, in French. Its publication in English beginning in 1971 reflected the oil consultants' understanding of the rising importance of their motivating ideas. *Arab Oil & Gas* had been founded on the premise that it was necessary to "reset the problems" of oil exploitation "within the framework of the interests of the producing countries," Sarkis wrote in the first English-language edition. Because those problems were of "world interest" and because English was "by far the most widely used language in the oil industry," he and Tariki had decided to launch the new edition.[16]

Sarkis printed Penrose's paper in full and issued a truculent riposte. He disagreed, above all, with her basic premise – that the imposition of new conditions for the oil concessions "in the name of sovereignty" was somehow "anti-economic." That international law and the international economy were inseparable was a point he had held since he had begun to read Gunnar Myrdal and Albert O. Hirschman as a student at the

[14] Edith Penrose, "Equity Participation and Sovereignty: Some Economic Aspects," *AOG* 1: 3 (November 1, 1971): 26–34.
[15] Penrose, "Equity Participation and Sovereignty," 26, 39–40.
[16] Sarkis, "Foreword," 3–4.

University of Paris, and he defended it with vigor. He found particularly injudicious her fear of a return, "in the name of sovereignty rights, to 'The Law of the Jungle.'" His response invoked the standard history petroleum colonization: "The oil countries, which are generally developing countries and most of which have just freed themselves from colonial domination, do not have the intention . . . to impose such a law. Quite to the contrary, they only hope to get out of it."[17]

Such language was not confined to oil elites. The concepts that held meaning for Sarkis – decolonization, permanent sovereignty, unequal exchange, changing circumstances, economic emancipation, and others – also remained commonplaces of anticolonial thought outside of the oil nations. The Indian lawyer Krishna Rao, who wrote a doctoral thesis supporting Mossadegh's interpretation of national jurisdiction at New York University in 1955, oversaw the production of a document collection on the Non-Aligned Movement for the Indian Society of International Law in 1970. For him, the emergence of Asian and African nations "as independent sovereign states" had removed international law from "the exclusive domain of Christian European nations." One driver of that change was the recognition of sameness among the poorer states of "the community of nations," a shared perception of economic subjugation that led to mutually recognized "interests, purposes, objectives, aspirations and ideals." Declarations of solidarity, as expressed in the many minutes and communiqués he collected, thus reflected new "international norms." Among these was "the concept of permanent sovereignty over natural resources."[18]

Rao dealt proof like cards from a deck. In one example from April 1970, the same month Qaddafi hired Maghribi, the foreign ministers of the Non-Aligned Movement met in Dar-Es-Salaam. Prompted by the inaugural address of Tanzania President Julius Nyerere, they held an impromptu session on the international economy. The participants agreed that "the continuance of an outdated and iniquitous pattern of economic relationships" threatened their independence. They also held that nationalist economic programs could not be pursued in isolation. Rather, the poor nations needed to work in concert to bring the international economy in line with the political liberation that characterized the age of

---

[17] Nicolas Sarkis, "Opinion: Participation and Economic Development," *AOG* 1: 3 (November 1, 1971): 3–4.

[18] K. Krishna Rao, *The International Court of Justice and the Advisory Jurisdiction* (S.J.D. dissertation, New York University, 1955); K. Krishna Rao, "Foreword," *ISIL* (1970), v–vi.

decolonization. "[T]he progress of each member depends on the progress of all," the delegates wrote. Without "economic solidarity," imperialistic interests would continue "the expropriation of their natural resources and to the impairment of their future economic well-being."[19]

The ferment of anticolonial legal and economic thought echoed through the Third World. In another example from a year later, 1,500 representatives from 95 Asian, African, and Latin American countries gathered in Lima for the second ministerial meeting of the "Group of 77" developing countries, which had been formed at the first UN Conference on Trade and Development meeting in 1964. The "radical soldiers" of the Peruvian military government, who had nationalized their miniscule oil production when they came to power in 1969, invited Algerian Foreign Affairs Minister Abdelaziz Bouteflika to give the inaugural address. He presented cooperation among the oil-exporting countries as a model of common effort. "In 1971, the Third World countries, on the whole, lived through the battle that the oil producing countries had to fight," he said. In language redolent of the culture formed over the past two decades, Bouteflika drew the connection between past failure and future success. "World opinion acknowledged therein a decisive progress in the establishment of new economic relations based on justice," he said. The victory of OPEC was "therefore a victory which goes beyond the narrow circle" of the oil producers. Instead, it was "indeed a victory to all underdeveloped countries."[20]

The speech did more than just vibrate through so many translation earpieces with a consistent message. The Iranian Minister of Economy, Hushang Ansari, agreed with it later in the conference, albeit using not the language of saga but the softer, more technical tones of unequal exchange. OPEC's successes had taken a step to overturn "the deteriorating terms of trade" for oil, he said. That economic theory also pointed to the representativeness of the oil producers' experiences for Ansari, and he sought to link oil to the universal question of unequal exchange. The negotiations in Tehran and Tripoli were "a victory in the battle undertaken by underdeveloped countries to reach a fair solution to the difficult problem of raw materials export prices."[21]

---

[19] Preparatory Meeting of Non-Aligned Countries, April 17, 1970, in *ISIL* (1970), 55–60.
[20] "OPEC Presented as Example to Follow at the 'Group of 77' Conference of Lima," *AOG* 1: 4 (November 16, 1971): 18.
[21] "OPEC Presented as Example," 18.

The argument that the OPEC states were representative should not be taken too far, but it did have credibility at the time. On the one hand, as Penrose noted, oil was a unique commodity. But on the other, oil elites had consistently emphasized permanent sovereignty and unequal exchange since the early 1950s. And by the early 1970s the oil nations seemed more than ever to form a cohesive unit, a fact borne out by the almost circadian rhythm of successful negotiations after the Libyan breakthrough. Whenever an impasse arose, the OPEC negotiators threatened collective legislative enactments of their demands. A legal and intellectual shift that had begun two decades earlier in the United Nations at the advent of decolonization now seemed to amount to a transfer of economic power and the redistribution of wealth.

The meeting of the Group of 77 conveys a world of meaning about decolonization: the combination of economic and legal thought, the emphasis on international politics, and the belief that the oil countries could be representative. But most of all, the speeches illustrate that the transfer of power in the oil industry was not the work of insurrectionists alone. It would have been impossible without the support of gradualist oil elites. In mid-1971, in fact, a proposal that was initially a gradualist compromise moved to the front of the OPEC nations' collective agenda. The oil ministers passed a resolution in favor of the "natural right" to what was called "equity participation," or partial ownership in oil production, at the July 1971 meeting in OPEC's newly renovated Vienna headquarters. They were explicit in their argument that this sovereign right built on the previous assertions of others. Participation was a just means to redistribution, they said, "considering the change of circumstances which entails the implementation of Member Countries' right to participate in the existing oil concessions."[22]

The oil ministers named Saudi Oil Minister Ahmed Zaki Yamani as their negotiator in September. The State Department reported then that "OPEC's oil tax victory over the oil companies earlier this year marked a definite shift in bargaining power in favor of the exporting countries." Many American officials, like their British counterparts, understood participation as an expression of permanent sovereignty and thus an imperative of decolonization. It was "probably inevitable" in the long run, one wrote. But both governments initially took an uncompromising public

---

[22] OPEC Press Release, Vienna, December 8, 1971, OIC; "OPEC Presses on with Participation Demand," *MEES* 14: 38 (July 16, 1971): 1.

stance, in contrast to the earlier American accommodations, arguing that the demand for participation repudiated the stability enshrined in the Tehran and Tripoli contracts.[23]

Nadim Pachachi, now OPEC's Secretary General, responded that the oil producers had not flouted the previous agreements. Rather, changes in the international monetary system, in particular the recent US dollar devaluation, had made necessary a constant "revision of prices" to avoid a drop in the OPEC members' "purchasing power." Here, Pachachi drew on a new report conducted by OPEC on the terms of trade for oil, which the organization submitted to the UN Conference on Trade and Development in July 1970. According to that report, the "terms of trade of the Middle East oil producers" had fallen precipitously since 1958. The oil producers had again used their growing technical expertise, a crucial part of their sovereign rights program since the 1950s. This time they used it to make a new argument for greater control and upward revision of prices.[24]

British officials warned their American counterparts that the cancellation of the five-year promise threatened "to throw the producer governments' relations with the oil companies into turmoil." Still, by the end of 1971, the British ended on a policy that echoed American accommodation. This was because the British cabinet decided that diplomatic action would be "at best ineffective and at worst counter-productive." Their position was similar to the US argument during the 1970 Libyan push: "Creeping nationalization," as Ambassador to Iraq Glen Balfour-Paul had called participation, was "at least ... better than outright legislative measures." The Nixon administration agreed, and the hapless John Irwin was again tasked with the unenviable chore of telling company executives that the US government "did not want to get more and more involved" in the negotiations.[25]

[23] Bureau of Intelligence and Research, RECN-17, "Oil: New Confrontation over 'Participation'?" August 11, 1971, RG 59, Central Foreign Policy Files 1970–73, PET 3 OPEC, box 1483, NARA; Telegram 594, Jedda to FCO, August 8, 1971, Foreign and Commonwealth Office: Commodities and Oil Department, folder 560, UKNA 560; Hormats to Kissinger, "Oil Companies Faced with New OPEC Negotiating Demands," October 20, 1971, National Security Council, National Security Council Files, box 367, RNL.

[24] "Exclusive Interview with Dr. Pachachi," *AOG* 1: 1 (October 1, 1971), 5–7; OPEC Secretariat, "OPEC: An Example of Sub-Regional Cooperation and Trade Expansion," A Study Submitted to UNCTAD's International Group on Trade Expansion, Economic Cooperation and Regional Integration among Developing Countries, July 1970, OIC.

[25] Telegram 2214, FCO to Washington, August 20, 1971, Foreign and Commonwealth Office: Commodities and Oil Department, folder 560, UKNA; Fullerton to Gallagher,

The Libyan Revolutionary Command Council, on the other hand, sought to politicize the participation issue as much as possible. Libya "emerged as the leading hawk" on participation, one commentator wrote, when 'Izz al-Din al-Mabruk began to publicly insist on nothing less than immediate majority control. Even Iraqi Oil Minister Sa'doun Hammadi, who called for immediate 20 percent participation at the July 1971 meeting, had argued for a smaller percentage and more flexibility. The radicalism had consequences. In a statement similar to its five-year guarantee made and broken in Tehran, the Iranian government promised that the Gulf producers would not ask for more than 20 percent participation, even if Libya acted "unreasonably as it had in the past." Industry experts were now less sanguine about such pledges. If Mabruk extracted an agreement for majority participation, Iran and the other gradualist producers would "be bound to follow suit," one British official wrote.[26]

When the oil ministers met in Beirut that September, their meeting lasted just two hours. Owing to differences about the desired percentage of participation, their resolution was purposefully vague, allowing each country to negotiate according to "the objectives that best conform to its national interests." The OPEC ministers were emphatic that the resolution reaffirmed "the right of member countries" to ownership over existing concessions. The resolution boiled down to a simple phrase: "each for himself, and OPEC for all." An analyst from the British Oil Department analyst summarized the situation. The companies did "not have a leg to stand on" because the producers "would simply claim participation as a sovereign right." The State Department agreed that there was "no merit in a formal diplomatic approach."[27]

"Diplomatic Action in Support of the Oil Companies on Participation," August 9, 1971, Foreign and Commonwealth Office: Commodities and Oil Department, folder 560, UKNA; Baghdad to FCO, "OPEC and Participation," August 8, 1971, Foreign and Commonwealth Office: Commodities and Oil Department, folder 560, UKNA; Memorandum of Conversation, "The Oil Companies and OPEC Demands," December 2, 1971, *FRUS 1969–76*, vol. 36, doc. 96.

[26] *MEES* 14: 48 (September 24, 1971), 2–6; Telegram 430, Beirut to FCO, "OPEC Meeting," September 24, 1971, Foreign and Commonwealth Office: Commodities and Oil Department, folder 561, UKNA; Telegram 2614, FCO to Washington, October 8, 1971, Foreign and Commonwealth Office: Commodities and Oil Department, folder 560, UKNA.

[27] "Negotiations on Participation and Monetary Adjustments to Begin in October," *AOG* 1: 1 (October 1, 1971): 19–24; Oil Department, Meeting Record, August 3, 1971, Foreign and Commonwealth Office: Commodities and Oil Department, folder 560,

Mabruk thus returned to Tripoli with a mandate to keep Libya as the pacesetter. "The companies should now be prepared to change the out-dated concession agreements," he said in his first public statement after the meeting. Then, in a sudden turn of events, the formal processes of British decolonization gave Libyan authorities the chance to further press the issue. As British authorities undertook their final preparations to depart from the Trucial States on November 30, 1971, Iranian forces took the disputed islands of the Tunbs and Abu Musa in the Persian Gulf.[28]

The Shah had been empowered to conduct this endgame of the Gulf Scuttle largely for the same Cold War reasons that worked to his advan-tage in the oil revenue negotiations of the late 1960s. Fearing the estrange-ment of their essential ally, both the State Department and the Foreign and Commonwealth Office had worked, in the words of one official, "to solve the Gulf islands problem without alienating the Shah." According to the final agreement, Iran would take control of the Tunbs. On Abu Musa, Iran and Sharjah would share jurisdiction and split any offshore petrol-eum revenue. After discussions with the United States, King Faisal of Saudi Arabia reassured the British that he would not intervene and that Saudi remonstrations against the island seizure would be minimal.[29]

But the sheikh of tiny Ras al Khaimah never accepted Iranian jurisdic-tion and ordered his police forces to resist the Iranian landing party. On November 30, 1971, they did so, resulting in the death of four policemen and three members of the landing party. The sheikh invoked his treaty of protection with the United Kingdom, but the Foreign and Common-wealth Office ignored his plea and terminated all treaty relationships the next day as planned.

Most observers expected a relatively moderate Arab outcry, but they did not foresee what happened next. Libya nationalized all the holdings of British Petroleum, the largest of which was the 330,000 barrel-per-day

UKNA; Washington to FCO, "OPEC – Participation," August 23, 1971, Foreign and Commonwealth Office: Commodities and Oil Department, folder 560, UKNA.

[28] "Negotiations on Participation to be Conducted Separately with the Concession-aires," 17.

[29] Telegram 3147, FCO to Washington, December 10, 1971, Foreign and Commonwealth Office: Commodities and Oil Department, folder 610, UKNA; Rogers to Nixon, "Persian Gulf," December 16, 1971, *FRUS 1969–76*, vol. XXIV, doc. 112; Telegram 3147, FCO to Washington, December 10, 1971, Foreign and Commonwealth Office: Commodities and Oil Department, folder 610, UKNA; Elliot to Kissinger, "Persian Gulf Situation," December 1, 1971, National Security Council Files, box 647, RNL.

Sarir field. The nationalization was on the one hand a blunt response to a problem of regional power. The nationalization decree accused the British government of "collusion" in the Iranian occupation. But it also indicated more than a protest of the role of the exiting empire in the Iranian annexation. "It had, in any case, been on the cards for other reasons," British Foreign Minister Alec Douglas-Home told the cabinet. He briefed his prime minister even more explicitly. "Libya's desire to remain the front-runner" in OPEC was the major factor.[30]

Libya received support from the usual suspects, including the standard bearers of pan-Arabism. A message from Yasser Arafat was read on Libyan National Radio: "On behalf of all our people and all the Palestine revolution fighters, we congratulate you and shake your hand for the giant revolutionary step you have taken." The Voices of Fatah radio station, operating from Cairo, celebrated the nationalization as "moving far beyond the traditional Arab reaction to imperialist plotting." Other oil elites agreed. "Your decisions rightly represent a new gain acquired by the glorious Libyan Revolution in the field of recuperating and liberating the resources of the Arab Nation," Boumedienne wrote to Qaddafi. "It is also a big victory to the common cause for whose triumph we are all fighting." Nicolas Sarkis likened the Libyan nationalization to "a heavy fist-blow … on the international oil chess-board." It toppled some of the master pieces and further opened the breach in "the whole set of relationships." Even the Cuban publicity organ, *El Tricontinental*, expressed its satisfaction of "the measures undertaken to place the economy in government hands."[31]

Among the Arab oil elites, support for Libya was universal. For his part, Iraqi Oil Minister Sa'doun Hammadi told the Iraq News Agency that the Libyan nationalization was "a natural outcome of the

---

[30] Annex, "The Dispute over the Sovereignty of Abu Musa and the Tunbs and Drilling Rights in the Area," January 14, 1972, Foreign and Commonwealth Office: Commodities and Oil Department, folder 743, UKNA; Telegram 3146, FCO to Washington, "BP and Libya," December 10, 1971, Foreign and Commonwealth Office: Commodities and Oil Department, folder 610, UKNA; PMV(BER)(71)28, "Talks between the Prime Minister and the President of the United States – Oil, Libya," December 10, 1971, Foreign and Commonwealth Office: Commodities and Oil Department, folder 610, UKNA.

[31] Summary of World Broadcasts, December 10, 1971, Foreign and Commonwealth Office: Commodities and Oil Department, folder 610, UKNA; "Algeria and Iraq Support BP's Nationalization," *AOG* 1: 6 (December 16, 1971): 15–16; Nicolas Sarkis, "Participation and Nationalization," *AOG* 1: 6 (December 16, 1971): 3; "Libya: The Conquest of Its Sovereignty," *Tricontinental* 5: 57 (December 1970): 36, Reference Center for Marxist Studies, Pamphlet Collection, box 2, Tamiment Library, New York University.

intransigence of the oil trusts vis-à-vis national demands." *Al-Thawra*, the official daily newspaper of Iraq's Ba'ath Party, linked Libyan policy to the Iraqi refusal to settle its dispute over Rumaila, where the concession had been written in a way that had "sold Iraq out to the imperialist oil monopolies at the cheapest price."[32]

In Iraq, Hammadi was prepared to act, and the drive for sovereign rights seemed to become an uncontrollable stampede when Iraq nationalized the Iraq Petroleum Company sixth months later. Neither the nationalization nor its success were foretold. In the 1960s, most policymakers in the US State Department had underestimated the gravity of the Iraq oil situation. "The hard-line intransigence" of Iraqi oil policy was little more than the "trite slogans of 'Arab oil for the Arabs,'" one official wrote in a typical analysis. But American decision makers were becoming more aware of the changing circumstances by 1971. In the second half of 1971 and again in early 1972, they took note when the Iraq Petroleum Company limited the flow of Iraqi oil to the Syrian port of Banias. The company cited lower Persian Gulf freight rates as its economic logic, a result of the uptick in "supertanker" construction following the 1967 closure of the Suez Canal. The cutbacks nevertheless upset the Ba'ath leaders. The young vice president of the Revolutionary Command Council, Saddam Hussein, complained to the head French member of the IPC that the reduction was a heavy-handed negotiating ploy.[33]

Meanwhile, the hand of the Iraqi government continued to improve. Importantly, the continued closure of the Suez Canal made Iraqi oil of greater interest to Asian markets. Ceylon concluded an agreement in February 1971 on barter grounds, exchanging future oil for Ceylonese tea. India also signed a two-year agreement directly with the Iraq National Oil Company in September 1971. As had the earlier contracts with Western and Eastern European consumers, the agreement dealt in future oil in return for contribution to industrial projects in Iraq, including a steel plant, a cement factory, and the extension of the railway network.[34]

---

[32] "Algeria and Iraq Support BP's Nationalization," 15–16; "Dr. Hammadi: 'No Compromises about Law No. 80," *AOG* 1: 6 (December 16, 1971): 18.

[33] Kuwait A-79, "Some Observations on the Sixth Arab Petroleum Congress," March 28, 1967, RG 59, Central Foreign Policy Files 1967–69, PET IRAQ, box 1359, NARA; "Note of a Meeting Held at 1 Victoria Street on 13 September 1972," UKNA, FCO 67/781.

[34] "India will be INOC's Second Asian Customer," *AOG* 1: 2 (October 16, 1971): 14–15.

Against that immediate backdrop, the national oil company finally began production in Rumaila in April 1972. When the nationalized oil first began to flow, the multinational Iraq Petroleum Company restated its ownership claim and further limited Iraq's Mediterranean off-take at the Syrian port of Banias, cutting Iraqi oil revenues by a third. The IPC once more denied that the action was in retaliation for Rumaila, but most observers assumed that it was. The Ba'ath government decried the "pressure tactic" and issued an ultimatum: The IPC could abandon its bountiful Kirkuk fields or allocate part of its pipeline capacity to oil from Rumaila.[35]

OPEC supported Iraq in these endeavors. First, the Secretariat labeled the production cuts "political." When the IPC did not budge on its claim to Rumaila, promising only to reinstate production, OPEC and Iraqi officials noted that the company counterproposal did not even address the fundamental assertion of Iraqi sovereignty. The Revolutionary Command Council brusquely rejected it, and Iraq nationalized all IPC operations on June 1, 1972.[36]

The *Journal of World Trade Law* provided a concise summary of the consequences of the nationalizations. Like British and American officials' increasing use of the concepts of sovereign rights, the journal's reporting indicates the reach of the economic culture of decolonization. Libya and Iraq had followed "the path laid out by history." The old concessions were dead letter, the journal's analyst continued. "The traditional concession surrendering huge areas to the oil interests now seems a thing of the past." Actors across the world joined the oil elites in hailing the Libyan and Iraqi breakthroughs as the culmination of two decades of progress for sovereign rights. The UN Economic and Social Council passed a resolution approving the nationalizations. The Brazilian ambassador, Sergio Frazao, linked the nationalizations at that meeting to his notion of Third World mutualism. "The peoples of the world were all in the same economic boat," he said.[37]

---

[35] Smolansky and Smolansky, *Soviet Quest*, 46; Chalmers, Oil Department, "The Dispute between the Iraq Petroleum Co. and the Iraqi Government," October 20, 1972, Foreign and Commonwealth Office: Commodities and Oil Department, folder 781, UKNA .

[36] Amembassy Vienna to SecState, "OPEC Supports Iraq vis-a-vis IPC Oil Production Drop," May 31, 1972, RG 59, Central Foreign Policy Files 1970–73, PET 3 OPEC, box 1484, NARA; Wolfe-Hunnicutt, "The End of the Concessionary Regime," 256–62.

[37] Barraz, "The Legal Status of Oil Concessions," 630; UNOPI, *Weekly News Survey*, May 4, 1973, UN doc. WS/605.

That the boat was getting bigger seemed evident to many as they observed another instance of successful diplomacy from Iraq and Libya when the multinational companies failed to blacklist the sale of nationalized oil in 1972 and 1973. This inability to prevent the oil's arrival to market further indicated the viability and visibility of sovereign rights as oil diplomacy.

The day after the nationalization in Libya, both BP and the British embassy in Tripoli officially agreed that the Libyan government "had the right as a sovereign state to nationalize." However, the company and its parent government protested the nationalization on the basis that the decree had not provided for compensation. The British government presented a note to the Revolutionary Command Council that called on them to "act in accordance with the established rules of international law" and either restore the company's operations or make reparations. The Foreign and Commonwealth Office requested that the State Department issue a similar note "deploring" the nationalization. Douglas-Home wrote to US Secretary of State William Rogers, "If the Libyan government's action does not meet with any retribution, both the Libyans and the governments of the other oil producing countries will be encouraged to take action against other concessions." The cascade effect would throw "the existing international oil machinery into complete disarray and consequently jeopardize the security of oil supplies to the western world." Over some protests from the Bureau of Near Eastern Affairs, the State Department agreed to "black" the oil from the Sarir concession, making its sale illegal in the United States and by US companies.[38]

BP took legal measures throughout the first half of 1972 to prevent the nationalized oil from arriving to market and "providing a precedent that others, like Iraq, might rapidly follow." The US Justice Department, for its part, lifted antimonopoly regulations on the major US oil companies,

---

[38] File Note, "Events affecting BP interests in Tripoli," December 13, 1971, Foreign and Commonwealth Office: Commodities and Oil Department, folder 610, UKNA; Telegram 521, FCO to Moscow, June 6, 1972, Foreign and Commonwealth Office: Commodities and Oil Department, folder 795, UKNA; Telegram 4229, Washington to FCO, December 15, 1971, Foreign and Commonwealth Office: Commodities and Oil Department, folder 610, UKNA; Telegram 3147, FCO to Washington, December 10, 1971, Foreign and Commonwealth Office: Commodities and Oil Department, folder 610, UKNA; Brief by the FCO, "Talks between the Prime Minister and the President of the United States – Oil, Libya," December 15, 1971, Foreign and Commonwealth Office: Commodities and Oil Department, folder 610, UKNA; DOS to Embassy Libya, December 17, 1971, *FRUS 1969–76*, vol. 36, doc. 100; DOS to Certain Diplomatic Posts, December 22, 1971, *FRUS 1969–76*, vol. 36, doc. 101.

which allowed them to meet in New York and design a "Libyan safety net" to offset BP's production loss. When the Revolutionary Command Council requested that the Spanish national oil company, Hispanoil, run the nationalized concession, both governments pressured the Franco regime to reject their entreaty. The Spanish foreign affairs ministry waffled initially, expressing concern that its interests would also be expropriated "if they did not play the Libyan game." But after an emotional quarrel between the executives of BP and Hispanoil in New York, in which Eric Drake accused his counterpart of "poaching" and "piracy," the Spanish company signed on to the joint action directed from New York.[39]

BP pursued the black oil successfully in the first half of 1972. It resolved over thirty cases of legal action in Italian courts and conducted a series of backroom conversations with General Anastasio Somoza of Nicaragua. In the latter case, Somoza finally yielded to the British ambassador's arguments and agreed in May 1972 not to purchase oil directly from Libya, even though he was "fighting a rearguard action with the petroleum companies against price increases." Somoza's submission maintained BP's "100% success record" in preventing non-Communist countries from buying nationalized oil.[40]

But similar inhibitions did not exist behind the iron curtain. In a countercurrent to the much-ballyhooed détente between the United States and the Soviet Union, both Libya and Iraq used the Cold War to beat the blacklist. In this case, it was Libya that followed the Iraqi lead. The rulers in Baghdad had continued the Iraqi–Soviet economic relationship, which now culminated in a state visit by Saddam Hussein to Moscow in February 1972. The joint communiqué published after the meeting stressed Soviet readiness to help Iraq "exploit its oil wealth independently." The statement was typical of Soviet policy, but the Jordanian ambassador in Moscow informed his American counterpart that Hussein's primary goal had been a substantial agreement on the marketing of Rumaila oil. Iraq, according to his sources, had acquired fifteen Soviet oil tankers as

---

[39] Record of a meeting held at the FCO, December 17, 1971, Foreign and Commonwealth Office: Commodities and Oil Department, folder 610, UKNA; Telegram 571, Madrid to FCO, "Libyan Oil," Foreign and Commonwealth Office: Commodities and Oil Department, folder 610, UKNA; Telegram 574, Madrid to FCO, "Libyan Oil," Foreign and Commonwealth Office: Commodities and Oil Department, folder 610, UKNA.

[40] I. P. S. Vincent to G. B. Chalmers, "General Somoza's Interest in BP/Libyan Oil," May 19, 1972, Foreign and Commonwealth Office: Commodities and Oil Department, folder 795, UKNA.

a result of the visit, which would make "harassment of their operations by oil companies more difficult."[41]

Soviet Premier Alexei Kosygin paid a return visit to Iraq in April 1972 to sign a Treaty of Friendship and Cooperation. The visit and treaty were timed to overlap with the commencement of national production in Rumaila. At the ribbon-cutting ceremony, Hussein and Kosygin smiled for pictures and then gave brief speeches. Hussein's opening provides a unique window into the national and international politics of sovereign rights in the age of decolonization. "We and the masses of the people everywhere in this country are today celebrating an important event in our national history – the beginning of the direct national exploitation of oil," he said. The industry had been dominated for "about half a century by foreign monopolistic companies." With the beginning of production in Rumaila, he continued, the Ba'ath Party had at last cast off "imperialist influence and raised the national slogan 'Arab oil belongs to the Arabs.'" The slogan the State Department had written off as "trite" during the 1967 oil embargo now was less so. Kosygin's shorter speech discussed Rumaila as an example of Iraq "strengthening its sovereignty" – part of a broader struggle to ensure that "natural resources, and above all oil, belong to their true owners."[42]

The next month, in an echo of the Iraqi–Soviet deals of the previous years, the Libyan News Agency announced a marketing contract with Moscow. Soviet tankers would now also lift the oil from the former BP terminal in Tobruk. Libya cut the production of BP's former partner in the Sarir field, Bunker Hunt, to free oil for the Soviet deal. A Russian tanker arrived on May 31 to take the first consignment, and Libyan press reports trumpeted the triumph over the "imperialist oil monopolies."[43]

The British embassy in Washington pointed out the ramifications of the Libyan–Soviet deal. It would be impossible to "take any kind of legal action in the Soviet courts." Just as it had in the months before the

[41] AmEmbassy Soviet Union to DOS, February 18, 1972, *FRUS 1969–76*, vol. E-4, doc. 298.

[42] ME/3959/E/1, "E. Kosygin's Visit to Iraq," April 10, 1972, Foreign and Commonwealth Office: Commodities and Oil Department, folder 774, UKNA.

[43] G. B. Chalmers to I. P. S. Vincent, "BP/Libya," June 1, 1972, Foreign and Commonwealth Office: Commodities and Oil Department, folder 795, UKNA; S. L. Egerton, British Embassy, Tripoli, "BP/Libya," May 25, 1972, Foreign and Commonwealth Office: Commodities and Oil Department, folder 795, UKNA; Meeting Record, May 25, 1972, Foreign and Commonwealth Office: Commodities and Oil Department, folder 795, UKNA; Telegram 649, Tripoli to FCO, "BP/Libya," June 2, 1972, Foreign and Commonwealth Office: Commodities and Oil Department, folder 795, UKNA.

Rumaila nationalization, the entry of the Soviet Union into Sarir broke the back of the companies' black oil strategy. Yugoslavia followed in Soviet footsteps in June 1972, when a national company signed a deal for a half-million tons of Sarir crude per year. Bulgaria and Romania also concluded agreements. When the British ambassador in Tripoli remonstrated to his Yugoslavian counterpart over dinner, the response was curt: "The nationalization of BP had been legitimate."[44]

The Cold War dealings precipitated an agreement on compensation between BP and the Revolutionary Command Council. The Egyptian government conveyed a "top level message" to BP via the directors of Pan American Oil on the possibility of compensation from Libya in November 1972. Although Drake was reluctant to "upset the participation apple cart" – the ongoing discussions over partial ownership between oil executives and Saudi Oil Minister Ahmed Zaki Yamani, on behalf of his OPEC counterparts – he agreed to talk. Hispanoil began to work as a quiet conduit between 'Izz al-Din al-Mabruk and Drake, and they arrived at an agreement that would allow the Spanish company to produce and market the nationalized oil. By then, Mabruk had also signed marketing contracts with the French and Italian national oil companies.[45]

Back in Baghdad, the attempts to blacklist Iraqi oil ran along a similar track. The Ba'ath government already had preestablished markets in both the Eastern and Western blocs by dint of the future oil contracts it had signed since 1968. The largest of these were with the Italian, Brazilian, and Spanish national oil companies. After the nationalization, the members of the Iraq Petroleum Company filed cases in in each of those national legal systems. Each case failed, and despite a worldwide advertising campaign by the IPC in August 1972 warning consumers not to take Iraqi oil, private and public companies from many more nations – including Greece, Japan, and several Eastern European states – signed contracts with the national oil company. When World Bank President

[44] M. R. Melhuish, British Embassy, Tripoli to J. C. Kay, North African and Near East Department, "Sarir Oil," June 5, 1972, Foreign and Commonwealth Office: Commodities and Oil Department, folder 795, UKNA; Telegram 637, Tripoli to FCO, June 2, 1972, Foreign and Commonwealth Office: Commodities and Oil Department, folder 795, UKNA; Telegram 713, Tripoli to FCO, "BP/Libya," June 25, 1972, Foreign and Commonwealth Office: Commodities and Oil Department, folder 795, UKNA.

[45] G. B. Chalmers, Oil Department, "BP/Libya," November 16, 1972, Foreign and Commonwealth Office: Commodities and Oil Department, folder 796, UKNA; Telegram 1068, FCO to Tripoli, "Marawan's Visit," December 15, 1972, Foreign and Commonwealth Office: Commodities and Oil Department, folder 796, UKNA.

Robert McNamara personally canceled a final attempt to pressure Iraq to raise its compensation through a "blocking operation" on an education loan in February 1973, the IPC officially accepted the 1961 and 1972 nationalization decrees. A US intelligence report recognized that Iraqi "efforts to arrange alternative supply contracts have been relatively successful."[46]

The French member company of the IPC, the *Compagnie Française des Pétroles* (CFP), played a key role in this success. Saddam Hussein led a delegation to Paris immediately after the June 1972 nationalization. To the consternation of the other members of the IPC, the delegation negotiated an agreement allowing the CFP to receive its formerly allotted share of oil for ten years under pre-nationalization conditions. But the other members of the concession, albeit begrudgingly, accepted the French connection when CFP executives assured them that they would use the relationship to negotiate "adequate" compensation for the nationalized property. But the final terms of compensation reveal that the IPC fared as poorly on that issue as it had in defending its concessionary rights. The IPC claimed that it had "quasi-property rights" over underground reserves and argued that the value of the expropriation, including oil in the subsoil, totaled $1 billion. The Ba'ath government rebutted the claim and offered a much lower compensation value, based on the net book value of $15 million.[47]

---

[46] Telegram 428, FCO to Santiago, "Nationalisation of the IPC," September 1, 1972, Foreign and Commonwealth Office: Commodities and Oil Department, folder 781, UKNA; Lockton, Oil Department, "Iraqi Oil Sales," August 22, 1972, Foreign and Commonwealth Office: Commodities and Oil Department, folder 781, UKNA; G. B. Chalmers, "IPC and Mediation with the Iraq Government," July 5, 1972, Foreign and Commonwealth Office: Commodities and Oil Department, folder 779, UKNA; Telegram 719, UK Director IMF/IBRD to FCO, November 8, 1972, Foreign and Commonwealth Office: Commodities and Oil Department, folder 781, UKNA; Oil Department, "Brief for Meeting with Directors of BP and Shell," November 6, 1972, Foreign and Commonwealth Office: Commodities and Oil Department, folder 781, UKNA; National Intelligence Estimate 36.2–72, December 21, 1972, *FRUS 1969–76*, vol. E-4, doc. 330. The Spanish national oil company, Hispanoil signed a 1970 deal to exchange seven 35,000-ton oil tankers for future North Rumaila crude. In 1971, the Brazilian national company, Petrobras and the Italian national company, ENI, followed suit. ENI made an unprecedented 10-year deal for 20 million tons of INOC oil. On the legal cases, see: "North Rumeila [sic] Oil Sales Go Ahead Despite Company's Legal Threats," *The Times* (London), April 13, 1972; "IPC Begins Legal Action to Bar oil for Brazil," *The Times* (London), June 29, 1972.

[47] Majid Khadduri, *Socialist Iraq: A Study in Iraqi Politics since 1968* (Washington: The Middle East Institute, 1981), 127; Telegram 1468, Paris to FCO, October 26, 1972, Foreign and Commonwealth Office: Commodities and Oil Department, folder 781,

Owing to his relationship with Hussein, the IPC members appointed the director of the CFP, Jan Duroc Danner, to mediate the compensation. British and American executives immediately regretted the decision, speculating that self-interest drove Danner, who recommended that the IPC settle for a depressed compensation value. The companies agreed in March 1973 to pay Iraq $350 million "as settlement of past debts" in return for fifteen million tons of Iraqi oil. Upon announcing the settlement, Iraqi president Ahmed Hassan al-Bakr stated that the agreement "guarantees our sovereignty over our natural resources and gives the companies the compensation they deserved."[48]

The courting of France and Spain by Iraq and Libya, as well as their successful use of the Cold War to break the blacklists, reflected the shared policy of using sovereign rights to their national advantages. At times, what one British oil analyst described as their "maverick behavior" had decidedly mixed results – he invoked the "sad" image of the lone Brazilian representative's suitcase spilling its contents "over the Syrian desert during his trip from Beirut to Baghdad." The State Department also held that Iraqi and Libyan diplomacy had serious limits. The OPEC countries had, after all, "promis[ed] an uninterrupted supply of oil to world customers at terms tolerable to both producers and sellers," an analyst wrote. For that reason, Iraq and Libya could not expect "wholehearted support" from their fellow oil-producing states.[49]

That assessment underestimated the strength of the oil producers' collective sovereignty. It also misgauged their desire to use it. For one, Iraq received material succor from its fellow oil producers at the crucial moment of nationalization. Kuwait made substantial loans to Iraq, despite their considerable differences, and the finance ministers of the members of the new Organization of Arab Petroleum Exporting

UKNA; Maarten H. Muller, "Compensation for Nationalization: A North-South Dialogue," *Columbia Journal of Transnational Law* 19: 1 (1981): 43–5.

[48] Telegram No. 55034 to AmEmb Paris, October 17, 1967, doc. CK3100344219, DDRS; Jacobs to Solomon, "New Iraqi Oil Legislation Finally Deprives IPC of Most of its Concession Area," August 11, 1967, RG 59, Central Foreign Policy Files 1967–69, PET 6 IRAQ, box 1360, NARA; Memorandum of Conversation, "IPC Report on Baghdad," October 8, 1968, *FRUS 1964–68*, vol. XXXIV, doc. 223; "Oil Takeover Pact Announced by Iraq," *New York Times*, March 1, 1973.

[49] "Background Brief on Iraq," n.d. (1974), Foreign and Commonwealth Office: Energy Department, folder 123, UKNA; Graham to Egerton, December 1, 1974, Foreign and Commonwealth Office: Energy Department, folder 123, UKNA; National Intelligence Estimate 36.2–72, December 21, 1972, *FRUS 1969–76*, vol. E-4, doc. 330.

Countries (OAPEC) also agreed to lend Iraq £54 million to make up for production shortages resulting from nationalization. Saudi Arabia and Kuwait, furthermore, slowed production to pressure the IPC to reach a quick settlement. OPEC released a public statement supporting the nationalization as "an act of sovereignty valid under international law." Iraq also received somewhere between $50 and $90 million in loans from Kuwait and Libya between June 1972 and January 1973.[50]

The easing of rivalries among the members of OAPEC, which was founded in January 1968, reflected the broader shift toward a collective position in the early 1970s. The official rationale of the Arab producers in founding the organization was to better coordinate their use of the "Arab oil weapon" in the ongoing battle with Israel. But in reality, that argument was window dressing to conceal a level of disharmony among the Arab members of OPEC. The monarchies of Saudi Arabia, Kuwait, and Libya actually founded the organization "chiefly to give the conservative oil-rich states a pan-Arab umbrella under which pressures from the radical Arab states might be more easily resisted," the State Department reported.[51]

But the 1969 coup in Libya perforated the umbrella. Serious strains between the founders surfaced when the new Libyan government accused the Saudi Arabia and Kuwait of opposing the admission of Algeria and Iraq, both of which qualified for membership as Arab countries for which oil was the principle source of income. To balance the radical presence, according to the British Oil Department, Saudi Arabia made great efforts "at King Faisal's personal command" to bring the smaller Gulf states into the organization. Abu Dhabi, Qatar, and Dubai, along with Algeria, joined in May 1970. By then OAPEC could boast that it represented 55 percent of global oil exports.[52]

Iraq applied for membership a month later, but Saudi Arabia blocked a decision, forcing the response to be deferred until December 1970 and

---

[50] Telegram 308, Baghdad to FCO, June 21, 1972, Foreign and Commonwealth Office: Commodities and Oil Department, folder 747, UKNA; National Intelligence Estimate 36.2–72, December 21, 1972, *FRUS 1969–76*, vol. E-4, doc. 330. An intricate description of Iraqi diplomatic labors within OPEC and OAPEC can be found in RG 59, Subject-Numeric Files 1970–73, PET 3 OAPEC, box 1481, NARA.

[51] Brewer to Battle, "Slow Start for Organization of Arab Petroleum Exporting Countries (OAPEC)," August 1, 1968, *FRUS 1964–68*, vol. XXXIV, doc. 222; Mary Ann Tetreault, *The Organization of Arab Petroleum Exporting Countries: History, Policies and Prospects* (Westport, CT: Greenwood Press, 1981), 29–32.

[52] Tetreault, *The Organization of Arab Exporting Countries*, 58–87.

again until June 1971. That meeting was suspended when the group's Secretary General, Suhail Sa'dawi of Libya, publicly tendered his resignation and warned that the organization might be dissolved. In December 1971 Saudi Arabia sought compromise through an amendment to the membership qualifications that allowed Arab oil producers to join regardless of whether oil was their principal source of income. The amendment opened the way for the admission of Egypt and Syria, as well as Iraq, in May 1972, just after the IPC nationalization.[53]

The gap between insurrectionists and gradualists had closed so much by then as to become almost inexistent. Sarkis, writing in *Le Monde Diplomatique* in July 1973, again turned to the Iranian nationalization of 1951 to explain this. The Iraqis and the Libyans had exorcized "from a psychological and political viewpoint ... the trauma created by Dr. Mossadegh's experience in Iran" two decades earlier, he wrote. Their nationalizations dispelled "the long-standing myths" that the oil producers "could not exploit their own resources."[54]

The ongoing negotiations over participation, led on behalf of the OPEC members by Saudi Oil Minister Yamani, further reveal the narrowing margin between gradualists and insurrectionists. Yamani himself had made a tactical move toward insurrection since the Libyan success of 1970, and his language and policies increasingly struck an *ultra* sovereign note in 1972 and after. The shift tells us something about the viability of sovereign rights and something about Yamani. He was the most stalwart gradualist among the OPEC members' oil ministers in the 1960s. He had angered Tariki and Sayid Abdul Aziz al-Wattari during the royalty negotiations, was a vocal critic of the 1967 Arab embargo, and had backed crablike into the politics of sovereign rights in 1968. In the last instance, he presented participation then as a more responsible alternative to nationalization. He had even called the relationship between the companies and the countries as "indissoluble, like a Catholic marriage" in a speech at the American University of Beirut that year.[55]

Yet even then the economic culture of decolonization had begun to tincture Yamani and, by the early 1970s, he found that set of ideas more

[53] Lockton, "OAPEC," March 23, 1972, Foreign and Commonwealth Office: Commodities and Oil Department, folder 747, UKNA .

[54] Nicolas Sarkis, "The Nationalisation of IPC: One Year After," *AOG* 44: 2 (July 16, 1973): 22–3.

[55] Sampson, *The Seven Sisters*, 276.

compelling than before. He began to join other oil elites in consistently discussing control over oil in terms that were once the provenance of insurrectionists. American officials at the embassy in Saudi Arabia first noted this shift when they described a new relationship of "fraternal good feeling" between Saudi King Faisal and Algerian President Boumedienne. After discussing oil at the December 1969 Arab summit, the two men had become the "strange bedfellows" of oil geopolitics, one official wrote. Faisal had since visited Boumedienne in Algiers, and Yamani and the Algerian oil minister, Belaid Abdessalam, began to work together "in asserting ... the need for producing countries to play a greater role in the destiny of the oil industry."[56]

As Yamani became more intransigent, he set a hard floor for the dialogue. He would never assail neocolonialism like the Iraqis, Algerians, or Libyans. But neither would he allow the sovereign breakthrough to remain solely within the radical purview. In striking that balance, he repeated the line that had been used for over a decade by other elites: he emphasized sovereignty as a matter of fact. The companies that held the old concessions had an obligation to abide by national mandates, he told the US ambassador. The changing circumstances were best explained as a meteorological imperative. "New winds were now blowing, as marked by Algerian action, and Libyan and Iraqi attitudes," he said. To the members of OPEC in 1972, he described the events since 1970 in collective terms: "Finally our efforts were coordinated and OPEC stood united, proving time and time again that it can enforce its demands."[57]

Yamani acted based on his assessment of Saudi national interest. But as he borrowed from the language of sovereign rights diplomacy, he helped sustain the program of the oil elites after 1970. In any case, his internationalist identification with the insurrectionists grew stronger as he sought to increase the power of Saudi Arabia to control its national oil production. And with good reason, for sovereign internationalism helped the cause of each nation, and even actors as different as Yamani and Abdessalam, the strange bedfellows, breathed the same atmosphere and drew on the same store of economic culture. They thus arrived at the same

---

[56] A-157 from Jidda, "Monthly Commentary for Saudi Arabia," July 6, 1970, RG 59, Subject-Numeric Files 1970–73, POL 2 SAUD, box 2584, NARA.

[57] AmEmbassy Jidda to SecState, "Discussion re Participation with Min-Pet Yamani," February 17, 1972, *FRUS 1969–76*, vol. XXXVI, doc. 112; "Participation," October 26, 1972, in Kubbah, *OPEC, Past and Present*, 118–19.

FIGURE 7.1 Algerian Minister of Industry and Energy Belaid Abdesselam and
Saudi Minister of Oil Ahmed Zaki Yamani meet with officials from Belgium at
Egmont Palace in Brussels in 1973. Yamani is second from the left, Abdesselam
second from the right.
Source: EC – Audiovisual Service, Photo: Jean-Louis Debaize, November 30, 1973,
© European Communities, 1973.

ultimate conclusion – the inward and outward conviction that the OPEC
members could control the supply and price of oil.

A good cop–bad cop analogy is too simple, but one can hardly argue
with the interpretation that the insurrectionists and gradualists of OPEC
had spun a web of reciprocal influence. They interlocked on their belief in
sovereign rights diplomacy and, as importantly, found that their goals of
oil control overlapped. In a meeting with James Akins in November 1972,
the managing director of the National Iranian Oil Company explained

that dynamic. The "radical Arab states of Iraq or Libya" would consistently impose stricter terms on the companies. The companies would yield to them and then, he predicted, "yield again" to Yamani in the discussions over participation.[58]

That is exactly what happened. By the end of 1972 it was Iran and Saudi Arabia that were competing with each other over which nation could extract the best deal on participation from the companies. Oil company executives reported to the State Department that the whipsaw between Libya and the gradualists was now complemented by "a political cross fire between Saudi Arabia and Iran." The Shah told the US ambassador that he had "no intention of coming out second best to Dr. Yamani" in February 1973. He added for good measure that the "United Nations [had] made clear that the way in which a nation handles and disposes of its natural resources is its business alone." As such, any new dictums to the companies from his government would be "non-negotiable."[59]

This time, the Shah was upset because Yamani had negotiated a new agreement on participation, signed in December 1972 by Saudi Arabia, Kuwait, and the other Arab states in the Gulf. According to the agreement, the governments immediately would take up to 25 percent participation in their concessions and end with 51 percent in 1982. This gradual and partial nationalization was considered less radical than the actions of Libya, Iraq, and Algeria. But sovereign rights diplomacy, even in this form, revealed the changed assumptions of the international economy. Compensation, for example, would be based on the new concept of "updated book value," approximately two and a half times the value the companies used for local taxes in the case of Saudi Arabia. Reflecting the victories of Iraq and Libya in their negotiations about compensation, this amount came nowhere near the compensation numbers the companies had initially put forward in earlier negotiations, which still took into consideration the value of oil in the ground.

---

[58] "Memcon, "New Iranian Approaches to Oil Company-Government Relationship," November 15, 1972, White House Special Files, Staff Member & Office Files, Flanigan Subject Files, box 3, RNL.

[59] Memcon, "Iranian Oil Crisis," January 30, 1973, White House Special Files, Staff Member & Office Files, Flanigan Subject Files, box 3, RNL; Helms to Rogers, February 7, 1973, White House Special Files, Staff Member & Office Files, Flanigan Subject Files, box 3, RNL.

Yamani's success displeased the Shah because he felt upstaged; the new terms superseded a 25-year participation agreement concluded with Iran in June 1972. Before the ink of the Yamani deal was dry on the page, the companies offered to "sweeten" the Iranian participation package. But the Shah was not happy being second best, and demanded that Iran's contract be converted into a sales agreement. In other words, Iran would own all of its oil and the companies would be required to purchase and market it. Iranian officials also offered to compensate the countries for their losses on the basis of a depreciated book value. In sharp contrast to the June 1972 agreement, the Shah's proposal envisaged full takeover of management, operating, and financing of production by 1979.[60]

These demands were another step toward full sovereign control. If the Shah could force the sales contract onto the companies, the US National Security Council reported, it would be tantamount to expropriation. This again raised the problem of precedent for American officials. The Iran deal would have an effect "throughout the Middle East and other developing country areas," NSC analysts wrote. In January 1973, John Irwin wrote to tell the US ambassador in Tehran to explain to the Shah the Nixon administration's "deep concern" with the sales agreement. Such a proposal would "inevitably generate another round of claims from other producer countries leaving the international petroleum scene in a continued state of unrest and uncertainty."[61]

Henry Kissinger and Peter Flanigan described the case to Nixon in January 1973. Acceptance of the principle of immediate confiscation with no negotiations and with compensation on the depreciated book value "would set a precedent not only in the oil industry, but in the entire extractive [sic] industry," they wrote. They drafted a letter from Nixon to the Shah, in which the president asked him not take any "unilateral step" in the negotiations. This was a far cry from his promise in 1969 to help the Shah in the annual revenue negotiations.[62]

---

[60] Kissinger and Flanigan to Nixon, January 18, 1973, White House Special Files, Staff Member & Office Files, Flanigan Subject Files, box 3, RNL.

[61] Memcon, "New Iranian Approaches to Oil Company-Government Relationship," November 15, 1972, White House Special Files, Staff Member & Office Files, Flanigan Subject Files, box 3, RNL; SecState to AmEmbassy Tehran, "Oil – GOI/Consortium Negotiations," January 10, 1973, White House Special Files, Staff Member & Office Files, Flanigan Subject Files, box 3, RNL; AmEmbassy Tehran to SecState, "Oil – GOI/ Consortium Negotiations," January 13, 1973, White House Special Files, Staff Member & Office Files, Flanigan Subject Files, box 3, RNL.

[62] Kissinger and Flanigan to Nixon, January 18, 1973, White House Special Files, Staff Member & Office Files, Flanigan Subject Files, box 3, RNL; "Nixon to the Shah,"

The Shah's response to Nixon revealed the extent to which circumstances had changed. It was "cool to the point of insult," one official complained. The Shah wrote, quite simply, that "he knew best." The next week, he gave the companies a public choice. They could either accept the previously secret option of giving Iran immediate participation and final national control by 1979 or immediate nationalization and a 25-year sales agreement ratified by the Majlis. The companies were thus caught between the "Scylla of suspended nationalization with no rights at all ... and the Charybdis of nationalization now on (presumably) better terms," NSC official Harold Saunders wrote. Even worse, the threat of nationalization came from a "friendly" country, which could not but cause "even more adverse effects on investments around the world."[63]

The gradualist crossfire points to the way in which the sovereign rights program was imbued in the minds of the oil elites. When read closely, the letter from the Shah to Nixon was more than just a nonchalant slight, although it certainly was that. The Iranian leader justified his position by steeping his policy in a quarter century of anticolonial law and economics. The oil companies had not presented reliable alternatives to state control over production. Time had run out for them. Now Iran would force them to "meet our legitimate rights and reasonable demands."[64]

Iranian Finance Minister Jamshid Amouzegar explained the basis for Iranian policy in more detail later that week. The work of UN delegates in the previous generation had enshrined in international law the "economic rights and duties of states and the permanent sovereignty of the governments over their natural resources." He thus found it "astonishing" that the Nixon administration would horn in on "such a fundamental and inalienable sovereign right of a nation over its most fundamental resource." This turn to sovereign rights, like that of other elites, was a natural one for Amouzegar. While employed as an analyst at the International Monetary Fund in 1968, he had written a letter to the editors of *The American Journal of Economics and Sociology* entitled "Comparative Advantage Revisited." His argument was Prebischean. It was, he wrote, "a curious reality of the mid-twentieth century" by which Western

January 18, 1973, White House Special Files, Staff Member & Office Files, Flanigan Subject Files, box 3, RNL.

[63] National Security Council, Saunders to Alins, Hullin, Bennett, and Critchfield, "Iran-Consortium Confrontation," February 5, 1973, White House Special Files, Staff Member & Office Files, Flanigan Subject Files, box 3, RNL.

[64] "Shah of Iran to Nixon," January 20, 1973, White House Special Files, Staff Member & Office Files, Flanigan Subject Files, box 3, RNL.

FIGURE 7.2 OPEC representatives in a 1973 meeting at OPEC headquarters in Vienna. Third from the left is Iranian Finance Minister Jamshid Amouzegar. Next to him are Saudi Oil Minister Ahmed Zaki Yamani and Iraqi Minister of Oil and Minerals Sa'doun Hammadi.
Source: OPEC Information Center, OPEC PICL-1973 (3).

governments paid for costly aid programs but were "reticent" to reexamine the prices of petroleum and other primary products.[65]

The insertion of Amouzegar into the economic culture of decolonization, like that of Yamani or the Shah, reminds historians that conclusions about policy motives can only be partial. A distinction exists between ideals and interests, one that a number of oil elites sought to gloss over in the early 1970s. That the concepts of permanent sovereignty and unequal exchange were widely touted does not, of course, mean that they alone drove policy. But neither did their existence as a set of beliefs stand in opposition to their use as a deliberate diplomatic instrument by different parties or for different reasons. The battle over who could get the best

---

[65] Amouzegar to Bexon, January 27, 1973, White House Special Files, Staff Member & Office Files, Flanigan Subject Files, box 3, RNL; Jamshid Amouzegar, "'Comparative Advantage' Reconsidered," *The American Journal of Economics and Sociology* 26: 2 (April 1967), 218.

deal between the "friendly governments" in the Persian Gulf, in fact, vividly dramatizes the pervasive influence of sovereign rights.

This was not lost on the most insurrectionist of the oil elites. "It is curious indeed that the Arab leaders (including Saudi Minister Mr. Ahmed Zaki Yamani) who today appear as the promoters of the participation principle are precisely those known for their 'moderation,'" Nicolas Sarkis wrote in 1971. Such a backhanded compliment was not without warrant – a half century later it remains difficult to distinguish the meritorious from the meretricious in the Saudi oil minister. For Sarkis and other insurrectionist opinion makers, Yamani carried an unhealthy pragmatic frisson in his rearguard politics. Yet he ably changed ships on the rising tide and fastened on to sovereign rights as firmly as his insurrectionist opponents-cum-counterparts. From 1971 to 1973 at least, Sarkis's criticism thus misses its mark. It is too atomizing – Yamani was no apostate and it was normal, not ironic, that his oil policies fell within the sovereign rights program.[66]

Belaid Abdessalam, the Algerian Minister of Industry and Energy who worked with both Mabruk and Yamani, addressed the opening session of an International Hydrocarbons Conference held in Algiers in October 1971. He told the conferees that he believed the OPEC nations were at the end of a long process of "regaining control of our natural resources." Soviet Premier Alexei Kosygin, who would soon do the same in Iraq and Libya, timed a visit to coincide with the conference. Upon receiving the microphone from Abdessalam, he added that the "essential purpose" of the new Arab political and technical wherewithal was to claim oil "as the national resource of producing countries." His presence in Algiers was emblematic of Soviet policy, which abetted the insurrectionist policies of Libya and Iraq by helping the nations dispose of oil that the multinational oil companies hoped to keep off the market.[67]

The failure to blacklist oil and the widespread support for the Iraqi and Libyan nationalizations, as well as the Iranian–Saudi crossfire, revealed that the insurrectionist vision of sovereign rights had won a test of wills by the beginning of 1973. The participation of Kosygin, though, is also significant in that it reveals again that the rise of sovereign rights did not occur in a geopolitical vacuum. In important ways, in fact, Cold War

---

[66] Nicolas Sarkis, "Participation: Political Manoeuvres and Economic Realities," *AOG* 1: 2 (October 16, 1971): 3–4.

[67] "Proceedings of the International Hydrocarbons Conference," *AOG* 1: 2 (October 16, 1971): 11–12.

politics had spurred along the rise of the sovereign rights program among the oil elites increasingly in the past half decade. Even so, the episodes described above did not by any means remain within the traditional superpower binary. To be sure, Soviet bloc countries abetted the production and sale of nationalized oil from Libya and Iraq. However, it could also be argued that the economic culture of decolonization blurred and twisted Cold War boundaries more than vice versa, as Western importers and other oil-producing nations in the Middle East acted independently of the Cold War to cultivate the Iraqi and Libyan capacity to successfully nationalize. Moreover, Saudi and Iranian policies revealed that their leaders did not understand their Cold War status as pro-American states as a reason to limit their demands for rapid change to the oil concessions. The Cold War threat, so useful in rationalizing the policy of accommodation, now was rarely used.

Many international observers in the era of détente saw the Cold War as a sideshow to the broader debate about decolonization and international capitalism. The directors of the IMF, the World Bank, and the UN Conference of Trade and Development addressed the "world economic situation" at a meeting of the UN Economic and Social Council in July 1971. Pierre-Paul Schweitzer, the President of the IMF Executive Committee, contrasted the nascent détente in the Cold War with the continuing problem of the "deterioration of the terms of trade": the Cold War seemed to be winding down, he said, while the problem of unequal exchange continued unabated. Hollis Chenery, an early supporter of the doctrine of unequal exchange in the 1950s and now Robert McNamara's economic adviser at the World Bank, emphasized the difficulty of spreading the material benefits of development to "the poorer countries." Manuel Pérez-Guerrero, a onetime Venezuelan oil minister who was now Raùl Prebisch's replacement as Secretary-General of the UN Conference on Trade and Development, agreed. The fact that the poor countries were "in the position of price-takers" in international markets exacerbated their poverty.[68]

In a television interview after meetings with the leaders of India, Pakistan, Bangladesh, and Thailand the next year, the UN Secretary General, Kurt Waldheim, repeated the motif. "The East-West confrontation was almost over," he said. "The problem of the future was relations between North and South, or rich and poor." Waldheim made such

[68] UNOPI, "Press Release," July 7, 1971, ECOSOC/3136, DHL.

a sweeping statement because he believed it. But it and others were too pat. The experiences of the oil elites in the late 1960s and 1970s show the many different ways in which the question of sovereign rights interacted with the Cold War policies of the United States and the Soviet Union. Nevertheless, the above statements also reveal a general perception of the times. According to the account of time and history that was pervasive among anticolonial elites, the oil producers' shared program was something of a foregone conclusion. Rather than happening entirely in the present, then, even the gradualist project of participation represented a reaching back in time to jerk the old concessions out of the darkness of the colonial past into the bright light of the sovereign future.[69]

The above statements also reveal that the belief in sovereign rights not only enveloped the politics of the oil elites, but that it also continued to extend beyond them. The UN Secretariat hired the Harvard political scientist Joseph Nye to write a report on "the concept of collective economic security" in 1973. After attending a number of meetings of the UN Economic and Social Council and the UN Conference for Trade and Development, he wrote that the concept was "very relevant to today's world." This was, in part, because the way people discussed how the relationship between traditional diplomacy and international capitalism had changed with the acceleration of decolonization. In the first half of the twentieth century and into the early Cold War, collective security meant a traditional balance-of-powers arrangement in which "the unlawful use of military force" of one nation would be deterred "by the combined force of all other states." But the notion had evolved to mean something else. The push for sovereign rights, in short, represented a new "moral view" that in turn meant that "economic issues have risen in importance on the agendas of world politics."[70]

The UN Conference on Trade and Development, what he elsewhere called "the Poor Nations' Pressure Group," was key to this process, Nye believed. Above all, this was because the group had shifted the question of "threats of state autonomy" from the territorial to the economic arena. Like the second-generation oil elites, he understood that decolonization had become and international force that shaped a certain way of looking at the world. For him, the Conference on Trade and Development and other groupings of anticolonial elites had done so by functioning "as

[69] UNOPI, *Weekly News Summary*, February 16, 1973, UN doc. WS/594.
[70] Joseph S. Nye, "Economic Security," *International Affairs* 50: 4 (October 1974): 584–5.

transmission belts transmitting policy sensitivities across national boundaries." Indeed, their constant communication and sense that their lives impinged upon each other would become central to Nye's burgeoning concept of "interdependence."[71]

The image of an internationalist conveyer belt captures well the propagation of the principles and policies of the economic culture of decolonization from the 1950s to the 1970s. Permanent sovereignty and unequal exchange were standard arguments spoken and heard across Africa, Asia, Latin America, and the Middle East. The anticolonial premises that were formed in the UN Economic and Social Council, at Bandung, among the Arab League oil experts, in OPEC, at the UN Conference of Trade and Development, by the heads of state of the Non-Aligned Movement, and elsewhere were now stated and repeated in the International Monetary Fund, the World Bank, and by American officials.

Nadim Pachachi tended to the votive candles in his last major statement as OPEC's Secretary General. "Over the last twenty years circumstances have changed," he said in late 1971, after expressing his admiration for Libyan policy. "Nowhere do governments accept the role of a sleeping partner. They want to have a direct role in the management and exploitation of national oil resources." That political awareness, which for Pachachi stretched back to his time as Iraqi oil minister in the mid-1950s, had been formed in an age dominated by decolonization. Sovereign rights had been marginal for much of that time. But now, with the swift success of the oil producers, it had an air of inevitability. "These countries consider their raw materials as their property," one Department of Defense official concluded. "That's just a fact of life."[72]

---

[71] Nye, "Economic Security," 586–7; Joseph S. Nye, "UNCTAD: Poor Nations' Pressure Group," in Robert Cox and Harold Jacobson, *The Anatomy of Influence* (New Haven, CT: Yale University Press, 1973). For a recent appraisal of different types of interdependence, see Victor McFarland, "The NIEO, Interdependence, and Globalization," *Humanity: An International Journal of Human Rights, Humanitarianism, and Development* 6: 1 (Spring 2015): 217–33.

[72] *Times* (London), November 9, 1971; Minutes of Senior Review Group Meeting, "Expropriation," August 4, 1971, *FRUS 1969–76*, vol. E-10, doc. 45.

8

The OPEC Syndrome

The Third World's Energy Crisis, 1973–1975

The OPEC action is really the first and at the same time the most spectacular illustration of ... the vital needs for the producing nations to have in hand the levers of price control and of the great potentialities of a union of raw material producing countries.[1]

Houari Boumedienne, 1974

The contemporary world can no longer be encompassed in traditional stereotypes. The notion of the northern rich and the southern poor has been shattered.[2]

Henry Kissinger, 1974

A week into the fourth Arab–Israeli war in a quarter decade, the Arab oil ministers hastily convened at the Kuwait Sheraton. They announced the imposition of an oil embargo on the United States, general supply cuts, and a 70 percent increase in Persian Gulf oil's posted price, from $3.01 to $5.11 per barrel. The rest of OPEC immediately followed suit and increased prices. The announcement marked the first time that the OPEC nations set the price of oil, a power reserved exclusively for the multinational companies until 1970 and subject to joint company–government determination after the 1971 agreements in Tehran and Tripoli. The OPEC nations had, of course, waged a protracted campaign to wrest pricing and production control from the grip of the multinationals. It

---

[1] "The OPEC Countries Expound at the UN Their Oil Policy Objectives," *AOG* 3: 63 (May 1, 1974): 25, 27.
[2] Department of State, No. 143, "The Challenge of Interdependence," April 15, 1974, RG 59, Policy Planning Council, Director's Files (Winston Lord), 1969–77, box 345, NARA.

had lasted over a decade. But after a complex and fitful time, their project gathered momentum. From September 1970, when the Libyan negotiations concluded, to September 1973, the world had already seen the posted price of Persian Gulf oil rise from $1.80 to $3.07, its first sustained increase since the late 1950s. Then, with the spark of the October 1973 war and Arab oil embargo, the top blew off. By January 1974, the members of OPEC had increased the posted price to $11.65 per barrel.

Throughout that rapid sequence of events, oil elites of different stripes depicted their campaign as a model of anticolonial opposition, seeking to make clear their own special role in the history of the search for an economic equivalent to decolonization. On December 24, 1973, two days after OPEC ministers met in Iran and decided to increase prices to $11.65, the Shah energetically employed the egalitarian rhetoric of sovereign rights to defend the price hikes: "It [was] only equitable and just that the oil producing countries" had ended the era in which the industrial powers were "able to buy oil at ridiculously low prices." When Algerian President Houari Boumedienne invoked UN procedure to call for a Special Session of the General Assembly in February 1974, he emphasized the radical potential for a "new equilibrium between developed and developing states" if more nations could "assert greater control over their natural resources."[3]

Of that context was born the call in the United Nations for New International Economic Order. To end "the systematic plundering" of the Third World, Boumedienne said in the opening speech of the Sixth Special Session in April 1974, poor nations needed "to follow the example of OPEC by uniting and presenting a common front facing the rich countries." The delegates responded by publishing a Declaration and Program of Action on the Establishment a New International Economic Order. The Declaration began with the core premises of the economic culture of decolonization. "The greatest and most significant achievement during the last decades has been the independence from colonial and alien domination," the delegates wrote. That overriding impulse was bound to continue to express itself after political independence, especially in the international economy. This could be done, in particular, through "full

---

[3] Telegram, AmEmbassy Vienna to SecState, "Shah's Press Conference," December 29, 1973, RG 59, Central Foreign Policy Files 1973–76, Electronic Telegrams, NARA; AmEmbassy Algiers to SecState, January 31, 1974, National Security Council Files, box 321, RNL.

FIGURE 8.1 Houari Boumedienne, President of the Revolutionary Council and of the Council of Ministers of Algeria, gives the opening address to the Sixth Special Session of the UN General Assembly on April 10, 1974.
Source: UN Photo/Teddy Chen. Courtesy of the United Nations Photo Library, Photo No. 190740.

permanent sovereignty of every State over its natural resources." At its broadest, the New Order thus called upon the collective use of national sovereignty "to correct the inequalities and redress the existing injustices" of the international economy, described as "the remaining vestige of alien and colonial domination."[4]

The sovereign rights challenge to the structure of the international economy had always been an existential one; unequal exchange questioned the basic dogma of comparative advantage, and permanent sovereignty was etched into international law to create "just" prices that reflected the "real" value of oil and other raw materials. All that was wrapped in a universal understanding of the deeply exploitative history of colonialism. In turn, what gave transcendent legitimacy to the price increases was their depiction as a belated correction of long-standing

---

[4] "Focus on Oil at the UN Special Session on Raw Materials." *AOG* 3: 62 (1974): 5–6; Resolution No. 3201 (S-VI), "Resolutions Adopted on the Report of the *Ad Hoc* Committee of the Sixth Special Session," May 1, 1974; United Nations, *Yearbook of the United Nations, 1974* (New York, 1975), 306.

inequity. From that perspective, the OPEC nations had subdued the characteristic threats faced by all poor nations. This was an elevating vision of international redistribution: a spirited people rose to defend the ramparts of economic equality and had triumphed. The coherence and force of the argument rested on a view of the past that had long smoldered in the breasts of many anticolonial elites.

The view was less provocative than widespread. For this reason, Henry Kissinger did not relish his April 28, 1974, dinner date with Boumedienne at the People's Palace of Algiers. His host had already described American pressure on the OPEC nations to lower prices in colonial terms – an attempt "to establish a protectorate over oil prices." Kissinger wholeheartedly rejected this, and the dinner conversation became rather curt. Boumedienne at one moment told Kissinger that his economic views were "outdated." Why did American officials complain so much about high prices, he asked, when they reflected the established sovereign right to control supply? Didn't Kissinger understand that sovereign rights and higher oil prices were to become permanent characteristics of the international economy? Kissinger responded sharply. He accepted neither Boumedienne's "demagoguery" in the United Nations nor, for that matter, "the idea of cartels." American policy against high oil prices was as resolute as that of "Brezhnev on world revolution."[5]

In other words, Kissinger would not compromise on either point. But in turning to the metaphor of the Brezhnev Doctrine, which elsewhere he had identified as out of line with the new global reality of superpower détente, his response was also as appreciative of sovereign rights as it was critical. The inflamed invocation of the Cold War paid homage to the depth of the challenge of the energy crisis and the New International Economic Order. The political forces underlying the energy crisis had a profound meaning to which Kissinger was not blind: ultimately, the Secretary of State could not ignore the economic impact of the crisis or the ideas that gave it meaning.

Kissinger spoke before the UN special session the same month. "The energy crisis" was not a problem of colonial economic domination protruding into the present, he said. The crisis could not be "perceived in

[5] AmInt Algiers to SecState, "President Boumediene's Le Monde Interview," February 5, 1974, RG 59, Central Foreign Policy Files 1973–76, Electronic Telegrams, NARA; "Conversation at Dinner at the Peoples' Palace," April 29, 1974, National Security Council Files, box 1028, RNL.

terms of a confrontation between the haves and the have-nots." That sort of "traditional stereotype" did not match the reality of the international economy. Kissinger's reaction is worth noting in part because it marks the definitive shift in the US policy of accommodation that occurred when sovereign rights became a legitimate threat to US national security. The disagreement between Boumedienne and Kissinger is interesting, in other words, because their arguments reflected the contemporary interpretations of the energy crisis. That Kissinger invoked the Cold War, always at the center of his world, conveyed his understanding of the high stakes. The dinner debate and UN speeches, to put it differently, reveal the meaning of the energy crisis as a real and symbolic confrontation between competing visions of the past, present, and future of the international economy. In that moment in April 1974, one sees the essences of those clashing views: the one, oil revolution, based on emancipation from colonial economic structures, the other, energy crisis, on the erasure of that unrestrained rhetoric. What was a desire for the Algerian – that the success of OPEC represented larger dynamics of historical change – was a fear for the American.[6]

From Kissinger's vantage point, sovereign rights was becoming a danger of a new magnitude. His economic adviser, Fred Bergsten, warned of a broader "threat of Third World commodity collusion" in a series of articles in *Foreign Policy* in 1973 and 1974. Intelligence analysts for the US State and Treasury Departments saw the crisis as a structural transformation: "the passing from an era of abundant supplies into one of constant shortage." The interpretation was not limited to government. The Club of Rome, the Ford Foundation, and Earthwatch all emphasized the need to martial scant "fossil fuels" and "non-renewable resources." The threat of a global "population bomb" loomed in academic and policy circles, and social scientists across fields predicted a nightmarish future of rising commodity prices. "We have to face the fact that the OPEC syndrome is catching on," the

---

[6] Department of State, No. 143, "The Challenge of Interdependence," April 15, 1974, RG 59, Policy Planning Council, Director's Files (Winston Lord), 1969–77, box 345, NARA. On US foreign policy toward the Third World in this period, see: Christopher R. W. Dietrich, "Oil Power and Economic Theologies: The United States and the Third World in the Wake of the Energy Crisis," *Diplomatic History* 40: 3 (2016): 500–29. For a synopsis of the question as it moved forward, see: Margot E. Saloman, "From NIEO to Now and the Unfinishable Story of Economic Justice," *International and Comparative Law Quarterly* 62: 1 (January 2013): 31–54.

British Prime Minister, Harold Wilson, worried in a summit meeting of Western leaders. "There are already phosphate-pecs, bauxite-pecs, banana-pecs and others."[7]

All this happened at the exact moment that the collective power of the oil producers reached a zenith. Yet, at the same time, the unification of the oil producers to the general plight of the other poor nations was an ambiguous prospect. In the end, the compressed energy of the contradiction between the internationalist vision of a more just economic order and the national containers for that vision exploded when high oil prices caused a more general sovereign debt crisis.

The rise of sovereign debt in the non-oil countries of the Third World was disastrous. High oil prices killed the New International Economic Order, midwifed by oil insurrectionists, at birth. This chapter holds that the longstanding contradictions of the sovereign rights program became overwhelming as oil prices rose to unprecedented levels. The program for a New International Economic Order frayed at the edges in 1974. By 1975 the redistributionist argument would unravel beyond repair. The oil revolution thus became a global transformation, but not the sort that the anticolonial elites called for. Rather it was a transformation marked by unrealized expectations and unintended consequences.

The energy crisis embroiled its actors in what they considered an epic struggle. A fact of great importance for the anticolonial side of that story is that nobody regarded it as arising out of thin air, even though at the time it was often depicted as sudden or violent. In fact, most anticolonial elites saw it as the logical culmination of a shared history. The broader clout of sovereign rights remained palpable in the late 1960s and early

---

[7] C. Fred Bergsten, "The Response to the Third World," *Foreign Policy* (1974): 3–34; C. Fred Bergsten, "The Threat from the Third World," *Foreign Policy* (1973): 102–24; "Critical Imported Materials: Study of Ad Hoc Group Established by NSSM 197," n.d. (July 1974), National Security Council Files, Institutional Files, box H-203, RNL; Donella H. Meadows, *The Limits to Growth: A Report for the Club of Rome's Project on the Predicament of Mankind* (New York: Universe Books, 1974); Ford Foundation, *A Time to Choose: America's Energy Future: A Final Report* (Cambridge, MA: Ballinger, 1974); UNOPI, *Weekly News Summary*, March 15, 1974, UN doc. WS/650; Paul Sabin, *The Bet: Paul Ehrlich, Julian Simon, and the Gamble over the Earth's Future* (New Haven, CT, 2013); Tom Robertson, "'This is the American Earth': The American Empire, the Cold War, and American Environmentalism," *Diplomatic History* 32: 4 (2008), 561–84; Memorandum of Conversation, November 16, 1975, L. William Seidman Files, box 312, GFL.

1970s, especially at the summit meetings of the UN Conference on Trade and Development in 1968 and 1972 and the summit of the Non-Aligned Movement in 1973.

The influence of sovereign rights had by then gained more of a theoretical voice with the elaboration of dependency theory among development economists. Unequal exchange had received a fillip in 1967 with the publication of André Gunder Frank's *Capitalism and Underdevelopment in Latin America*, which reached a wide audience. Gunder Frank noted in 1974 that the doctrine "penetrated ever wider circles," thanks to the "subjective intentions and self-perceptions" of a group of prominent "economists-ideologues" led by Prebisch and including himself, Aldo Ferrer, Celso Furtado, Maria de Conceção Tavares, Aníbal Pinto, and Osvaldo Sunkel. Frank, Immanuel Wallerstein, and Giovanni Arrighi would further delineate and popularize the theory with their discussions of "underdevelopment" in the "peripheral regions" of the "capitalist world-system," and North American Marxists Paul Baran and Paul Sweezy would add a Leninist critique of "natural comparative advantage" in the following half decade.[8]

One economist wrote in 1973 that Prebisch's basic critique merited the respect of his status as "the dean and elder statesmen among specialists." His life work had "generated a wider and more protracted discussion among specialists than any other proposition related to the field of Latin American economics." The shared analysis, and its stickiness with anticolonial elites, continued to cover the same basic ground as the political use of unequal exchange: the poverty of the poor lands was a result of the means used by the rich to achieve wealth. Moreover, the situation had been imposed by imperial control. Even critics of that core premise of ingrained inequality noted its political influence. "Conventional analysis accepts that behind the veil of nominal political sovereignty, LDCs [less developed countries] still lack much of the substance of real economic

[8] Gunder Frank, *Capitalism and Underdevelopment in Latin America; Historical Studies of Chile and Brazil* (New York: Monthly Review Press, 1967); Gunder Frank, "Dependence Is Dead, Long Live Dependence and the Class Struggle: An Answer to Critics," *Latin American Perspectives* 1: 1 (Spring 1974): 88; Baran and Sweezy, *Monopoly Capital: An Essay on the American Economic and Social Order* (New York: Monthly Review Press, 1966); Baran, *The Political Economy of Neo-Colonialism* (New York: Monthly Review Press, 1975); Sweezy, *Modern Capitalism and Other Essays* (New York: Monthly Review Press, 1972); Gunder Frank, *On Capitalist Underdevelopment* (New York: Oxford University Press, 1975); Wallerstein, *The Capitalist World-Economy* (Cambridge University Press, 1979).

independence," the political economist Benjamin Cohen wrote in one example. "Despite decolonization, relations with the advanced capitalist countries still spell dominance for the metropolitan center, dependence for the nations of the periphery."[9]

Prebisch summarized the general relationship between past subjugation and present poverty for a group of officials who gathered in preparation for the 1968 ministerial meeting of the UN Conference of Trade and Development. "This state of affairs is not due to particular circumstances, nor is it temporary," he said. Rather the problem of international inequality was general. It had "deep roots," he continued. "We must seek the explanation of present events in past years, and at the same time draw certain conclusions from them for the future." This interpretation was widely accepted as truth among the like-minded elites that occupied the highest positions in the UN and other organizations that pursued the sovereign rights program, whatever specific national or intellectual heritage they claimed. Citing the concept of the "colonial pact" first put forth in the mid-nineteenth century by Jean Baptiste Say in his *Dictionary of Political Economy*, analysts at the UN Secretariat added in their report of the meeting that the "long-standing pattern of trade" between the poor and rich nations had "well-known disadvantages."[10]

When over one hundred national delegations descended on New Delhi for the 1968 UNCTAD summit, its first global summit since the founding in 1964, a number of influential figures noted the dogged resilience of the colonial pact. More often than not, they used the conceptual apparatus of sovereign rights to describe it. Indira Gandhi, for one, used her inaugural speech to emphasize the problems "which all struggling nations face." She and other Indian leaders had long been "keenly aware of other nations and of peoples who also were oppressed." Because they shared that indignity of oppression, it was natural that they "forged a kinship" during and after formal decolonization. She also argued that the problem of economic inequality arose directly out of the imperial past. Every delegate

---

[9] Henry William Spiegel, "Review," *The Americas* 29: 3 (January 1973): 394; Benjamin J. Cohen, *Question of Imperialism: The Political Economy of Dominance and Dependence* (New York: Basic Books, 1971), 193.

[10] UN Economic and Social Council, General Discussion of International Economic and Social Policy, "Statement made by Dr. Prebisch," July 26, 1967, E/L.1170, ARR 40/2344, notebook 79, UNA-G; UNCTAD, Second Session, New Delhi, vol. V, Special Problems in World Trade and Development, TD/40, Report by the Secretariat of UNCTAD, "The International Division of Labour and Developing Countries," January 1, 1968, ARR 40/2344, box 127, UNA-G.

at the meeting, she said, knew exactly what she meant because they all were "familiar with the part colonialism has played in the exploitation of dependent countries." The connection between political independence and economic growth were thus inseparable. In fact, the rise to independence always had an economic end point. "Our fight for freedom was itself part of the greater fight to liberate our people from the grip of poverty," she said.[11]

Gandhi believed that the work of UNCTAD, regional economic meetings, the Non-Aligned Movement, and other groups meant that the question of economic emancipation, once a secondary concern, was now "projected on a giant screen." General Suharto of Indonesia agreed in his message to the conference. The meeting was a clear manifestation of the "political emancipation" that had occurred since World War II, but it was unfortunate that "the elimination of colonialism and imperialism" had not been "adequately matched by an equal rate of progress toward economic emancipation."[12]

The moral argument for a global redistribution of wealth thus existed well beyond Gunder-Frank's Latin American "economists-ideologues." It was also present in the minds of other influential national and international leaders. In his opening address to the 1972 UNCTAD summit, held in Santiago, Chilean President Salvador Allende reiterated "the basic mission" of sovereign rights: "to further the replacement of an outdated and essentially unjust economic and trade order by an equitable one based on a new concept of man and of human dignity."[13]

The vision of justice through a restructuring of the international economy was one that Barbara Ward understood well, to take another example. The well-known development economist attended the 1972 meeting as a member of the Vatican's delegation. Her reading of recent history – if less downtrodden than that of Allende, Suharto, or Gandhi – followed the same script. "It is perhaps easy to forget that in the broader stream of history of which UNCTAD III is a part, something unprecedented is happening to the human family," she told the

[11] UNCTAD, Second Session, New Delhi, vol. I, Report and Annexes, "Address by Mrs. Indira Gandhi," February 1, 1968, ARR 40/2344, box 127, UNA-G.

[12] UNCTAD, Second Session, New Delhi, vol. I, Report and Annexes, "Address by Mrs. Indira Gandhi," February 1, 1968, ARR 40/2344, box 127, UNA-G; UNCTAD, Second Session, New Delhi, vol. I, Report and Annexes, "Message dated 30 January 1968 from General Soeharto," ARR 40/2344, box 127, UNA-G.

[13] William F. Ryan, S. J., "And What about UNCTAD III, n.d. (July 1972), ARR 40/2344, notebook 56, UNA-G.

delegates. "A hundred years ago, the relatively small group of the developed states set up the structure of the world economy. Now they are beginning to accept the right of full participation by the developing world – and not a soul believes this to be the end of the process."[14]

But in the face of the results of the 1968 and 1972 conferences, in which the United States and other rich nations blocked what the Third World delegates considered meaningful reform, such optimism was not widespread. Upon receiving a report from Ward, Pope Paul VI wrote a letter to Manuel Pérez-Guerrero, the former Venezuelan oil minister who replaced Prebisch at the helm of UNCTAD. The Pope conveyed his disappointment that the conference had not resulted in gains that reflected the "legitimate hopes" of the developing nations. In particular, he noted the widespread feeling that the "numerous economic structures of domination" left over from imperial rule had not undergone "any sort of correction, regardless of the accession of people to political independence." Pérez-Guerrero agreed. "[L]ittle or nothing had been achieved concretely," he responded. "There is still much to do," he added in a letter to Salvador Allende.[15]

The Fourth Summit Conference of the Non-Aligned Movement, hosted by Algeria in September 1973, provides another example of the prominence of sovereign rights. The host delegation was more upbeat than Pérez-Guerrero or, for that matter, Ward. They presented a paper that argued that "a new phenomenon" had begun to replace the unjust economic system that had been established "between rich and poor countries during the colonial period." They leaned on the concepts of permanent sovereignty and unequal exchange in making their case. The relations between colonial rulers and colonized subjects, and then between the rich nations and the poor, had always been "dominated by problems" connected with raw materials, they said. They used language that was reminiscent of the basic problem George Kennan posed in 1950 – the fact that empires had successfully established "the idea that raw materials had no value other than that which they consented to give them." In other words, oil and other natural resources only became valuable in the moment when empires acquired them. The classical economists of nineteenth-century

---

[14] Quoted in William F. Ryan and Grant Maxwell, "Planet Earth after UNCTAD III," *America* (July 8, 1972), 9.

[15] Pope Paul VI to Pérez-Guerrero, April 7, 1972, ARR 40/2344, notebook 56, UNA-G; Pérez-Guerrero to Pope Paul VI, August 3, 1972, ARR 40/2344, notebook 56, UNA-G; Pérez-Guerrero to Allende, May 23, 1972, ARR 40/2344, notebook 56, UNA-G.

Western Europe had entrenched that idea so thoroughly that by the mid-twentieth century it had become an unexamined "pre-established principle." The centrality of raw material production to international economic inequality, as well as the new understanding of its intrinsic value, was evidenced in the rich countries' replacement of the label "abundance" with "shortage" in the 1970s, they added.[16]

Like other oil elites, the Algerian delegates used the raw material they knew best as evidence of that transformation. The rich nations had reached a sort of panicky zenith in their international politics when their leaders labeled "the energy crisis" a major concern, they said. That very name, and the way it shaped debate about the value of raw materials, was illegitimate for the Algerians. "The fears of the rich countries do not really arise from the possibility that oil and gas deposits may run out," they wrote. "Actually, the outstanding feature of the problem" lay in the fact that "rich countries are becoming aware ... that their dependence on the Third World" was bound to increase. OPEC, then, heralded the much-anticipated turn in the global "balance of power." The Algerian argument echoed the common rich nations–poor nations assessment of the geopolitics of decolonization. It was also an argument that the oil elites' collective diplomacy was not only, or even primarily, about doing away with the old concessions or taking control of prices. The work of the oil producers had changed the very understanding of the direction of benefits to be derived from raw material production. Never again would profits "ultimately revert ... to the rich countries."[17]

This was also a more elaborate version of Algerian Foreign Minister Abdelaziz Bouteflika's 1971 assertion in Peru that the OPEC success was "a victory to all underdeveloped countries." According to that reading, the oil elites had used their sovereign rights to detach themselves from the past and surge into the future. In doing so, they further argued, they and their commodity set an example for others.

It was the unique success of the oil producers that raised their profile to a level at which they could become illustrative of broader hopes. By early 1973, their victories had become important enough to the international economy that even an avowedly anti-economic thinker like Henry Kissinger had become more interested in the attempt to nullify the old

[16] "The Third World Countries and the Energy Crisis," *AOG* 2: 48 (September 16, 1973): 24–7.
[17] "The Third World Countries and the Energy Crisis," 24–7.

concessions. But to the most powerful actors in the Nixon administration, including Kissinger, the sovereignty of the oil producers had been little more than a trifle before the October 1973 Arab–Israeli war. Other issues – détente, the opening of China, the Vietnam War, the end of the Bretton Woods monetary system – were more important to them.

When they did turn their attention to the oil producers, they tended to discard their growing political and economic power. Secretary of the Treasury George Shultz told European finance ministers that their fear of OPEC's supply control was "overly alarmist." Sometimes this took the form of historical arguments. At a nationally televised press conference in September 1973, Nixon responded to a reporter's question about "oil as a club to force a change" in his support for Israel. "Oil without a market, as Mr. Mossadegh learned many, many years ago, does not do a country much good," he said. If Arab leaders pressed their oil weapon too hard, "the inevitable result is that they will lose their markets."[18]

Even Nixon could not but help muster up the memory of Mossadegh. But a vast gulf separated his interpretation from reality. Nixon's comment, in particular, ignored the recent string of successes for OPEC. A week after Shultz berated his European counterparts as alarmist, Saudi Oil Minister Yamani called it a "stark fact" that the multinational companies had yielded power to the producers. The oil ministers could "dictate the flow of oil and the price of oil" as they wished, he said. On the lower rungs of the American policy-making hierarchy, officials also found the confidence of their superiors unwarranted. The ambassador in Riyadh summarized this position in a September 1973 report. It was unlikely the "gradualist salami tactics" of OPEC would end at anything short of full nationalization, he predicted.[19]

OPEC leaders were already pressing the price issue before the Arab oil embargo gave them their golden opportunity. The most prominent figures continued to celebrate their ongoing success with the internationalist language of unequal exchange and permanent sovereignty. In a 1973 interview with Italian journalist Oriana Fallaci for *The New Republic*, the Shah of Iran emphasized that higher oil prices were a response to the high prices of finished goods from the West. "You've sent

---

[18] George Shultz, "Remarks at OECD Ministerial Meeting," June 6, 1973, White House Central Files Herbert Stein Materials, box 43, RNL; Richard Nixon, "News Conference," September 5, 1973, in *PPPUS*.

[19] *New York Times*, June 12, 1973, 45; DOS, Intelligence Brief, "Constraints on Oil Price Increases," September 26, 1973, RG 59, Subject-Numeric files 1970–73, PET 14, box 1485, NARA

petrochemical prices rocketing," he said. "You buy our crude and sell it back to us, refined as petrochemicals, at a hundred times the price you've paid us. You make us pay more, scandalously more, for everything, and it's only fair that, from now on, you should pay more for oil." So familiar had this trope become that it seemed like a natural progression, and Fallaci and her editors decided that the position needed no further explanation.[20]

By the time of the interview's December publication, her ellipses had become pregnant with meaning. In early 1974, as the permanency of the price increases began to settle in, many other oil elites took the same line. Boumedienne elaborated on the thesis in his opening speech to the Sixth Special Session. "The OPEC action is really the first and at the same time the most spectacular illustration of ... the vital needs for the producing nations to have in hand the levers of price control and of the great potentialities of a union of raw material producing countries," he said. "In order to recover the revenue which is our due, we must create, product by product, common fronts among the exporting countries, which will enable us to defend collectively our rights." Iranian Finance Minister Jamshid Amouzegar agreed. The imperial legacy had "repressed prices" for too long, he said. Whether the substitution of repression for depression was a Freudian slip or purposeful one mattered less than its consequences for the former World Bank economist. The price increase, he said, was "justified since it gave oil its real value."[21]

Saudi Oil Minister Yamani – normally more prosaic than most oil elites in his political rhetoric, despite his newfound penchant for the language of insurrectionism – echoed Boumedienne's argument and its imperial terms. He warned the special session delegates against "any trusteeship-type attempt to fix oil prices" led by the United States. Iraqi Oil Minister Sa'doun Hammadi had sparred with Yamani over the 1967 embargo. Seven years later, the circumstances had changed enough that, speaking directly after Yamani in the special session, Hammadi not only urged an end to all old oil concessions, he also celebrated the possibility of a new "balanced exchange of raw materials against capital goods." Okoi Arikpo, the foreign minister of Nigeria, agreed with his OPEC counterparts

[20] "An Oriana Fallaci Interview: The Shah of Iran," *The New Republic*, December 1, 1973.
[21] "The OPEC Countries Expound at the UN Their Oil Policy Objectives," *AOG* 3: 63 (May 1, 1974): 25–9; "Focus on Oil at the UN Special Session on Raw Materials," *AOG* 3: 62 (April 16, 1974): 7.

on prices. He too invoked the colonial past: the time had come to condemn the "gunboat diplomacy" by which the "strong dictated to the weak how much of their raw materials they must sell."[22]

If the battle for oil control comprised specific fights – the Shah against the consortium, the Iraqis over Rumaila, the Libyans against BP, as an Arab lever against Western support for Israel – it had also become part of a learned formula. Others joined in the invigorating atmosphere. The "monopolistic countries" had dug their own graves with their "insolent opulence," the foreign minister of Mexico, Emilio Rabasa, told the Special Session. According to one Latin American group, the oil crisis confirmed "the vulnerability of the powerful and the strengthened position of the weak." Almost thirty African and Asian leaders also gave speeches in support of OPEC. Pope Paul VI joined the Africans, Asians, and Latin Americans when he sent a message to the Special Session urging the end of "superfluous consumption in the wealthy nations" and calling for a "more just relation" between them and "the poor countries struggling to better their lot."[23]

The support for OPEC thus ranged from the militant to the folksy. In that expansive coverage, it was an expression of the shared attitudes that lay at the heart of the economic culture of decolonization. That interpretation of the oil revolution rested on the belief that it was a step toward a necessary change in the disposition of international wealth. The way the anticolonial elites talked about oil prices followed the doctrinal lines of permanent sovereignty, unequal exchange, and changing circumstances – concepts that had been dwelt on endlessly in the previous quarter century. The conjunction between oil and sovereign rights had not been accidental, from this perspective. Instead, the energy crisis crystalized a generation of political-economic thought which reached its high point with the call for a New International Economic Order.

For many, the Declaration on the Establishment of the New International Economic Order marked the fulfillment of an idea that had been deeply embedded in a quarter-century movement for an economic equivalent to decolonization. The anticolonial elites' awareness, their

---

[22] UNOPI, *Weekly News Summary*, April 19, 1974, UN doc. WS/655.

[23] UNOPI, *Weekly News Summary*, April 19, 1974, UN doc. WS/655; Hal Brands, "Third World Politics in an Age of Global Turmoil: The Latin American Challenge to U.S. and Western Hegemony," *Diplomatic History* 32: 1 (January 2008): 112; UNOPI, *Weekly News Summary*, April 12, 1974, UN doc. WS/654.

pattern of ideas and attitudes, had developed over time as historical phenomena in their own right. The sovereign rights program originated from the political equality inherent in decolonization, was carried forward with additions and modifications, and framed the mind-set with which the international community of elites approached the energy crisis.

The interpretation of OPEC as reproducible, the twin image of the narrative of the "OPEC syndrome," was an alluring one because it was familiar in a general way to Third World leaders everywhere. Yet it was also different. This was in part because the oil producers' collective strategy could not be effectively shared across different sectors. It was different also because the shared national interest of the OPEC members ended up opposing that of the other Third World nations. This was because the price increases did the national economies of oil importers irreparable harm.

That tension was evident to UNCTAD Secretary General Manuel Pérez-Guerrero, whose career in international politics spanned the middle half of the twentieth century and was characteristic of the international class of anticolonial elites. Like many others, he developed a strong moral sense of justice and injustice early in his career that worked on both national and international scales. He studied law at the University of Paris, earning his doctorate in 1936 with a dissertation on Latin American policy in the League of Nations. Although he modestly described the work as "an almost exclusively descriptive study" of Latin American contributions to the different organs of the League, it was more than that. Latin American delegates, he argued, had undertaken great efforts "to increase the prestige of the young nations and give them a platform" from which they could proclaim the idea of a "universal international law" that would guarantee political independence and territorial integrity. Throughout, he emphasized the consistency of the Latin American opposition to what one Venezuelan diplomat described as "accords designed to limit the sovereignty of member states." Every nation, Pérez-Guerrero wrote, had the right to its independence and its sovereignty. Without adherence to the notion of the equality of nations, and equal respect for national law among nations, he continued, sovereignty was at risk of becoming "a word without meaning."[24]

---

[24] Manuel Pérez-Guerrero, *Les Relations des États de l'Amérique Latine Avec la Société des Nations* (Thèse pour le Doctorat, Université de Paris – Faculté de Droit, 1936), v–vi, 1, 86–7.

He then joined the Department of Economics, Finance, and Legal Procedure at the League of Nations, where he worked until 1940. Afterwards, he returned to Venezuela, where he held a number of different ministerial positions, including serving as the Venezuelan representative to the Bretton Woods conference in 1944 and the founding meeting of the United Nations in 1945. He became Venezuela's Minister of Finance in 1947. In 1949, he described the program he helped design to use national taxes to increase oil income, the famous 50/50 provision, as an attempt to "place the State in a position similar to that of a partner to the corporations." He then left Venezuela to accept a position as the Executive Secretary of the UN Technical Assistance Mission, first to Egypt and then to Tunisia, from 1953 to 1958. This experience, and the fact that he learned Arab during it, made him a perfect candidate to join Egaña and Juan Pablo Pérez Alfonso as a member of the Venezuelan delegation to the First Arab Petroleum Congress.

After that meeting Pérez-Guerrero became more involved in oil policy and replaced Pérez Alfonso as oil minister in 1963, after which he consistently emphasized the solidarity of the OPEC members. "In spite of the distance that separates some of our countries, we have come to find out that there is a lot that we have got in common," he told representatives from the national oil companies of the OPEC member nations in a 1967 meeting in Caracas. By working together, he hoped the producers could collectively "conquer, in a peaceful way, their place under the sun in the international market." In 1968, he accepted the position to replace Prebisch at the UN Conference of Trade and Development.[25]

Pérez-Guerrero's life traversed two generations of anticolonial and oil elites. His long career left him in a perfect position to analyze the link between oil and the New International Economic Order. In February 1974, after Houari Boumedienne called for the UN Special Session, he wrote a letter to Enrique Iglesias, a Prebisch student who now directed the Economic Commission for Latin America. The letter from one anticolonial elite to another is telling both in its adhesion to the principles of sovereign rights and in its attempt to escape the tension between sovereign interest and international solidarity. Pérez-Guerrero understood, perhaps better than anyone by dint of the never-ending stream of reports and statistics that flowed through his

---

[25] Manuel Pérez Guerrero, "El Progreso Económico de Venezuela," *El Trimestre Económico* 16: 62 (April–June 1949): 223; Manuel Pérez Guerrero, *Petróleo: Hechos y Consideraciones* (Caracas: Oficina Central de Información, 1965), Inside Flap; "Opening Session," *OPEC Record*, January 1967, OIC.

FIGURE 8.2 The first meeting of the Joint Second and Third Committee of the
UN General Assembly, November 18, 1946. Manuel Pérez-Guerrero, who served
then as the Director of the Division of Coordination with the UN Department of
Economic Affairs, is on the far right.
Source: UN Photo. Courtesy of the United Nations Photo Library, Photo No. 292897.

office, that the rising price of oil exacerbated the daunting challenges faced by
the non-oil poor nations. There was no doubt by this time that high oil prices
would add to most nations' financial deficits. Many of these were already
acute. Yet the former Venezuelan oil minister was still warmed by the
"possibility of taking advantage of the new negotiating power in the hands
of the OPEC nations to the benefit of all of the Third World." He continued:
"The current crisis offers a singular opportunity to restructure interregional
economic relations along more just and firm bases."[26]

But, lest Iglesias judge him as naïve, he also wrote in closing that his
letter had begun to sound too much like a speech. The self-aware send-off
suggests that he understood that the reality of the energy crisis fit the
narrative of OPEC as syndrome, but with a crucial caveat. On the one
hand, oil elites had couched their critique of the oil concessions in
the universalist language of sovereign rights and had attended the same
conferences and meetings as the other anticolonial elites since the first

[26] Pérez-Guerrero to Iglesias, February 27, 1974, ARR 40/2344, notebook 58, UNA-G.

FIGURE 8.3 Gamani Corea and Manuel Pérez-Guerrero, February 1, 1974. The two men shake hands after Corea (right) was announced as Pérez-Guerrero's successor as Secretary-General of the UN Conference on Trade and Development. *Source*: UN Photo. Courtesy of the United Nations Photo Library, Photo No. 87878.

discussions at the UN Economic and Social Council and at the Afro-Asian conference in Bandung. But on the other, Pérez-Guerrero knew that he was guilty of attempting to normalize what was actually a sort of oil exceptionalism. Despite the attempts by Tariki, Zakariya, Francisco Parra, Feisal al-Mazidi, and many others to liken the concessions to the broader plight of economic inequality, oil had always been a unique commodity. It had exceptional strategic value and, given its outsize role in the industrial and consumer-driven global economy of the mid-twentieth century, it also had an inelastic demand.

Pérez-Guerrero knew that without a doubt. The preparatory report for the 1968 UNCTAD ministerial meeting in New Delhi, held right before he replaced Prebisch, noted that the share of developing countries in total world trade had declined steadily between 1950 and 1966. If oil exports were excluded, the analysts pointed out, the decline was even more notable. Analysts from the UN Secretariat pointed out at the same meeting that petroleum constituted an important exception to the rule of weak commodity-based growth. Moreover, its benefits were limited to a number of countries that could be "counted on two hands." Prebisch excluded petroleum from his presentation of the general terms of trade problem in 1968, he said, "for obvious reasons." When IMF Executive Committee President Pierre-Paul Schweitzer discussed unequal exchange with the UN Economic and Social Council in 1973, on a panel on which Pérez-Guerrero also sat, he too noted the common failure of commodity producers to shift their terms of trade – "with the exception of the oil producing countries."[27]

The problem of divergent economic interests among developing countries was not a new one. To take just one example, the oil insurrectionists and gradualists had long disagreed. But what makes the oil price hikes after October 1973 different was that the problem of contradictory interests was more acute on a larger scale. Indeed, the energy crisis revealed in full the great contradiction of the sovereign rights program: the rise of decolonization might have been a clarion call for its economic equivalent, but it also resulted in a world that often pitted newly independent countries against one another on the basis of their divergent economic interests. In other words, the widespread support for political decolonization resulted in the consecration of an immense number of different national economic interests. Although the oil producers touted their experience as an example of how national and international objectives could align, their policies worked against the possibility of further transnational cooperation.

This was because high oil prices hurt the bottom line of the non-oil nations, and the energy crisis crippled the larger effort at redistributive economic justice. Importantly, the foreign policy of the United States, directed by Henry Kissinger, used that contradiction to disparage OPEC and undermine the New International Economic Order. Before 1973, the

---

[27] UNCTAD, Second Session, New Delhi, vol. I, Report and Annexes, Part I, Introduction, ARR 40/2344, box 127, UNA-G; UNCTAD, Second Session, New Delhi, vol. V, Special Problems in World Trade and Development, TD/40, Report by the Secretariat of UNCTAD, "The International Division of Labour and Developing Countries," January 1, 1968, ARR 40/2344, box 127, UNA-G; Statement Made by Dr. Raul Prebisch," June 15, 1967, ARR 40/2344, notebook 79, UNA-G; UNOPI, *Weekly News Summary*, February 16, 1973, UN doc. WS/594.

US government had done little to help the multinational oil companies withstand the pressure of the oil elites, whether it came from gradualists or insurrectionists. In fact, US policy had mostly abetted the OPEC members' drive for control. But after the price of oil increased – and raised the stakes of what Kissinger in 1969 had called the "North-South gap" – he took the ideas of the sovereign rights program into greater account.[28]

Initially, Kissinger responded with vigor to what the State Department called the "heavily biased" UN Declaration, ordering the US delegation to the United Nations to express its dissent. It did so, speaking most strongly against what it called the "heart" of the New Order resolution: articles allowing for nationalization, calling for "just and equitable relationships" between raw material export prices and import costs, and urging the creation of more cartels. Kissinger also lashed out at OPEC at the United Nations in his April 1974 speech to the special session. High oil prices were "not the result of economic factors," he said. Rather, they were "artificial," based on "a political decision" that had no economic viability.[29]

Kissinger crusaded against high oil prices in close consultation with Treasury Secretary George Shultz and his replacement, William Simon. In their most incisive moments, the three men labeled expensive oil an economic and ideological menace of cosmic proportions. The energy crisis was "a change in economic circumstances without precedent in magnitude and suddenness in peacetime," Shultz told the Executive Board of the International Monetary Fund in January 1974, in one typical instance. The "capricious" oil producers had forsaken "their responsibilities as custodians of Nature's bounty." In another example, Kissinger told a group of congressmen that "the OPEC cartel pushed prices far beyond the level that economics would dictate." US President Gerald Ford also accused the OPEC nations of shirking their "international responsibility." They had not only cited "artificial economic justifications" to increase prices but had ignored "the destructive consequences of their actions."[30]

---

[28] Kissinger to Nixon, "NSC Meeting on Foreign Aid," March 25, 1969, National Security Council Files, Institutional Files, box H-021, RNL.

[29] Airgram A-4568 From the Department of State to All Diplomatic Posts, June 5, 1974, *FRUS 1969–76*, vol. E-14, part 1, doc. 16; "An Age of Interdependence: Common Disaster or Community," *Department of State Bulletin* 71: 1842 (October 14, 1974), 503.

[30] Herbert Stein, "Meeting with Shultz, Ash, and Stein," January 21, 1974, White House Special Files, President's Office Files, box 93, RNL; "Draft Rome Remarks by Secretary Shultz," January 1974, Arthur F. Burns Papers, box B86, GFL; Memorandum of

Before and after the Sixth Special Session, statements such as these echoed a more widespread fear of the OPEC syndrome. A poll of Treasury analysts expressed the prevalent belief that "the 1972–1974 period might mark the dawn of a new era for which past commodity policy was no longer suited." Kissinger found the potential consequences of further applications of collective supply control disturbing enough to request studies from the State Department and the National Security Council on "the use of raw materials as a weapon against the West."[31]

The results were comforting. The State Department responded that "cartel-like action" from other raw material producers was not "a general problem." In a more detailed report, NSC staffers wrote that the probability of cartelized "price gouging" was highly unlikely in materials other than oil. In fact, their painstakingly accumulated evidence revealed that collective action at OPEC levels was not an option for other Third World commodity producers. The distance between the oil producers and the rest emasculated at its innermost core the idea of OPEC as representative. Armed with the knowledge that the oil elites had erected an idol, Kissinger shifted tactics after the Sixth Special Session. He would continue to attack the oil producers, but rather than condemn the New Order itself, he instructed the State Department to undermine it. "The LDCs are weak reeds," he told his staff upon reading the raw materials reports.[32]

"No period in the postwar era has been as turbulent for the balance of payments of the non-oil less developed countries," wrote another observer. The combined deficit of those nations grew from $10 billion in 1972 to $38 billion in 1975, according to his conservative estimate. Other estimates were higher, and the rise in the deficits was widely attributed to the oil price increases. In the year following the Sixth Special Session, the US government began to develop policies to help the "hardest hit" poor countries cope with their massive "oil-related debt" through loans on the

Conversation, June 10, 1975, *FRUS 1969–76*, vol. XXXVII, doc. 65; DOS to All Diplomatic Posts, December 22, 1976, *FRUS 1969–76*, vol. XXXVII, doc. 113.

[31] US Treasury, "Summary of Report to Economic Policy Board on Commodity Policy for Non-Fuel Minerals," n.d. (April 1975), US Council of Economic Advisers Records, Alan Greenspan Files, box 58, GFL; Decision Memorandum, "The Secretary's Regional Staff Meeting," March 9, 1975, Kissinger Transcripts, DNSA.

[32] Lord to Kissinger, "Critically Imported Materials," March 22, 1974, RG 59, Policy Planning Staff Director's Files (Winston Lord), 1967–77, box 345, NARA; Lord, "Critical Imported Materials: NSSM/CIEPSM Study," July 11, 1974, RG 59, Policy Planning Staff Director's Files (Winston Lord), 1967–77, box 345, NARA; Secretary's Staff Meeting, March 18, 1974, Kissinger Transcripts, DNSA.

private financial market. That policy would be packaged as a compromise. But it was still relatively combative in essence, as revealed by policy toward the UN Emergency Relief Fund and the Oil Facility of the International Monetary Fund.[33]

In a move freighted with symbolism, UN Secretary General Kurt Waldheim called Raúl Prebisch out of retirement to promote and manage the UN Emergency Relief Fund, which the delegates of the Sixth Special Session designed to mitigate the difficulties of the nations that were most seriously affected by high oil prices. The promise of solidarity was as seductive to Prebisch as ever, and the 74-year-old worked with what his biographer has called "youthful energy" to solicit donations. But the mission was more of an emotional tonic than an actual one. He had gathered only $5 billion as of September 1974, an amount that he reported to Waldheim was "very small" compared to the problem of oil-related deficits for the poor, non-oil-producing nations. Furthermore, heavy borrowing already added "markedly to the indebtedness of these countries" because other forms of aid were increasingly unavailable.[34]

Had Prebisch been party to private conversations in the White House and the State Department, he would have been more indignant. His fundraising failure in part owed to US opposition. A slew of internal memos argued against the Emergency Fund in 1974. The General Assembly had "properly identified [the] major task of relief for the poor countries hardest hit by oil," State Department Policy Planning Director Winston Lord told Kissinger. But the delegates had passed the task "to a UN forum which neither the industrial countries nor the oil producers have shown a strong inclination to support." Writing with greater urgency a month later, Lord and Assistant Undersecretary of State Thomas Enders held that it was "politically necessary" to direct present and future financial initiatives "to an international coordination point other than" the UN Fund, which was "unwieldy and loaded against us."[35]

---

[33] Millard Long, "Balance of Payments Disturbances and the Debt of the Non-Oil Less Developed Countries: Retrospect and Prospect," *Kyklos* 33: 3 (1980): 475; "Tab B: Assistance to the Hardest-Hit," May 1974, RG 59, Policy Planning Staff Director's Files (Winston Lord), 1967–77, box 345, NARA.

[34] Edgar J. Dosman, *The Life and Times of Raúl Prebisch, 1901–1986* (Montreal: McGill-Queen's Press, 2008), 471; UNDP, "Current Situation on the United Nations Emergency Operation," August 22, 1974, Papers of Sidney Dell, Special Collections, Bodleian Library; United Nations Emergency Operation, Report to the Secretary General, June 16, 1975, Papers of Sidney Dell, Special Collections, Bodleian Library.

[35] Lord to Kissinger, "Briefing Memorandum: Your Lunch with Outside Experts," May 31, 1974, RG 59, Policy Planning Staff Director's Files (Winston Lord), 1967–77, box 345,

FIGURE 8.4 Press conference by Raúl Prebisch for the UN Emergency Relief
Fund, May 23, 1974.
Source: UN Photo/Teddy Chen. Courtesy of the United Nations Photo Library, Photo
No. 145313.

In a hook-and-ladder movement, Kissinger proposed a "Development
Security Fund" at a meeting of the Organization of American States in
May 1974. He described the program as seeking the same objectives as
the UN fund. However, Enders had designed it to supplant Prebisch's
effort by enveloping UN aid within a larger mix of public and private
capital directed through a new International Development Council staffed
by World Bank and International Monetary Fund officials. Success in this
venture would "diminish pressure to make the UN General Assembly ...
the central point for coordination," Lord and Enders wrote. The Development Security Fund would continue to form part of US foreign policy in
the following year, and would be presented as one of several key compromises at the next UN Special Session in November 1975.[36]

NARA; Briefing Memorandum, Lord and Enders to Kissinger, "Following Up Your UN
and OAS Speeches," May 1974, RG 59, Policy Planning Staff Director's Files (Winston
Lord), 1967–77, box 345, NARA.
[36] Briefing Memorandum, Lord and Enders to Kissinger, "Following Up Your UN and OAS
Speeches," May 1974, RG 59, Policy Planning Staff Director's Files (Winston Lord),

The US followed a similar strategy in its policy toward a new loan program at the International Monetary Fund. There, Kissinger and Simon worked to limit the size and effectiveness of the so-called Oil Facility, proposed by IMF managing director Johannes Witteveen to mitigate "the very large deterioration" the price increases threatened in the current accounts of "the overwhelming majority of countries" through the provision of low-interest loans. US officials dissented on the basis that this endorsed "the unnatural phenomenon" of OPEC's price increases. For Simon, the new credit line "put OPEC in the driving seat" by legitimizing their actions. Shultz agreed and told Nixon that the United States should not "too readily bail out oil-importing countries ... lest that weaken the resolve to get the price down."[37]

As a first step to limit the Fund's role in 1974, Simon pushed for a series of mandatory conditions for countries that borrowed from the Oil Facility. The central requirement was that borrowing should be allowed only for countries that relaxed their capital controls, as the United States had done since 1971. Simon abolished the remaining capital controls in the United States in 1974, a decision that allowed more American banks to accept greater quantities and amounts of deposits, including those from the increasingly rich oil producers. Larger deposits in turn meant that more nations would be able to borrow from those banks. At the same time, Simon hoped that the "liberalizing" capital would direct the growing flows of oil money to American banks, solidifying a dominant position for the United States in international finance. He reported to the Senate in September 1974 that, because capital controls no longer limited the size of short-term deposits in New York, the US financial market had grown massively since the beginning of the energy crisis. Of the $17.2

1967–77, box 345, NARA; Minutes of the Rambouillet Economic Summit Meeting, November 16, 1975, *FRUS 1969–76*, vol. XXXVII, doc. 88.

[37] Benjamin Cohen, "When Giants Clash: The OECD Financial Support Fund and the IMF," in Vinod K. Aggarwal, ed., *Institutional Designs for a Complex World: Bargaining, Linkages, and Nesting* (Ithaca, NY: Cornell University Press 1998), 161–94; Staff Report, "A Facility to Assist Members in Meeting the Initial Impact of the Increase in Oil Import Costs," February 19, 1974, Oil Facility Records, IMFA; "Respective Roles of Private Markets, Oil Facility, Described by Witteveen," IMF *Survey*, May 6, 1974; William Simon, "Oil Prices: Why They Should Come Down," US Information Service, US Embassy, London, November 5, 1974, Foreign and Commonwealth Office: Energy Department, folder 96, UKNA; Sir Donald Maitland, "Oil and the World Economy," October 17, 1974, Foreign and Commonwealth Office: Energy Department, folder 96, UKNA; Herbert Stein, Memorandum for the President's File, "Meeting with Shultz, Ash, and Stein," January 21, 1974, White House Special Files, President's Office Files, box 93, RNL.

billion inflows of short-term capital reported by US banks, he estimated that $7 billion came from OPEC nations.[38]

Many observers questioned Simon's interpretation of the problem and his solution. IMF analysts worried about "marked break in the customary patterns of international capital flows" in a 1974 report. As oil prices increased, the "structural problem" of the growing deficits of the oil-producing nations would only increase in severity. The debtors' deficits would grow, investment would become more risky, and capital would dry up. "There is no assurance, and indeed little likelihood, that the aggregate flow of funds . . . will be adequate, in direction and volume, from the point of view of the world economy," the Fund team concluded.[39]

As the energy crisis entered its second full year, IMF officials became more anxious about oil-related debt and feared that the Oil Facility was too small. Their prediction came true when the Fund announced that it had reached its lending limits in October 1974. One British official summed up the sense of disquiet in December when he argued that increased IMF lending was a better option than Simon's "ad hoc, not to say anarchic" approach. British Chancellor of the Exchequer Denis Healey, who later described Simon as "far to the right of Genghis Kahn and totally devoted to the freedom of financial markets," thus proposed a second and open-ended Oil Facility.[40]

After getting Witteveen's support, Healey brought the proposal to Simon and the finance ministers of France, Germany, Japan, and the

---

[38] Eric Helleiner, *States and the Reemergence of Global Finance* (Ithaca, NY: Cornell University Press 1994),107–26, 444; Alan Matusow, *Nixon's Economy: Booms, Busts, Dollars, and Votes* (Lawrence: University Press of Kansas, 1997), 117–48. George Shultz first pushed for the lifting of capital controls as the director of the Office of Management and Budget, based on Arthur Laffer and Eugene Fama's arguments about how "prestige costs" and "economic costs" of controls far outweighed their balance of payments benefits. See: Shultz to the Members of the Council on International Economic Policy, "Capital Control Programs," March 2, 1971, National Security Council Files, box 218, RNL; Eugene F. Fama and Arthur Laffer, "Information and Capital Markets," *The Journal of Business* 44: 3 (July 1971): 289–98.

[39] Research Department, "Adequacy of Present Financing Arrangement of Oil Surplus Funds," November 12, 1974, *Oil Facility Records*, IMFA; Secretary to Executive Board, "Oil Facility – Further Review for 1974," November 29, 1974, *Oil Facility Records*, IMFA.

[40] Edwin L. Dale, "20 Finance Chiefs Meet," *New York Times*, October 4, 1974, p. 53; US Congress, House, Committee on Banking and Currency, Ad Hoc Committee on the Domestic and International Monetary Effect of Energy and Other Natural Resource Pricing, "Petrodollars: Recycling and Aid Prospects," 93rd Congress, 2nd session, December 12, 1974; Denis Healey, *Time of My Life* (New York: W W Norton, 1989), 419.

United Kingdom at a summit in September 1974. At the meeting, he sought to disabuse American policy of what Healey believed was "a misconceived link between the issue of oil prices and that of recycling." For him, the spillover of the American policy of "brinksmanship" on OPEC's price control into debates about international lending was "dangerously imprudent." Healy hoped the new Oil Facility would attract at least $30 billion, and reminded Simon that this relatively small amount would leave the majority of petrodollars in private capital markets.[41]

The US did not budge. Meanwhile, Simon began to formulate a plan to substitute the new proposal with a "closed-circuit Common Trust" managed by officials at the Paris offices of the Organization of Economic Cooperation and Development. Simon elaborated on the ramifications of what he promoted as the "Kissinger Solidarity Fund" in December 1974. The fund was a "safety net" for the free market, he said. As such, it was "not intended to provide free, unlimited or unconditional aid." Instead, it offered "standby support" that was available only when a nation took "reasonable measures to resolve its difficulties."[42]

The IMF Executive Board welcomed the Kissinger Solidarity Fund as evidence that "the extent and urgency of the need for official recycling facilities seemed at last to be widely recognized." However, the board also correctly speculated that the proposal was "an attempt to prevent a Fund oil facility ... from being established." If that were true, US policy represented "a serious departure from international solidarity." They thus voted "to press ahead" with the design of a new Oil Facility. Simon stopped that effort in its tracks by using US voting power to ensure its existence "on a much more limited basis than had been proposed by the Europeans and others," he told Ford. He forced the option in a January 1975 IMF board meeting when he used US voting power to limit the fund to $5 billion, a far cry from Healy's initial $30 billion proposal.[43]

---

[41] H.M. Treasury, "Brief for Discussions with the Americans: Recycling," October 9, 1974, Foreign and Commonwealth Office: Energy Department, folder 6, UKNA; Meeting Record, "Oil and the World Economy," October 2, 1974, Foreign and Commonwealth Office: Energy Department, folder 6, UKNA.

[42] "Statement by the Honorable William E. Simon, Secretary of the Treasury," Before the Subcommittee on International Finance, House Committee on Banking and Currency, December 3, 1974; US Congress, Senate, *Financial Support Fund Act*, Hearings before the Senate Committee on Banking, Housing and Urban Affairs, June 4, 1976.

[43] "Minutes of the Executive Board Meeting," November 18, 1974, Executive Board Minutes, IMFA; Simon to Ford, "Results of the International Meetings this Week on Monetary and Development Issues," January 18, 1975, L. William Seidman Files, box

"Unfortunately, the figure proposed by Dr. Witteveen was cut by the US delegation," Prebisch wrote UN Secretary General Kurt Waldheim the same month. It was an "important problem" for him that neither an IMF nor a UN fund would meet the yawning deficits of the poorest oil importers. "There will be a vacuum that has to be filled in one way or another to avoid a very difficult situation for the hardest hit developing countries," he concluded.[44]

Money from the private capital market would fill the void. Kissinger convened a meeting to set diplomacy toward the New International Economic Order in February 1975 with that expectation in mind. Flush from the UN Emergency Fund and IMF victories, Assistant Secretary of State Thomas Enders delineated the overarching goal: "The main point is political; breaking up the bloc of 77," a reference to the ever-growing group of developing countries that comprised the UN Conference on Trade and Development. He suggested that the US balance "anti-cartel provisions" with a series of concessions that included "provisions relating to access to markets and access to financing." To put it bluntly, the US government would offer compromise in the form of "money on the table," a tactic that Enders hoped would curb the ability of "UNCTAD, the Algerians, and others ... to exploit [high oil prices] as a North-South issue."[45]

The call to subvert the New International Economic Order rather than confront it dismayed Simon. Accommodation placed the United States "in danger of compromising our basic commitment to the free enterprise system," he wrote Ford. Kissinger defended the shift toward accommodation when he met with the president. "My role is to project an image of the US which is progressive," he said. A strident ideological line did not serve that purpose. Instead of "vindicating" the international economy, which he told Ford was "a system which no one will support," he hoped to "fuzz it up" and make gains with little sacrifice. "I don't want to accept a New Economic Order," he said, "but I don't want to confront Boumedienne." Ford agreed: "I see no reason to talk theory when we can in a practical way just screw up the negotiations." Days later,

206, GFL; Shultz Report, "Private Group of Five Meeting," February 2–3, 1975, National Security Adviser's Files, Memoranda of Conversations, box 9, GFL.

[44] Prebisch to the Secretary General, "Recent Financial Discussions in Washington, D.C.," January 21, 1975, Papers of Sidney Dell, Special Collections, Bodleian Library.

[45] Memcon, "Commodity Initiative," February 22, 1975, RG 59, Central Foreign Policy Files 1973–76, doc. PD820123-0999, NARA.

Kissinger tried to calm the still simmering Simon, telling him, "We can use the ambiguities to accomplish our objectives."[46]

Kissinger made public the new strategy of accommodation in a speech delivered from Milwaukee in June 1975. Parts of the speech were designed for the consumption of anticolonial elites, Kissinger wrote to UN Ambassador Daniel Patrick Moynihan. He directed Moynihan to call on "those responsible for their countries' policies at the Seventh Special Session" and "invite their attention" to the "positive aspects" he presented. In particular, Moynihan was to depict American policy as a concerted effort at "dialogue with the developing world."[47]

Political confrontation was not completely taken off the table, though. But Kissinger's North–South quarrel would not be on the topic of sovereign rights and the international economy. Instead, he hoped to move the debate away from the question of economic decolonization and toward human rights. Moynihan was an obvious choice for that mission. He had just written a widely distributed article for *Commentary* magazine arguing that the United States did not hold a monopoly on contemporary injustice. "The new nations" in particular "were subordinating freedom and denying the rights of individuals" at egregious levels, he said. The United States needed not to "appease" these human rights abusers but to display toughness in the face of anti-American hostility. In his first meeting as ambassador with the President, Moynihan told Ford he planned to "play hard ball." For Kissinger, the new emphasis on human rights was also tailored to enable the counteroffensive against the sovereign rights program and the New International Economic Order. This was because it would enable a quieter and more effective response to the problem. He explained this to Simon in May 1975: "On the broader North/South question, I want to split them... That is why we have Moynihan going up there to take them on."[48]

Kissinger sought to shift the agenda from redistributive economic justice to human rights, a realignment that he believed would supplement

[46] Simon and Seidman, "Memorandum for the President," n.d. (May 1975), Papers of the Council on Economic Affairs, box 58, GFL; Memorandum of Conversation, May 24, 1975, National Security Adviser's Files, Memoranda of Conversation, box 12, GFL; Memorandum of Conversation, May 26, 1975, National Security Adviser's Files, Memoranda of Conversation, box 12, GFL.

[47] SecState to USUN, "Secretary's July 14 Speech on UN," July 19, 1975, National Security Adviser's Files, Presidential Agency File, box 21, GFL.

[48] Daniel Patrick Moynihan, "The United States in Opposition," *Commentary* (March 1975), 31–40; Memcon, August 27, 1975, National Security Adviser's Files, Presidential Agency Files, box 20, GFL; Memorandum of Conversation, "IEA and OECD Meetings," May 24, 1975, *FRUS 1969–76*, vol. XXXI, doc. 293.

the policies suggested by Enders. To that end, Kissinger created a joint National Security Council and Economic Policy Board task force. Its objective was to create a "flexible approach" for the Seventh Special Session of the UN General Assembly, which would meet in October 1975. Flexible, it turned out, was a relative term. The Ford administration would continue to oppose the more outright forms of sovereign economic control – including price indexation, most commodity agreements, and any other actions "that attempt to maintain prices above long-term market levels."[49]

The chair of the joint committee, Assistant Treasury Secretary Gerald Parsky, and the other members developed policy with that goal in mind. Two proposals, developed in addition to the Kissinger Solidarity Fund, reveal their strategy: first, a case-by-case approach to commodity discussions and, second, a proposal for increased World Bank support for investment in raw material production. A brief discussion of commodities reveals the contours of the overall strategy. It also indicates the weakness of OPEC-style collective action for raw materials other than oil. Based on the task force report, Kissinger instructed Moynihan to accede to consumer–producer forums for major commodities such as tin, coffee, and cacao. American willingness to review specific commodity prices would blunt the sense of solidarity that infused the New Order, task force members hoped. The policy would demonstrate to the developing countries that "they are an artificial grouping" and that "they have much less in common than many recognize," one official explained.[50]

As with the UN Emergency Fund and the IMF Oil Facility, Kissinger's foreign policy team had devised a fudge. A change in policy toward the International Tin Agreement in August 1975, which would impose voluntary export controls if global prices dropped severely, followed the prescription. The United States, alone among major consuming nations, had declined to ratify the previous four agreements. But now it supported it for the first time. Changing tack was both a safe economic move and an effective political one for at least four reasons. First, the US government owned a tin stockpile equivalent to one year's world consumption. Second, American participation was unlikely to have any material impact on prices.

---

[49] Memorandum of Conversation, May 26, 1975, cited in *FRUS 1969–76*, vol. XXXI, doc. 295.

[50] Butler to Scowcroft, "Secretary Kissinger's Speech to the Seventh Special Session: Tin Agreement," August 28, 1975, National Security Adviser's Files, Presidential Agency Files, box 20, GFL.

Third, the task force reported, the agreement lacked "the negative features frequently associated with international controls," in large part because a majority of producers and consumers had to approve any export controls. Last, the six tin producers in the agreement – Indonesia, Thailand, Malaysia, Bolivia, Nigeria, and Zaire – were all "politically significant moderates." Signing the agreement would thus cultivate their support on other issues and enhance "US credibility among the developing countries." Ford approved Kissinger's request to announce that the United States would join the agreement at the Seventh Special Session.[51]

A second example of the new strategy came with American proposals for a variety of mixed-capital investment funds. These proposals confirm again that the United States had designed a different sort of policy of accommodation, which sought to weaken the sovereign rights program and the New International Economic Order. In 1975, Kissinger requested approval for a $200 million contribution of the International Fund for Agricultural Development, originally proposed by the OPEC nations at the 1974 World Food Conference, and a $450 million outlay for the International Finance Corporation. Again, the ideological emphasis from the US side was clear. The money would "complement private investment" rather than replace it, Kissinger told Ford, by allowing the World Bank to establish a trust that would "expand the access of . . . the middle-level developing countries to international capital." The funding decisions were part of the widespread promotion of what the State Department called "semi-commercial banks," which would provide finance for countries that otherwise might be "crowded out of international capital markets." Such policies to tie Third World nations more securely to the global capital market were "very much in our interest," a task force member wrote.[52]

---

[51] Seidman to Ford, "U.S. Participation in the International Tin Agreement," August 28, 1975, Presidential Handwriting File, box 6, GFL; Economic and Energy Meeting, Memorandum of Decisions, August 30, 1975, Presidential Handwriting File, box 6, GFL. Later, when the administration signed the Third International Coffee Agreement, the same policy was used. See: Seidman and Scowcroft, "U.S. Participation in the Third International Coffee Agreement," February 11, 1976, Presidential Handwriting File, box 6, GFL; Connor to Seidman and Scowcroft, "U.S. Participation in the Third International Coffee Agreement," February 18, 1976, Presidential Handwriting File, box 6, GFL.

[52] Memorandum from Gardner to Simon, August 20, 1975, *FRUS 1969–76*, vol. XXXI, doc. 298; Memorandum from Kissinger to Ford, August 27, 1975, *FRUS 1969–76*, vol. XXXI, doc. 297; Butler to Scowcroft, "UN Seventh Special Session: IFAD and IFC Issues," August 28, 1975, National Security Adviser's File, Presidential Agency File, box 20, GFL.

At the same time, it remained a standing policy to attack the OPEC nations, which US officials identified as market deviants and adversaries of Third World solidarity. Kissinger continued to complain about "price-gouging," culminating in a December 1974 interview, in which he told *Business Week* that he could not rule out the use of force against oil-producing nations "in the gravest emergency." Kissinger explained the policy to European leaders later that year. The United States hoped to convey to the OPEC members, especially "the moderate countries ... who are most psychologically dependent on the U.S.," that they could not underwrite higher oil prices "without paying an economic and political price." In particular, it became US policy to "document publicly the adverse impact" of high oil prices on the less-developed countries.[53]

But the United States could not be sure that its strategy – reviling OPEC and undercutting the New International Economic Order – would be successful. For one, the vilification of OPEC did not seem to pay immediate dividends. Even the hardest-hit developing nations continued to support the price increases in principle. The Sudanese government, for example, made it official policy to "not deny the right of our Arab brothers to have the best prices for their primary commodity." Sudanese officials were joined by many others. Even the president of tiny Madagascar declared "that it was a victory for the nations of the Third World that OPEC could impose ... a price it judged equitable."[54]

In addition, oil elites continued to hammer away at their argument about structural inequality in the international economy. The Organization of Arab Petroleum Exporting Countries took on an especially active role in the Seventh Special Session of November 1975. Twenty years after helping inscribe permanent sovereignty into international law, the permanent representative of Saudi Arabia, Jamil Baroody, served as the cochairman of the OAPEC delegation at the session. He was more adamant than ever about the structural roots of global economic injustice. He accused Moynihan and Kissinger of attempting to divert attention from

---

[53] Editorial Note, *FRUS 1969–76*, vol. XXXVII, doc. 30; Memorandum of Conversation, September 9, 1975, *FRUS 1969–76*, vol. XXXVII, doc. 88; Katz to Kissinger, "Preliminary Strategy for Dealing with the OPEC Price Increase," January 4, 1977, *FRUS 1969–76*, vol. XXXVII, doc. 115.

[54] AmEmbassy Khartoum to SecState, "Sudanese Reaction to OPEC Price Increases," December 22, 1976, RG 59, Central Foreign Policy Files 1973–76, Electronic Telegrams, NARA; AmEmbassy Tananarive to SecState, "Demarche on OPEC Price Decision," November 30, 1976, RG 59, Central Foreign Policy Files 1973–76, Electronic Telegrams, NARA.

the larger problem of unequal exchange and "make the oil producing countries their scapegoat." Blaming the OPEC nations for the greater woes of the international economy was laughable, he told the delegates, if taking into account his "humble experience" of three decades in the UN. Instead of the "spurious" aid programs suggested by the United States, more trade between commodity producers and consumers "at genuinely fair prices" should be used to prop up the development programs of the Third World.[55]

Algerian Foreign Minister Abdelaziz Bouteflika, who served as the OAPEC delegation co-chair and the President of the Session, argued again that the OPEC price actions had "illustrated spectacularly" the need "to put an end to several centuries of plunder by fixing themselves, as sovereign countries, the price of that resource." Their decision was proof that, "when judiciously employed," the natural resources of the poor nations could become a "decisive instrument of their economic liberation." Sa'doun Hammadi, the Iraqi oil minister who had worked so closely with the Libyans and Algerians in 1970 and 1971, agreed. "The capitalist industrialized countries," had tried to place the blame "for the incurable evils to be found in their own economic system" on high oil prices, he said. For him too, greater fault lay with the structure of the international economy. The problem of economic injustice faced by the poor nations was a longer one related to the terms of trade for raw materials, one that had until recently "prevailed in regard to the fixing of the price of crude oil."[56]

Despite the familiarity of these arguments, guided by the long-brewing assumptions of the economic culture of decolonization, the United States gained support for its initiatives. It could do so, in large part, because of another success in the strategy of accommodation. In short, Moynihan and the US delegation were able to move the debate about the international economy outside the United Nations to a new Conference on International Economic Cooperation, a program first suggested by the French government in 1974. Comprised of economic officials from eight industrialized countries, eight OPEC members,

---

[55] OAPEC, Oil in the Seventh Special Session of the United Nations (Kuwait, 1976), "H. E. Mr. Jamil Baroody," ARR 40/1842, box 167, TD 440 OAU, UNA-G.

[56] OAPEC, *Oil in the Seventh Special Session of the United Nations* (Kuwait, 1976), "The President H. E. Abdelaziz Bouteflika" and "H. E. Dr. Saadoon Hammadi," both in ARR 40/1842, box 167, TD 440 OAU, UNA-G.

and eleven developing countries, US officials believed the CIEC would be a more manageable group.

A major US objective in the CIEC in 1975 and after continued to be to emphasize the "severe impact" of high oil prices on the non-oil developing countries. By the time they began to plan for the first meeting of the CIEC in late 1975, US officials believed that their strategy had paid direct dividends. The US Mission in Geneva reported that the policies designed for the Seventh Special Session successfully "generated severe strains within the G-77 and fracture lines in the Non-Aligned Movement." The "moderates" among the poor nations, including three of the tin producers, had opted for "cooperation with the West." For the Federal Reserve analysts who observed the session, the US delegates had been able to capitalize on that "more constructive environment for North-South relations" to continue to push "private markets and IMF financing as the best response" to the rising debt burdens of the poor nations.[57]

Accommodation, now with different objectives than the similar policy toward individual oil producers in the late 1960s and early 1970s, established solid groundwork for a "North–South dialogue" on the basis of American objectives, National Security Adviser Brent Scowcroft wrote Ford in December 1975. Public diplomacy, "our intention to be conciliatory," had paved the way for future initiatives that would weaken the New Order. In conclusion, Scowcroft turned to the earlier theme of a deviant OPEC. American policy had weakened the "unnatural" alliance between the oil producers and the other developing countries.[58]

But in the end, the success in breaking what Kissinger called "the unholy alliance of OPEC and the Third World" depended less on US policy and more on the negative effect of high oil prices on the economies of the non-oil nations. To put it differently, anticolonial elites did not need Kissinger, Moynihan, or Enders to bring the debit side of the oil revolution to light. The majority of nations simply were powerless in the face of high oil prices and their financial corollary, sovereign debt. Money poured out of their national treasuries with devastating consequences as OPEC continued to increase prices in 1974 and after, and

---

[57] DOS to Selected Diplomatic Posts, May 12, 1975, *FRUS 1969–76*, vol. XXXVII, doc. 62; DOS to Kissinger in Oslo, May 22, 1976, *FRUS 1969–76*, vol. XXXVII, doc. 98; Ferguson to Moynihan, "U.S. Policy Re: 7th Special Session," July 11, 1975, Moynihan Papers, series I, box 335, LOC; Briefing Papers, International Economic Summit, "Relations with Developing Countries," November 1975, Arthur S. Burns Papers, box B62, GFL.

[58] Scowcroft to Ford, n.d. (December 1975), *FRUS 1969–76*, vol. XXXI, doc. 300.

many of the same people who publicly applauded OPEC privately wrung their hands.[59]

The positions of anticolonial elites in the "hardest hit" nations, which US officials also labeled "the new casualty cases," revealed the extent of the sovereign debt problem in every continent at the end of 1975. Kifle Wodajo, fifteen years after first promoting sovereign rights in the Organization of African Unity, was now the Ethiopian ambassador in the United States. He told US officials that the "greatly increased prices of oil and fertilizer" had caused serious dislocations in his country. In Pakistan, which received concessionary rates for oil and aid from the OPEC countries, the price increases raised the import bill by almost half of national export earnings. "The increased oil prices are having a disastrous effect," Prime Minister Zulfikar Ali Bhutto told Kissinger when the Secretary of State visited Islamabad in October 1974.[60]

In Latin America and the Caribbean, consuming nations faced similar problems. The military government in Chile managed to bridge its sizable oil deficit through austere fiscal policies, what the Pinochet regime framed as "a year of sacrifice." The government extended that year "by twelve months" in December. Michael Manley, the Jamaican prime minister who had recently been celebrated by Fidel Castro for his attempts to "consolidate complete and political and economic independence," had his reform attempts limited by oil prices. Fuel costs rose to a quarter of total import costs in 1974, a dilemma that forced him to announce a "survival package" of loans and lower government spending.[61]

---

[59] Memorandum of Conversation, November 16, 1975, L. William Seidman Files, box 312, GFL.

[60] Department of State, Memcon, "Secretary's Lunch with Outside Experts," May 31, 1974, RG 59, Policy Planning Staff Director's Files (Winston Lord), 1967–77, box 345, NARA; DOS to the Embassy Ethiopia, October 9, 1974, FRUS 1969–76, vol. E-6, doc. 113; AmEmbassy Islamabad to SecState, "Concessionary Rates for Oil," February 10, 1975, RG 59, Central Foreign Policy Files 1973–76, Electronic Telegrams, NARA; AmEmbassy Islamabad to SecState, "Petroleum Prices and Balance of Payments," September 30, 1975, RG 59, Central Foreign Policy Files 1973–76, Electronic Telegrams, NARA; Memorandum of Conversation, October 31, 1974, FRUS 1969–76, vol. E-8, doc. 183.

[61] AmEmbassy Santiago to SecState, "Balance of Payments Review – Chile," December 17, 1975, RG 59, Central Foreign Policy Files 1973–76, Electronic Telegrams, NARA; AmEmbassy Kingston to SecState, "Visit to Cuba of PM Manley," July 16, 1975, RG 59, CFP 1973–76, Electronic Telegrams, NARA; AmEmbassy Kingston to SecState, "Jamaican Economic Situation," October 18, 1975, RG 59, CFP 1973–76, Electronic Telegrams, NARA.

Even nations with relatively manageable oil deficits were negatively affected. Oil consumption in India was very low, for example, but the crisis struck at important economic sectors. Particularly hard hit was agriculture, which also faced a poor monsoon year. High fuel and fertilizer costs and other factors produced an unprecedented inflation rate and growing hardship. Huge political demonstrations against the Congress government led Indira Gandhi to unilaterally declare a state of emergency and suspend democratic institutions in June 1975. To take another example, the government of Thailand, which already faced protests from labor unions over rising rice and sugar prices, could do little to mollify increased labor and student activism when they lifted their price subsidy for retail gasoline in January 1976. In Ghana, too, government economists predicted that the cost of oil would amount to over one-fifth of total import costs, despite the existence of substantial hydro-electric capability at the Volta Dam. The situation there, as in many African countries, gave "the impression of drift and deep malaise ... with no prognosis of near-term improvement."[62]

Some anticolonial elites could be "unusually forthright" about the problem of high oil prices with their American counterparts, as one US official noted. Their statements revealed the growing fissure between internationalist ideals and nationalist practice. In one case, a cabinet member of the Ivory Coast called OPEC's price increases "disastrous for less developed African nations" and described the idea of "Non-Aligned solidarity" in the hands of OPEC as "idiotic." In another example, the Tanzanian Minister of Commerce accused the OPEC nations of "turning their backs on the developing countries, particularly the least developed." The Director of Economic Affairs for the Organization of African Unity added that he believed the oil producers "used promises of compensation through aid programs as a form of blackmail." Nonetheless, his organization could not "in good conscience" oppose the price increases because it was "committed ideologically to obtaining price increases for all raw materials."[63]

---

[62] Raju G. C. Thomas, "Energy Politics and Indian Security," *Pacific Affairs* 55: 1 (Spring 1982): 28–38; AmEmbassy Bangkok to SecState, "Thai Government Faces Series of Political, Economic Tests," December 29, 1975, RG 59, Central Foreign Policy Files 1973–76, Electronic Telegrams, NARA; AmEmbassy Accra to Secstate, "Ghana's Economy," May 31, 1975, RG 59, CFP 1973–76, Electronic Telegrams, NARA.

[63] AmEmbassy Abidjan to SecState, "Ivorian Attitudes on OPEC Price Decision," December 3, 1976, RG 59, Central Foreign Policy Files 1973–76, Electronic Telegrams, NARA; AmEmbassy Lome to SecState, "Demarche on OPEC Price Increase," November 30,

Such protestations bespeak an uneasiness to the sovereign rights program. By its universal nature, its key concepts and rationale could brook little ideological opposition. But in the hands of the oil producers, the problem of sovereign debt opened cracks in the notion of solidarity among anticolonial elites. The arguments by Baroody and other elites in the Seventh Special Session seemed more like smudged carbon copies than legitimate arguments in that context. In a statement to UN General Assembly delegates in October 1975, Mexican President Luís Echeverría summarized the new problem. He began by defending the righteousness of the price increases. The success of OPEC was evidence of a "new mentality" brought about by the rise of the United Nations as "a forum for the implantation of an authentic international and political democracy." But he also called on OPEC to recognize the "serious imbalance" high prices caused. It was fine for "affluent nations" like the United States to pay a "fair price" for oil and other raw materials, but the "debt burden" for the majority of nations threatened a greater concentration of power in the international economy, not a redistribution of it.[64]

The attorney general of Kenya put it differently at a parliamentary debate in Nairobi. Noting the effect of high oil prices on transportation, utilities, manufacturing, and tourism, he held that the OPEC nations were "milking" their non-oil counterparts. The "betrayal" was twofold in the case of Saudi Arabia, whose citizens' purchases of massive amounts of smuggled Kenyan charcoal had converted the country into "a treeless wasteland – a desert without oil."[65]

Such statements gave vent to the anxieties that permeated the sovereign rights program after the energy crisis. Disillusionment was hastened by the impact of debt on economic development. There was little those nations, labeled the NoPECs or the EDDCs (Energy Deficient Developing Countries) in thankfully short-lived neologisms, could do to improve their balance of payments position. Spurred on by the need to finance their

---

1976, RG 59, Central Foreign Policy Files 1973–76, Electronic Telegrams, NARA; AmEmbassy Dar Es Salaam to SecState, "Tanzania's Oil Problems and Their Spillover," September 30, 1975, RG 59, Central Foreign Policy Files 1973–76, Electronic Telegrams, NARA.

[64] USMission UN to SecState, "30th UNGA," October 8, 1975, RG 59, Central Foreign Policy Files 1973–76, Electronic Telegrams, NARA.

[65] AmEmbassy Nairobi to SecState, "Kenyan Reaction to Latest OPEC Price Increase," November 6, 1975, RG 59, Central Foreign Policy Files 1973–76, Electronic Telegrams, NARA.

development and, in most cases, their debt, they increasingly took out private loans.

The question of external national debt, of course, was not an entirely new one. During the 1960s, the UN Conference on Trade and Development tracked the debt of eighty nations, and concluded that their combined sovereign debt amounted to $59 billion at the end of 1969. But the issue reached unprecedented proportions immediately after the energy crisis, when the non-oil Third World became major borrowers of private capital for the first time. The indebtedness of the Third World nations doubled between December 1969 and December 1973, according to the World Bank. After that, the annual NoPEC deficit of soared, from $9.1 billion in 1973 to $27.5 billion in 1974 to $35 billion in 1975, according to the International Monetary Fund. In total, it is estimated that the non-oil developing countries borrowed over $200 billion between 1974 and 1980 from banks and bondholders.[66]

The all-important qualification to the oil producers' endorsement of anticolonial solidarity was glaring. Notwithstanding declarations of unity, the OPEC nations preferred to keep their money in American and European banks, who then "recycled" their petrodollars in the form of loans elsewhere. The flood of debt of this kind, lent by private investors directly to the governments of the poor nations, was unlike anything seen before. The consequences of these loans in 1974 and after are straightforward. As a number of scholars have argued, the lending plans of those banks dovetailed with the surge of international liquidity provided by the oil money surplus and the vacuum left by oil-related debt. Much of the liquidity was used for interbank loans, leading to a growing dependence on volatile, short-term deposits. Volatility, in turn, led banks to apply variable interest rates. The changing rates allowed banks to shift costs to their borrowers. Many of those borrowers were sovereign states.[67]

---

[66] UNCTAD, Official Record, "Debt Problems of Developing Countries," UN doc. TD/11/ suppl. 6; IMF, *World Economic Outlook. Development and Prospects in the Non-Oil Primary Producing Countries*, Table 1, World Reports, IMFA; Frieden, *Global Capitalism*, 370.

[67] Richard P. Mattione, *OPEC's Investments and the International Financial System* (New York: Brookings Institution, 1987), 22–37; Paul Hallwood and Stuart W. Sinclair, *Oil, Debt, and Development: OPEC in the Third World* (London: Allen & Unwin, 1981), 11–24; Karin Lissakers, *Banks, Borrowers, and the Establishment: A Revisionist Account of the Debt Crisis* (New York: Basic Books, 1993), 20–22, 36. For the perspective of the banks: David Rockefeller, *Memoirs* (New York: Random House, 2002), 281–302; Walter B. Wriston, *Risk and Other Four Letter Words* (New York: HarperCollins, 1987), 144–50.

TABLE 8.1 *Trends in Terms of Trade and Current Account Balances, Developed, OPEC, and NoPEC Nations, 1973–1980*

	1973	1974	1975	1976	1977	1978	1979	1980
Terms of Trade (%)								
Developed	-1	-11	-2.5	-1	-1	-3	2.5	-6
OPEC	15	137	-5	4.5	1	-10.5	28	39
NoPEC	7.5	-8	-9.5	3.5	3	-4	-2.5	-0.5
Current Account Balances ($ billion)								
Developed	19.3	-11.6	17.9	-0.5	-4.1	33.4	-9.8	-50
OPEC	6.6	67.8	35	40	31.9	50	68.4	115
NoPEC	-11.5	-36.9	-45.9	-32.9	-28.6	-35.8	-52.9	-70

Source: Chandra Hardy, "Adjustment to Global Payments Imbalances: A Tripartite Solution," April 1981. MS. Eng. c. 5826, Papers of Sidney Dell, Special Collections, Bodleian Libraries. Data from IMF *Annual Report, 1980* and IMF, *World Economic Outlook,* May 1980.

The growth of sovereign debt in the poorer nations thus troubled a number of people, including the members of the Development Committee of the World Bank. For them, this was primarily because the bulk of new financing was concentrated in private loans rather than direct investment or official aid. Both the Bank and the International Monetary Fund made strong pleas for increased flows of official capital in 1975. The outlook for the poorest countries was "particularly bleak," Robert McNamara told his officials. In a meeting of the Joint Ministerial Committee of the Bank and the Fund, IMF Director Johannes Witteveen endorsed the position that "substantial increases in capital flows" were necessary to prevent "the continued deterioration of the position of most of the developing countries." But those options simply did not exist on a large enough scale. IMF analysts predicted in 1977 that the poor nations' "exposure" to commercial credit would have drastic negative effects on their overall development.[68]

Under such circumstances, the inability of sovereign rights to reform the international economy in the grandiose manner envisioned by anticolonial elites was patently obvious. Raúl Prebisch himself grimly noted the gravity of the situation. Private financing of oil debt had "political meaning," he wrote UN Secretary General Waldheim. He feared that the rise of sovereign debt would limit the poor nations' independence more than ever.[69]

The economic culture of decolonization developed into a Third World consensus on sovereign rights over a period of more than two decades. But pessimism and debt overrode the consensus in less than two years after the oil revolution. A new UN Institute for Training and Research had begun a "worldwide research effort" on international economic inequality in 1967, in conjunction with the Center for Economic and Social Studies of the Third World in Mexico City. The groups settled on

---

[68] Robert McNamara's Opening Statement to Development Committee, June 12, 1975, Robert S. McNamara Papers, part I, box 23, LOC; Press Communique, Draft, June 12, 1975, Robert S. McNamara Papers, part I, box 23, LOC; Development Committee, "Measures to Facilitate Access to Capital Markets by Developing Countries," May 8, 1975, Robert S. McNamara Papers, box I, part 23, LOC; SM/77/111, prepared by the Exchange and Trade Relations Department, "International Banking: Recent Developments and Prospects for 1977," World Reports, IMFA.

[69] "UN Interoffice Memorandum, Prebisch to the Secretary General, Recent Financial Discussions in Washington, D.C.," January 21, 1975, Papers of Sidney Dell, Special Collections, Bodleian Library.

the objective of creating a "NIEO Library" in early 1975. The goal of the project was to explain the New Order as "a process which has deep historical precedents, and an undisputed historical significance."[70]

The project leaders began with the standard history of economic colonialism. The significance of the New Order lay within the "decisive event" of decolonization. But that "great wave" had been limited by continued and systemic poverty. "The newly independent states were said to be sovereign and equal to all other states, old and new, large and small," the project director wrote. "However, the fresh political and juridical status of the new countries was far from matched by their actual economic conditions. The majority felt that their *de jure* political colonization ended only to be replaced by a *de facto* economic colonization." The oil producers, in this particular recounting, had proved "the ability of the Third World to wield economic and political power effectively." But the consequences had been great, because such an "OPEC-type exercise" had thus far been unrepeatable.[71]

The earliest volumes commissioned for the NIEO Library emphasized the obstacles to the New Order rather than the possibility of its achievement. The victory of OPEC had "splintered Third World solidarity," one report said. The "long-term historical process of democratization" in international society may have brought into sharp relief the inequities of the international economy, but calls for structural reforms to international capitalism had been negated by the rise of sovereign debt. The resolution of that problem likely would be entrusted to the mechanisms of the free market, said another, a situation that would continue to produce "widening gaps between the rich and the poor nations." That problem and all of its corollaries served to create "more injustice, suffering, and conflict."[72]

[70] Information Note, UN Institute for Training and Research, "The 16-Volume NIEO Library," S-0913-0022-08, UNA-NY.

[71] Information Note, UN Institute for Training and Research, "The 16-Volume NIEO Library," S-0913-0022-08, UNA-NY.

[72] Ervin Laszlo, ed., *The Obstacles to the New International Economic Order* (New York: Pergamon Press, 1980); Jorge Lozoya and Hector Cuadra, eds., *Africa, the Middle East, and the New International Economic Order* (New York: Pergamon Press, 1980); Jorge Lozoya and A. K. Bhattacharya, eds., *Asia and the New International Economic Order* (New York: Pergamon Press, 1981); Information Note, UN Institute for Training and Research, "The 16-Volume NIEO Library," S-0913-0022-08, UNA-NY; UNITAR, "Progress in the Establishment of a New International Economic Order: Obstacles and Opportunities," December 16, 1978, S-0913-0022-08, UNA-NY; "The Obstacles to the New International Economic Order," August 25, 1980, Official Record, UN doc.

Sovereign debt and sovereign rights were intimate counterparts, according to that consensus. The high levels of sovereign debt were associated in the minds of many with the oil price increases. The oil revolution thus also cast into doubt the broader effectiveness of the sovereign rights program, in particular, the state-guided national development projects that dominated development discourse from the 1950s to the 1970s. As historians and other scholars have argued, sovereign debt helped pave the way for the rise of global capitalism and its more intrusive violations of sovereignty in the late twentieth and early twenty-first centuries. For some of the earliest proponents of anticolonial law and economics, the stratospheric rise of privately owned sovereign debt was a bitter pill to swallow. The early dons of development economics, William Arthur Lewis and Albert O. Hirschman, wore their opinions like mourning garments by the early 1980s. In his presidential address before the American Economic Association, entitled "The State of Development Theory," Lewis described the field as "in the doldrums." Hirschman discussed "The Rise and Decline of Development Economics" in the first chapter of *Essays on Trespassing*, emphasizing the latter. A young Amartya Sen wrote that development economists, "would-be dragon slayers," felt that they "had fallen on their swords."[73]

Sovereign rights, it seemed, had failed not only in the realm of political-economic practice but also in the terrain of the imagination. As in so many areas of human experience, what the anticolonial elites expected

UNITAR/11/SS/02. This view was, of course, contested. For arguments that attribute underdevelopment to state planning and other endogenous factors and propose market-based solutions, see: Gregory Clark, *Farewell to Alms: A Brief Economic History of the World* (Princeton University Press, 2008); William R. Easterly, *The Elusive Quest for Growth: Economists' Adventures and Misadventures in the Tropics* (Cambridge, MA: MIT Press, 2001). As noted in Chapter 1, the critique of state-led economic development has a long history. See, for more: P. T. Bauer, *Equality, the Third World, and Economic Delusion* (Cambridge, MA: Harvard University Press, 1981), Daron Ademoglu and James A. Robinson, *Economic Origins of Dictatorship and Democracy* (New York: Cambridge University Press, 2005).

[73] W. Arthur Lewis, "The State of Development Theory," *The American Economic Review* 74: 1 (March 1985): 1; Albert O. Hirschman, *Essays in Trespassing: Economics to Politics and Beyond* (New York: Cambridge University Press, 1981), 1–11; Amartya Sen, "Development: Which Way Now?" *The Economic Journal* 93: 372 (December 1983): 745. On the oil crisis, globalization, and sovereignty, see: Mark T. Berger, "The Nation-State and the Challenge of Global Capitalism," *Third World Quarterly* 22: 6 (2001): 889–907. For an overview, see: Daniel J. Sargent, *A Superpower Transformed: The Remaking of American Foreign Relations in the 1970s* (New York: Oxford University Press, 2015); Hal Brands, *The Unipolar Moment: U.S. Foreign Policy and the Rise of the Post-Cold War Order* (Ithaca, NY: Cornell University Press, 2016).

and what actually happened were two different things. The notion of national interest that lay at the root of the sovereign rights program – the same force that made economic anticolonialism a collective and egalitarian theme since the 1950s – helped unleash that world. In other words, if the process of decolonization marked one of the great turning points of the twentieth century, the energy crisis marked the expiration of its most egalitarian strain.

Conclusion

Dead by Its Own Law

Sovereignty either is or is not.[1]
                    Mohammed Bedjaoui, 1969

The remarkable 1966 short story by Julio Cortazar, "The Southern Highway," takes place on the road from Fontainebleau to Paris. On the last day of a summer weekend, masses of people are on their return to the city. Twelve lanes of traffic slow, placed under "the regimen of a camel caravan," and then stop. After that, the rows of cars move "practically in bloc" if they move it all. The protagonist, known simply as "the engineer," feels as if "an invisible gendarme in the floor of the highway ordered the simultaneous advance, in which no one could obtain an advantage."

Day turns to night and night to day, again and again. Time passes, the traffic jam endures, food is measured out, and units of leadership created. When the engineer sets out to find water, he discovers that "beyond his group, they were creating other cells with similar problems." The leaders of each meet to take stock of their situation in a series of "war councils." Seasons pass, romances begin and end, the elderly die, children are born. Throughout it all, the engineer can come to only one surefire conclusion: "the situation was analogous in all parts." Then, suddenly, engines turn and the traffic jam clears. The gear shift

---

[1] UNGA, Official Records, "Second Report on Succession of States in Respect of Matters Other Than Treaties; Economic and Financial Acquired Rights," (1969), 60, UN doc. A/CN.4/216.

feels "incredible" in the engineer's hand. But the accelerating march forces him to an unwelcome conclusion. The premises of his new life had been constructed in the dark shadow of an unfounded solidarity. In minutes, his group "dislocated itself, no longer existed."

Deeply critical of the naiveté inherent to the utopian idea of solidarity in its very subject matter, an infinite traffic jam, Cortazar's dream-fable is a fine allegory for the fragility of the bond between the individual and the collective in the modern era. The final uncoupling also provides a useful metaphor for the history of the economic culture of decolonization, oil elites, and sovereign rights. The New International Economic Order, a grand gesture of unity based on the shared experience of decolonization, splintered into nothingness in what seemed like no time at all. Anticolonial elites were forced into the realization that the refraction of sovereign rights through a simplified morality tale became unfeasible. The fact was that sovereign rights had always been an alloy of possibilities and limits, never entirely pure. Oil flowed over, around, and through its tensions, which could not be more vividly reflected than in its many multicolored distortions.

More explicitly, Henry Kissinger's "unholy union" of OPEC and the Third World captured the tension between national interests and international idealism. The contradiction between the oil price increases and the New International Economic Order was too much in the end. High oil prices caused a grave economic crisis for most Third World nations, and the collective vision of sovereign rights buckled under the burden of expensive oil. The soaring expectations of the New International Economic Order were littered with the wreckage of reality by 1976. This is not a story with a heroic arc.

But the story of sovereign rights was always one that welded hope and despair, so the failure of the New Order was also a diffident one. The rise of sovereign debt should not obscure the essential achievement of the anticolonial elite class, including the oil elites, in the quarter century before. To advance sovereign rights in the place of colonialism was a profound change in human history, after all, and the economic culture of decolonization shaped the mentality of two generations of anticolonial elites while sovereign rights formed their primary political-intellectual matrix. In addition, when sovereign debt moved in the opposite direction of sovereign rights, that shift revealed once and for all that decolonization was not an absolute condition but a set of international relations characterized by success and failure, drastic change accompanied by equally stubborn continuity.

Recognizing that, we must likewise recognize that the energy crisis was not just an international economic event. It was also political, intellectual, and cultural one.

In February 1976, the Group of 77 held a ministerial meeting in the Philippines. Much had changed since Raúl Prebisch addressed the inaugural meeting in 1964. In his opening speech, Ferdinand Marcos proposed the transformation of UNCTAD into a "more militant organization" to be renamed the Third World Economic System. The new group would be based on the principle of what he called "collective economic self-reliance." The birth and growth of this new system, the dictator said, arose from the growing acceptance by "the family of nations that the theories of Adam Smith, which still haunt us, have been replaced by the developmental principles of Gandhi, Myrdal, and Prebisch."[2]

Such statements – whether by autocratic or socialist leaders, their technical experts, or elites employed by international organizations – came up against searching opposition after the oil revolution. In particular, the basic elements of US policy toward the Conference on International Economic Cooperation in 1976 and after were predictable extensions of the logic of undermining the New International Economic Order formed in early 1974. For one, the strategy of depicting the OPEC members as wanton agitators continued intact into the presidential administration of Jimmy Carter. US officials also continued to emphasize the glaring effects of high oil prices on different national economies. The oil price increases were "unwarranted by market conditions and harmful to the world economy," Secretary of State Cyrus Vance wrote in one example.[3]

More importantly, the Carter administration used those discrepancies to continue the US effort "to change the thrust" of North–South relations, in particular in the CIEC. Carter's UN ambassador Andrew Young, a man who shared little in terms of his personal history or outlook with Daniel Patrick Moynihan, followed the line of argument laid out by his predecessor when he told CIEC delegates in 1977 that the United States would only accept the NIEO as "an evolving concept." This statement arose from the State Department's continued policy of directing negotiations toward a "long-term and evolving North/South dialogue in ways

---

[2] EmEmbassy Manila to SecState, "Group of 77 Meeting Manila; UNCTAD," February 5, 1976, RG 59, Central Foreign Policy Files 1973–76, Electronic Telegrams, NARA.
[3] DOS to Selected Diplomatic Posts, November 4, 1977, *FRUS 1969–76*, vol. XXXVII, doc. 136.

that will improve rather than fundamentally change the international economic structure." The Carter administration's policy – led by Julius Katz, who directed the State Department Economics Bureau – envisioned the CIEC as a "cooperation program," but understood that cooperation would emphasize the "role of private capital" and the expectation that the developing nations would improve "their investment climate." Vance himself reminded CIEC delegates at their April 1977 meeting that "official aid should not – and as a practical matter cannot – substitute for the flows of private investment capital to the LDCs."[4]

The phrase "North–South Dialogue" itself became a bone of contention at the conference. For many Third World leaders, what the Brazilian delegate called the "so-called 'Dialogue'" was anything but. For him, the negotiations led "to a low common denominator." The United States and the other industrialized countries refused even to consider the Third World's primary objective – official financial assistance to bridge "oil-related" payment deficits. In a reiteration of the Ford administration's opposition of the UN Emergency Fund and the IMF Oil Facility, the northern countries at the meeting declined to discuss this and other measures of official adjustment aid for the South. Instead, following Vance's lead, they emphasized the private capital market. The continuity of this strategy from Kissinger's was plain to anticolonial elites. The position of the United States revealed a lack of "any desire to compromise," one UN official wrote Gamani Corea, the Oxford-trained Sri Lankan economist who had taken over UNCTAD from Manuel Pérez-Guerrero. Another UN official added that US policy was "an attempt to regain initiative and define the final shape of the outcome."[5]

---

[4] Paper Prepared in the DOS for President Carter, n.d. (September 1977), *FRUS 1977–80*, vol. 3, doc. 275; Katz to Cooper, "CIEC: Your Lunch with Manuel Perez-Guerrero," February 5, 1977, RG 59, Policy Planning Staff: Office of the Director, Records of Anthony Lake, box 2, NARA; DOS to Selected Diplomatic Posts, March 8, 1977, *FRUS 1969–76*, vol. XXXVII, doc. 120; DOS to Embassy Switzerland, June 17, 1977, *FRUS 1969–76*, vol. XXXVII, doc. 125; Lake to Vance, Talking Points, "Third World Economic Relations," April 15, 1977, RG 59, Policy Planning Staff: Office of the Director, Records of Anthony Lake, box 2, NARA.
[5] CIEC, Statement by Antonio Francisco Azeredo da Silveira, May 31, 1977, Papers of Sidney Dell, Special Collections, Bodleian Library; Report of the Conference on International Economic Cooperation, June 2, 1977, Papers of Sidney Dell, Special Collections, Bodleian Library; Adib al-Jadir to Gamani Corea, "Conference on International Economic Co-operation," July 13, 1977, ARR 40/1862, box 305, TDO 525(1), UNA-G; Iqbal Haji to Gamani Corea, "CIEC Resumed," May 2, 1977, ARR 40/1862, box 305, TDO 525(1), UNA-G, Geneva. See also: Gamani Corea, *The Economic Structure in Ceylon in Relation to Fiscal Policy* (D.Phil., University of Oxford, 1952).

The final report of the conference concluded "with regret that most of the proposals for structural changes in the international economic system" had not been agreed upon. The anticolonial elites had fallen far short of the objectives envisaged for "a comprehensive and equitable program of action" for the New International Economic Order. The dawning realization of defeat completed a profound reorientation for some anticolonial elites in how they understood their collective power. The meeting signaled "the death of the Prebisch-inspired UN Conference on Trade and Development scheme" for Enrique Iglesias, the director of the Economic Commission for Latin America. The refusal of the United States to negotiate had successfully reinforced the economic status quo, which Iglesias continued to see as a stultifying hierarchy preserved from the colonial past – "a significant relapse in the sense that it is a straight-forward and open neo-colonialist arrangement."[6]

Pérez-Guerrero, who was the spokesman for the eight "poor nations" at the CIEC, agreed. Rather than "fundamental changes," he wrote, the United States had put forward no more than "isolated gestures." The Iranian economist Jahangir Amouzegar added in his "Requiem for the North-South Conference" that the poor nations had lost "the ideological tug of war between the supporters and the opponents of the status quo."[7]

The language of death and defeat was widespread. But it had a different meaning for US officials. In its own "post-mortem," the State Department celebrated the fact that relations with the poor nations "lacked the acrimony and even the hostility that accompanied the North-South dialogue two years ago." Carter's National Security Adviser, Zbigniew Brzezinski, ordered a Presidential Review of the "North-South dialogue" after the meeting. The State Department responded with a strategy designed to further enfeeble the New International Economic Order. It engaged Moynihan and Kissinger's human rights smokescreen and drew a tighter link between the rise of human rights and the decline of sovereign rights. The United States could use the doctrine of "Basic Human Needs"

---

[6] "Report of the Conference on International Economic Cooperation," June 2, 1977, ARR 40/1862, box 305, TDO 525(1), UNA-G; Ferguson to Moynihan, "U.S. Policy Re: 7th Special Session," July 11, 1975, MP, series I, box 335, LOC.

[7] CIEC, "Statement by Mr. Manuel Perez Guerrero on Behalf of the Group of Nineteen Developing Countries," May 31, 1977, Papers of Sidney Dell, Special Collections, Bodleian Library; Jahangir Amuzegar, "A Requiem for the North-South Conference," *Foreign Affairs* (October 1977). For a trenchant critique of U.S. policy during the conference, see: M. P. Garrity, "Implications of the Lomé Convention for African Trade and Development," *The Review of Black Political Economy* 8: 1 (1977).

to close the "values gap" between the North and the South on the topic of "basic economic rights," analysts suggested. Human rights would thus supplant and, hopefully, consume the idea of "'fairness' among nation-states" in international discussion.[8]

Many oil elites had an altogether different perspective. The sovereign rights program had been profitable for them in the 1970s, despite serious misgivings between Saudi Arabia and the other producers and a host of other problems. "In view of the radically changed circumstances since the establishment of OPEC in 1960," the oil ministers collectively began to formulate a long-term strategy in 1978 and 1979. They and their "group of experts" met nine times, and in his introduction to their final committee report Saudi Oil Minister Ahmed Zaki Yamani noted that OPEC had "more than achieved its initial objectives." They now had "full control over all aspects of their oil industries, including the key decisions of pricing, production levels, and investment."[9]

For oil elites, the economic culture of decolonization had transformed from an elusive mind-set into a particular policy program and, now, into an unequivocal mandate. But even as the oratorio of self-praise welled high, chords of dissatisfaction could be heard. As the Acting Director of the OPEC's Information Department, Amir Kubbah wrote a semiofficial history of OPEC in 1974. Kubbah had shut down his journal and left Iraq in 1968 upon the Ba'athist ascension in national politics and Francisco Parra, then serving as Secretary General of OPEC, hired him to continue his earlier work on building "oil consciousness." His position gave him a front-row seat to the major events of the 1970s, and his analysis of that moment modeled itself on the histories of petroleum colonization and decolonization written in the previous two decades. The old oil concessions had been granted "under duress" and were therefore fundamentally illegitimate, he wrote. When the Third World nations "finally shook off the yoke of foreign suzerainty and achieved political independence," they found themselves heirs to these and other "very unjust" agreements. It was not surprising that under those circumstances the producing countries were imbued by a "growing oil consciousness" and sought to amend the terms

---

[8] Cooper to Vance, June 11, 1977, *FRUS 1977–80*, vol. III, doc. 266; Lake to Vance, "Supplementary Information for PRM-8 (North-South)," July 27, 1977, RG 59, Policy Planning Staff: Office of the Director, Records of Anthony Lake, box 2, NARA.

[9] OPEC, Report of the Group of Experts, Submitted to and Approved by the Fourth Meeting of the Ministerial Committee on Long-Term Strategy, February 22, 1980, Papers of Sidney Dell, Special Collections, Bodleian Library.

of trade for their oil. Key to that sensibility was the emergence of a new class of experts. That group – "through education, experience, and frequent consultations among themselves" – became increasingly aware that they had the means to redirect the past.[10]

The success of the oil producers had begun with the First Arab Petroleum Congress in 1959, Kubbah wrote, when "hundreds of Arab and non-Arab oil technocrats, company executives, government representatives and others attended that mammoth meeting." The ability of the oil producers to control price, which he dated to the 1970 negotiations between Maghribi and the oil companies, also softened his criticism of OPEC in the 1960s as hidebound by national difference. Rather than a reflection of the weakness of what he had once called the "sick colossus in Geneva," the early victories were now described as "hard-won." Nevertheless, Kubbah held a certain counterfactual resentment. Had the member countries "manipulated supply" in the mid-1960s, as Tariki had suggested forcefully at the 1965 Arab Petroleum Congress, the problem of sovereign debt might have been less acute. For him, the "history of OPEC and the pattern of relationships between the Third World and developed countries would have now been different beyond recognition." Unfortunately, given the course of events after 1973, the international economy was still characterized by gross injustice.[11]

But most other oil elites were less wistful. Rene Ortiz, the Secretary General from 1979 to 1980, emphasized the historical link between the oil producers and the Third World in a 1979 press conference in Quito, Ecuador. His history of petroleum colonization lined up with the earlier ones. OPEC had been founded as "a justified reaction" to the loss of power that resulted from the old concessions. Gradual gains characterized its first decade, and the 1970s marked the "major achievements" of the organization. A "new and deeper dimension" of that historical path had been laid out by Libya in 1970, and then by the other OPEC members in the 1971 Tehran and Tripoli agreements, and finally in the enforcement of "the sovereignty of the Member Countries to determine petroleum prices" in late 1973 and early 1974.[12]

---

[10] Kubbah, *OPEC, Past and Present*, 9–10, 87.
[11] Kubbah, *OPEC, Past and Present*, 8, 37.
[12] "OPEC: The Unparalleled Achievements of an Organization of Third World Countries," *Viewpoint, Selection of Speeches by Rene G. Ortiz, OPEC Secretary General, 1979–80*, OIC.

The achievements of OPEC, for Ortiz, were part of "a quiet revolution" that enveloped the organization and, more to the point, "the historical forces it represents." Then he took the history further. The use of collective sovereignty to overturn economic injustice was "a seed, planted by OPEC" that in turn "grew its roots with the establishment" of the New International Economic Order.[13]

In a way, such statements rang hollow by the late 1970s. By then most observers agreed that the victory of the OPEC nations marked the end of an era of heroic expectations for decolonization. Carlos Romulo, who a quarter century earlier had provided an important firsthand account of the Afro-Asian conference in Bandung, wrote to Gamani Corea in December 1978 that he hoped but doubted the UN Conference on Trade and Development could "harmonize the positions of the developing countries in Africa, Asia, and Latin America" in its 1979 meeting in Arusha, Tanzania.[14]

The conference had many of the trappings of the ones that had preceded it in previous decades. To host the meeting, the Tanzanian government contracted the construction of a new "village hotel." The organizers also ensured that the local staff at the new Arusha conference center, especially typists and telephonists, had working knowledge of at least two or more of the official languages of the meeting – English, French, Spanish, and Arabic.[15]

But the Arusha conference was also different. It had a more circumspect and, at the same time, urgent tone. The delegates noted the difficulty of finding agreement on "action-oriented" policies that would "contribute effectively to the establishment of the New International Economic Order." Similarly, the ministers of foreign affairs of the Group of 77 pointed out their "grave concern [about] the aggravation of the negative trends in international economic relations." The situation, which they described as the most serious one since the end of World War II,

[13] *OPEC Chronology, 1960–1980*, OIC; "OPEC: The Unparalleled Achievements," OIC.
[14] Romulo to Corea, December 29, 1978, ARR 40/1842, box 171, TDO 444/1(4), UNA-G; E. Mbuli, Note for the File, July 31, 1978, ARR 40/1842, box 171, TDO 444/1(4), UNA-G; Report of the UNOG/UNCTAD Mission to Tanzania, June 29, 1978, ARR 40/1842, box 171, TDO 444/1(4), UNA-G.
[15] Romulo to Corea, December 29, 1978, ARR 40/1842, box 171, TDO 444/1(4), UNA-G; E. Mbuli, Note for the File, July 31, 1978, ARR 40/1842, box 171, TDO 444/1(4), UNA-G; Report of the UNOG/UNCTAD Mission to Tanzania, June 29, 1978, ARR 40/1842, box 171, TDO 444/1(4), UNA-G.

resulted largely from the "persistent lack of equity in international economic relations" and the refusal of the United States and other industrialized nations "to recognize the right of developing countries in international economic relations." That problem had been exacerbated by higher oil prices. Not only had the Ford administration and then the Carter administration placed upon the poor nations a "disproportionately large share of the burden of adjustment" to oil prices, the United States had hardened its attitude toward the New Order. This killed progress on the laundry list of past-cum-present ills: "colonialism, imperialism, neocolonialism, interference in internal affairs, apartheid, racism, racial discrimination, and all forms of foreign aggression . . . which constitute major obstacles to the economic emancipation of the developing countries." In short, the OPEC members made unconvincing Robin Hoods, while the United States and other industrial powers had resisted calls for economic justice. Moreover, US strategy had effectively shifted the focus of the international community away from "genuine economic problems and the negotiations on the establishment of a New International Economic Order" to the contrary concept of sovereign debt.[16]

The problem was evident to Julius Nyerere, the president of Tanzania, and Michael Manley, the Prime Minister of Jamaica. The two men met in Arusha, and during their conversation they both attacked the continuity of the old economic order and the failure of the new. For Nyerere in particular, the "terms of trade" for raw materials other than oil had worsened. New proposals for relieving national debt that had come out of the US Treasury and, more recently, the International Monetary Fund ignored the structural problems of the international economy. They were "market-oriented," he said, "and, therefore, not ideologically neutral." Manley agreed. Such market-oriented prescriptions, while preaching their objective neutrality, were "designed for developed capitalist economies," not the poor nations.[17]

Despite this widespread sense of failure, others attempted to rescue something from the wreckage. One final example stands out. Jean Schwoebel,

---

[16] Draft Resolution, Report of the UN Conference on Trade and Development on Its Fifth Session, n.d. (October 30, 1979), ARR 40/1842, box 170, TDO 444, Correspondence with or Concerning Group of 77, UNA-G; "Declaration of the Ministers for Foreign Affairs of the Group of 77," n.d. (September 28, 1979), ARR 40/1842, box 170, TDO 444, Correspondence with or Concerning Group of 77, UNA-G

[17] Michael J. Stopford, Summary of Issue No. 2 of "Development Dialogue, September 1, 1980, S-0972-0004-12, UNA-NY.

the radical editor of *Le Monde*, wrote to UN Secretary General Kurt Waldheim in 1977 to suggest the mass publication of a newspaper insert for "major world newspapers" that explained the objectives of the New International Economic Order. When Schwoebel wrote, he had already lined up editors in Belgrade, Cairo, Mexico City, Milan, Frankfurt, New Delhi, London, Tokyo, and Dakar – all of whom were willing to publish translated versions of the insert. Waldheim agreed that the creation of a world newspaper insert designed to "advocate and promote a new world economic order" was a good idea. But he balked at Schwoebel's estimated cost of nearly $1 million dollars.[18]

Then Japanese shipbuilding magnate and Nippon Foundation philanthropist Ryoichi Sasakawa agreed to pay for the insert, and Waldheim gave the project a green light. By the beginning of 1979, Schwoebel had also secured agreements from newspapers in Spain, Brazil, Algeria, Hungary, Pakistan, and the United States. The insert would be a "dramatic means to bring to light the fundamentally innovative character of this enterprise of unprecedented cooperation for the common good of humanity," Schwoebel wrote Waldheim. He estimated the total circulation in the sixteen countries to be greater than 10 million copies.[19]

Schwoebel wrote in the lead article of the supplement, "Towards One World," that the New Order "measured up to the breadth of the challenges of modern times." But Waldheim's tone in the initial draft of his introductory message was strikingly less positive. "The world economic situation, regrettably, gives us no cause of optimism," he wrote. Awareness of the need for "far reaching modifications in the framework to international economic relations" had, quite simply, not translated into "positive joint action." The editor of the Algerian newspaper *El Moudjahid*, Mohamed Benchicou, spoke in even harsher terms in his introduction to the Algerian insert. "Time moves on, however, and brings out the truth," he wrote. His truth was that "the secular process

---

[18] Schwoebel to Waldheim, January 23, 1978, S-0972-0005-1, UNA-NY; Waldheim to Schwoebel, February 22, 1978, S-0972-0005-1, UNA-NY; Francois Giuliani, Interoffice Memorandum, "Mr. Schwoebel's Letter," February 11, 1978, S-0972-0005-1, UNA-NY; Francois Giuliani, "Note for the Secretary General," June 22, 1978, S-0972-0005-1, UNA-NY; Genichi Akatani to Waldheim, Interoffice Memorandum, "World Newspaper Supplement," June 19, 1978, S-0972-0005-1, UNA-NY.

[19] Telegram, Sasakawa to Waldheim, August 9, 1978, S-0972-0005-1, UNA; Waldheim to Sasakawa, September 14, 1978, S-0972-0005-1, UNA-NY; Schwoebel to Waldheim, January 23, 1978, S-0972-0005-1, UNA-NY; Yasushi Akashi, UN Department of Public Information, to Sasakawa, August 14, 1979, S-0972-0005-1, UNA-NY.

euphemistically known as unequal exchange, but generally amounting to systematic plunder of the Third World's riches," continued unabated.[20]

In a very real and profound sense, Waldheim and Benchicou believed that the elites had failed to develop a political solidarity that could overcome their economic differences. UN Conference on Trade and Development Secretary General Gamani Corea shared that opinion. He addressed the foreign ministers of the Non-Aligned Movement the same year in Belgrade, where they had convened to discuss the New International Economic Order. The purveyors of sovereign rights had "registered a measure of success" in securing the consent of the international community "to make these issues the subjects of a serious and intensive negotiating process," he admitted. Yet this meant little to him because no new agreements had been reached. "We cannot really be satisfied with what has been attained so far," he said. The failure of the poor nations to develop sustained and collective commodity policies was "one of the notable symptoms of the malfunctioning and malaise of the international economy."[21]

The proclamation of a New International Economic Order was like an incandescent light bulb that flares just before fizzling out. That OPEC's success was so thoroughly imbued with the spirit of sovereign rights meant that the subsequent failures to emulate it, not to mention the rise of sovereign debt, were all the more devastating. To make matters worse, as Corea noted, the problems of the Third World were wrapped in the mantle of the economic culture of decolonization. The taking on of sovereign debt, which transformed in scale because of high oil prices, was literally the giving away of sovereignty. The anticolonial elites' sense of this problem was acute and, often, their despair was viral. This was in part because sovereign debt discredited the universal claims about the ineluctable power of sovereignty.

Sovereign rights thus foundered on the shoals of its own contradiction between loyalty based on political principle and the capacity of economic circumstances to compel choice in the opposite direction. The right to

[20] Jean Schwoebel, "Towards One World," *One World: Supplement for a New International Economic Order*, Number 1, July 1979, S-0972-0005-1, UNA-NY; UN Cable, Rohan to UNIDO (Vienna), May 16, 1979, S-0972-0005-1, UNA-NY; Mohamed Benchicou, "Basic Truths," *One World: Supplement for a New International Economic Order*, Number 1, July 1979, S-0972-0005-1, UNA-NY.
[21] Conference of Ministers for Foreign Affairs of Non-Aligned Countries, "Statement by Mr. Gamani Corea," July 26, 1978, ARR 40/1862, box 305, TD 525(2), UNA-G.

sovereignty – considered all at once the rejection of colonialism, the epitome of the age of decolonization, and a prolific weapon in the fight for development – was now a liability. The cursed reality was that once-illuminating ideas were now imprisoning.

That sort of conclusion, common at the time, raises an interesting set of question for historians. For even if the sovereign rights program was so easily snuffed out, its history is more than a narrative of the life and death of a set of beliefs. When the sovereign rights program took form in the 1950s and 1960s, it corresponded to the new realities of the age of decolonization. For the anticolonial elites poised at the end of empire, the drive to make statehood more meaningful was a cultural and intellectual project that existed on an international scale. It may have been, at times, a muddled amalgam of utopian ideas and moral indignation, but it was never just a prelude to failure. Rather, the oil revolution, the fall of sovereign rights, and the rise of sovereign debt reveal that the idea of a more moral, decolonized economy was precisely that – an idea.

For the Algerian jurist Mohammed Bedjaoui, the fact that the consensus on the New International Economic Order was partly fictive mattered less than another consideration. This was that colonialism had been deprived of political legitimacy for all time. In a 1976 tract on the Non-Aligned Movement and international law, again written under the auspices of the Carnegie Foundation, he made that argument. He dedicated the book to former Chilean President Salvador Allende, using the phrase coined by Régis Debray in his martyr's tribute – *mort dans sa loi*, "dead by his own law." The coup in Chile thus had a meaning that extended far beyond its geographic location. "[T]he major revolution of our time that began with decolonization" had not ended, Bedjaoui wrote. The process of self-assertion instead was a first step that "enriched the content of cardinal notions like that of sovereignty." That way of looking at the world, ingrained over a quarter century and expressed in the New Order, promised lasting consequences. Chief among them was the belief that, even if "economic imperialism" continued to mold the structure of international relations, the "new political phenomenon" of decolonization continued to enrich international affairs. New laws would continue to help overcome the tensions of the sovereign rights program, he predicted, if anticolonial elites could only show "solidarity and . . . a minimum of loyalty."[22]

---

[22] Bedjaoui, *Non-Alignment et Droit International*, 347, 349–50, 380, 444.

Bedjaoui reminds us that much remained of the spirit of the economic culture of decolonization and the sovereign rights movement. The New International Economic Order was not just a back eddy in the tide of time. The abstract and historical visions of oppression and liberation and the doctrines of unequal exchange, permanent sovereignty, and changing circumstances held a certain primacy in the world of ideas. From that optimistic perspective, the marginality of sovereign rights can be interpreted as being deceptively powerful. It ultimately compelled the prevailing hierarchies of power to take it into account and even seek accommodation with it.

In a later work commissioned by the United Nations, Bedjaoui described "the deterioration of the terms of trade" as "the new form of slavery of modern times." Like other anticolonial elites, he understood the international order as an oligarchic one driven by a historical relationship between exploiters and the exploited. That history was driven by what he described as the colonial right of confiscation, was based on the supremacy of Europe and the subjugation of non-Europeans, and was as decisive a turning point in world history as the constitution of colonial empires following the industrial revolution. But by the same token first decolonization and then "the strength conferred upon the LDCs by their joint action in world affairs" could also be a turning point and, as it already had, could continue to offer the elites opportunities to be "instruments of change."[23]

Bedjaoui found truth, then, not just in the harsh fact of failure. Truth was also in the conceptual and moral stakes that stood behind decolonization, its economic culture, and the program of sovereign rights. The oil revolution and the New Order were not discrete events from this perspective, but rather parts of an ongoing and complex process of decolonization that had begun a quarter century earlier. More than that, sovereign rights was the first broad-based program to seriously address the economic legacy of formal and informal imperialism. From the 1950s to the 1970s, the anticolonial elites had created a program that sought to be at once radical and humane – they insisted that the international community had some responsibility for the common welfare and, in doing so, they built a full-fledged project to those ends that cut across traditional barriers. If there was a past for such an effort, Bedjaoui and others believed, there might be a future.

---

[23] Mohammed Bedjaoui, *Towards a New International Economic Order* (London: Meier, 1979), 13–4, 34–6.

Appendix I

Chronology

1949 Meeting of the Economic Commission of Latin America, Havana, Cuba
1951 International Court of Justice hears Anglo-Iranian Oil Case
1951 Mossadegh addresses the UN Security Council
1952 Meetings of the Economic and Financial Committee, UN General Assembly, New York
1955 Meetings of the Third Committee, UN General Assembly, New York
1955 Afro-Asian Summit, Bandung, Indonesia
1955 Meeting of the Arab League's Oil Experts Committee
1955 Libyan Petroleum Law passed
1957 Meeting of the Arab League's Oil Experts Committee
1958 Iraqi Revolution
1958 First Meeting of the Economic Commission, Afro-Asian People's Solidarity Organization
1958 United Nations, Convention on the Territorial Sea
1959 First Arab Petroleum Congress, Cairo, Egypt
1959 First Meeting of the UN Permanent Sovereignty Commission
1959 Meeting of the Arab League's Oil Experts Committee
1960 Founding of the Organization of Petroleum Exporting Countries, Baghdad, Iraq
1960 Second Arab Petroleum Congress, Beirut, Lebanon
1961 First Report of UN Permanent Sovereignty Commission
1962 First Meeting of the Nonaligned Movement's Economic Commission, Cairo, Egypt
1963 First Meeting of OPEC on Royalty Negotiations
1963 Fourth Arab Petroleum Congress, Beirut, Lebanon

1963 Meeting of the Economic Committee of the Organization of African Unity, Naimey, Niger

1963 Meetings of the UN Economic and Social Council, New York

1964 First Summit of the UN Conference on Trade and Development, Geneva, Switzerland

1964 Non-Aligned Movement, Summit Meeting, Cairo, Egypt

1964 OPEC Ministerial Meeting, Djakarta, Indonesia

1965 Fifth Arab Petroleum Congress, Beirut, Lebanon

1966 Permanent Sovereignty Revolution passed by UN General Assembly, New York

1967 Arab Oil Embargo

1967 Meetings of the Economic Commission for Africa, the Economic Commission for Asia and the Far East, and the Economic Commission for Latin America

1967 Ministerial Meeting of the Group of 77, Algiers, Algeria

1968 OPEC Declaratory Statement published

1968 Second Summit of the UN Conference on Trade and Development, New Delhi, India

1968 Founding Meeting of the Organization of Arab Petroleum Exporting Countries, Beirut, Lebanon

1969 Libyan Revolution

1970 Meeting of Foreign Ministers of the Non-Aligned Movement, Dar es-Salaam, Tanzania

1970 OPEC Ministerial Meeting, Algiers, Algeria

1970 OPEC Ministerial Meeting, Caracas, Venezuela

1971 OPEC Oil Agreements signed, Tehran, Iran, and Tripoli, Libya

1971 Meeting of the Algerian Bar Association, Algiers, Algeria

1971 International Hydrocarbons Conference, Algiers, Algeria

1971 Ministerial Meeting of the Group of 77, Lima, Peru

1971 Libyan Oil Nationalization

1972 Iraqi Oil Nationalization

1972 Third Summit of the UN Conference on Trade and Development, Santiago, Chile

1973 Arab Oil Embargo begins

1974 Sixth Special Session of the United Nations General Assembly

1975 Seventh Special Session of the United Nations General Assembly

1975 First Meeting of the Conference on International Economic Cooperation

1976 Ministerial Meeting of the Group of 77, Manila, Philippines

1977 Last Meeting of the Conference on International Economic Cooperation

Appendix II

Anticolonial Elites
(In Order of Appearance)

Name	Nationality, Education	Position(s)	Percent of National Population with Tertiary Schooling[1]
Djalal Abdoh	Iran; SJD, University of Paris, 1937	UN Representative, Iran	.55
Mostafa Fateh	Iran; MA, Columbia University, 1919	Anglo-Iranian Oil Company	.55
Raúl Prebisch	Argentina; PhD, University of Buenos Aires, 1922	Secretary, Economic Commission for Latin America; Secretary, UN Conference on Trade and Development	3.00

(continued)

[1] Statistics for the population aged 25 and over in the year 1960 that had any post-secondary education. Data from Robert J. Barro and Jong-Wha Lee, "Educational Attainment for Total Population, 1950–2010," data set version 1.3, attached to "A New Data Set of Educational Attainment in the World, 1950–2010," *NBER* Working Paper 15902 (April 2010). In the starred cases, nation-specific data were not available and I have substituted the regional average. The ratio of female-to-male tertiary students in the Middle East and North Africa was 41.5 percent, in Latin America and the Caribbean, 86.7 percent.

(continued)

Name	Nationality, Education	Position(s)	Percent of National Population with Tertiary Schooling[1]
Hla Myint	Burma; PhD, London School of Economics, 1945	Professor, Rector, University of Rangoon	.34
Jamil Baroody	Lebanon; MA, American University of Beirut, 1926	UN Representative, Saudi Arabia	1.2*
Abdul Rahman Pazhwak	Afghanistan; Habibia, Lycee, 1930	UN Representative, Afghanistan	.59
Abdul Khalek Hassouna	Egypt; PhD, Cambridge University, 1925	President, Arab League	1.79
Mohammed Salman	Iraq; Education not known by author	Director, Arab League Petroleum Committee; Oil Minister, Iraq	.78
Abdullah al-Tariki	Saudi Arabia; MA, The University of Texas at Austin, 1948	Minister of Petroleum and Mineral Resources; Independent Consultant	4.52
Anes Qasem	Palestine; LL.M, University of London, 1949; PhD, University of London, 1969	Group of Experts, Arab League Petroleum Bureau; Lawyer, Libya	1.2*
Juan Pablo Pérez Alfonso	Venezuela; PhD, Universidad Central de Venezuela, 1925	Director of Mines and Hydrocarbons, Venezuela	1.50
Ashraf Lufti	Palestine; BA, Scots College, Safa, Palestine, 1937	Director of Oil Affairs, Kuwait; OPEC, Secretary General	1.2

Name	Nationality, Education	Position(s)	Percent of National Population with Tertiary Schooling[1]
Fuad Rouhani	Iran; SJD, University of London, 1925	OPEC, Secretary General	.55
Nadim Pachachi	Iraq; PhD, Imperial College of Science and Technology, University of London, 1938	Director of Oil Affairs, Iraq; Secretary General, OPEC; Consultant, Iraq and Libya	.78
Feisal Mazidi	Kuwait; BA, Keele University, 1958	Finance Ministry, Kuwait	3.77
Francisco Parra	Venezuela; PhD, Graduate Institute of International Studies, Geneva, 1966	Secretary General, OPEC	1.50
Abdul Amir Kubbah	Iraq; ABD, New York University, 1954	Department of Petroleum Affairs, Libya; Information Office, OPEC	.78
Ahmed Zaki Yamani	Saudi Arabia; MA, NYU Law School, 1955; MA, Harvard Law School, 1956	Oil Minister, Saudi Arabia	4.52
Kifle Wodajo	Ethiopia; MA, University of Wisconsin, 1959	Secretary General, Organization of African States	1.2*
Mohammed Mughraby	Lebanon/Palestine; SJD, Columbia University, 1966	Professor, American University, Beirut; Lawyer and Activist	1.2*

(*continued*)

(*continued*)

Name	Nationality, Education	Position(s)	Percent of National Population with Tertiary Schooling[1]
Jorge Castañeda	Mexico; JD, Universidad Nacional Autónoma de México, 1943	UN, International Law Commission	1.34
Mohammed Bedjaoui	Algeria; SJD, Centre National de la Recherche Scientifique, Paris, 1958	UN, International Law Commission	.33
Hasan Zakariya	Iraq; SJD, Harvard Law School, 1954	OPEC, Director of Legal Department	.78
Mahmood Maghribi	Libya; SJD, George Washington University, 1966	Standard Oil; Revolutionary Command Council, Libya	.20
Jamshid Amouzegar	Iran; MA, University of Washington; PhD, Cornell	International Monetary Fund; Finance Minister, Iran	.55
Nicolas Sarkis	Lebanon; PhD, University of Paris, 1960	Independent Consultant	1.2*
Pérez-Guerrero, Manuel	Venezuela; PhD, University of Paris, 1936	United Nations, Conference on Trade and Development	.15

Bibliography

PRIMARY SOURCES

Archives

Archives of the International Monetary Fund, Washington, DC
Country Reports
Executive Board Minutes
Oil Facility Records
World Reports

Dolph Briscoe Center for American History, The University of Texas at Austin, Austin, TX
ExxonMobil Historical Collection
Texas Independent Producers and Royalty Owners Association Records

Gerald Ford Presidential Library, Ann Arbor, MI
Arthur F. Burns Papers
L. William Seidman Files
National Security Adviser's Files: Kissinger-Scowcroft West Wing Office Files, 1974–77
National Security Adviser's Files: Memoranda of Conversations, 1973–77
National Security Adviser's Files: Presidential Agency Files, 1974–77
Presidential Handwriting File
Records of the Council of Economic Advisers: Alan Greenspan Files

Library of Congress, Manuscripts Division, Washington, DC
Daniel Patrick Moynihan Papers
NBC Television Collection
Robert S. McNamara Papers

Lyndon Baines Johnson Presidential Library, Austin, TX
National Security Files
White House Central Files

National Archives of the United Kingdom, Kew, England
Foreign and Commonwealth Office: Commodities and Oil Department, 1968–73
Foreign and Commonwealth Office: Energy Department, 1974–81
Prime Minister's Office: Correspondence and Papers, 1964–70
Prime Minister's Office: Correspondence and Papers, 1970–74

Nettie Lee Benson Library, The University of Texas at Austin, Austin, TX
Raúl Prebisch Working Papers

Organization of Petroleum Exporting Countries, Information Center, Vienna, Austria
Inter-OPEC Newsletter
Official Resolutions and Press Releases
OPEC *Annual Review and Record*
OPEC Seminar Papers
Public Relations Pamphlets
Public Relations Department: Photo Archive
Selected Documents on the International Petroleum Industry

Richard Nixon Presidential Library, Yorba Linda, California
National Security Council Files: Country Files
National Security Council Files: Institutional Files
National Security Council Files: Subject Files
White House Special Files: Staff Member Office Files: Flanigan Subject Files
White House Special Files: President's Office Files

National Archive and Records Administration of the United States, College Park, MD
Record Group 59: Department of State Records, Central Files
Central Foreign Policy Files, 1967–69
Electronic Telegrams, 1973–76
Policy Planning Council, Director's Files, 1969–77
Policy Planning Council, Director's Files, 1977–80
Subject-Numeric Files, 1970–73
Subject-Numeric Files, 1973–76

Seely G. Mudd Manuscript Library, Princeton University, Princeton, NJ
George Kennan Papers

Special Collections, Bodleian Library, Oxford University, Oxford, England
Papers of Sidney Dell

Tamiment Library Archives, New York University, New York, NY
Printed Ephemera Collection of Government Publications
Reference Center for Marxist Studies, Pamphlet Collection

United Nations Library, Geneva, Switzerland
Commission on Permanent Sovereignty over Natural Resources, Official Records
Conference on the Law of the Sea, Official Records

Conference on Trade and Development, Official Records
Conference on Trade and Development, Summary Records
Economic and Social Council, Official Records
General Assembly, Official Records
General Legal Division, Official Reports
International Court of Justice, Official Records
International Law Commission, Official Reports
Office of Public Information, Weekly News Summaries
Security Council, Minutes

United Nations Organization Archive, New York, NY
Records of the Secretary General
Records of the United Nations Institute of Training and Research

United Nations Organization Archive, Geneva, Switzerland
Records of the Conference on Trade and Development, Boxes
Records of the Conference on Trade and Development, Inter-Office Memoranda
Records of the Conference on Trade and Development, Notebooks

Document Collections, Print

Barrows, Gordon H. *Middle East Basic Oil Laws and Concession Contracts: Original Texts* (New York: Petroleum Legislation, 1959).
Burdett, A.L.P., ed. *OPEC: Origins and Strategy, 1947–1973, Volumes I and II* (London: Archive Editions, 2004).
Indian Society of International Law. *Non-Aligned and Developing Countries (Basic Documents)* (New Delhi: Indian Society of International Law, 1970).
    The Asian-African States: Texts of International Declarations (New Delhi: Indian Society of International Law, 1965).
International Association of Democratic Lawyers. *Le Droit Pétrolier Et La Souveraineté Des Pays Producteurs, Alger, Octobre 1971* (Paris: Librairie Générale de Droit et de Jurisprudence, 1973).
League of Arab States, The Secretariat General, Department of Petroleum Affairs. *Papers of the First Arab Petroleum Congress*, 2 vols. (Cairo: The Egyptian Book Press, 1959).
League of Arab States, Second Arab Petroleum Congress. *Collection of Papers Submitted to the Congress, vol. I., Petroleum Economics, Legislation, and Other General Topics* (Cairo, 1961).
League of Arab States, Secretariat General. *Papers of the Fourth Arab Petroleum Congress* (Cairo, 1964).
    Papers of the Fifth Arab Petroleum Congress, March 16–23, 1965 (Cairo, 1965).
League of Arab States. *Study on the Fifth Arab Petroleum Congress* (Beirut: Bureau des Documentations Libanaises at Arabes, 1965).
    Seventh Arab Petroleum Congress, Volume I: Economics (Papers), March 16–22, 1970 (Cairo, 1970).

Moss, Alfred George and Harry M. N. Winton, eds. *A New International Economic Order, Selected Documents, 1945–1975*, vol. I (New York: United Nations Institute for Training and Research, 1975).

Non-Aligned Movement. *The Conference on the Problems of Economic Development* (Cairo, 1962).

Venezuela, General Secretariat of the Presidency of the Republic. *Venezuela and OPEC* (Caracas, 1961).

Document Collections, Digital

Cold War International History Project, Digital Archive

Declassified Documents Reference Service

Department of State, Historian's Office, *Foreign Relations of the United States*
  1952–1954, vol. X, *Iran, 1951–54*
  1958–1960, vol. IV, *Foreign Economic Policy*
  1961–1963, vol. XVII, *Near East, 1961–62*
  1964–1968, vol. XII, *Western Europe*
  1964–1968, vol. XXI, *Near East Region; Arabian Peninsula*
  1964–1968, vol. XXII, *Iran*
  1964–1968, vol. XXXI, *South and Central America; Mexico*
  1964–1968, vol. XXXIV, *Energy Diplomacy and Global Issues*
  1969–1976, vol. XXIV, *Middle East Region and Arabian Peninsula, 1969–72; Jordan, September 1970*
  1969–1976, vol. XXXI, *Foreign Economic Policy, 1973–76*
  1969–1976, vol. XXXVI, *Energy Crisis, 1969–74*
  1969–1976, vol. XXXVII, *Energy Crisis, 1974–80*
  1969–1976, vol. E-4, *Documents on Iran and Iraq, 1969–72*
  1969–1976, vol. E-6, *Documents on Africa, 1973–76*
  1969–1976, vol. E-8, *Documents on South Asia*
  1977–1980, vol. III, *Foreign Economic Policy*

Digital National Security Archive
  Iran: The Making of U.S. Policy, 1977–80
  Kissinger Transcripts
  Presidential Directives on National Security, Part II

Public Papers of the Presidents of the United States
  Papers of Lyndon Johnson
  Papers of Richard Nixon

Periodicals

  American Journal of International Law
  Arab Information: Newsletter of the Arab Information Center
  Arab Oil & Gas

Arab World: A Monthly Review of Progress in the Arab Countries
Barrow's Petroleum Legislation
Department of State Bulletin
Financial Times
International Affairs
Le Gaz et Le Pétrole Arabe
Middle East Forum
Middle East Economic Digest
Middle East Economic Survey
New York Times
Oil and Gas Journal
OPEC Bulletin
OPEC Record
Petroleum Intelligence Weekly
Petroleum Press Service
Petroleum: Journal of the European Oil Industry
Platt's Oilgram News
Review of Arab Petroleum Economics
The Arab World: The Journal of the Anglo Arab Association
The Economist
The Petroleum Economist
The Times (London)
The Washington Post
World Petroleum

Unpublished Theses and Published Primary Sources

Abdoh, Djalal. "L'élément psychologique dans les contrats suivant la conception iranienne," Thèse pour le doctorat, Universitè de Paris, Facultè de Droit (1937).

Badre, Albert Y. and Simon G. Siksek, *Manpower and Oil in Arab Countries* (Beirut: American University Beirut, 1959).

Baroody, Jamil M. "Middle East-Balance of Power versus World Government," *Annals of the American Academy of Political and Social Science* 264: *World Government* (July 1949).

Bedjaoui, Mohammed. *Fonction Publique Internationale et Influences Nationales*, Dotation Carnegie pour la Paix Internationale, Centre Européen (Paris: A. Pedone, 1958).

Law and the Algerian Revolution (Brussels: International Association of Democratic Lawyers, 1962).

Towards a New International Economic Order (London: Meier, 1979).

Castañeda, Jorge. *Mexico and the United Nations* (New York: Manhattan Publishing Company, 1958).

"Naciones Unidas y Derecho Internacional," *Foro Internacional* 1: 2 (October–December 1960).

"The Underdeveloped Nations and the Development of International Law," *International Organization* 38 (1961).

Corea, Gamani. *The Economic Structure in Ceylon in Relation to Fiscal Policy*, DPhil thesis, University of Oxford (1952).

Egaña, Manuel. *Tres Décadas de Producción Petrolera* (Caracas: Tipografía Americana, 1947).

Fateh, Mostafa Khan. "Taxation in Persia: A Synopsis from the Early Times to the Conquest of the Mongols," *Bulletin of the School of Oriental Studies* 4: 4 (1928): 723–43.

Friedmann, Wolfgang. *The Changing Structure of International Law* (New York: Columbia University Press, 1962).

"The Position of Underdeveloped Countries and the Universality of International Law," *Columbia Journal of Transnational Law* 2: 2 (1963): 78–86.

Furtado, Celso. *Dialectica do Desenvolviminto* (Rio de Janeiro: Fundo de Cultura, 1964).

Hammadi, Sadun Lawlah. *"Agricultural Taxation in Iraq,"* PhD dissertation, University of Wisconsin – Madison (1957).

Hassouna, Mohamed Abdel Khalek, *The First Asian-African Conference Held at Bandung Indonesia* (League of Arab States, 1955).

Hirschman, Albert O. "Investment Policies and 'Dualism' in Underdeveloped Countries," *The American Economic Review* 47: 5 (1957): 550–70.

The Strategy of Economic Development (New Haven: Yale University Press, 1958).

Hourani, Albert. "The Decline of the West in the Middle East," *International Affairs* 29: 1 (January 1953): 22–42.

Jessup, Philip C. *Parliamentary Diplomacy: An Examination of the Legal Quality of the Rules of Procedure of Organs of the United Nations* (Leyden: A. W. Sijhoff, 1956).

The Use of International Law (Thomas M. Cooley Lectures, University of Michigan Law School, 1959).

Transnational Law (New Haven, CT: Yale University Press, 1956).

Khadduri, Majid. "The Anglo-Egyptian Controversy," *Proceedings of the Academy of Political Science* 24: 4 (January 1952): 82–100.

Kubbah, Abdul Amir Q. *Libya: Its Oil Industry and Economic System* (Baghdad: The Arab Petro-Economic Research Centre, 1965).

OPEC, Past and Present (Vienna: Petro-Economic Research Centre, 1974).

Lewis, W. A. *Economic Survey, 1919–1939* (London: Tinling and Co., 1949).

Lufti, Ashraf. *Arab Oil: A Plan for the Future*, Middle East Monographs No. 3 (Beirut: The Middle East Research and Publishing Center, 1960).

Maghribi, Mahmood S. "Petroleum Legislation in Libya," SJD thesis, George Washington University (June 1966).

Malaviya, H. D. *Report on Problems of Economic Development of Afro-Asian Countries*, presented to the Second Conference of Afro-Asian Peoples' Solidarity, Conakry (Cairo: Dar el Hana Press, April 1960).

McFarland, Victor. *"The United States, Saudi Arabia, and Oil in the 1970s,"* PhD dissertation, Yale University (2013).

Mughraby, Muhamad. *Permanent Sovereignty over Oil Resources: A Study of Middle East Oil Concessions and Legal Change*, Middle East Oil Monographs No. 5 (Beirut: The Middle East Research and Publishing Center, 1966).

Myint, Hla. "The 'Classical Theory' of International Trade and the Underdeveloped Countries," *The Economic Journal* 68: 270 (1958): 317–37.

"The Gains from International Trade and the Backward Countries," *The Review of Economic Studies* 22: 2 (1954): 129–42.

"An Interpretation of Economic Backwardness," *Oxford Economic Papers* 6 (June 1954): 132–44.

Myrdal, Gunnar. *Asian Drama: An Enquiry into the Poverty of Nations*, vol. 1 (London: Pantheon, 1968).

The Dyason Lectures: Economic Nationalism and Internationalism (Canberra: The Australian Institute of International Affairs, 1957).

Economic Theory and Under-Developed Regions (London: Duckworth, 1957).

An International Economy: Problems and Prospects (New York: Harper and Brothers, 1956).

The Political Element in the Development of Economic Theory (London: Harper and Brothers, 1953).

Rich Lands and Poor: The Road to World Prosperity (New York: Harper and Brothers, 1957).

Nurkse, Ragnar. *Problems of Capital Formation in Underdeveloped Countries* (New York: Oxford University Press, 1953).

Pachachi, Nadim al-. *Iraqi Oil Policy: August 1954–December 1957* (Beirut: The Research and Translation Office, 1958).

Pazhwak, Rahman. *Aryana: Ancient Afghanistan* (London: Key Press, 1950).

Petroleum Commission. *Petroleum Development in Libya, 1954 through Mid-1960* (Tripoli: Government Press, n.d. [1960]).

Petroleum Development in Libya: 1954 through 1958 (Tripoli: Government Press, 1958).

Petroleum Development in Libya: 1954 through Mid-1961 (Tripoli: Petroleum Commission, 1961).

Prebisch, Raúl. *The Economic Development of Latin America and Its Principal Problems* (New York: United Nations, 1949).

Qasem, Anes Mustafa. "Habeas Corpus," L. L. M. thesis, University of London (1949).

"Petroleum Legislation in Libya," PhD dissertation, University of London (1969).

Rao, K. Krishna. *"The International Court of Justice and the Advisory Jurisdiction,"* SJD thesis, New York University (1955).

Republic of Iraq, *Oil and Minerals in Iraq* (Baghdad, 1970).

Rouhani, Fuad. *A History of O.P.E.C.* (New York: Praeger, 1971).

Sarkis, Nicolas. *"Le Pétrole Facteur D'Intégration et de Croissance Économique,"* Thése pour le Doctorat en Droit, Universite de Paris, Faculte de Droit et des Sciences Economiques (1962).

Siksek, Simon G. *The Legal Framework for Oil Concessions in the Arab World*, Middle East Oil Monographs No. 2 (Beirut: The Middle East Research and Publishing Center, 1960).

"Oil Concessions – An Arab View," *Middle East Forum* (July 1960): 36–8.

Siles, Luis Adolfo. *Bolivia en la ONU* (La Paz: Imprenta del Estado, 1966).

Wodajo, Kifle. "Ethiopia's Treaty Relations with Britain, France and Italy, 1884–1914," MA thesis, University of Wisconsin – Madison (1959).

Wolfe-Hunnicut, Brandon. *"The End of the Concessionary Regime: Oil and American Power in Iraq, 1958–1972,"* PhD dissertation, Stanford University (2011).

Zakariyya, Hasan S. "State Liability in Tort: A Comparative Study of the Development of Its Theory and Practice in the Anglo-American and French Laws," SJD thesis, Harvard Law School (1954).

BOOKS AND ARTICLES

Abdelrehim, Neveen, Josephine Maltby, and Steven Toms. "Corporate Social Responsibility and Corporate Control: The Anglo-Iranian Oil Company, 1933–1951," *Enterprise and Society* 12: 4 (2011): 824–62.

Abraham, Itty. "From Bandung to NAM: Non-Alignment and Indian Foreign Policy, 1947–65," *Commonwealth and Comparative Politics* 46: 2 (April 2008): 195–219.

Abrahamian, Ervand. *The Coup: 1953, the CIA, and the Roots of Modern U.S.-Iranian Relations* (New York: The New Press, 2013).

Iran between Two Revolutions (Princeton University Press, 1982).

Ademoglu, Daron and James A. Robinson. *Economic Origins of Dictatorship and Democracy* (New York: Cambridge University Press, 2005).

Akins, James E. "The Oil Crisis: This Time the Wolf Is Here," *Foreign Affairs* 51: 3 (1973).

Alnasrawi, Abbas. *Arab Nationalism, Oil, and the Political Economy of Dependency* (Westport, CT: Greenwood Press, 1991).

Alvandi, Roham. *Nixon, Kissinger, and the Shah: The United States and Iran in the Cold War* (New York: Oxford University Press, 2014).

Amouzegar, Jamshid. "'Comparative Advantage' Reconsidered," *The American Journal of Economics and Sociology* 26: 2 (April 1967).

Anderson, Irvine. *Aramco, the United States, and Saudi Arabia: A Study of the Dynamics of Foreign Oil Policy, 1933–1950* (Princeton University Press, 1981).

Anghie, Antony. *Imperialism, Sovereignty, and the Making of International Law* (New York: Cambridge University Press, 2004).

Arndt, H. W. "Development Economics before 1945," in J. Bhagwati and R. S. Eckhaus, eds., *Development and Planning: Essays in Honour of Paul Rosenstein-Rodan* (London: Allen & Unwin, 1972).

Economic Development: The History of an Idea (University of Chicago Press, 1987).

Aydin, Cemil. *The Politics of Anti-Westernism in Asia: Foundations of World Order in Pan-Islamic and Pan-Asian Thought* (New York: Columbia University Press, 2007).

Bablawi, Hazem. *The Rentier State in the Arab World* (Berkeley: University of California Press, 1990).

Balfour-Paul, Glen. *The End of Empire in the Middle East: Britain's Relinquishment of Power in Her Last Three Arab Dependencies* (New York: Cambridge University Press, 2004).

Bamberg, James H. *The History of the British Petroleum Company: Volume II, The Anglo-Iranian Years, 1928–1954* (Cambridge University Press, 1994).

Barbier, Edward B. *Natural Resources and Economic Development* (New York: Cambridge University Press, 2007).

Barrows, Gordon H. *Middle East Basic Oil Laws and Concession Contracts: Original Texts* (New York: Petroleum Legislation, 1959).

Bauer, P. T. *Equality, the Third World, and Economic Delusion* (Cambridge, MA: Harvard University Press, 1981).

Berger, Mark T. "After the Third World? History, Destiny and the Fate of Third Worldism," *Third World Quarterly* 25: 1 (2004): 9–39.

"The Nation-State and the Challenge of Global Capitalism," *Third World Quarterly* 22: 6 (2001): 889–907.

Bergsten, C. Fred. "The Response to the Third World," *Foreign Policy* (1974): 3–34.

"The Threat from the Third World," *Foreign Policy* 11 (1973): 102–24.

Bialer, Uri. *Oil and the Arab-Israeli Conflict* (New York: Palgrave Macmillan, 1998).

Bill, James A. *The Eagle and the Lion: The Tragedy of American-Iranian Relations* (New Haven, CT: Yale University Press, 1992).

Block, Fred "Political Choice and the Multiple 'Logics' of Capital," *Theory and Society* 15: 1/2 (January 1986): 175–92.

Bordo, Michael, Michael Oliver, and Ronald MacDonald, "Sterling in Crisis: 1964–1967," *NBER Working Paper Series* 14657 (January 2009), 8–10.

Borgwardt, Elizabeth. *A New Deal for the World: America's Vision for Human Rights* (Cambridge, MA.: Belknap Press, 2005).

Borstelmann, Thomas. *The Cold War and the Color Line: American Race Relations in the Global Arena* (Cambridge, MA: Harvard University Press, 2003).

Boué, Juan Carlos. "OPEC at (More Than) Fifty: The Long Road to Baghdad, and Beyond," *Oxford Energy Forum* 83 (2011): 16–18.

Bourdieu, Pierre and Loïc Wacquant. *The State Nobility: Elite Schools in the Field of Power* (Palo Alto, CA: Stanford University Press, 1998).

Bowie, Robert. *Suez 1956: International Crises and the Role of Law* (New York: Oxford University Press, 1974).

Bradley, Mark. *Imagining Vietnam and America: The Making of Postcolonial Vietnam, 1919–1950* (Chapel Hill: University of North Carolina Press, 2000).

Brands, H.W. *The Specter of Neutralism: The United States and the Emergence of the Third World, 1947–1960* (New York: Columbia University Press, 1989).

Brands, Hal. "Third World Politics in an Age of Global Turmoil: The Latin American Challenge to U.S. and Western Hegemony," *Diplomatic History* 32: 1 (January 2008).

The Unipolar Moment: U.S. Foreign Policy and the Rise of the Post-Cold War Order (Ithaca: Cornell University Press, 2016).

Bryce, Robert. *Cronies: Oil, the Bushes, and the Rise of Texas* (New York: PublicAffairs, 2005).

Byrne, Jeffrey James. *Mecca of Revolution: From the Algerian Front of the Third World's Cold War* (New York: Oxford University Press, 2015).

Chafer, Tony. "Education and Political Socialisation of a National-Colonial Political Elite in French West Africa, 1936–47," *The Journal of Imperial and Commonwealth History* 35: 3 (September 2007): 437–58.

Chamberlin, Paul T. *The Global Offensive: The United States, the PLO, and the Making of the New International Order* (New York: Oxford University Press, 2012).

Citino, Nathan J. *From Arab Nationalism to OPEC: Eisenhower, King Saud, and the Making of U.S.-Saudi Relations*, 2nd edn (Bloomington: Indiana University Press, 2005).

"Defending the 'Postwar Petroleum Order': The US, Britain, and the 1954 Saudi-Onassis Tanker Deal," *Diplomacy and Statecraft* 11 (July 2000): 137–60.

"Internationalist Oilmen, the Middle East, and the Remaking of American Liberalism, 1945–1953," *Business History Review* 84: 2 (2010): 227–51.

Clark, Gregory. *Farewell to Alms: A Brief Economic History of the World* (Princeton University Press, 2008).

Coates, Benjamin. *Legalist Empire: International Law and American Foreign Relations in the Early Twentieth Century* (New York: Oxford University Press, 2016).

Cohen, Benjamin J. *Question of Imperialism: The Political Economy of Dominance and Dependence* (New York: Basic Books, 1971).

"When Giants Clash: The OECD Financial Support Fund and the IMF," in Vinod K. Aggarwal, ed., *Institutional Designs for a Complex World: Bargaining, Linkages, and Nesting* (Ithaca, NY: Cornell University Press, 1998), 161–94.

Cooley, John K. *Libyan Sandstorm* (New York: Holt, Rinehart and Winston, 1982).

Cooper, Frederick. *Citizenship between Empire and Nation: Remaking France and French Africa, 1945–1960* (Princeton University Press, 2014).

Coronil, Fernando. *The Magical State: Nature, Money, and Modernity in Venezuela* (University of Chicago Press, 1997).

Cullather, Nicholas J. *The Hungry World: America's Cold War Battle Against Poverty in Asia* (Cambridge, MA.: Harvard University Press, 2010).

Illusions of Influence: The Political Economy of United States-Philippines Relations, 1942–1960 (Palo Alto, CA: Stanford University Press, 1994).

"Development? It's History," *Diplomatic History* 24: 4 (2000).

Dietrich, Christopher R. W. "'Arab Oil Belongs to the Arabs': Raw Material Sovereignty, Cold War Boundaries, and the Nationalisation of the Iraq

Petroleum Company, 1967–1973," *Diplomacy & Statecraft* 22: 3 (2011): 450–79.

"Oil Power and Economic Theologies: The United States and the Third World in the Wake of the Energy Crisis," *Diplomatic History* 40: 3 (2016): 500–29.

Dosman, Edgar J. *The Life and Times of Raúl Prebisch, 1901–1986* (Montreal: McGill-Queen's University Press, 2008), 471.

Dunning, Thad. *Crude Democracy: Natural Resource Wealth and Political Regimes* (New York: Cambridge University Press, 2008).

Easterly, William R. *The Elusive Quest for Growth: Economists' Adventures and Misadventures in the Tropics* (Cambridge, MA: MIT Press, 2001).

Elm, Mostafa. *Oil, Power, and Principle: The Iranian Nationalization and Its Aftermath* (Syracuse University Press, 1994).

Emerson, Rupert. *From Empire to Nation: The Rise to Self-Assertion of Asian and African Peoples* (Cambridge, MA: Harvard University Press, 1960).

Feis, Herbert. "Oil for Peace or War," *Foreign Affairs* 32: 3 (April 1954): 416–29.

Finnie, David H. *Desert Enterprise* (Cambridge, MA: Harvard University Press, 1958).

Ford Foundation, *A Time to Choose: America's Energy Future: A Final Report* (Cambridge, MA: Ballinger, 1974).

Ford, Alan W. *The Anglo-Iranian Oil Dispute of 1951–1952: A Study of the Role of Law in the Relations of States* (Berkeley: University of California Press, 1955).

Foucault, Michele. *Discipline and Punish: The Birth of the Prison*, trans. Alan Sheridan (New York: Pantheon, 1977).

Frank, Alison Fleig. *Oil Empire: Visions of Prosperity in Austrian Galicia* (Cambridge, MA: Harvard University Press, 2007).

Frank, Andre Gunder. *Capitalism and Underdevelopment in Latin America: Historical Studies of Chile and Brazil* (New York: Monthly Review Press, 1967).

  On Capitalist Underdevelopment (New York: Oxford University Press, 1975).

  "The Development of Underdevelopment," *Monthly Review* 18 (September 1966): 17–30.

Frankel, Herbert. *The Economic Impact on Underdeveloped Societies* (Cambridge, MA: Harvard University Press, 1953).

Frieden, Jeffry A. *Global Capitalism: Its Fall and Rise in the Twentieth Century* (New York: W. W. Norton, 2006).

Friedmann, Wolfgang. *The Changing Structure of International Law* (New York: Columbia University Press, 1962).

  "The Position of Underdeveloped Countries and the Universality of International Law," *Columbia Journal of Transnational Law* (1963): 76–86.

Furtado, Celso. *Dialectica do Desenvolviminto* (Fundo de Cultura: Rio de Janeiro, 1964).

Gallagher, John and Ronald Robinson, "The Imperialism of Free Trade," *Economic History Review* 6 (1953): 1–15.

Galpern, Steve. *Money, Oil, and Empire in the Middle East: Sterling and Postwar Imperialism, 1944–1971* (Cambridge University Press, 2009).

Galtung, Johan. "A Structural Theory of Imperialism," *Journal of Peace Research* 8: 2 (1971): 81–117.

Garavini, Giuliano. *After Empires: European Integration, Decolonization, and the Challenge from the Global South, 1957–1986* (Oxford University Press, 2012).

Gavin, Francis J. *Gold, Dollars, and Power: The Politics of International Monetary Relations* (Chapel Hill: University of North Carolina Press, 2004).

Gilman, Nils. *Mandarins of the Future: Modernization Theory in Cold War America* (Baltimore: Johns Hopkins University Press, 2003).

Golan, Galia. "The Soviet Union and the Outbreak of the June 1967 Six-Day War," *Journal of Cold War Studies* 8: 1 (2006): 3–19.

Gorman, Daniel. *The Emergence of International Society in the 1920s* (New York: Cambridge University Press, 2012).

Haberler, Gottfried. "Integration and Growth of the World Economy in Historical Perspective," *The American Economic Review* 54: 2, part 1 (March 1964), 1–22.

Hahn, Peter. *The United States, Great Britain, and Egypt, 1945–1956: Strategy and Diplomacy in the Early Cold War* (Chapel Hill: University of North Carolina Press, 1991).

Hallwood Paul, and Stuart W. Sinclair. *Oil, Debt, and Development: OPEC in the Third World* (London: Allen & Unwin, 1981).

Hancock, William Keith. *Wealth of Colonies* (Cambridge University Press, 2012 [1950]).

Harmer, Tanya. *Chile and the Inter-American Cold War* (Chapel Hill: University of North Carolina Press, 2011).

Hartshorn, J. E. *Politics and World Oil Economics* (New York: Praeger, 1962), 301.

Heiss, Mary Ann. *Empire and Nationhood: The United States, Great Britain, and Iranian Oil, 1950–1954* (New York: Columbia University Press, 1997).

Helleiner, Eric. *States and the Reemergence of Global Finance* (Ithaca, NY: Cornell University Press, 1994).

Hirschman, Albert O. *Essays in Trespassing: Economics to Politics and Beyond* (New York: Cambridge University Press, 1981).
  "Rival Interpretations of Market Society: Civilizing, Destructive or Feeble," *Journal of Economic Literature* 20: 4 (December 1982): 1463–84.
  The Strategy of Economic Development (New Haven, CT: Yale University Press, 1958).

Hobson, John A. *Imperialism: A Study* (London: Nisbet, 1902).

Hossain, Kamal and Subrata Roy Chowdhury, eds. *Permanent Sovereignty over Natural Resources in International Law: Principle and Practice* (New York: Pinter, 1984).

Huei, Pang Yang. "The Four Faces of Bandung: Detainees, Soldiers, Revolutionaries and Statesmen," *Journal of Contemporary Asia* 39: 1 (2009): 63–86.

Hunt, Lynn. *Politics, Culture, and Class in the French Revolution* (Berkeley: University of California Press, 1984).

Hurewitz, J. C. *Diplomacy in the Near and Middle East, A Documentary Record: 1914–1956*, vol. 2 (Princeton University Press, 1956).

Hurrell, Andrew. *One Global Order: Power, Values, and the Constitution of International Society* (New York: Oxford University Press, 2007).

Iriye, Akira. *Cultural Internationalism and World Order* (Baltimore: Johns Hopkins University Press, 2000).

Irwin, Ryan. *The Gordian Knot: Apartheid and the Unmaking of the Liberal World Order, 1960–1970* (New York: Oxford University Press, 2012).

Janson, G. H. *Nonalignment and the Afro-Asian States* (New York: Prager, 1966).

Jessup, Philip C. *The Use of International Law* (Thomas M. Cooley Lectures, University of Michigan Law School, 1959).

Johns, Andrew. "The Johnson Administration, the Shah of Iran, and the Changing Pattern of U.S.-Iranian Relations, 1965–1967: 'Tired of Being Treated like a Schoolboy,'" *Journal of Cold War Studies* 9: 2 (Spring 2007): 64–94.

Kahin, George McT. *The Asian-African Conference: Bandung, Indonesia, April 1955* (Ithaca, NY: Cornell University Press, 1956).

Kapstein, Ethan. *The Insecure Alliance: Energy Crises and Western Politics since 1944* (Oxford University Press, 1990).

Karl, Terry Lynn. *The Paradox of Plenty: Oil Booms and Petro-States* (Berkeley: University of California Press, 1997).

Kennedy, David. *A World of Struggle: How Power, Law, and Expertise Shape Global Political Economy* (Princeton University Press, 2016).

Khadduri, Majid. *Socialist Iraq: A Study in Iraqi Politics since 1968* (Washington DC: The Middle East Institute, 1981).

Koskenniemi, Martti. *The Gentle Civilizer of Nations: The Rise and Fall of International Law, 1870–1960* (New York: Cambridge University Press, 2001).

Kunz, Diane B. *The Economic Diplomacy of the Suez Crisis* (Chapel Hill: University of North Carolina Press, 1991).

Kuznets, Simon. *Economic Growth of Nations: Total Output and Production Structure* (Cambridge, MA: Harvard University Press, 1971).

Ladjevardi, Habib. *Labor Unions and Autocracy in Iran* (Syracuse University Press, 1985).

Laron, Guy. *Origins of the Suez Crisis: Postwar Development Diplomacy and the Struggle over Third World Industrialization, 1945–1956* (Washington, D.C.: Woodrow Wilson Center Press, 2013).

Laszlo, Ervin, ed. *The Obstacles to the New International Economic Order* (New York: Pergamon Press, 1980).

Latham, Michael E. *The Right Kind of Revolution: Modernization, Development, and US Foreign Policy from the Cold War to the Present* (Ithaca, NY: Cornell University Press, 2011).

Lawrence, Mark Atwood. "The Rise and Fall of Nonalignment," in *The Cold War in the Third World*, ed. Robert J. McMahon (New York: Oxford University Press, 2013).

Lee, Christopher J., ed. *Making a World after Empire: The Bandung Moment and Its Political Afterlives* (Columbus: Ohio University Press, 2010).

Leuchtenburg, William E. "Progressivism and Imperialism: The Progressive Movement and American Foreign Policy, 1898–1916," *The Mississippi Valley Historical Review* 39: 3 (1952): 483–504.

Levallois, Clement. "Why Were Biological Analogies in Economics 'A Bad Thing'? Edith Penrose's Battles against Social Darwinism and McCarthyism," *Science in Context* 24 (2011): 465–85.

Lewis, David Levering. *W. E. B. Du Bois: Biography of a Race, 1868–1919* (New York: Henry Holt, 1993).

Lewis, W. Arthur. "The State of Development Theory," *The American Economic Review* 74: 1 (March 1985).

Lissakers, Karin. *Banks, Borrowers, and the Establishment: A Revisionist Account of the Debt Crisis* (New York: Basic Books, 1993).

Little, Douglas. "Nasser Delenda Est: Lyndon Johnson, the Arabs, and the 1967 Six-Day War," in H. W. Brands, ed., *The Foreign Policies of Lyndon Johnson: Beyond Vietnam* (College Station: Texas A&M University Press, 1999).

"To the Shores of Tripoli: America, Qaddafi, and Libyan Revolution, 1969–1989," *The International History Review* 35: 1 (2013): 70–99.

Lodge, David. *Small World: An Academic Romance* (London: Secker and Warburg, 1984).

Lorca, Arnulf Becker. "Sovereignty Beyond the West: The End of Classical International Law," *Journal of the History of International Law* 13: 1 (2011): 7–73.

Louis, William Roger. "The British Withdrawal from the Gulf, 1967–71," *Journal of Imperial and Commonwealth History*, 31: 1 (2003): 83–108.

"The Imperialism of Decolonization," *Journal of Imperial and Commonwealth History* 22: 3 (1994): 462–511.

Love, Joseph. *Crafting the Third World: Theorizing Underdevelopment in Rumania and Brazil* (Palo Alto, CA: Stanford University Press, 1996).

Lozoya, Jorge, and A. K. Bhattacharya, eds. *Asia and the New International Economic Order* (New York: Pergamon Press, 1981).

Lozoya, Jorge, and Hector Cuadra, eds. *Africa, the Middle East, and the New International Economic Order* (New York: Pergamon Press, 1980).

Lukes, Steven. *Power: A Radical View*, 2nd edn (New York: Palgrave Macmillan, 2004 [1974]).

Maier, Charles. *In Search of Stability: Explorations in Historical Political Economy* (Cambridge University Press, 1987).

Manela, Erez. *The Wilsonian Moment: Self-Determination and the International Origins of Anti-Colonial Nationalism* (New York: Cambridge University Press, 2007).

Mattione, Richard P. *OPEC's Investments and the International Financial System* (New York: Brookings Institution, 1987).

Matusow, Alan. *Nixon's Economy: Booms, Busts, Dollars, and Votes* (Lawrence, University Press of Kansas, 1997).

Maxfield, Sylvia, and James H. Nolt. "Protectionism and the Internationalization of Capital: U.S. Sponsorship of Import Substitution Industrialization in the Philippines, Turkey and Argentina," *International Studies Quarterly* 34: 1 (March 1990): 49–81.

McAlister, Melani. *Epic Encounters: Culture, Media, and U.S. Interests in the Middle East since 1945* (Berkeley: University of California Press, 2005).

McFarland, Victor. "The NIEO, Interdependence, and Globalization," *Humanity: An International Journal of Human Rights, Humanitarianism, and Development* 6: 1 (Spring 2015): 217–33.

McMahon, Robert J. *Colonialism and Cold War: The United States and the Struggle for Indonesian Independence, 1945–49* (Ithaca, NY: Cornell University Press, 1981).

The Cold War on the Periphery: The United States, India, and Pakistan (New York: Columbia University Press, 1994).

Meadows, Donella H. *The Limits to Growth: A Report for the Club of Rome's Project on the Predicament of Mankind* (New York: Universe Books, 1974).

Miles, Kate. *The Origins of International Investment Law: Empire, Environment and the Safeguarding of Capital* (New York: Cambridge University Press, 2013).

Miller, Aaron David. *Search for Security: Saudi Arabian Oil and American Foreign Policy, 1939–1949* (Chapel Hill: University of North Carolina Press, 1980).

Mitchell, Timothy. *Carbon Democracy: Political Power in the Age of Oil* (New York: Verso, 2011).

Moon, Parker Thomas. "Raw Materials and Imperialism," *Proceedings of the Academy of Political Science in the City of New York* 12: 1, International Problems and Relations (July 1926), 180–7.

Syllabus on International Relations (New York: Macmillan, 1926).

Moyn, Samuel. "Knowledge and Politics in International Law," *Harvard Law Review* 129: 8 (June 2016): 2164–89.

Moynihan, Daniel Patrick. "The United States in Opposition," *Commentary* (March 1975), 31–40.

Muller, Maarten H. "Compensation for Nationalization: A North-South Dialogue," *Columbia Journal of Transnational Law* 19: 1 (1981): 43–5.

Nguyen, Lien-Hang T. *Hanoi's War: An International History of the War for Peace in Vietnam* (Chapel Hill: University of North Carolina Press, 2012).

Nye, Jr., Joseph S. "Energy Nightmares," *Foreign Policy* (1980): 132–54.

"UNCTAD: Poor Nations' Pressure Group," in Robert Cox and Harold Jacobson, *The Anatomy of Influence* (New Haven, CT: Yale University Press, 1973).

Odom, William. "The Cold War Origins of the U.S. Central Command," *The Journal of Cold War Studies* 8: 2 (2006).

Packenham, Robert A. *The Dependency Movement: Scholarship and Politics in Development Studies* (Cambridge, MA: Harvard University Press, 1998).

Pahuja, Sundhya. *Decolonising International Law: Development, Economic Growth, and the Politics of Universality* (New York: Cambridge University Press, 2011).

Painter, David S. "Oil and World Power," *Diplomatic History* 17 (Winter 1993): 159–70.

Oil and the American Century: The Political Economy of U.S. Foreign Oil Policy, 1941–1954 (Baltimore: Johns Hopkins University Press, 1986).

Parker, Jason. "Cold War II: The Eisenhower Administration, the Bandung Conference, and the Reperiodization of the Postwar Era," *Diplomatic History* 30: 5 (November 2006): 867–92.

Pederson, Susan. "Getting Out of Iraq – in 1932: The League of Nations and the Road to Normative Statehood," *The American Historical Review* 115: 4 (2010): 975–1000.

Penrose, Edith. *The Large International Firm in Developing Countries: The International Petroleum Industry* (Cambridge, MA: MIT Press, 1970).

Pham, Phuong. *Ending "East of Suez": The British Decision to Withdraw from Malaysia and Singapore, 1964–1968* (Oxford University Press, 2010).

Pocock, J.G.A. *The Machiavellian Moment: Florentine Political Thought and the Atlantic Republican Tradition* (Princeton University Press, 2009).

Polanyi, Karl, C. M. Arensberg, and H. W. Pearson, eds. *Trade and Markets in the Early Empires* (Glencoe, IL: Free Press, 1957).

Popp, Roland. "Stumbling Decidedly into the Six-Day War," *Middle East Journal* 60: 2 (Spring 2006): 281–309.

Priest, Tyler. *Global Gambits: Big Steel and the U.S. Quest for Manganese* (New York: Praeger, 2003).

Rabe, Stephen G. *The Killing Zone: The United States Wages Cold War in Latin America* (New York: Oxford University Press, 2012).

   The Road to OPEC: United States Relations with Venezuela, 1919–1976 (Austin: University of Texas Press, 1982).

Rajak, Svetozar. "No Bargaining Chips, No Spheres of Interest: The Yugoslav Origins of Cold War Non-Alignment," *Journal of Cold War Studies* 16: 1 (2014): 146–79.

Rakove, Robert B. *Kennedy, Johnson, and the Nonaligned World* (New York: Cambridge University Press, 2013).

Ramazani, Rouholla K. *Iran's Foreign Policy: A Study of Foreign Policy in Modernizing Nations* (Charlottesville: University of Virginia Press, 1975).

Robertson, Tom. "'This is the American Earth': The American Empire, the Cold War, and American Environmentalism," *Diplomatic History* 32: 4 (2008), 561–84.

Robinson, Jeffrey. *Yamani: The Untold Story* (London: Simon and Schuster, 1988).

Rodgers, Daniel. *Atlantic Crossings: Social Politics in a Progressive Age* (Cambridge, MA: Belknap, 1998).

Rodman, Kenneth A. *Sanctity vs. Sovereignty: The United States and the Nationalization of Natural Resource Investments* (New York: Columbia University Press, 1988).

Romulo, Carlos. *The Meaning of Bandung* (Chapel Hill: University of North Carolina Press, 1956).

Rosenberg, Emily S. *Spreading the American Dream: American Economic and Cultural Expansion, 1890–1945* (New York: Hill and Wang, 1982).

Rubino, Anna. *The Queen of the Oil Club: The Intrepid Wanda Jablonski and the Power of Information* (Boston: Beacon Press, 2008).

Sabin, Paul. *The Bet: Paul Ehrlich, Julian Simon, and the Gamble over the Earth's Future* (New Haven, CT: Yale University Press, 2013).

Saloman, Margot E. "From NIEO to Now and the Unfinishable Story of Economic Justice," *International and Comparative Law Quarterly* 62: 1 (January 2013): 31–54.

Sampson, Anthony. *The Seven Sisters* (New York: Viking, 1975).

Sargent, Daniel J. "Lyndon Johnson and the Challenge of Economic Globalization," in *The United States and the Dawn of the Post-Cold War World*, eds. Francis Gavin and Mark Lawrence (New York: Oxford, 2015).

A Superpower Transformed: The Remaking of American Foreign Relations in the 1970s (New York: Oxford University Press, 2015).

Sato, Shohei. *Britain and the Formation of the Gulf States: Embers of Empire* (Manchester University Press, 2016).

Saul, Samir. "Masterly Inactivity as Brinksmanship: The Iraq Petroleum Company's Road to Nationalization," *International History Review* 29: 4 (2007): 746–92.

Schachter, Oscar. "The Development of International Law through the Legal Opinions of the United Nations Secretariat," *British Yearbook of International Law* 25 (1948): 91–132.

"The Invisible College of International Lawyers," *Northwest University Law Review* 72: 2 (1977): 217–26.

Schneider, Steven A. *The Oil Price Revolution* (Baltimore: Johns Hopkins University Press, 1983).

Schrijver, Nico. *Development without Destruction: The UN and Global Resource Management* (Bloomington: Indiana University Press, 2010).

Sovereignty over Natural Resources: Balancing Rights and Duties (New York: Cambridge University Press, 2008).

Schumann, Christoph. "The Generation of Broad Expectations: Nationalism, Education, and Autobiography in Syria and Lebanon," *Die Welt des Islams* 41: 2 (July 2001).

Schumpeter, Joseph A. "John Maynard Keynes, 1883–1946," *The American Economic Review* 36: 4 (September 1946): 500–1.

Semmel, Bernard. "The Philosophic Radicals and Colonialism," *The Journal of Economic History* 21: 4 (1961): 513–25.

Sen, Amartya. "Development: Which Way Now?" *The Economic Journal* 93: 372 (December 1983).

Seymour, Ian. *OPEC: Instrument of Change* (London: Macmillan, 1980).

Shwadron, Benjamin. *The Middle East, Oil, and the Great Powers*, 3rd edn (New York: Wiley, 1974).

Silverfarb, Daniel. "The Revision of Iraq's Oil Concessions, 1949–1952," *Middle Eastern Studies* 23 (1996): 69–95.

Simpson, Bradley R. *Economists with Guns: Authoritarian Development and U.S.-Indonesian Relations, 1960–1968* (Palo Alto, CA: Stanford University Press, 2008).

Skeet, Ian. *OPEC: Twenty-Five Years of Prices and Politics* (New York: Cambridge University Press, 1988).

Smith, Benjamin. *Hard Times in the Lands of Plenty: Oil Politics in Iran and Indonesia* (Ithaca, NY: Cornell University Press, 2007).

Smith, Simon C. *Britain's Revival and Fall in the Gulf: Kuwait, Qatar, and the Trucial States* (New York: Routledge, 2004).

"French Imperial Outposts in Post-Imperial India, 1947–54," *European History Review* 3: 2 (1996): 187–97.

Smolansky, Oles, and Bettie Smolansky. *The USSR and Iraq: The Soviet Quest for Influence* (Durham, NC: Duke University Press, 1991).

Staples, Amy L. S. *The Birth of Development: How the World Bank, Food and Agriculture Organization, and World Health Organization Changed the World, 1945–1965* (Kent State University Press, 1998).

Sternfeld, Lior. "Iran Days in Egypt: Mosaddeq's Visit to Cairo in 1951," *British Journal of Middle Eastern Studies* 43: 1 (2016): 1–20.

Stoff, Michael B. *Oil, War, and American Security: The Search for a National Policy on Foreign Oil, 1941–1947* (New Haven, CT: Yale University Press, 1980).

Stork, Joe. *Middle East Oil and the Energy Crisis* (New York: Monthly Review Press, 1975).

Suri, Jeremi. *Power and Protest: Global Revolution and the Rise of Détente* (Cambridge, MA: Harvard University Press, 2003).

Tetreault, Mary Ann. *The Organization of Arab Petroleum Exporting Countries: History, Policies and Prospects* (Westport, CT: Greenwood Press, 1981).

Thomas, Raju G. C. "Energy Politics and Indian Security," *Pacific Affairs* 55: 1 (Spring 1982): 28–38.

Tignor, Robert. *W. Arthur Lewis and the Birth of Development Economics* (Princeton University Press, 2006).

Toprani, Anand. "The French Connection: A New Perspective on the End of the Red Line Agreement, 1945–1948," *Diplomatic History* 36: 2 (April 2012): 261–99.

Toye, John. "Herbert Frankel: From Colonial Economics to Development Economics," *Oxford Development Studies* 37: 2 (2009): 171–82.

Toye, John, and Richard Toye. *The UN and the Global Political Economy* (Bloomington, IN: Indiana University Press, 2004).

Turner, Louis. *The Oil Companies in the International System* (London: George, Allen & Unwin, 1978).

Uche, Chibuike. "Oil, British Interests, and the Nigerian Civil War," *The Journal of African History* 49 (2008): 111–35.

Veblen, Thorstein. *The Theory of the Business Enterprise* (New York: Scribner's Sons, 1904).

Viner, Jacob. *International Trade and Economic Development* (London: Clarendon, 1953).

The Role of Providence in the Social Order (Princeton University Press, 1972).

Vitalis, Robert. *America's Kingdom: Mythmaking on the Saudi Oil Frontier* (Palo Alto, CA: Stanford University Press, 2006).

"The Midnight Ride of Kwame Nkrumah and Other Fables of Bandung (Bandoong)," *Humanity* 4: 2 (2013).

von Bismarck, Helene. *British Policy in the Persian Gulf, 1961–1968: Conceptions of Informal Empire* (London: Palgrave Macmillan, 2013).

Wallerstein, Immanuel. *The Capitalist World-Economy* (Cambridge University Press, 1979).

Watt, D. C. "The Decision to Withdraw from the Gulf," *Political Quarterly* 39: 3 (1968): 310–21.

Westad, Odd Arne. *The Global Cold War: Third World Interventions and the Making of Our Times* (New York: Cambridge University Press, 2005).

Whelan, Daniel J. "Under the Aegis of Man": The Right to Development and the Origins of the New International Economic Order," *Humanity: An International Journal of Human Rights, Humanitarianism, and Development* 6: 1 (2015).

White, Nicholas J. "Reconstructing Europe through Rejuvenating Empire: The British, French, and Dutch Experiences Compared," *Past and Present* 210 (2011): 211–36.

Willetts, Peter. *The Non-Aligned Movement: The Origins of a Third World Alliance* (New York: Pinter Publishing, 1978).

Williams, John H. "The Theory of International Trade Reconsidered," *The Economic Journal* 39: 154 (1929): 195–209.

Williams, William Appleman. "The Frontier Thesis and American Foreign Policy," *Pacific Historical Review* 24: 4 (1955): 379–95.

Wolfe, Patrick. "History and Imperialism: A Century of Theory, from Marx to Postcolonialism," *The American Historical Review*, Vol. 102, No. 2 (1997): 388–420.

Wood, Robert E. "From Marshall Plan to the Third World," in Melvyn P. Leffler and David S. Painter, eds., *The Origins of the Cold War: An International History*, 2nd edn (London: Routledge, 2005), 239–50.

Woolf, Leonard. *Economic Imperialism* (New York: Harcourt, Brace & Howe, 1920).

Wright, Richard *The Color Curtain: A Report on the Bandung Conference* (New York: World Publishing, 1956).

Yaqub, Salim. *Containing Arab Nationalism: The Eisenhower Doctrine and the Middle East* (Chapel Hill: University of North Carolina Press, 2004), 237–67.

Yergin, Daniel. *The Prize: The Epic Quest for Oil, Money and Power* (New York: The Free Press, 2008 [1991]).

Zabih, Sepehr. *The Communist Movement in Iran* (Berkeley: University of California Press, 1966).

Index